IDEAS IN CONTEXT

THE TAMING OF CHANCE

IDEAS IN CONTEXT

Edited by Richard Rorty, J. B. Schneewind, Quentin Skinner and Wolf Lepenies

The books in this series will discuss the emergence of intellectual traditions and of related new disciplines. The procedures, aims and vocabularies that were generated will be set in the institutions. Through detailed studies of the evolution of such traditions, and their modification by different audiences, it is hoped that a new picture will form of the development of ideas in their concrete contexts. By this means, artificial distinctions between the history of philosophy, of the various sciences, of society and politics, and of literature, may be seen to dissolve.

This series is published with the support of the Exxon Education Foundation

A list of books in the series will be found at the end of the volume.

THE TAMING OF CHANCE

IAN HACKING

*Institute for the History and Philosophy of
Science and Technology, University of Toronto*

The right of the
University of Cambridge
to print and sell
all manner of books
was granted by
Henry VIII in 1534.
The University has printed
and published continuously
since 1584.

CAMBRIDGE UNIVERSITY PRESS
Cambridge
New York   Port Chester
Melbourne   Sydney

Published by the Press Syndicate of the University of Cambridge
The Pitt Building, Trumpington Street, Cambridge CB2 1RP
40 West 20th Street, New York, NY 10011, USA
10 Stamford Road, Oakleigh, Melbourne 3166, Australia

First published 1990

Printed in Great Britain by
The Bath Press, Avon

British Library cataloguing in publication data
Hacking, Ian, *1936–*
The taming of chance. – (Ideas in context).
1. Probabilities – Philosophical perspectives
I. Title II. Series
121′.63

Library of Congress cataloguing in publication data
Hacking, Ian.
The taming of chance / Ian Hacking.
p.   cm. – (Ideas in context)
ISBN 0-521-38014-6. – ISBN 0-521-38884-8 (pbk.)
1. Chance. 2. Necessity (Philosophy)
I. Title. II. Series.
SD595.H33   1990
123′.3–dc   89-36411 CIP

ISBN 0 521 38014 6 hard covers
ISBN 0 521 38884 8 paperback

CE

Curiosities for the Ingenious
In memory of H. E. H.

CONTENTS

Determinism was eroded during the nineteenth century and a
space was cleared for autonomous laws of chance. The idea of
human nature was displaced by a model of normal people with
laws of dispersion. These two transformations were parallel and
fed into each other. Chance made the world seem less capricious:
it was legitimated because it brought order out of chaos. The
greater the level of indeterminism in our conception of the world
and of people, the higher the expected level of control.

These events began with an avalanche of printed numbers at
the end of the Napoleonic era. Many kinds of human behaviour,
especially wrongdoings such as crime and suicide, were counted.
They appeared astonishingly regular from year to year. Statistical
laws of society seemed to spring from official tables of deviancy.
Data about averages and dispersions engendered the idea of
normal people, and led to new kinds of social engineering, new
ways to modify undesirable classes.

In the early years of the century, it was assumed that statistical
laws were reducible to underlying deterministic events, but the
apparent prevalence of such laws slowly and erratically
undermined determinism. Statistical laws came to be regarded as
laws in their own right, and their sway was extended to natural
phenomena. A new kind of 'objective knowledge' came into
being, the product of new technologies for gaining information
about natural and social processes. There emerged new criteria
for what counted as evidence for knowledge of this kind. The
statistical laws that could thus be justified were used not only for
description but also for explaining and understanding the course
of events. Chance became tamed, in the sense that it became the
very stuff of the fundamental processes of nature and of society.

In 1800 'chance', it was said, was a mere word, signifying
nothing – or else it was a notion of the vulgar, denoting fortune
or even lawlessness, and thus to be excluded from the thought of
enlightened people. Every event followed necessarily, at least in

the phenomenal world, from an antecedent set of conditions.
Even students of vital medicine, who rejected universal laws
within their domain, held to particular and individual trains of
necessary causation, and would not countenance fundamental
chance.

was a controversy: who is more suicidal, Parisians or Londoners? It could not be settled then; a decade later it could, because new institutions had been established for collecting and publishing data.

Suicide is a recurring theme in statistics. In one instance of medical imperialism, there was an implicit syllogism: madness was to be treated by physicians, suicide was a kind of madness, hence the suicide statistics were treated like other medical statistics. As a result, theories of medical causation were appropriated to suicide. These were then applied to all statistics of deviancy.

rearranged in order to make statistical laws consistent with
determinism.

physiology, here represented by Broussais, and then was transformed into part of a political agenda by Comte. Normality displaced the Enlightenment idea of human nature as a central organizing concept, but evolved two roles. One is the Quetelet-Durkheim conception of the normal as the right and the good. The other is the Galtonian notion of the normal as the mediocre, and in need of improvement. In either role, the idea of the normal presents itself as the seal of objectivity and impartiality, a neutral bridge between 'is' and 'ought'.

believed in absolute chance, and in a universe in which laws of
nature are at best approximate and evolve out of random
processes. Chance was no longer the essence of lawlessness, but
at the core of all laws of nature and all rational inductive
inference. His radical indeterminism is less striking when seen as
a corollary of the probabilizing of the world and our knowledge
of it. He concluded that we live in a chance universe not because
of an argument, but because probability and statistics were
coming to permeate every aspect of life.

ACKNOWLEDGEMENTS

Family, friends and foundations have been unstinting in their help during the decade it has taken to finish this book. In 1980–1 the US National Science Foundation and a sabbatical leave from Stanford University allowed me to accept a Visiting Fellowship at Peterhouse, Cambridge, where I began serious work. In 1982-3 the Zentrum für interdisziplinäre Forschung, Bielefeld, generously supported the research group on the probability revolution: many thanks to Lorenz Krüger who organized this, and to all those colleagues whom he and the ZiF brought together. Thanks also to Dr Hilary Gaskin, my subeditor at Cambridge University Press, for help in making my final text presentable.

1

The argument

The most decisive conceptual event of twentieth century physics has been the discovery that the world is not deterministic. Causality, long the bastion of metaphysics, was toppled, or at least tilted: the past does not determine exactly what happens next. This event was preceded by a more gradual transformation. During the nineteenth century it became possible to see that the world might be regular and yet not subject to universal laws of nature. A space was cleared for chance.

This erosion of determinism made little immediate difference to anyone. Few were aware of it. Something else was pervasive and everybody came to know about it: the enumeration of people and their habits. Society became statistical. A new type of law came into being, analogous to the laws of nature, but pertaining to people. These new laws were expressed in terms of probability. They carried with them the connotations of normalcy and of deviations from the norm. The cardinal concept of the psychology of the Enlightenment had been, simply, human nature. By the end of the nineteenth century, it was being replaced by something different: normal people.

I argue that these two transformations are connected. Most of the events to be described took place in the social arena, not that of the natural sciences, but the consequences were momentous for both.

Throughout the Age of Reason, chance had been called the superstition of the vulgar. Chance, superstition, vulgarity, unreason were of one piece. The rational man, averting his eyes from such things, could cover chaos with a veil of inexorable laws. The world, it was said, might often look haphazard, but only because we do not know the inevitable workings of its inner springs. As for probabilities – whose mathematics was called the doctrine of chances – they were merely the defective but necessary tools of people who know too little.

There were plenty of sceptics about determinism in those days: those who needed room for freedom of the will, or those who insisted on the individual character of organic and living processes. None of these thought for a moment that laws of chance would provide an alternative to strictly causal laws. Yet by 1900 that was a real possibility, urged as fact by an adventurous few. The stage was set for ultimate indeterminism. How did that happen?

This is not a question about some sort of decay in knowledge or management. The erosion of determinism is not the creation of disorder and ignorance – quite the contrary. In 1889 Francis Galton, founder of the biometric school of statistical research, not to mention eugenics, wrote that the chief law of probability 'reigns with serenity and in complete effacement amidst the wildest confusion'.[1] By the end of the century chance had attained the respectability of a Victorian valet, ready to be the loyal servant of the natural, biological and social sciences.

There is a seeming paradox: the more the indeterminism, the more the control. This is obvious in the physical sciences. Quantum physics takes for granted that nature is at bottom irreducibly stochastic. Precisely that discovery has immeasurably enhanced our ability to interfere with and alter the course of nature. A moment's reflection shows that a similar statement may be attempted in connection with people. The parallel was noticed quite early. Wilhelm Wundt, one of the founding fathers of quantitative psychology, wrote as early as 1862: 'It is statistics that first demonstrated that love follows psychological laws.'[2]

Such social and personal laws were to be a matter of probabilities, of chances. Statistical in nature, these laws were nonetheless inexorable; they could even be self-regulating. People are normal if they conform to the central tendency of such laws, while those at the extremes are pathological. Few of us fancy being pathological, so 'most of us' try to make ourselves normal, which in turn affects what is normal. Atoms have no such inclinations. The human sciences display a feedback effect not to be found in physics.

The transformations that I shall describe are closely connected with an event so all-embracing that we seldom pause to notice it: an avalanche of printed numbers. The nation-states classified, counted and tabulated their subjects anew. Enumerations in some form have been with us always, if only for the two chief purposes of government, namely taxation and military recruitment. Before the Napoleonic era most official counting had been kept privy to administrators. After it, a vast amount was printed and published.

The enthusiasm for numerical data is reflected by the United States census. The first American census asked four questions of each household. The tenth decennial census posed 13,010 questions on various schedules addressed to people, firms, farms, hospitals, churches and so forth. This 3,000-fold increase is striking, but vastly understates the rate of growth of printed numbers: 300,000 would be a better estimate.

The printing of numbers was a surface effect. Behind it lay new technologies for classifying and enumerating, and new bureaucracies with the authority and continuity to deploy the technology. There is a sense in which many of the facts presented by the bureaucracies did not even exist ahead of time. Categories had to be invented into which people could conveniently fall in order to be counted. The systematic collection of data about people has affected not only the ways in which we conceive of a society, but also the ways in which we describe our neighbour. It has profoundly transformed what we choose to do, who we try to be, and what we think of ourselves. Marx read the minutiae of official statistics, the reports from the factory inspectorate and the like. One can ask: who had more effect on class consciousness, Marx or the authors of the official reports which created the classifications into which people came to recognize themselves? These are examples of questions about what I call 'making up people'. This book touches on them only indirectly.[3]

What has the avalanche of printed numbers to do with my chief topic, the erosion of determinism? One answer is immediate. Determinism was subverted by laws of chance. To believe there were such laws one needed law-like statistical regularities in large populations. How else could a civilization hooked on universal causality get the idea of some alternative kind of law of nature or social behaviour? Games of chance furnished initial illustrations of chance processes, as did birth and mortality data. Those became an object of mathematical scrutiny in the seventeenth century. Without them we would not have anything much like our modern idea of probability. But it is easy for the determinist to assume that the fall of a die or the spin of a roulette work out according to the simple and immutable laws of mechanics. Newtonian science had no need of probabilities, except as a tool for locating underlying causes. Statistical laws that look like brute, irreducible facts were first found in human affairs, but they could be noticed only after social phenomena had been enumerated, tabulated and made public. That role was well served by the avalanche of printed numbers at the start of the nineteenth century.

On closer inspection we find that not any numbers served the purpose. Most of the law-like regularities were first perceived in connection with deviancy: suicide, crime, vagrancy, madness, prostitution, disease. This fact is instructive. It is now common to speak of information and control as a neutral term embracing decision theory, operations research, risk analysis and the broader but less well specified domains of statistical inference. We shall find that the roots of the idea lie in the notion that one can improve – control – a deviant subpopulation by enumeration and classification.

We also find that routinely gathering numerical data was not enough to make statistical laws rise to the surface. The laws had in the beginning to be read into the data. They were not simply read off them. Throughout this book I make a contrast of a rough and ready sort between Prussian (and other east European) attitudes to numerical data, and those that flourished in Britain, France, and other nations of western Europe. Statistical laws were found in social data in the West, where libertarian, individualistic and atomistic conceptions of the person and the state were rampant. This did not happen in the East, where collectivist and holistic attitudes were more prevalent. Thus the transformations that I describe are to be understood only within a larger context of what an individual is, and of what a society is.

I shall say very little about mathematical conceptions of probability. The events to be described are, nevertheless, ingredients for understanding probability and for grasping why it has been such an incredible success story. Success story? A quadruple success: metaphysical, epistemological, logical and ethical.

Metaphysics is the science of the ultimate states of the universe. There, the probabilities of quantum mechanics have displaced universal Cartesian causation.

Epistemology is the theory of knowledge and belief. Nowadays we use evidence, analyse data, design experiments and assess credibility in terms of probabilities.

Logic is the theory of inference and argument. For this purpose we use the deductive and often tautological unravelling of axioms provided by pure mathematics, but also, and for most practical affairs, we now employ – sometimes precisely, sometimes informally – the logic of statistical inference.

Ethics is in part the study of what to do. Probability cannot dictate values, but it now lies at the basis of all reasonable choice made by officials. No public decision, no risk analysis, no environmental impact, no military strategy can be conducted without decision theory couched in terms of probabilities. By covering opinion with a veneer of objectivity, we replace judgement by computation.

Probability is, then, *the* philosophical success story of the first half of the twentieth century. To speak of philosophical success will seem the exaggeration of a scholar. Turn then to the most worldly affairs. Probability and statistics crowd in upon us. The statistics of our pleasures and our vices are relentlessly tabulated. Sports, sex, drink, drugs, travel, sleep, friends – nothing escapes. There are more explicit statements of probabilities presented on American prime time television than explicit acts of violence (I'm counting the ads). Our public fears are endlessly debated in terms of probabilities: chances of meltdowns, cancers, muggings, earthquakes, nuclear winters, AIDS, global greenhouses, what next? There is nothing to fear (it may seem) but the probabilities themselves. This obsession with the chances of danger, and with treatments for changing the odds, descends directly from the forgotten annals of nineteenth century information and control.

This imperialism of probabilities could occur only as the world itself became numerical. We have gained a fundamentally quantitative feel for nature, how it is and how it ought to be. This has happened in part for banal reasons. We have trained people to use numerals. The ability to process even quite small numbers was, until recently, the prerogative of a few. Today we hold numeracy to be at least as important as literacy.

But even compared with the numerate of old there have been remarkable changes. Galileo taught that God wrote the world in the language of mathematics. To learn to read this language we would have to measure as well as calculate. Yet measurement was long mostly confined to the classical sciences of astronomy, geometry, optics, music, plus the new mechanics. T.S. Kuhn has iconoclastically claimed that measurement did not play much of a role in the 'Baconian' sciences that came to be called chemistry and physics.[4] He urged that measurement found its place in physics – the study of light, sound, heat, electricity, energy, matter – during the nineteenth century. Only around 1840 did the practice of measurement become fully established. In due course measuring became the only experimental thing to do.

Measurement and positivism are close kin. Auguste Comte coined the word 'positivism' as the name of his philosophy, holding that in all the European languages the word 'positive' had good connotations. His own philosophy did not fare especially well, but the word caught on. Positive science meant numerical science. Nothing better typified a positive science than a statistical one – an irony, for Comte himself despised merely statistical inquiries.

The avalanche of numbers, the erosion of determinism, and the invention of normalcy are embedded in the grander topics of the Industrial Revolution. The acquisition of numbers by the populace, and the professional lust for precision in measurement, were driven by familiar themes of manufacture, mining, trade, health, railways, war, empire. Similarly the idea of a norm became codified in these domains. Just as the railways demanded timekeeping and the mass-produced pocket watch, they also mandated standards, not only of obvious things such as the gauge of the lines but also of the height of the buffers of successive cars in a train. It is a mere decision, in this book, to focus on the more narrow aspects that I have mentioned, a decision that is wilful but not arbitrary. My project is philosophical: to grasp the conditions that made possible our present organization of concepts in two domains. One is that of physical indeterminism; the other is that of statistical information developed for purposes of social control.

This study can be used to illustrate a number of more general philosophical themes. I have mentioned one above: the idea of making up people. I claim that enumeration requires categorization, and that defining new classes of people for the purposes of statistics has consequences for the ways in which we conceive of others and think of our own possibilities and potentialities.

Another philosophical theme is reasoning. In thinking about science we have become familiar with a number of analytic concepts such as T.S. Kuhn's paradigms, Imre Lakatos's research programmes and Gerald Holton's themata. Following A.C. Crombie I have thought it useful to employ the idea of a style of reasoning.[5] Crombie had in mind enduring ways of thinking such as (a) the simple postulation and deduction in the mathematical sciences, (b) experimental exploration, (c) hypothetical construction of models by analogy, (d) ordering of variety by comparison and taxonomy, (e) statistical analysis of regularities of populations, and (f) historical derivation of genetic development.[6]

Each of these styles has its own sources and its own pace. Those who envisage continuity in the growth of knowledge see each style evolving at its own rate. Catastrophists see sharp beginnings and radical mutations. One need not dogmatically adhere to either extreme in order to see styles of reasoning coming together. Each contributed to what Crombie calls 'the growth of a research mentality in European society'.

My topic is Crombie's style (e) which, of the six that he distinguishes, is quite the most recent. Despite various discernible precursors and anticipations, our idea of probability came into being only around 1660, and the great spurt of statistical thinking did not occur until the nineteenth century. The statistical example makes plain that the growth of a style of reasoning is a matter not only of thought but of action. Take so seemingly unproblematic a topic as population. We have become used to a picture: the number of people in a city or in a nation is determinate, like the number of people in a room at noon, and not like the number of people in a riot, or the number of suicides in the world last year. But even the very notion of an exact population is one which has little sense until there are institutions for establishing and defining what 'population' means. Equally there must be ways of reasoning in order to pass from cumbersome data to sentences with a clear sense about how many were such and such. Most professionals now believe that representative sampling gives more accurate information about a population than an exhaustive census. This was unthinkable during most of the nineteenth century.[7] The very thought of being representative has had to come into being. This has required techniques of thinking together with technologies of data collection. An entire style of scientific reasoning has had to evolve.

Its development was intimately connected with larger questions about what a society is, and thus leads to speculation and historical study of the formation of the western concept of a community.[8] But it also invites more abstract analytical philosophy, because styles of reasoning are curiously self-authenticating. A proposition can be assessed as true-or-false only when there is some style of reasoning and investigation that helps determine its truth value. What the proposition means depends upon the ways in which we might settle its truth. That innocent observation verges nervously on circularity. We cannot justify the style as the way best to discover the truth of the proposition, because the sense of the proposition itself depends upon the style of reasoning by which its truth is settled. A style of thinking, it seems, cannot be straightforwardly wrong, once it has achieved a status by which it fixes the sense of what it investigates. Such thoughts call in question the idea of an independent world-given criterion of truth. So the seemingly innocent notion of a style of reasoning can lead to deep waters, and it is wiser to enter them by wading into examples than by a high dive into abstraction. The development of statistical thinking may be our best example available – because most recent and enduring and now pervasive.

Historians will see at once that what follows is not history. One may pursue past knowledge for purposes other than history of science or history of ideas. A noncommittal account of what I am attempting might be: an epistemological study of the social and behavioural sciences, with consequences for the concept of causality in the natural sciences. I prefer a less expected description. This book is a piece of philosophical analysis. Philosophical analysis is the investigation of concepts. Concepts are words in their sites. Their sites are sentences and institutions. I regret that I have said too little about institutions, and too much about sentences and how they are arranged.

But what sentences? I use only the printed word, a minuscule fraction of what was said. The distinguished statistician I. J. Good noted in a review that 'the true history of probability or of science in general will never be written because so much depends on unrecorded oral communication, and also because writers often do not cite their sources'.[9] The true historian of science is well able to solve the second problem, but not the first. One may nevertheless make a good stab at it by consulting the ample Victorian troves of notebooks, letters and other ephemera. I do not do so, for I am concerned with the public life of concepts and the ways in which they gain authority. My data are published sentences.

But which ones? I omit many pertinent words because one cannot do everything. I leave out Malthus and Mendel, for example, A.A. Cournot, Gustav Fechner, Florence Nightingale and ever so many more modest participants in the taming of chance. Very well: but I say nothing of Maxwell, Bolzmann or Gibbs, although statistical mechanics is critical to the spread of chance and probability not only into physics but also into metaphysics. I say nothing of Charles Darwin, although evolutionary theorizing was to import chance into biology. I say nothing of Karl Marx fabricating an iron necessity out of the very same numerals, the identical official statistics, that I have incorporated into an account of the taming of chance.

There is an uncontroversial good reason for silence about these figures. Scholars and teams of scholars dedicate their lives to the study of one or another. It would be folly to venture a short story here, a mere chapter. But it is not only prudence and respect, but also method, that makes me hold my tongue. Transformations in concepts and in styles of reasoning are the product of countless trickles rather than the intervention of single individuals. Marx, Darwin and Maxwell worked in a space in which there was something to find out. That means: in which various possibilities for truth-or-falsehood could already be formulated. This book is about that space. So although a lot of sentences are reproduced in this book, they are the words not of heroes, but of the mildly distinguished in their day, the stuff of the more impersonal parts of our lives.

Sentences have two powers. They are eternal, and they are uttered at a moment. They are anonymous, and yet they are spoken by flesh and blood. I have tried to answer to these two facts. On the one hand, I do regard the sentences as mere material objects, inscriptions. But to do that, and only that, is to become lost in vain abstraction. As counterbalance, my epigraphs to each chapter are dated, to recall that on a real day important to the speaker, those very words were uttered, or are said to have been uttered. My footnotes (marked with asterisks) are anecdotes that would be improper in the more solemn text.* They give some tiny glimpse of who the speakers were. But there is seldom anything personal about the footnotes. They address the individual as official, as public writer, even if his behaviour may strike us, so much later, as strange.

Thus although many chapters have a central character or text, it is not because Salomon Neumann, A.-M. Guerry or John Finlaison is 'important'. They are convenient and exemplary anchors for a particular organization of sentences. I use the antistatistical method, that of Frédéric Le Play, topic of chapter 16. After having interminably trekked across the

---

* Notes at the end of the book provide references, and, rarely, numerical formulae. They are marked with numerals. A numeral after an asterisk (as *³) indicates that note 3 at the end of the book bears on the material in the footnote marked *.

written equivalent of his Hartz mountains, I take what I think is the best example of one speaker. Much like Le Play, I include a few stories, but the personages whom I use are in some ways like his household budgets, if, alas, less thorough.

There is one exception among these chapters. The final one is twice as long as the others, and is a rather full account of one side of one writer, namely C.S. Peirce. He really did believe in a universe of absolute irreducible chance. His words fittingly end this book, for as he wrote, that thought had become possible. But I argue that it became possible because Peirce now lived a life that was permeated with probability and statistics, so that his conception of chance was oddly inevitable. He had reached the twentieth century. I use Peirce as a philosophical witness in something like the way that I used Leibniz in *The Emergence of Probability*.[10] But Leibniz was a witness to the transformation that I was there describing, namely the emergence of probability around 1660 and just afterwards. Here Peirce is the witness to something that had already happened by the time that he was mature. That is why he is the topic of the last chapter, whereas in *Emergence* the name of Leibniz recurred throughout.

Although other philosophers are mentioned in the two books, only Leibniz and Peirce play a significant part. The two works do, however, differ in structure in other ways. *Emergence* is about a radical mutation that took place very quickly. Doubtless, as Sandy Zabell and Daniel Garber have shown in an exemplary way, the book underestimated various kinds of precursors.[11] My central claim was, however, that many of our philosophical conceptions of probability were formed by the nature of the transition from immediately preceding Renaissance conceptions. Accounts of the methodology have been given elsewhere.[12] *Taming*, in contrast is about a gradual change. Hence the geological metaphors: avalanches, yes, but also erosion.

Most of my selections and omissions – such as my long treatment of Peirce and my neglect of any other philosopher – have been deliberate. But sloth and good fortune have also played their part. When I began work there was hardly any recent secondary material; now there is a great deal. I am particularly glad of new books by my friends Lorraine Daston, Ted Porter and Stephen Stigler, and of earlier ones by William Coleman and Donald MacKenzie. We all participated in a collective inspired and guided by Lorenz Krüger. The joint work of that group has also appeared. Hence there is now a number of brilliant and often definitive accounts of many matters that overlap with mine.[13] They have made it unnecessary for me to examine a good many matters. And aside from specific histories, there are also points of great generality that I have allowed myself to gloss over in the light of that collective work. For example, another virtue of my geological metaphor is that the erosion of determinism took place at markedly different rates on different terrains. Not uncommonly the least deterministic of disciplines most fiercely resisted indeterminism – economics is typical. This phenomenon emerges from the individual studies of the research group, and is further emphasized in a recent summing up of some of its results.[14]

I have mentioned a number of more specific topics on which I have only touched, or have entirely avoided: making up people; styles of reasoning; great scientists; philosophers; mathematical probability. There is a more glaring omission. I write of the taming of chance, that is, of the way in which apparently chance or irregular events have been brought under the control of natural or social law. The world became not more chancy, but far less so. Chance, which was once the superstition of the vulgar, became the centrepiece of natural and social science, or so genteel and rational people are led to believe. But how can chance ever be tamed? Parallel to the taming of chance of which I speak, there arose a self-conscious conception of pure irregularity, of something wilder than the kinds of chance that had been excluded by the Age of Reason. It harked back, in part, to something ancient or vestigial. It also looked into the future, to new, and often darker, visions of the person than any that I discuss below. Its most passionate spokesman was Nietzsche. Its most subtle and many-layered expression was Mallarmé's poem, 'Un Coup de dés'.[15] That graphic work, whose words are more displayed than printed, began by stating that we 'NEVER . . . will annul chance'. The images are of shipwreck, of a pilot whose exact mathematical navigation comes to naught. But the final page is a picture of the heavens, with the word 'constellation' at its centre. The last words are, 'Une pensée émet un coup de dés', words that speak of the poem itself and which, although they do not imagine taming chance, try to transcend it.

2

The doctrine of necessity

In 1892 the iconoclastic American philosopher C.S. Peirce proposed 'to examine the common belief that every single fact in the universe is determined by law'.[1] 'The proposition in question' – he called it the doctrine of necessity – 'is that the state of things existing at any time, together with certain immutable laws, completely determines the state of things at every other time.' His examination was venomous. At the end: 'I believe I have thus subjected to fair examination all the important reasons for adhering to the theory of universal necessity, and shown their nullity.'[2] That was only the negative beginning. Peirce positively asserted that the world is irreducibly chancy. The apparently universal laws that are the glory of the natural sciences are a by-product of the workings of chance.

Peirce was riding the crest of an antideterminist wave. As is so often the case with someone who is speaking for his time, he thought himself alone. 'The doctrine of necessity has never been in so great a vogue as now.' He did warn against supposing 'that this is a doctrine accepted everywhere and at all times by all rational men.' Nevertheless he had to peer back into the distant past to find people with whom he agreed. The philosophy of Epicurus and the swerving atoms of Lucretius were, in his opinion, precursors of the statistical mechanics of Maxwell, Boltzmann and Gibbs. He had more allies than he imagined, but he was right in thinking that his examination of the doctrine of necessity would have been unthinkable in the eighteenth century.

For a before-and-after portrait, we inevitably contrast Peirce with the greatest of probability mathematicians, Laplace, author of the classic statement of necessity. 'All events, even those which on account of their insignificance do not seem to follow the great laws of nature, are a result of it just as necessarily as the revolutions of the sun'.[3] With those words Laplace opened his *Philosophical Essay on Probabilities*, a text that goes back to his introductory lectures at the Ecole Polytechnique in 1795.[4] It was full of memorable passages like this:

Given for one instant an intelligence which could comprehend all the forces by which nature is animated and the respective situation of the beings who compose it – an intelligence sufficiently vast to submit these data to analysis – it would

11

embrace in the same formula the movements of the greatest bodies of the universe and those of the lightest atom; for it, nothing would be uncertain and the future, as the past, would be present to its eyes.[5]

Philosophers were in complete agreement with the great physicist. In his *Foundations of the Metaphysics of Morals* Kant took as a commonplace that it is 'necessary that everything that happens should be inexorably determined by natural laws'.[6] Free will became a pressing problem because of the conflict between necessity and human responsibility. One resolution broadly followed the thought of Descartes, who had supposed there are two essentially distinct substances, mind and body, or thinking substance as opposed to spatially extended substance. Everything that happens to spatial substance is inexorably determined by law. Hence all spatio-temporal phenomena are necessarily determined. That might leave room for human freedom, so long as it is mental. Kant's account of human autonomy was a sophisticated version of this. The two substances, spatial and mental, were replaced by two worlds, one knowable, one not. The free self dwells in an unknowable realm of noumena. Kant was so convinced a necessitarian that he had to devise an entire other universe in which free will could play its part. Even that world did not escape universality, the concomitant of necessity in the phenomenal realm: the only principles that could govern rational beings must themselves be universal, just like the laws of nature.

What role could chance have in the deterministic world of phenomena? There had always been plenty of suggestions. There was the long-standing idea of intersecting causal lines. Suppose that you and I meet 'by chance' at the market. There may be a causal story of why I am at the market at ten past nine in the morning, choosing cantaloupes. A different but equally causal account will explain why you are there at that time, picking your peaches. Because the two sets of causes together entail that we will cross paths at 9.10, there was nothing 'undetermined' about our meeting. We call it chance, but not because the event was uncaused. Chance is a mere seeming, the result of intersecting causal lines. This face-saving, necessity-saving idea has been proposed again and again, by Aristotle, by Aquinas, and by the nineteenth-century probabilist A.A. Cournot, for example.[7]

Probability textbooks were less philosophically subtle but they too posed no threat to necessity. Prior to Laplace the best one was Abraham De Moivre's *The Doctrine of Chances*. It went through three editions, in 1711, 1738 and 1756. De Moivre's fundamental chances were equipossible outcomes on some sort of physical set-up. Everything that happened was itself determined by physical properties of the set-up, even if we did not know them. Any other idea of chance is wicked:

Chance, in atheistical writings or discourse, is a sound utterly insignificant: It imports no determination to any *mode of Existence*; nor indeed to *Existence* itself, more than to *non existence*; it can neither be defined nor understood: nor can any Proposition concerning it be either affirmed or denied, excepting this one, 'That it is a mere word.'[8]

That paragraph appeared just as Hume was finishing his *Treatise of Human Nature*. What the devout De Moivre had condemned as atheistical, Hume dismissed as vulgar: ''tis commonly allowed by philosophers that what the vulgar call chance is nothing but a secret and conceal'd cause'.[9] Later, in his *Enquiry Concerning Human Understanding*, he explicitly employed De Moivre's epithet, that chance is a mere word:

It is universally allowed that nothing exists without a cause of its existence, and that chance, when strictly examined, is a mere negative word, and means not any real power which has anywhere a being in nature.[10]

De Moivre's atheistical writers, and (Hume's vulgar people,) took chance to be a positive power, along with luck, fortune and the like. That was the only space left for chance, a space repugnant to reason.

Hume did not care for chance, but would not Hume, the famous sceptic about causation and necessity, doubt the doctrine of necessity? Not at all.

'Tis universally acknowledged, that the operations of external bodies are necessary, and that in the communication of their motion ... in their attraction and mutual cohesion, there are not the least traces of indifference or liberty. Every object is determin'd by absolute fate to a certain degree and direction of its motion ... The actions, therefore, of matter are to be regarded as instances of necessary actions.[11]

Perhaps Hume did sow a seed of doubt about determinism. Why does each of my quotations begin ''Tis commonly allowed', 'It is universally allowed', ''Tis universally acknowledged'? Do these phrases put the onus on the convictions of other philosophers, rather than express Hume's concurrence? But what Hume did expressly doubt was something different, not about the reality of necessity but about our knowledge of it. He scoffed only at claims to know the inner workings of nature. He was faithful to his countryman John Locke, whose *Essay* held that the real essence of things is their 'inner constitution' – but human beings can never know anything about that. He admired Robert Boyle, that 'great partizan of the mechanical philosophy; a theory which by discovering some of the secrets of nature, and allowing us to imagine the rest, is so agreeable to the natural vanity and curiosity of men'.[12] Newton's genius lay not only in his celestial mechanics but also in his implication that gravity in itself is unknowable. Thus, as Hume continued, Newton put an end to vain presumption: 'While he seemed to draw off the veil from some of the mysteries of nature, he showed at the same time the imperfections of the mechanical philosophy, and thereby restored her ultimate secrets to that obscurity, in which they ever did and ever will remain.'

That 'ever did and ever will' of this ironic paragraph has a profoundly sceptical ring that few physicists would echo. Laplace was optimistic. Out of ignorance we may have had recourse to final causes or to chance, 'but such imaginary causes have gradually receded with the widening bounds of knowledge and disappear entirely before sound philosophy, which sees in them only the expression of our ignorance of the true causes'.[13]

Not everyone agreed with the healthy philosophy of physics. Xavier Bichat, lecturing down the street at the Ecole de Médecine, warned his pupils that 'There are in nature two classes of beings, two classes of properties, and two classes of sciences. The beings are either organic or inorganic, the properties vital or non-vital, and the sciences either physiological or physical.'[14] Bichat postulated a realm of vital organic stuff. The Laplace story holds only of the physical sciences and inorganic matter. 'Physical laws are constant, invariable', wrote Bichat, but physiological ones are not. Physical phenomena 'can, consequently, be foreseen, predicted and calculated. We calculate the fall of a heavy body, the motion of the planets, the course of a river, the trajectory of a projectile, etc. The rule being once found it is only necessary to make the application to each particular case.'[15] Organic life is very different:

all the vital functions are susceptible of numerous variations. They are frequently out of their natural state; they defy every kind of calculation, for it would be necessary to have as many different rules as there are different cases. It is impossible to foresee, predict, or calculate, anything with regard to their phenomena; we have only approximations towards them, and even these are very uncertain.

Even a supreme intelligence could not compute the future state of a vital organism. An omniscient creator could foretell the course of life, but not by applying a universal law to some boundary conditions. Events in an organism are caused, but each cause must be particular and peculiar. Each antecedent condition is unique, and so is its effect.

Bichat's doctrine dissents from the doctrine of necessity, as defined by Peirce. Bichat did not think that every single fact in the universe is determined by law (not unless the doctrine is trivialized, making up a special law, case by case, for each individual event). His opposition to law was not, however, an opposition to order or causality. It left no place for chance. Irreducible probabilities were as alien to Bichat's scheme as to that of Laplace. Nor does the erosion of determinism occur as a sort of mutation from Bichat's vitalism. On the contrary, organic philosophies were quite resistant to chance. Chance gradually worked its way into the fissures and the crevices found in the rock of physical law, but it found no place in living matter until vitalism had been largely discredited.

This is not to say that the erosion of determinism had nothing to do with life. It had everything to do with life: living people. Not living people regarded as vital organic unities, but rather regarded as social atoms subject to social laws. These laws turn out to be statistical in character. They could be seen as statistical only when there were, literally, statistics. There could be statistics only when people wanted to count themselves and had the means to do so.

Let us then turn to counting. First I shall take up the counting that existed during the lifespan of Hume and Kant. It was largely of two kinds: secret and official, or public but amateur. The numbers disseminated by amateurs, when combined with available public records, were sufficient for an alert observer like Kant. Just as he finished *The Foundations of the Metaphysics of Morals* (with its noumenal account of the will) he received the first part of Herder's book on the idea of history.[16] He put that together with current reading of popular German statistics, and wrote a small essay on the idea of universal history. It began:

Whatsoever difference there may be in our notions of the *freedom of will* metaphysically considered, it is evident that the manifestations of this will, viz. human actions, are as much under the control of universal laws of nature as any other physical phenomena. It is the province of History to narrate these manifestations; and, let their causes be ever so secret, we know that History, simply by taking its station at a distance and contemplating the agency of the human will upon a large scale, aims at unfolding to our view a regular stream of tendency in the great succession of events – so that the very same course of incidents which, taken separately and individually, would have seemed perplexed, incoherent, and lawless, yet viewed in their connection and as the actions of the human *species* and not of independent beings, never fail to discover a steady and continuous, though slow, development of certain great predispositions in our nature. Thus, for instance, deaths, births, and marriages, considering how much they are separately dependent on the freedom of the human will, should seem to be subject to no law according to which any calculation could be made beforehand of their amount: and yet the yearly registers of these events in great countries prove that they go on with as much conformity to the laws of nature as the oscillations of the weather.[17]

3

Public amateurs, secret bureaucrats

Trento, 11 September 1786 I console myself with the thought that, in our statistically minded times, all this has probably already been printed in books which one can consult if the need arises.

Edinburgh, 1 January 1798 Many people were at first surprised at my using the words, *Statistics* and *Statistical* ... In the course of a very extensive tour, through the northern parts of Europe, which I happened to take in 1786, I found that in Germany they were engaged in a species of political inquiry to which they had given the name of *Statistics*. By statistical is meant in Germany an inquiry for the purpose of ascertaining the political strength of a country, or questions concerning matters of state; whereas the idea I annexed to the term is an inquiry into the state of a country, for the purpose of ascertaining *the quantum of happiness enjoyed by its inhabitants and the means of it future improvement.*[*][1]

Every state, happy or unhappy, was statistical in its own way. The Italian cities, inventors of the modern conception of the state, made elaborate statistical inquiries and reports well before anyone else in Europe. Sweden organized its pastors to accumulate the world's best data on births and deaths. France, nation of physiocrats and probabilists, created a bureaucracy during the Napoleonic era which at the top was dedicated to innovative statistical investigations, but which in the provinces more often perpetuated pre-revolutionary structures and classifications. The English inaugurated 'political arithmetic' in 1662 when John Graunt drew demographic inferences from the century old weekly Bills of Mortality for the City of London. England was the homeland of insurance for shipping and trade. It originated many other sorts of provisions guarding against contingencies of life or illness, yet its numerical data were a free enterprise hodge-podge of genius and bumbledom.

Visionaries, accountants and generals have planned censuses in many times and places. Those of the Italian city-states now provide historians

---

[*] Goethe at the start of his *Italian Journey*. Sir John Sinclair at the completion of his *Statistical Account of Scotland*. Goethe and Sinclair were travelling at almost exactly the same time.

with a rich texture of information. In the modern era, however, a census was an affair more of colonies than of homelands. The Spanish had a census of Peru in 1548, and of their North American possessions in 1576. Virginia had censuses in 1642–5 and a decade later. Regular repeated modern censuses were perhaps first held in Acadie and Canada (now the provinces of Nova Scotia and Québec) in the 1660s. Colbert, the French minister of finance, had instructed all his regions to do this, but only New France came through systematically and on time. Ireland was completely surveyed for land, buildings, people and cattle under the directorship of William Petty, in order to facilitate the rape of that nation by the English in 1679. The sugar islands of the Caribbean reported populations and exports to their French, Spanish or English overlords. New York made a census in 1698, Connecticut in 1756, Massachusetts in 1764. The United States wrote the demand for a decennial census into the first article of their Constitution, thus continuing colonial practice, and even extending it, as westward the course of empire took its way, across the continent and in due course to the Philippines. Going east, the British took the same pains to count their subject peoples. India evolved one of the great statistical bureaucracies, and later became a major centre for theoretical as well as practical statistics.

Thus there is a story to be told about each national and colonial development, and each has its own flavour. For example the first Canadian enumerations were possible and exact because the people were few and frozen-in during midwinter when the census was taken. There was also a more pressing concern than in any of the regions of mainland France, for whereas the population of British North America was burgeoning, the number of fecund French families in Canada was small due to the lack of young women. To take a quite different concern, the 1776 Articles of Confederation of the United States called for a census to apportion war costs, and the subsequent Constitution ordered a census every ten years to assure equal representation of families (as a sop to the southern plantations, blacks were to be enumerated as $\frac{3}{5}$ of a person). Six and seven decades later, those who interpreted the Constitution strictly insisted that a census could ask no question not immediately connected with representation.

No one will doubt that each region, once it takes counting seriously, becomes statistical in its own way. Stronger theses wait in the wings. For example, the nineteenth century statistics of each state testify to its problems, sores and gnawing cankers. France was obsessed with degeneracy, its interpretation of the declining birth rate.[2] The great crisis in the United States Census occurred after 1840, when it was made to appear that the North was full of mad blacks, while in the South blacks were sane and healthy – strong proof of what was good for them.[3] Chapter 22 below is entitled 'A chapter from Prussian statistics', a phrase taken from a pamphlet of 1880. It is about antisemitism.

A survey of even one set of national statistics would be either superficial or vast. In either case it would provide excessive preparation for a reading of nineteenth-century counting. But for fear that we become fixated upon the avalanche of printed numbers that occurred after 1820 or so, I shall start with one regional example from an earlier period. I ended the last chapter by quoting Kant, writing in 1784. He wrote of the yearly registers of deaths, births and marriages which go in 'conformity to the laws of nature'. I began the present chapter quoting Goethe, who in 1786 spoke of 'our statistically minded times'. I shall use the German-speaking world, especially Prussia, as my example of those times. Graunt and the English began the public use of statistics. Peoples of the Italian peninsula and elsewhere had promulgated the modern notion of the state. But it was German thinkers and statesmen who brought to full consciousness the idea that the nation-state is essentially characterized by its statistics, and therefore demands a statistical office in order to define itself and its power.

Leibniz, my favourite witness to the emergence of probability in the seventeenth century, was the philosophical godfather of Prussian official statistics. His essential premises were: that a Prussian state should be brought into existence, that the true measure of the power of a state is its population, and that the state should have a central statistical office in order to know its power. Hence a new Prussian state must begin by founding a bureau of statistics.

He formulated this idea of a central statistical office about 1685, a few years after William Petty had made the same recommendation for England.[4] Leibniz saw a central office as serving the different branches of administration: military, civil, mining, forestry and police. It would maintain a central register of deaths, baptisms and marriages. With that one could estimate the population, and hence measure the power of a state. A complete enumeration was not yet deemed to be practicable. The population of a country, as opposed to a walled city or a colony, was in those days not a measurable quantity. Only institutions could make it one.

Leibniz had a lively interest in statistical questions of all sorts, and pursued an active correspondence on issues of disease, death and population. He proposed a 56-category evaluation of a state, which would include the number of people by sex, social status, the number of able-bodied men who might bear weapons, the number of marriageable women, the population density and age distribution, child mortality, life expectancy, distribution of diseases and causes of death.[5] Like so many of Leibniz's schemes, such a tabulation was futurology that has long since become routine fact.

Leibniz brought these strands together in a memorandum of 17 August 1700. Prince Frederick of Prussia wanted to be king of a united Brandenburg and Prussia, and Leibniz urged his case. The argument is heavy with the future. A kingdom must be a viable unit, and its heartland must be its most powerful part. The true measure of strength is the number of people, for where there are people, there are resources for sustaining the population and making it productive. It had been contended by Frederick's opponents that Prussia could provide only a small portion of the power of a proposed Brandenburg-Prussia, and hence that the ruler should not be Prussian. That, countered Leibniz, was an error. According to the Prussian registers of births (commenced in 1683) 65,400 people were born every year in the entire region, 22,680 in Prussia. Hence Prussia was vital. Leibniz then used a multiplier of 30 to deduce that Brandenburg-Prussia had 1,962,000 inhabitants, or roughly two million. Even England, rich in people, could claim only five and a half million inhabitants.[6]

Leibniz wrote this advice in 1700. The kingdom of Brandenburg-Prussia was created next year, but, as one historian of Prussian statistics put it, with a royal court, but no state.[7] Certainly there was no statistical office. Prussian enumerations began only with the reign of Friedrich Wilhelm I, 1713–1740, famed for administrative skills and controlled militarism. His agents had first to figure out how to count, for available numbers were far less reliable than Leibniz's rhetoric had made it appear.

Reorganization was undertaken piecemeal, starting with a machinery for registering births, deaths and marriages in the four (royal) residence cities of Brandenburg-Prussia. In 1719 an abortive enumeration of the entire state was attempted. Various systems of reporting were experimented with, and an initial summary of results was issued on 3 March 1723. By 1730 people were officially sorted into the following nine categories: landlords, goodwives, male and female children; then household members classified as journeymen, farmhands, servants, youths and maids. The rubrics endured but the subclassifications exploded. Workmen became classified according to 24 occupations, and special categories were created for the chief industry: cloth makers, fabric makers, hat makers, stocking makers etc. Quantities of worked wool were fitted into the tables. Buildings were meticulously sorted (roofed with tile or straw, new or repaired, barns or decaying), and cattle, land and roads were described. For what purpose? Often, of course, for taxation; hence the way buildings were classed. Leibniz's phrase was regularly used: determine the power of the state. What might the numbers reveal to enemies? A decree of 2 January 1733 forbade publication of the population list. It became a state secret.

If there is a contrast in point of official statistics between the eighteenth and nineteenth centuries, it is that the former feared to reveal while the latter loved to publish. An anecdote will illustrate. The energetic editor, geographer and traveller A.F. Busching published, along with much other material, two journals bulging with information about the German states and their neighbours. One, a 'magazine for new history and geography', ran steadily during 1762–93, and the other, a 'weekly news', between 1773 and 1787.[8] When Busching asked Frederick the Great for help in coordinating and publishing information already collected in the royal ministries, the king replied that he would not hinder Busching, who could publish anything he knew. But neither the king nor his agents would lift a finger to help him find anything out.[9]

A long string of private individuals like Busching collected and published myriad numbers. It was above all they to whom Goethe referred when, in his 1786 travelogue, he spoke of 'our statistically minded times'. Travel books less well remembered than that of Goethe would count anything. Take Johann Bernoulli's adventures in Brandenburg, Prussia, Pomerania, Russia and Poland, about the time of Goethe's more famous trip. You might expect a Bernoulli to be discerning with numbers, but not at all. When he went into a room with old master paintings, he would not describe the pictures; he whipped out his yardstick and measured their dimensions. He told the reader more about the (quite unexceptional) sizes of these paintings, than about what they depict or who made them.[10] The contents of every local statistical news-sheet were reported as he passed through. He was shocked to find that no one in Warsaw knew how many people lived in town, but was relieved to be able to insert a footnote, while the work was in press: the March 1780 issue of Busching's weekly cleared the matter up.[11]

The most systematic private statistical enterprise of mid-eighteenth-century Germany was J.P. Süssmilch's *Divine Order*. This was an intensely detailed study of births, deaths and sex ratios which revealed Providence at work.[12] He painstakingly studied parish registers and other unused data, following the model of the Englishman, Graunt: 'All that was needed' to start this kind of inquiry 'was a Columbus who should go further than others in his survey of old and well-known reports. That Columbus was Graunt.'[13]

Pastor Süssmilch was one of the finest exponents of natural religion, of the idea that arrangements here on earth themselves prove the existence of a benevolent creator.*[14] Here too he followed the English, for the application of birth rates to natural theology began with a bizarre twist in English political arithmetic. In 1710 John Arbuthnot had proved Divine Providence from the constant regularity between male and female births. More boys are born than girls. This could not result from chance (i.e. equal chances) so must be arranged by God to make allowance for the excess of young men killed off at sea, in war, etc.[15] The idea was transmitted by the Boyle lectures in the first decade of the eighteenth century, lectures dedicated to the proof of the existence of God on the basis of His Works.[16]

Süssmilch's demographic theology appeared in three editions, 1741, 1747, and posthumously 1775–6. It was a prodigious compilation of facts, combining church registers and mortality statistics. The second edition of 1747 noted royal approbation; belatedly, at his life's close, he was elected to the Berlin Academy. His immense book had much straightforward moralizing, the higher mortality rate of cities being attributed more to sin than to bad sanitation. But there was also a good deal of comment on population management. The marriage rate and the age of marriage were seen to depend upon the availability of farmland. This in turn was held to fix fecundity. He predicted fluctuating birth rates. As a population grows, land is less valuable, marriage is delayed, the birth rate drops. But in due course there is a shortage of labour and land is more available, so the marriage age decreases and the birth rate climbs. If we leave out the Seven Years' War, for which statistics were lacking, the prediction was true of Prussian numbers from the time of Süssmilch's first edition until 1800. Naturally this model requires numerous constraints, such as negligible (or cancelling) immigration and emigration, and relatively minor changes in agricultural technology.

Süssmilch was one of a long and open-ended line of actors on the stage of what Michel Foucault called a biopolitics 'that gave rise to comprehensive measures, statistical assessments, and interventions aimed at the entire social body or at groups as a whole'.[17] That pairs with an anatomopolitics

---

* In 1766 Süssmilch published 'an attempt to prove that the first language has its origin not in men, but on the contrary derives from the creator'. With the vigour of a Noam Chomsky he urged that in principle human beings cannot invent language from scratch, nor indeed can they even acquire one as infants by mere empirical generalization from the words of their parents. Linguistic competence derives from innate skills, the gift of the Creator. This thesis was so striking that the Berlin Academy set its 1769 prize essay topic on the alleged divine origin of language. Of the nineteen candidates, we remember only the winner: J.G. Herder. His essay is the announcement of the new German conception of language as a social and cultural phenomenon. It is not a matter of, as Hobbes put it, 'mental discourse', that for convenience is cast into spoken words. It is essentially public. Although Herder owed much to his mentor J. G. Hamann, and although the triumph of his views lay in the work of his successor Wilhelm Humboldt, this prize essay response to Süssmilch marks a fundamental transition in European thought: language, once essentially in the mind, a matter of mental discourse, became inherently communal and public.

focussed on the body, on 'biological processes: propagation, births and mortality, the level of health, life expectancy and longevity'. Foucault regarded these as 'two poles of development, linked together by a whole intermediary cluster of relations'. The distinction between the body politic and the body of the person sounds fine, but in fact I don't see Foucault's polarization in the texts that concern us. Süssmilch's statistical assessments (the biopolitical pole) are directed exactly at propagation, births, mortality, health, life expectancy (the anatomopolitical pole). But no matter how we take Foucault's polarization, biopolitics in some form has been rampant in western civilization from the eighteenth century or earlier.

The most famous piece of biopolitics is the Malthusian debate. This originated well before Malthus published in 1798, as his subtitle made plain: *With Remarks on the Speculations of Mr Godwin, M. Condorcet and Other Writers*. His celebrated proof, that production increases arithmetically while population grows geometrically, did, however, introduce a nineteenth-century preoccupation. His conclusion was that the poor must, at their own peril, have few children. Karl Pearson's eugenics presented the same theme at the start of our century, not in order to help the poor but to save the rich.

Biopolitics has the standard feature of a risk portfolio, namely that at almost the same time opposite extremes are presented as dire perils (today it is nuclear winter/greenhouse effect).[18] The 'population problem' denotes both the population explosion of other peoples and too low a birth rate of one's own people. During the nineteenth century in France, one's own people were French, the others German and British. In Prussia, as discussed in chapter 22, the others were Jewish. Today the others are the Third World. In late-Victorian England, the others were the labouring classes.

German biopolitics began in earnest after the Seven Years' War in 1757–63, and here the issue was underpopulation. Perhaps a third of the people had died, and many regions were left almost empty. They required colonization in order to restore ravished farmland. Many features of Prussian statistics originate with this objective concern, augmented by the zealous administration-for-its-own-sake of Frederick the Great.

A list of the categories of things that were counted during his reign required seven pages.[19] Many were 'natural', to be expected in any agricultural state whose economic development was comparable to Prussia's. But there were idiosyncrasies. First, a fundamental distinction was imposed upon the population. Every person had to be either civil or military. The military included not only the soldiers, but also their dependants and servants. The civil list was sorted according to the nine rubrics mentioned above: the military list had five divisions. This sorting was enduring. When we examine the excellent yearbooks published by the Prussian statistical bureau throughout the latter half of the nineteenth century we find the first division in the population: military on the left, civil on the right. You were first of all civil or military, then you were male or female, servant or master, Mennonite or Old Catholic. There was of course an unstated rationale. People were counted, as they still are, by geographic area. The civilian population stayed in one place, while the military were mobile and in garrisons. Military and civil were different aspects of the national topography. But in all of Europe, it was only Prussian official statistics that saw this as a first principle of all labelling of citizens, more fundamental, even, than their gender.

A second innovation began in 1745, probably in response to queries posed in the first edition of Süssmilch's book. We find the beginnings of tables for immigration, emigration, nationality and race. On the civilian side of the list, the nine basic categories had a subtabulation for people who were Walloons, French, Bohemians, Salzburgers or Jews. Although East Prussia was part of the kingdom, Poles, Lithuanians, Latvians etc. were not mentioned. This was partly because East Prussia was indifferently administered, and partly because it was not contiguous with Prussia proper so that migration between these two parts was less easy than between the other Prussian 'islands' in the west. Specific migration questions developed piecemeal. The Silesian towns began to record bourgeois movements from 1750. Some tables of colonists were made in 1753, but they became serious only during the reconstruction period following 1763. They started in Minden in 1768, and soon the tables covered the entire kingdom.

Most designations of minority groups were local and haphazard, the exception being Jews. They show up in the tables in 1745, and, at that time, not as a religious group. Soon there was to be a completely separate and regular enumeration of all Jewish households. Complete tables, known as the *General-Judentabellen* or *Provinzial-Judenfamilie-Listen*, became a routine part of Prussian numbers in 1769.

Aside from the tables of births, marriages and deaths, official statistics were private, for the eye of the king and his administrators. There were of course all kinds of documentation in commercial affairs, although even these tended to follow the patterns of counting people.[20] They ran parallel to the diligent productions of enthusiastic amateurs, of whom Süssmilch and Busching provide two different kinds of example. The third force in German statistical activity was the 'university statistics' from which our subject is said to take its name.

It is unclear (and unimportant) how far back the tradition of university statistics can be traced. Herman Conring, the great Jena professor of

politics and geography – and correspondent on these topics with Leibniz –
is said to have given enthralling lectures on the economic states of various
nations, and is often properly called the founder of the 'university
statistics'. He called his lectures *notitia statuum Germaniae*. A successor in
Jena, B.G. Struve, lectured on *de statu regni germanici*, and then, *notitia
statuum Germaniae*. Martin Schmeitzel at the same university had a
Collegium politico-statisticum in 1725.[21]

Words on which our word 'statistics' could draw are hardly original
with these professors, and probably have a better Italian pedigree than a
German one. But it was undoubtedly a Göttingen scholar who fixed the
very word 'Statistik'. Gottfried Achenwall thought of what he called
statistics as the collection of 'remarkable facts about the state'.[22] The
successor to his chair valiantly defined statistics in the words, 'History is
ongoing statistics, statistics is stationary history.' The Göttingen statisticians had a strong positivist bent:

Strictly speaking, one wants only facts from the statistician; he is not responsible
for explaining causes and effects. However, he must often seize upon effects in
order to show that his fact is statistically important – and moreover his work will
be entirely dry, if he does not give it some life and interest by introducing, at
suitable points, a mixture of history, cause and effect.[23]

The work of these men was seldom quantitative. They were opposed to
number-crunching of the sort represented by Süssmilch. They thereby
stand for an antinumerical and anti-averaging tradition that emerges from
time to time in our history. They produced giant pull-out tables, but here
one found descriptions of climates (for example) more often than measures
of cloudiness. Despite this, I find a very substantial continuum between the
historical-political-economic-geographic-topographical-meteorological-
military surveys of the university statisticians, and, for example, the
contents of Busching's two journals. Busching was thoroughly numerical
– statistical in our sense of the word – but on the title pages or in the titles
of many of his books he called himself an historian-geographer – a statistician in the Achenwallian sense of the word.

German culture demands definitions of concept and object. It requires
an answer to the question: is X an (objective) science? Is statistics, then, a
science? If so, what science is it, and what are its concepts, what its objects?
'Until now, there have been 62 different definitions of statistics. Mine will
make it 63', wrote Gustav Rumelin in 1863.[24] He was director of the
Württemberg statistical office, a political scientist and staunch Malthusian.
I don't know which 62 he had in mind – I think that by 1863 I can do twice
as well as he can, in the German literature alone. But already there had
been the correct move taught by professors of philosophy: distinguish!
There are two sciences. One is descriptive and non-numerical, namely the

work of the university statisticians. Then there is the heir to English political arithmetic, commenced seriously in Germany by Süssmilch. C.G.A. Knies's 1850 *Statistik als selbständige Wissenschaft* furthered this conclusion, recommending that although we owe the word 'statistics' to Achenwall, we should transfer it, and use it to name the numerical studies of the political arithmeticians.[25] We ought then to say that Achenwall did something other than *Statistik*; let us call it (said Knies) *Staatskunde*.

So what? All this seems like word-play. Harald Westergaard ironically recounted this 'saga' of the word 'statistics', concluding that 'but for the curious change of names which has taken place, and which has often puzzled students of statistics, little interest would have attached to it'.[26] Westergaard implied that we would never even notice Achenwall were it not for his having institutionalized the word 'statistics' which we now use to name something numerical and non-Achenwallian.

Perhaps that opinion underestimates the university statisticians. For example, Austria established a statistical office, on the Prussian model, only in 1829. This was a systematic bureaucracy for the compilation of numerical data. Who would it employ? The staff was taken straight from the universities, where old-style university statistics continued to be taught. The subject was part of the curriculum at the six Austrian universities – Innsbruck, Padua, Pest, Prague, Venice and Vienna. It was also standard at numerous colleges and lycées. Rightly or wrongly, the Austrian administrators did not see teachers and students as doing something essentially different from what a statistical bureau should do.

The Austrian example is an objective item from bureaucratic history. At a more impressionistic level it looks as if the Prussian statistical bureaucracy was remarkably continuous with the old university statisticians. It was numerical, yes, but also descriptive. There was a great deal of resistance to theoretical French notions of 'statistical law'. The Prussian tabulations resembled those of Achenwall and Schlozer, although with numbers instead of words. Bureaucratic efficiency was combined with mathematical naiveté. The Prussian bureau was heir to university statisticians, just as it was heir to the administrative expertise of the ministries of Frederick the Great, and heir to the army of amateurs of numbers.

It was however the amateurs of numbers that most struck literary travellers such as Goethe and Bernoulli. The travel books constantly referred to local periodicals more ephemeral than Busching's, crammed with numerical tid-bits, collected with an indiscriminate enthusiasm not equalled in Britain or France. Travellers with an eye to policy and public affairs could also learn. None toured more diligently in the continent of Europe than gentlemen from the British Isles. Arthur Young's travels in Europe, and his subsequent role in agricultural reform, are well known.

But such travellers did not import only agricultural technique. As we have seen from my second epigraph, they acquired an enthusiasm for statistics. The very word entered English by way of one of the greatest of the Scottish agricultural reformers, Sir John Sinclair. He was the author-editor of the stupendous 21-volume *Statistical Account of Scotland*, the result of compendious answers to mighty questionnaires. The respondents were the ministers of the 938 parishes of the Church of Scotland.*[27] Sinclair set about this project only after his German travels. His German lessons were not confined to Scotland, however. Here is a laconic diarist of the London scene:

August 20th, 1793: Farmer George has left his harvests and come to town – not to gape at the sights but to make his voice heard in high places – Sir John Sinclair, a Scottish laird, and a group of other large landowners, have induced Mr. Pitt to form a Board of Agriculture. Arthur Young, editor of the *Annals of Agriculture*, has been appointed secretary ... its first duty, I hear, will be to collect the agricultural statistics of the country, based upon returns from every parish.[28]

---

* The *Account* does provide much information that we would still call statistical, for example an analysis of the age distribution, life expectancy and estimates of the total population and its rate of change. There is also much information about lifestyles, for example the fishwives of Fisherow in Inveresk who carry 200-pound baskets of fish on their backs to the Edinburgh market, often covering the five miles in less than an hour, women who take the dominant role in their family and the community, swear much, but, according to their minister, otherwise sin seldom, who play golf on Sundays and have football matches between the married and unmarried women, the former of whom invariably win.

4

Bureaux

Potsdam, 12 November 1805 [In statistical work] the main
requirement is order, completeness and reliability. To achieve these
ends, German diligence, laboriousness and perseverance are more to
the point than brilliant talent, so long as they do not actually
destroy the latter.*¹

Numerical amateurs became public administrators. Sir John Sinclair came
to town in 1793 to found the Board of Agriculture, establishing one of
numerous bureaucracies whose tasks were in part statistical.² A great
landowner and a public man, caught up in the vibrant movement for
agricultural reform in Scotland, he had been convinced in Europe that facts
and numbers were the handmaiden of progress. Nothing was known of his
country: he would change that. 1799 saw the completion of the 21-volume
Statistical Account of Scotland that he had started directly after the
European tour, 1788.³ He wrote to each minister of the Church of
Scotland requesting a detailed schedule of facts about his parish. Some
were obliging, some recalcitrant. He begged, bullied, made jocular threats.
'*Large parties* of the Rothsay and Caithness fencibles are to be *quartered*
upon all the clergy, who have not sent their statistical account, on or before
the term of Martinmass, so that the ministers have it in their choice, either
to write to the Colonel, or to treat his soldiers.'⁴ When at last only six of
the 938 parishes were deficient, he wrote in blood-red, to suggest by 'the
Draconian colour of his ink' what would attend the delinquents.⁵

Sinclair was a one man statistical office. His fellow agricultural
reformers established the Highland and Agricultural Society, which
collected numbers on anything connected with the land. It was a society of
landowners and factors performing functions later assumed by the state.
Its data on the health of farm labourers became the first systematic
statistics of disease. These, as we shall see in chapter 6, created something

---

* Friedrich Wilhelm III, King of Prussia, writing to his minister of trade, Stein, about the
establishment of a statistical bureau. Stein was desperately trying to reform the Prussian
bureaucracy at that time, but was inneffectual until after the disastrous defeat of Prussia at
Jena in 1806. By 1807 he became a principal architect of the new Prussian state.

27

of a sensation when drawn to the attention of the London actuaries. When Sinclair went south to invigorate the bureaucracy, it was a board of agriculture that he wanted. It would do officially much of what he had been doing privately. Under his presidency it duly issued, from London, the *General Report of Scotland* (along with much else). Sinclair became part of the evolving British system of official statistics. It was piecemeal, pragmatic, by turns sensible or bungling, occasionally a source of radical reform, more often the handiwork of the Circumlocution Office. When an authority was needed to gather a new kind of information, some committee or other would establish a board with a designated mission or tack a department on to an existing bureaucracy.

The British kept people separate from stuff. Vital statistics in the south were prepared by the Registrar-General for England and Wales, an office established in 1837. Stuff was managed by the Board of Trade, an old institution with a chequered lineage. Advisory councils on trade had been set up from time to time since the fourteenth century. A permanent council established by Cromwell barely survived the Commonwealth as an American arm, serving as a colonial committee on trade and plantations. Abolished in 1675, it was revived twenty years later to prepare reports on the poor, on obstacles to trade, and on the value of silver. The coinage was a particular concern of its secretary, John Locke. But when Locke retired in 1700, the council once again became largely a colonial office. It doddered on until a celebrated speech by Edmund Burke, who in 1780 denounced the incompetence and profligacy of such mouldering bureaucracies. So the board was abolished for six years, and then reinstituted in 1786 by an order in council which has in a loose way determined the character of the Board of Trade ever since. It hived off various departments as needed, for example a railway department in 1840. Marine departments, harbour departments, finance departments – a bankruptcy department in 1886. Throughout this time there remained more or less in place a variously-called commercial, labour and statistical department, which meant 'whatever is left after the other departments'. There was no conception of centralized number-gathering facilities, and offices were shuffled to suit practical or political needs. Sinclair's Board of Agriculture, which came in with a clear enough mandate of agricultural reform, lost steam with its very success. It spun off a veterinary department in 1865, which became the core of the Board of Agriculture late in the century, a Board that in 1903 became agriculture and fisheries by taking over fisheries from the jurisdiction of the Board of Trade. These moves were characteristically belated responses to practical problems. As for statistics, the numbers were to be collected by the agency that needed them. The British way with numbers reflected a resistance to centralized management, but it was also the 'natural' thing to do. A central bureau dedicated to the pure science of numbering for its own sake: that would be an anomaly.

Prussia inaugurated the anomaly that became the wave of the future. It is tempting to describe the Prussian statistical bureau as an office of numbers-in-general. The bureau was a resource for all the other branches of government. Such an institution presupposes that there is a special type of knowledge, and a new kind of skill, the ability to collect, organize and digest numerical information about any subject whatsoever. That skill will present itself as neutral between parties, as independent of values, as objective.

We do not here want a history of institutions like the Board of Agriculture in London or the Royal Statistical Bureau in Berlin. We need notice only that new kinds of authorities were created, with new kinds of mandate. The transition was commonly effected by coopting the talents of the amateurs. Prussia provides the purest example of synthesizing the talents of secret governmental eighteenth century collectors of information with those of the fetishistic amateur enthusiasts of numbers. One man well represents the combination. Leopold Krug began as one of the greatest of the amateur geographer-statisticians, and became one of the first of the new breed of officially appointed numerators who made public digests of almost all that they counted. Krug had neither the wealth nor the status of a Sinclair. He could not found an organization; he could only accept a call. When the official, secretive bureaucracy was floundering he was an amateur ready to step in to change its methods and aims.

In honour of the coronation of Friedrich Wilhelm II, there was proposed in 1787 a new enumeration of the Prussian people and their dwellings. The motivation was explicit: let the new king and his ministers be told of their power. Unfortunately this was a time of national mismanagement and fading authority. Prussia looked grand on the map, having vastly expanded in the east thanks to successive annexations of parts of Poland. By the third partition of Poland in 1795, Prussia had doubled in size. Yet in that same year it relinquished to revolutionary France, with curious indifference, the prosperous German-speaking lands west of the Rhine. So it was trying to absorb an impoverished, alien and alienated people while losing a good number of its literate artisans. Frederick the Great's erstwhile freedom of the press and religion were terminated, but order diminished and effective control became rare. The bureaucracy seemed unable to achieve even minor goals. In particular, it could not enumerate its own heartland, let alone its disaffected subjects in East Prussia. The secretive bureaucrats had very little information about which to be secretive. Matters were left to the amateurs, among whom none was more notable than Krug.

He had been trained at Halle as a theologian but soon devoted his energies to describing the nation. Between 1796 and 1803 he produced a thirteen-volume *Topographical-Statistical-Geographical Dictionary of the entire Prussian State*, which provided a summary of people and production from every village in the realm.[6] He had the usual battle of an amateur with the censors. In 1796, in conjunction with his dictionary, he began his own journal, which was immediately censored for its article on 'Prussian Military Organization'.*[7] But on the death of Friedrich Wilhelm II he was given a post in the finance department, possibly because of the attention that his banned essay had attracted.[8] This post gave him access to more information than the previous generations of amateurs. He put it to good use. His labours culminated in two remarkable volumes called *Observations on the National Wealth of Prussia*.[9] This was a marvellous condensed model of what could be told by numbers-in-general about every locale in the kingdom. It moved the king to issue a decree on 28 May 1805:

A bureau shall be established to collect and integrate statistical tables from the different departments and offices, the special directories, and from the Silesian finance ministry. His majesty decrees that this department shall be administered by councillor Krug, with direct responsibility to Minister of State Stein.[10]

Stein himself wanted some sort of statistical office, but not one run by an amateur.[11] He had a keen eye on the innovations of France under the emperor, and knew that the time for numbers had come. But he wanted ministries run on a firm but traditional line. Statistics should be retained in a standard ministry directed by a standard official. He had his own favourite from Finance for the job. Krug, he told his king, had neither the status nor the ability to handle complex state affairs. The king was unmoved. I have quoted part of his reply at the head of this chapter, to the effect that we don't want brilliance, we want German diligence. The resulting brief compromise between Stein and the king collapsed with everything else when Napoleon's armies triumphed at Jena in 1807.

Stein, engineering the reconstruction of the shattered Prussian state, knew that statistics would have to play a part. But how? In a circular letter to provincial administrators he invited proposals for a new statistical

---

* Krug's enthusiasm for publication was hard to dampen. In 1804 he teamed up with L.H. Jakob, a philosophy professor at his old university, Halle, to found another periodical. Jakob wrote extensively on immortality, ethics, God, as well as intervening in or maybe inventing a controversy between Moses Mendelssohn and Kant. His true love was finance, and he proposed a new science of national economy that was to be furthered by the new periodical. Jena was more effective than mere censorship: Napoleon abolished the university at Halle. Professor Jakob went off to St Petersburg to advise the imperial government and to found his new science.

office. The response from Königsberg attracted his attention. One of its citizens, J.G. Hoffmann, a man armed with numerous diplomas but of no fixed profession, had been assigned the job of reporting to Berlin. His remarks on Krug's work were derisive. Had Krug given ample information on crops in all the regions of Prussia? Farmers, said Hoffmann, always lie to evade taxes: Krug's figures were 'thoroughly false and consequently thoroughly useless'.[12]

Hoffmann wrote to Stein's taste. His immediate reward from his own city was a chair at Königsberg.[13] He drew up an elaborate reasoned structure for numbering, based on six main categories and 625 subcategories. He stated an official rationale for a central statistical office which became incorporated into a memo from Dohna, the minister of the interior, to the interim chancellor, Altenstein:

> The Bureau shall have as its purpose the most complete collection possible of material bearing on the Prussian state ... the power of the state lies partly in its territory, partly in its people ... the one provides the raw material, and the other by capital and labour transforms it ... Hence the collection of data naturally falls under two main heads, one geographical and one anthropological. It is then natural to appoint two officers, one for each branch ... but the work of these two collectors, no matter how extensive, can be used only with difficulty, unless we appoint a third officer over these two, an officer armed with the necessary skills and tools to engage in political arithmetic in the most general sense of the words. He will transform the material of the first two officers so that they can be put to immediate use by the highest administrators in the land.[14]

The third man was to be a new kind of bureaucrat, doing a new kind of job. Dohna nominated Krug for anthropologist, student of people, as well as proposing a geographer, and a mathematician for the new political-arithmetical task of digesting information. Altenstein cared for Krug's type of person no more than did Stein. 'I don't fail to recognize the diligence and loyalty with which he has for so many years toiled for the Prussian state, but it would not be right to assign him the role of an independently thinking worker ... He has far too narrow a conception of political economy.'[15] None of the individuals suggested by Dohna were suitable leaders. They should be regarded as mere 'tools'.

There was a lot of bickering back and forth. Although the disputes were local, personal, petty matters of power and patronage, they reflected a genuine malaise. What *is* a statistical office? What kind of task does it perform, and what kind of person directs it? Hoffmann was waiting in the wings. His civil service status as professor was higher than that of Krug's in the finance department. He negotiated a dual role as director of the new bureau of statistics and as professor of a new chair of political science in Berlin, where he would teach the theory of the new science that he

directed. The director maintained this role and source of income until
1860. Even then the new director, Ernst Engel, no longer *ex officio* a
professor, established a famous 'statistical seminar' that trained most of the
new generation of German economists of the 1860s.[16] Achenwallian
university statistics was not abolished but transformed.

In the new administration Krug got the secondary, anthropological
post. He had *de facto* control of the bureau during 1814–21, when
Hoffmann was engaged in larger games, such as assisting Hardenburg at
the Congress of Vienna. These details are trifling, in themselves only an
accidental sequence of facts. But some such sequence had to embody the
creation of the new kind of institution. What was being resolved on paper
and in the disposition of persons was the very nature of a general
all-purpose statistical office. Friedrich Wilhelm, in 1804, and Dohna, in
1809, saw it, albeit dimly, as a new type of organization with a new kind of
worker providing a new kind of direction. The traditional and no-
nonsense ministers Stein and Altenstein preferred something that fit into a
streamlined version of the old order. They saw it as an organ to assist the
finance ministry. The taxonomic tree of government had to be maintained,
and an office that in principle might serve all ministries could not fit.
Dohna and the king won. Prussia was being rebuilt from the foundations,
and had a place for new institutions.

A man may float and make his way in a dual role. The formal position of
Hoffmann, both director of the bureau and professor in Berlin, nicely
signalled that the bureau was not part of an old order. But unlike a man, a
government office cannot exist in free suspension; it must report to
someone. It must have a place in the structure of administration. Since
nobody, not even Hoffmann, knew what this new entity was, no one knew
how to lodge it. In 1805 it had briefly reported to Stein, minister of state
for trade. In 1810 it went to the *Polizei* of the ministry of the interior. In
1812 it was placed directly under the new and powerful chancellor, von
Hardenburg. He kept it until 1823, when it went to the interior ministry. It
stayed there until Hoffmann died at the age of 79, in 1844. Under the
directorship of his successor C.F.W. Dieterici it moved to the ministry of
commerce; on his death it reverted to the interior.

One characteristic feature of the new kind of bureau was little affected
by its administrative home. It published and published and published,
combining the eighteenth-century enthusiasm for making numbers public
with the power of orderly government. It needed no Sinclairian letters in
blood-red ink to get responses. Hoffmann himself, professor-bureaucrat,
published over 300 statistical papers, as well as numerous monographs and
official and semi-official handbooks. The numbers, then, were out for all
who would read. A specific publication of the statistical office did not,

however, emerge during Hoffmann's long lifetime. That was left for his pupil and successor, Dieterici.[17] There was not, during the half-century 1810–60, a real dedication towards centralizing the publishing of numbers. Hoffmann's bureau was still gentlemanly and very much under a regime run by men whose ideas, however radical in their day, had been formed before 1810. The requisite new broom was Ernst Engel, brought in from Saxony. A man of energy, before he was 30 he had organized the first world trade fair at Leipzig (1850, the year before the Great Exhibition in London, and establishing Leipzig's tradition summed up in its motto today, *Die Messestadt*). He had established the Saxon statistical bureau, founded two statistical journals, invented mortgage insurance as a means to solving the housing problem, and so on. He started three new periodicals as soon as he was called to Berlin, and in one of them provided, with some dismay, a list of official government statistical periodicals current in 1860. These were regular publications, not occasional papers or special reports; they were published material, not in-house documents; these were not city or provincial papers, but ones issued by the central government in Berlin. It took him 21 pages to list the 410 periodical publications.[18] There were effectively none such in 1800. Is my phrase 'avalanche of printed numbers' an hyperbole?

One might think that an Engel, confronted by this ceaseless statistical activity, might want to call a halt. Not at all. He did indeed want to centralize the publication of statistical data, and moved swiftly to establish a Central Statistical Commission, to correlate the work of all other departments and ministries. Appointed on 1 April 1860, he presented the complete plans for the Commission to his minister on 24 June. But he wanted all the work done by the numerous national authorities replicated on the local scale. Every city, and in particular the free cities of Germany, should do in their domain what his office would do for the kingdom. Each of the 25 regional administrations of Prussia should do the same. The final goal would be that every district, every *Kreis*, every village, should have its own statistical office. This never did happen, but the pattern was there, each major city vying for its own statistical administration: Berlin 1862, Frankfurt-am-Main 1865, Hamburg 1866, Leipzig 1867; Lubeck, Breslau and Chemnitz 1871, Dresden 1874, and 27 major city offices by 1900. There was nothing peculiarly German about this; compare Vienna and Rome in the same year as Berlin, New York and Riga 1866, Stockholm 1868, Buda, 1869.

I shall lay great stress on the very first published civic statistics of a 'modern' sort, those begun by Paris and the Department of the Seine in the 1820s. I shall not even sketch that institutional history, noting only that every country was statistical in its own way. The history of Prussian numbers does not furnish a model for the development of the statistics of other nations. It is instead one among many parallel developments. Germany had special needs deriving from the customs union of 1833. Excise taxes for trade between states were apportioned according to the number of people in each state. Populations were to be assessed every three years. Hence the German states needed frequent raw population data for reasons unknown elsewhere in Europe. Prussia, as the most powerful and as one of the first in the statistical field, established the technology that was to be used, although other German states such as Baden and Württemberg were by no means inactive. Other nations and groups of nations followed other paths. Yet each, in its own way, created similar institutions to create its own public numbers. Since different administrations counted different things, the numbers that were heaped up differed from case to case. National conceptions of statistical data varied, and I argue for important differences between the ideas of Prussia and those of France, for example. Yet Engel perhaps best spoke for an international vision of statistics as a higher calling, the pure science of the numerical facts about the citizen. The institutions brought a new kind of man into being, the man whose essence was plotted by a thousand numbers:

in order to obtain an accurate representation, statistical research accompanies the individual through his entire earthly existence. It takes account of his birth, his baptism, his vaccination, his schooling and the success thereof, his diligence, his leave of school, his subsequent education and development; and, once he becomes a man, his physique and his ability to bear arms. It also accompanies the subsequent steps of his walk through life; it takes note of his chosen occupation, where he sets up his household and his management of the same; if he saved from the abundance of his youth for his old age, if and when and at what age he marries and who he chooses as his wife – statistics looks after him when things go well for him and when they go awry. Should he suffer a shipwreck in his life, undergo material, moral or spiritual ruin, statistics takes note of the same. Statistics leaves a man only after his death – after it has ascertained the precise age of his death and noted the causes that brought about his end.[19]

5

The sweet despotism of reason

Paris, 15 germinal de l'an IV   Isolated, and almost without any
support, with neither public schools nor elementary textbooks,
deprived of most of the means of propagation and influence, the
moral and political sciences – strong only in the energy that is
provoked by oppression, and using time and again the resources
that arise from an instinct for liberty – the moral and political
sciences, whether deceiving tyranny or defying it, prepared our
century for the overwhelming revolution that brings it to a close
and which recalls 25 millions of humankind to the exercise of their
rights, to the study of their interests, and to their duties.[*][1]

Published tabulations freeze the assembled numerical facts of a nation in
cold print. The tables exhibit regularities from year to year. Can that new
kind of thing, a statistical law of human nature, be far behind? Yes and no.
It depends where you are. The Prussia that overthrew Napoleon created a
conception of society that resolutely resisted statistical generalization. It
gathered precise statistics to guide policy and inform opinion, but any
regularities they might display fell far short of laws of society. The
Prussians created a powerful bureau but failed to achieve the idea of
statistical law. That was left for the France that survived Napoleon ('If you
want to attract the attention of the emperor, just recite some statistics').
  Statistical law needed two things. One was the avalanche of printed

---

[*] P.-C.-F. Daunou, at the inauguration of the Institut national, whose second section was
that of moral and political science. It was a great occasion, a celebration of the end of terror.
The entire Directory was present, as were almost all the notable artists and scientists who
had 'survived the storms of revolution'. The ambassadorial corps attended, as did 1,500
amateurs, women and men in almost equal numbers. In addition to Daunou's stirring
speech, the event included, among many other things, a recitation of 184 lines of allegory
on the unity of the arts and sciences, 124 lines of translation from Livy (Hannibal meets a
savage but republican senate), statistical estimates of the population of France, abstracts of
papers from all three sections of the Institut, a peroration from Cabanis on the unity of
physics and metaphysics, a lecture by Fourcroy on a new explosive, accompanied by much
lamentation on the loss of France's greatest chemist (although Fourcroy was widely
believed to have engineered the downfall and guillotining of Lavoisier). There was a lecture
by Cuvier on the fossils of Asian elephants and the event ended with fireworks, namely a
demonstration of Fourcroy's explosive.

numbers that occurred throughout Europe. Without the post-war bureaucracies there would have been no tabulations in which to detect
law-like regularity. But there also had to be readers of the right kind,
honed to find laws of society akin to those laws of nature established by
Newton. Prussia was and will remain our 'crucial experiment', the state
with exquisite statistics and a resistance to the idea of statistical law.

What made the difference between France and England on the one
hand, and Prussia on the other? I shall briefly mention a simplistic
East/West contrast, made familiar by some historians of European
culture, and then, in this chapter, point to a specific fact of French
intellectual history.

East/West is gross but convenient. The dominant languages and institutions of the West were French and English, its capitals Paris and
London. The chief language and institutions of the East were German,
and Berlin increasingly became its centre of gravity. Mainline western
thought was atomistic, individualistic and liberal. The eastern, in contrast,
was holistic, collectivist and conservative.

The western sovereign, whether it be a king or the people, was constituted by the individuals in its domain, just as Hobbes had taught. Further
east, as Herder's successors were to insist, the group – its civilization and
language – conferred identity upon the individuals who comprised it.
Western individuals (so ran their philosophy) constitute their sovereign.
Eastern states (so said their philosophers) constitute the individuals.

The liberal West held that industrial society with all its problems and
successes was best run by a combination of free individual competition
and philanthropy. The conservative East created the welfare state. Berlin
introduced workmen's compensation for industrial accidents, health and
unemployment insurance, and other aspects of the social net. Many of the
men who did the spadework for this Prussian collectivism worked in the
bureaux that collected statistical data and resisted any idea of statistical
law.

How far can one take this caricature of a contrast beyond the political
arena? Norton Wise has pushed it as far as physics.[2] He urges a fundamental divide between western and eastern physics that endured
throughout the nineteenth century, and which parallels the differences
between liberals and conservatives. His analysis spans the entire field, but
an example will suffice. Boltzmann and Maxwell converged on 'the same'
statistical mechanics. They did so by substantially different routes.
Maxwell was open to the idea that this science is indeterministic. Its laws
might be purely probabilistic in character. Boltzmann, on the other hand,
held deeply to a belief that statistical mechanics is deterministic. One of
his chief results, the *H*-theorem, was intended to confirm this.

Obviously, not all easterners rejected the idea of statistical law, nor did all westerners think that there are statistical laws. It does however happen that the German advocates of statistical law were typically in the liberal minority, while those French and English opponents of the very idea were commonly in the conservative camp. I shall from time to time draw attention to notable examples.

It is misleading to say that the dominant Prussian reaction to the French idea of statistical law was to reject it. 'Law' itself was understood differently. Here is a judicious French observer, writing in the article *Loi* for *La Grande Encyclopédie* at the end of the nineteenth century.

The English ... envisage law, in itself, as a given fact, and their reasoning implies that it is a product of the will of individuals. The Germans (historians and metaphysicians) attacked the problem [of law] at its origins ... they regard law as a social product, at the same level as custom and language; it is never fixed, but in constant evolution and transformation.

Why, if you are a conservative, who regards law as a social product, are you disinclined to think that statistical laws can be read into the printed tables of numerical data, or obtained from summaries of facts about individuals? Because laws are not the sort of thing to be inferred from individuals, already there and counted. Laws of society, if such there be, are facts about the culture, not distillations of individual behaviour.

Why, if you are a liberal who regards law (in the political sphere) as a product of the will of individuals, are you content to find statistical laws in facts about crime and conviction published by the ministry of justice? Because social laws are constituted by the acts of individuals.

This model indicates where many nineteenth-century incoherencies arise. To begin with, if, as many today will tell you, probabilistic law applies to populations, *ensembles*, or *Kollectivs*, ought not the collectivist, holistic attitude be the one that invites the notion of statistical law? Conversely, if the liberal thinks that statistical laws are laws of society, akin to laws of nature, then what freedom is left to the individuals en masse? This question of statistical fatalism reared its confusing head in mid-century.

The broad issues of statistical fatalism and East/West will occupy us much in the sequel. Here I turn to a more specific antecedent for the idea of statistical law. It was a pre-statistical, even antistatistical, notion of laws of society. It was a conception of the moral sciences. Daunou's declamation in my epigraph is a ringing statement of faith. The moral sciences are reasonable, liberating, and the foes of tyranny.

Science morale does not denote that priggish entity that we in English call morals. It is more to be understood as a science of *mœurs*, of customs, of society. In the course of effecting its mid-nineteenth-century reforms,

Cambridge University introduced a faculty of moral sciences to embrace
economics, politics, psychology, metaphysics and ethics. This classification in a single faculty was a borrowing from the French, who had in
turn invented the idea of moral science by idealizing their two English
heroes.

Newton had provided celestial and rational mechanics. The French
took from him everything but his theism. Locke's theory of ideas
investigated the human mind and its faculty of reason. Many of the chief
philosophers of the French Enlightenment cheerfully accepted the label of
idéologues, not ideologues or ideologists but idea-ists, Locke-ites. It was in
this matrix that there arose a conception of *science morale*, at first a rational
theory of individuals and society. 'We understand by this term all those
sciences that have as their object either the human mind itself, or the
relations of men one to another.'[3]

Those are the words of Condorcet, preeminent spokesman of the moral
sciences. The last of the *philosophes*, he was also a student, friend and
adviser of the greatest of the *physiocrats*, Turgot. Drafter of constitutions,
noblest (and most romantic) of the moderate revolutionaries, reformer of
educational systems and advocate of the rights of women, it was he who
would say that 'the American, breaking his own chains, acquires the duty
to break those of his slaves'. That utterance was just one of many
declaimed in his acceptance speech upon election to the Academy in 1782.
In the midst of such classic liberal sentiments he prophesied a glowing
future for the moral sciences:

Those sciences, created almost in our own days, the object of which is man himself,
the direct goal of which is the happiness of man, will enjoy a progress no less sure
than that of the physical sciences; & this idea so sweet, that our nephews will
surpass us in wisdom as in enlightenment, is no longer an illusion. In meditating on
the nature of the moral sciences, one cannot help seeing that, as they are based like
the physical sciences upon the observation of fact, they must follow the same
method, acquire a language equally exact & precise, attaining the same degree of
certainty.[4]

In unpublished revisions of the acceptance speech he made his convictions more plain. 'The moral sciences are founded upon facts and
reasoning; their certainty will therefore be the same as the physical
sciences.' The physical sciences are contrasted to the mathematical ones;
they have 'only that kind of certainty which is a true probability
mathematically expressed'. The theorems of rational mechanics are part of
mathematics and can be 'understood intuitively at a particular instant'. But
propositions about real existence are only probable. 'Thus it is from the
more or less constant order of facts observed in moral as in physical
phenomena that the kind of certainty that pertains to reality is derived.'[5]

The moral sciences aimed at studying people and their social relationships. But how? Not by anticipating empirical psychology or survey-sample sociology. Condorcet's moral science meant chiefly two things, and thereby hangs a tale not yet unravelled even today. He mapped out what have become two distinct terrains. One is moral-science-as-history, the other, moral-science-as-(probability, statistics, decision theory, cost-benefit analysis, rational choice theory, applied economics, and the like).

Moral-science-as-history is not chronology but that overarching structure presented in Condorcet's most famous work, his long-projected theory of human progress, *Esquisse d'un tableau historique des progrès de l'esprit humaine*. It was finished while he was in hiding towards the end of 1793, and published in 1795, a year after he died. It is a story of human development through nine stages, and of its entry into the tenth, the one inaugurated by the French Revolution. It is a model taken perhaps poetically by Saint-Simon, and taken quite literally by Auguste Comte, founder of positivism. Comte's seemingly interminable *Cours de philosophie positive*, published between 1830 and 1842, took human knowledge into the stage of positive science, the state achieved by the likes of Lagrange and Cuvier, Bichat and Laplace. The model of Condorcet's *Esquisse* was transformed by Hegel into historical dialectic; it is a model given new muscle by Marx.

The other terrain of moral science has no one on show as prodigious as Hegel and Marx. In the last of his works to be printed in his lifetime, Condorcet named it 'social mathematics'. 'I prefer the term "social" to the terms "moral" or "political" because the sense of these latter words is less comprehensive and less precise .'[6] Always a classifier, he divided social mathematics under five heads. First is the study of compound interest and other time series. Then comes permutations and combinations, then induction, then the calculus of probabilities and finally the theory of mean values. Although I shall emphasize the statistical inheritance of the social mathematics side of moral science, one could as well emphasize economics. That taxonomy confirms my slight modernization of terminology and interests: the second terrain of moral sciences was moral-science-as-(probability, statistics, decision theory, cost-benefit analysis, rational choice theory, applied economics, and the like).

The two terrains of moral science, historicist and numerical, diverged briskly in the early nineteenth century. Comte was the explorer of one, the statistician Quetelet of the other. They fought over various labels such as 'social mechanics' and 'social physics'. In each case the name apparently proposed by Comte for his historical epistemology was snapped up by Quetelet as a name for the statistical study of people (anathema to Comte). In desperation Comte invented the word 'sociology', holding it to be so

ugly that the statistical students of humankind would never deign to steal
it. He was proven wrong once again.[7]

It may seem that Condorcet's social mathematics, his numerical side,
must be the one that concerns our quest for the origins of statistical law.
That was the view of Karl Pearson, who much admired Condorcet, a
kindred spirit, no great mathematician, but with a 'mind strong in imagination, which can grasp new problems which can be solved mathematically'. He thought that Condorcet was 'the first writer who had a philosophy of his science [statistics], and indicated that our belief in the
stability of statistical ratios is precisely the same as our belief in the so-
called natural laws'.[8] Yes, but what mattered was Condorcet's firm
philosophe/physiocrat conviction that there do exist laws of society. For
him these were not statistical, but the principles of reason itself. The truth
in Pearson's judgement is this: the future field of statistics inherited the
idea of law from a moral science born of Enlightened Reason.

Pearson spoke of stable statistical ratios. Condorcet had precious few to
hand.[9] They were biological more than social. They were propositions
about birth and death, and included for example some speculation about
smallpox prevention. The first statistical law is this: with great regularity,
the ratio of male to female births is about 13:12. At any rate it exceeds $\frac{1}{2}$;
more boys are born than girls. I mentioned that John Arbuthnot established this in 1710, arguing that the preponderance of male births shows
Divine Providence at work. The idea had many consequences, including
the labours of J. P. Süssmilch. The study of death had more potential practical importance. By 1670 it was evident to the enlightened leaders of the
brief Dutch Republic that mortality data should be used to guide rates for
selling life annuities – the standard way of raising capital for the state. The
idea did not really take off, for reasons well elaborated by Lorraine
Daston, but it was a viable idea of actuarial data as applied science.[10]

Even though mortality statistics were of little practical importance until
the nineteenth century, they were conceptually significant. They gave rise
to the idea of a law of mortality, and to the very phrase '*law* of mortality'.
The fascination induced by these laws is well illustrated by J. H. Lambert,
who in 1765 made the most fastidious of eighteenth-century attempts at
fitting a mathematical equation to death. He was a notable self-taught geo-
meter, astronomer, philosopher, contributor to the probabilistic theory of
measurement and error, and a founder of photometry, the science that
measures the properties of light. He wrote a little textbook on practical
applications of mathematics. An edition of Süssmilch had recently
appeared, so he appended a ninth chapter of remarks on mortality, life
tables, births and marriages, using the information provided in *Die gottliche Ordnung*.[11]

One problem in representing mortality by a single formula was that the death rate for infants in those days was immense and for children very great; it was hard to smooth this into the more regular mortality of later years. Lambert proposed to embrace the entire life span in a curve of some complexity, a combination of a parabola and two logarithmic curves.[12] This law was admiringly picked up in 1787 by E.-E. Duvillard de Durand.[13] He was an important civil servant to whom I shall return, the man who introduced systematic life insurance to France. Duvillard's use of Lambert was in turn repeated as late as 1825, in the first volume of Quetelet's journal, founded in part to carry statistical news.[14] There the author stated that Lambert's equation 'gives, with astonishing precision, the law of mortality for London'. (It doesn't.) We do, however, get a graphic way of comprehending the above equation: 'The human species dies in the same way that a prismatic vase, or vertical cylinder, empties itself through a tiny hole in its base.'

Laws of birth and mortality abounded. Lambert serves me only as an example. Because death curves were not seen as a matter of *mœurs*, or customs, they gave little foothold for moral science or social mathematics. But they did furnish data for the solution of problems in social mathematics: ideally, for example, the correct rates at which a government should sell life annuities when a given rate of interest is prevalent.

Other statistics were, however, coming upon the scene: the distribution of age at marriage, for example. Was that not a consequence of customs, or moral choice? Here Süssmilch was central. Just as Lambert fitted a bizarre curve to Süssmilch's mortality data, so he drew digests of Süssmilch's marital tables, stating that these are also law-like. We move into the domain of the voluntary. What other human choices might display regularities?

a collection of men is made up of a certain number of persons of all kinds, and this brings about a roughly similar result, for one must take note that in these cases which are most dependent on chance one may, when the chances are numerous, calculate the outcome. For example it has been discovered in the Canton of Berne, that the number of divorces is very much the same from one decade to the next, and there are cities in Italy where one can calculate exactly how many murders will be committed from year to year. Thus, events which depend on a multitude of diverse combinations have a periodic recurrence, a fixed proportion, when the observations result from a large number of chances.[15]

These words of Mme de Staël were published just two years after Condorcet's death, and yet they jump beyond his ideas. She prophetically spoke of divorce and murder rates. Those stable ratios of deviancy are the stuff of early nineteenth-century French statistical thought. Condorcet's moral sciences stood upon an entirely different footing. They had the optimistic aim of subjecting social relations to 'the sweet despotism of reason'.[16] Their province was not that of empirical ratios of perversions but of the *a priori* solutions of sweet reason.

On the historicist side, Condorcet's posthumously published *Sketch* of the progress of the human spirit is his most famous work. On the statistical side his best known but still obscure work was a treatise on voting.[17] It analysed rational behaviour, where the word 'rational' bears less the sense of 'reasonable' than the meaning it has in 'rational mechanics', the deductive science of a Newton or a Lagrange. It had practical ambitions. Condorcet knew that France would soon demand assemblies and jury trials. It could adopt the ancient haphazard English models. But why prefer exactly twelve good men deciding by unanimous vote? Is the English jury derived from Babylonian superstition about the number twelve? Just as the Revolution would soon decimalize coinage, distances and the antique calendar, any reasonable man could query such primitive legal customs. What are the mathematically best sizes for groups that decide by majorities, and what are the best voting procedures?

Condorcet's essay was long neglected but has recently gained some fame as a precursor of Arrow's paradox about voting behaviour, an honour that it shares with lesser-known work by J. C. de Borda.[18] Arrow's paradox is an *a priori* observation about the impossibility of satisfactory voting procedures under certain circumstances. It is precisely an affair of the reason. In later chapters I show how Condorcet's proposals for juries engaged his successors, Laplace and then Poisson. Poisson's analysis of juries has been revived of late, for it embarked on a statistical study of conviction rates for juries of various sizes and voting rules. That was literally impossible for Condorcet, because he had no access to records of convictions. Only after 1829, when there were printed tabulations of French jury decisions, could Poisson form the idea of probabilistic laws of voting behaviour. It was the printed numbers that turned Condorcet's *a priori* studies into Poisson's empirical ones.

Condorcet is important to the student of probability for all sorts of reasons. Among others, it was probably he who interested Laplace in the topic, thus making him the godfather of modern probability theory.[19] It was he who picked up, from Laplace's early paper of 1781, the mode of inference first proposed by Thomas Bayes, and then made of it a major tool in his *a priori* analysis of voting procedures. Despite all these tidy anticipations, I here would emphasize his attempt to institutionalize a new *kind* of science. He little realized that it would turn into several kinds of knowledge. He lived to see none of that. Jacobin overcame Girondin, and the Jacobin constitution became law on 24 June 1793. Condorcet denounced it. He was proscribed on 8 July. Between those two dates his journal on public instruction had printed his account of social mathematics. He went into hiding, where he wrote his sketch of human progress. Being warned that he was discovered, he made for the country, was caught, and died during his first night in the village jail, possibly of a suicide pill he acquired from his medical friends a couple of years earlier.*

Condorcet was dead, but his projects continued. He had a dream for the moral sciences: they would be embodied in institutions alongside the natural sciences upon which they were modelled. If the mathematical and physical sciences comprised the first class of an academy, then the moral sciences should constitute the second. He broke this second class into five sections (metaphysics and morals, natural right and the social sciences, legislation and public obligations, political economy, history).

His plan had effect. The old academies were abolished in 1791. The Institut national came into being in 1796, heralded with the words of Daunou, my epigrapher. Daunou said it was to be a 'national temple whose doors, always closed to intrigue, would be open only to the clamour of true fame'. The Institut, with its second class for moral sciences organized roughly on Condorcet's lines, flourished all too briefly. In 1801 it elected its first foreign associate: Thomas Jefferson. The second class was filled not with statisticians but with *idéologues*. Napoleon had no use for them. In 1803 he put them out to pasture on pensions, abolishing the second class. Daunou's words were recalled, ineffectually: 'despotism, whose destiny it was to persecute the moral and political sciences ...' Napoleon reorganized the Institut. He barely allowed history: very ancient history. He was about to invade Egypt with 170 scientists. He then styled himself 'Bonaparte, general-in-chief and member of the Institute'. It took another revolution, that of 1830, to recreate an Academy of Moral Sciences. The first foreign member it elected was no Jefferson but rather the spry but ageing Thomas Malthus, welcomed by survivor Daunou, five years his senior.†[20]

---

* Tall tales should not be entirely discarded. Condorcet's safe house near the Luxembourg was found for him by his friend, the *idéologue* physician Cabanis, whose pupil, Pinel, the psychiatric reformer of Bicêtre, took Condorcet to the landlady of Pinel's student days. The good Mme de Vernet tried to keep him there after his cover was blown: 'Sir, the Convention may declare you *hors la loi*, but not *hors de l'humanité*.' There is also the story of being caught in the village inn. The landlord became a trifle suspicious when this putative rough citizen with his elegant white hands sat there reading Horace and ordered an omelette. 'How many eggs?' 'Twelve.'

† We have seen that Daunou had a way with words. He was ordained in 1787, the year in which he won the prize of the Berlin Academy for his essay on the authority that parents can exercise over their children. In 1789 he was on the steps of the Oratory, preaching the panegyric for those who had died storming the Bastille. In 1792 he was elected without contest to the assembly as a member for Arras. He voted with Condorcet for abolition of the monarchy but no execution: not a politic vote. He carried on as a scholar, adviser, archivist with Napoleon. He was an almost unrepentant *idéologue* – indeed, when Destutt de Tracy died in 1836, the very last one alive. And distinctly not moribund: in his late

Alas for Condorcet, this revived academy has never been of the least significance. Moral science was of the generation of Daunou, Malthus and Condorcet. It was succeeded by its progeny, which included empirical statistics. Condorcet's end-of-enlightenment fantasy of an academy or class of moral sciences was doomed, in part, by its *idéolog*-ical baggage. Napoleon was the future. It was his novel institutions, not those of Condorcet, that would survive. Yet there is a falsehood in this simplistic assertion. For what survived was set in motion by Turgot, and outlasted Napoleon by many a year. A single career serves to illustrate this.

Let us place beside Condorcet a man twelve years his junior, Duvillard de Durand. I have already mentioned how he took up Lambert's law of mortality in a study of life annuities. Such proto-statisticians were stabilizers who kept the state ticking over in those days of turmoil. Condorcet's vision of numerical moral science never took serious hold in the Academy of Moral Sciences. It had of necessity to follow another path, a bureaucratic one.

Turgot appointed people like young Duvillard to the controller-general's office in 1776. When Turgot was removed, Duvillard was sent to the treasury. He lasted in that bureau until year VIII of the Revolution. Then he went to the Senate, and in 1805 to the statistical office of the interior ministry. In 1812 he had another promotion, becoming head of the general services bureau. Who actually gave France the metric system or the new coinage? Duvillard worked on both projects and without his like neither would have succeeded.

In revolutionary times intellectuals and bureaucrats did mingle. Both Duvillard and Condorcet were members of the 1789 Club, which seems to have begun as a group of highly placed radical intellectuals (Lafayette, Dupont de Nemours, Sieyès, etc.). It soon attracted bankers and became identified with the right. It was elitist and secret, and may have had the following words inscribed above the door of its clubhouse: 'The little fish are always eaten by the bigger ones.'[21] Condorcet defended the elitism on the ground that the club had to be for equals, and hence strict admission rules were necessary. They would make it free of faction, a place where the best minds of the nation would preserve the state while transforming it to a better society. Hence it failed. Even Condorcet rejoined the Jacobin Club in 1791, and the 1789 Club disappeared. But for a civil servant such as Duvillard it had briefly been a perfect place to listen and influence.

Duvillard did influence. His statistical analysis of debt, annuities and

sixties and throughout his seventies he provided a course of study, mostly at the Collège de France, that, published after his death, ran to 20 volumes. He resumed his seat in the Academy of Moral Sciences on its refounding in 1832. Always an academician in the section for beaux-arts and inscriptions, he became its permanent secretary when he was 77.

the like was admired in the academy of sciences in 1786. He headed the commission to draw up a plan of life insurance, which had hitherto been something of an English speciality.[22] While in the finance ministry he became head of an office for political arithmetic in 1790. Of the three mathematicians who reviewed his plans for national life insurance, one was Condorcet, and a second was another member of the 1789 Club.

Condorcet did not survive the Terror. Duvillard did. While in the interior ministry he made the first deep analysis of the actuarial consequences of the great discovery of the age, Jenner's vaccination for smallpox. What effect would this have on national longevity? The matter was pressing when the state raised capital by selling life annuities.[23]

He appears to have been a sensible administrator who asked what we now think of as the right theoretical questions. For example, his paper on the mathematical statistics of the population was the first attempt, in France, to obtain systematic breakdowns of the laws of mortality not just according to age but also by sex, marital status, and, tentatively, location and even occupation.[24] Such a question entailed new echelons of clerks, enumerators, calculators, printers that would in time create the avalanche of numbers. Duvillard was also a prophet. He did not in general get what he wanted. He believed that it would be possible to obtain exact although incomplete figures, and then use the probability calculus to infer estimates of populations, age distribution and the like. Early on, the Consulate rejected his proposals for a highly mathematical board, preferring a more descriptive statistics based on exhaustive surveys made in the provinces, and not inferred by calculations made in the metropolis.[25]

Duvillard aspired after recognition. His work on vaccination statistics had him elected to the academies of St Petersburg and Haarlem. France had other standards, however. He competed for election to the first class of the *Institut* in 1803 and 1813, but failed. He did not live long enough to enter the Academy of Moral Sciences when it was restored in 1832, although he had been promoted as a possible member. It would not have mattered much to him: he wanted to be recognized among the mathematicians, which he was not. He did something much more significant. Toiling away, organizing the metric system, the new coinage, and above all the new bureaucracies for collecting statistical data, he had more effect on post-revolutionary France than we can ever trace directly to Condorcet.

The Duvillards were the functionaries required by Condorcet's vision of social mathematics. Duvillard's plans for a centralized office using the best technology of probability theory did not succeed. Other factions dominated many of the statistical bureaux of France.[26] They too could be disgraced. When in 1811 Napoleon asked for a complete table of manufactures of France within a week, they were, not surprisingly, ineffectual.[27]

The statistics of Duvillard and his immediate rivals had been motivated by *idéologues* and a desire to improve society by applying reason to facts. Towards the end of the Empire the bodies for collecting data were made increasingly efficient but their mission changed. The high ambitions of the old moral science were forgotten. Statistics became, once again, 'state oriented and intended to give the state its means of direction and control. Consequently, the statistics were no longer to be published.'[28]

These varied forces created the institutions that generated the data that transformed the very conception of social mathematics. Imperial statistics may have become increasingly secretive, but too many interests had been released in the world of officialdom for any one strand to dominate. When the wars were at an end, the city of Paris set the model for publication of social data, and the avalanche of printed public numbers was under way. But without Condorcet's enlightenment vision of law, of moral science, and of the sweet despotism of reason, those number-collecting offices might merely have manufactured tables in the Prussian style. French numeration and social mathematics were instead sired by Newtonian ambitions of laws of society. Without the avalanche of numbers set in motion by the Duvillards, there would have been no idea of statistical laws of society. But without the *a priori* belief that there are Newtonian laws about people, probabilistic laws would never have been read into those numbers.

6

The quantum of sickness

London, 11 March 1825 'When you say that sickness is incapable of valuation, you mean that there are no data whereon a calculation can be made?'

'I mean that life and death are subject to a known law of nature, but that sickness is not, so that the occurrence of the one event may be foreseen and ascertained, but not so the other.'*[1]

Seldom does the irregular become regular before our very eyes. Yet here it is. The witness was John Finlaison. In March he testified as above. In April the MPs gave him a hard time. When they made their report in July:

> Your Committee request particular attention to the evidence of Mr. *Finlaison*, Actuary to the National Debt Office, who having at his first examination before the Committee, signified an opinion that sickness does not follow any general law, and having, in consequence of suggestions from the Committee, paid further attention to the subject, has finally expressed his conviction, that sickness may be reduced to an almost certain law.[2]

The Committee exaggerated. Finlaison did not come round. He did produce tables of sickness rates for various ages, for he was told to do so, but nothing can be more guarded than his surrounding prose: 'If, in our present uncertainty as to the fact of the frequency and duration of Sickness among the labouring classes, we were permitted to assume, what may seem a reasonable hypothesis, the following might perhaps be hazarded, merely as speculation . . .'[3] His reaction to the new data appearing in the 1820s was to conclude, by 1829, that there is not even a law of mortality.[4] The spirit of the day ran otherwise. Whereas in 1825 there was quite literally no

---

* John Finlaison, chief actuary at the National Debt Office, replying to a question from a Select Committee of the House of Commons. He was something of an *enfant terrible*, becoming factor (manager) at the age of nineteen of the enormous Scottish estate of Sir Benjamin Dunbar. In his twenties he took a series of positions in the administration of HM Dockyards, and devised a system of information retrieval for this sprawling bureaucracy. Its accounts always had been eighteen months in arrears, but under his regime all bills were settled within three weeks. During his eleven years in the dockyards his accounting is thought to have saved the nation £2,000,000. He was just the man to be handed the national debt disaster.

known law of sickness of any kind, by 1840 the periodicals were full of laws classified by sex, location, disease and occupation. This was not an abstract, intellectual event, but, as always in the taming of chance, a practical attack on an immediate and material problem. There had long been small local mutual benefit clubs for groups of artisans, freehold farmers or labourers. Members would make small weekly subscriptions in exchange for support when ill, or for widows and orphans after death. In 1793 Parliament finally provided legislation for these friendly or benefit or benevolent societies, as they were called. A club was entitled to register under the Act, and receive some public scrutiny of its financial affairs, which had hitherto been open to much reported abuse. These little societies were ill-organized, but they were everywhere. In 1825 there was speculation that 'one eighth of the whole population of the empire' was enrolled in such organizations, and that they distributed one and a half million pounds annually. The Select Committee stated that by 1802, 9,672 societies had registered under the 1793 Act, and that in 1815 there were 925,429 members.[5]

The well-intentioned Act of 1793 was often revised during the next 30 years. There were difficulties. One regulation allowed the dissolution of a society by a majority vote of five to one. The members would then split the assets. This made a prosperous society of dotards attractive bait for a takeover bid by young men, who would then leave the old and infirm in dismal straits. Secondly, it was natural for clubs to convene in public houses. The publican was often the only man in the place used to dealing with money. He was commonly elected secretary or treasurer and would then encourage spending subscriptions on 'entertainment'.

There were political worries. Combinations of working men (future trade unions) were illegal. Employers imagined that the friendly societies were fronts: 'the Committee regret to find from the evidence that societies, legally enrolled as benefit societies, have been frequently made the cloak, under which funds have been raised for the support of combinations and strikes attended with acts of violence and intimidation'.[6] Because of these concerns the prosperous classes paid more attention to the friendly societies than might otherwise have been the case.

Fraud, drink and agitation were not the main difficulties. The problem was actuarial. No one had any idea of what premiums to charge. Moreover, except when insurance companies got into the act, the English clubs were small and local. This put them in double jeopardy. A society of 80 men gives little room for any 'law of large numbers' to come into play. Secondly, should a disease strike a village or a factory, an entire society might be wiped out financially. Moreover the tables used to compute the premiums were typically signed by 'petty schoolmasters and accountants' who had no idea of 'the probability of sickness'. Such are the critical words of the Select Committee. Their more profound question was: who does have an idea of the probability of sickness? Is there, indeed, such a thing at all?

There were experts. The most famous , Richard Price, had died in 1791, but he had left the Northampton tables, which provided a law of mortality based on the eighteenth-century records of the city of Northampton.* They became the British standard for a century, enacted into laws regarding premiums for life insurance and life annuities. Many American states followed the British example. This was not such a good idea, because Price overestimated mortality. He set life expectancy at birth at 24 years; in his day it was more like 30 and may have been increasing. Hence governments that had relied on life annuities to raise capital were in a bad way. No one was more aware of this than Finlaison. He desperately tried to change the mortality tables in 1819 and 1821, but was prevented in law from doing so.

Price's tables may have been unjust but they made a deep impression upon the English mind. We now think that work done in Sweden was much better.[7] The Select Committee asked nearly all its expert witnesses about what it called the 'Swedish tables', but the experts knew little. Much information can be deduced from published work on French tontines (in a tontine, 100 of us put so much in a fund; the last survivors take all the principal plus interest for themselves).[8] But the English complacently supposed that Price had provided the true empirical basis for mortality tables and although tables for other cities such as Carlisle were drawn up, Northampton ruled.

Finlaison had every ground for worry. Britain, like many other states, raised much capital by selling life annuities. There had been a gigantic annuity sale in 1808. In 1816 the national debt was £900 million. After the Napoleonic wars Britain conducted its affairs by deficit financing. By the standard of all other states its debt was grotesque. Finlaison's job was to ensure that the annuity side of the debt was serviced, given that millions upon millions of pounds had been purchased at disastrous bargain basement rates.

---

* Price constructed these tables after being consulted by the first life insurance company, the Equitable. The probabilist knows him as the man who presented Thomas Bayes's famous essay to the public in 1763, thus conveying one of the main theories of statistical inference. The philosopher knows him as the author of the 1758 *Review of the Principal Questions and Difficulties in Morals*. The historian knows him as the outspoken pamphleteer who in 1789 eulogized the French Revolution, who earlier had preached against the war in America, and who created the very name 'United States of America'. His support of the revolutionary colonists earned him the freedom of the city of London. His actuarial expertise and his sympathies led him to be invited to Philadelphia to be financial adviser to the Congress. He declined for reasons of health and family.

Now Price had also conjectured a schedule of sickness as well as mortality. He made the sickness rate proportional to the mortality rates as shown by his table. It was certainly tidy. Up to age 32 he anticipated one working day of illness every eight weeks, which (after deducting days of holiday standardly allowed agricultural workers) comes to almost exactly one working week per year off sick. Then by increments we are led to two weeks a year for a man of 60.[9] These could not have been entirely foolish rules of thumb for life insurance companies. The Equitable used them without complaint, or so testified Morgan, Price's nephew. So too did the Rock, according to its witness, as did the Royal Union:

The Committee: Dr. Price's tables, I apprehend, were not formed upon any actual observation of the quantity of sickness prevailing?
Mr. Glenny of the Royal Union: No, I think not.
The Committee: Having yourself constructed tables in a great degree from actual observation, you are confirmed in the opinion that Dr. Price's tables were correct?
Mr. Glenny: The nearest to correctness.
The Committee: Do not you think that health has improved by the improvement of the medical science since the time of Dr. Price?
Mr. Glenny: Not much more in adults, but very much in children.[10]

The Committee wanted firmer tables of illness and incapacity than such testimony, and racked all sources. It wrote to Baron Delessert, secretary of the Société Philanthropique in Paris, concerning the French *sociétés de prévoyance*. In reply it received the 1824 statistical reports for Paris and the Seine department, together with the sad news that 'unfortunately, we have as yet made so little progress in institutions of this nature, that I fear you will find little to interest you in the documents which I send'.[11]

Matters stood differently in Scotland. One key witness, Charles Oliphant, was active in the Highland Society, the mighty organ of agricultural reform that numbered Sir John Sinclair among its founders. He was the convener, in 1820, of a systematic study of the 'Scotch benefit societies'. His report of 1824 began with the courteous pride that characterized his testimony in London the next year. The members of a benefit club, he stated, 'have formed themselves into a society with a view to mutual assistance, and *not* as a charitable institution (as some meanly denominate societies) but out of brotherly love for one another, as each providing for himself'.[12]

The object of the Highland Society was precisely that to which the Select Committee addressed itself. 'Generally speaking, it would intro-duce a new idea among the members of Friendly Societies, could a belief be implanted that the schemes of these institutions are in any degree susceptible of calculation.'[13] A questionnaire was sent to every known society in Scotland. Two prizes of twenty guineas in plate or coin were offered.[14] In the end, only 73 societies had enough records, and enough trust that the Society would not abuse them, to respond. That amounted to 104,218 members, classified according to age by decades, and with the number of days off sick for a member. It will be noticed that these were large societies and thereby already on a sounder footing than their English counterparts. In consequence the Highland Society could exhibit the 'law of sickness from 20 to 70 years of age', or '*the quantum of sickness which an individual on an average experiences each year , from 20 to 70 years of age*'.[15] It is a quiet sign of the transition that occurred in statistical thinking that Sinclair had sought the 'quantum of happiness' in Scotland, while a quarter-century later the very society that he had helped found was asking about the quantum of sickness. How did these Scottish figures compare with Price's rule of thumb? For men under 50, Price's formula gave about half a week more of sickness per year per man than was found in the Scottish tabulations. Only in the sixties was there more illness than Price predicted.

The English actuaries for the big companies did not take kindly to the Scottish report. Thus the committee: 'Are you acquainted with the report on friendly or benefit societies lately published by a committee of the Highland Society of Scotland?' Mr Glenny: 'Yes.' 'Have you examined the tables annexed to that report?' 'Yes.' 'State your opinion of them?' 'My opinion is, that the data are too low.'[16] When asked if he thought the data were incorrect Glenny gave a 'qualified answer'. He suspected that the societies that did not report had far greater rates of sickness than those that did report, so the data were skewed. Glenny was actuary for the Royal Union. Were the Scottish figures to be publicly authorized, sickness insurance premiums issued by his company would have to drop by a third.

Finlaison took the stand the next day. He first set eyes on the Highland report in the committee room. He was convinced that there could not be a law of sickness. A week later, 18 March:

Upon further consideration of the question, I am still of the opinion, that, with the materials now existing, we are unable to reduce the event of sickness to a certain determinate law; but nevertheless, I apprehend that it might be considered analogous to insurance against fire and sea risque, and judged of by experience with tolerable accuracy.[17]

On 22 April Finlaison was again asked about the Scottish tables, and replied, 'I think that the data must be considered as far too limited to deduce tables from them.' His previous testimony was read, and judged not consistent with his present stance. Had the Highland Society at least used the correct methods? 'I am not exactly prepared to give an opinion on

that question; I don't know that it is the best mode that could be adopted.'
But Oliphant was on hand to testify that day, and the next. The two men
were called alternately to the stand, with Oliphant to rebut or qualify each
of Finlaison's criticisms as they were made. A dour Scot and an eloquent
one: Oliphant won.*[18]

Finlaison was ordered to compute premiums for friendly societies upon
the Scottish model. He did so grudgingly. Moreover it is plain that he did
not believe the Scottish tables. By 7 June he had obtained the sickness rates
for the army. Each week there is a muster, and the number of men ill on
that day is noted. He obtained 313,695 rank and file from 24 musters (i.e., a
population of about 13,000 soldiers, divided among cavalry, infantry and
footguards). Finlaison noted that only healthy men are admitted to the
army, that all the men are under 45, and that there are sergeants to rouse
malingerers. It stands to reason that the sickness rate in the army will be
much less than for the miserable labourers and crofters in the highlands
and lowlands of Scotland.

> But on the whole two years the rate of sickness [in the army] is remarkably
> constant and uniform, and being equal to 4.78553 per cent, this is the same as if 100
> soldiers had sustained among them 233 weeks of sickness every year, or as if each
> had been sick 2.33 weeks, which is more than thrice the quantum of sickness
> prevailing among benefit societies according to the returns from the Highland
> Society.[19]

Finlaison thought that this observation sufficed to discredit the Scottish
results. We now know better. The best way for a young man to get sick
was to join the British army, but it took 50 years and a Florence
Nightingale to bring the point home.

Finlaison did indeed lose. The British became convinced that there are
regular laws of sickness akin to those for mortality. Statistical law was on
the march, conquering new territory. The Select Committee reconvened in
1827, but the issue was already closed. The witnesses were theoretically
minded men such as Charles Babbage, or men with a medical rather than
an actuarial training.[20] Within a decade a new generation was churning out
laws of sickness. Once the thought of such laws had made an impression,
people found data under their noses. For example, the clerks of the East
India Company had kept great ledgers of all the London workers for that

---

* The committee asked canny Oliphant if the Scottish societies would furnish information to
a government office or department, and he replied, 'I incline to think they would not be so
willing.' Well what if the government then agreed to invest their money securely,
providing 4½ per cent interest (compared to the standard 3 per cent)? No. 'The circum-
stance which would disincline them would be a vague impression, which would not easily
be reduced to calculation; and, on the other hand, the advantage offered they would not
fully appreciate under present circumstances; for I believe in general, though the rate of
interest has fallen, they contrive, by purchasing house property, to receive a larger return
than 4½ per cent.'

gigantic enterprise, resulting in a 'large volume containing a list of 2,461 labourers employed in the month of April, 1823, with a statement of the number of days illness experienced by these labourers one by one, year by year, for the ten succeeding years'.[21]

The most celebrated author of laws of sickness was William Farr, compiler of abstracts in the office of the Registrar-General for England and Wales.[22] Appointed in 1838, the year after the office was formed, he used it to institutionalize British vital statistics until his angry resignation in 1879. (He had hoped that he would finally become Registrar-General in name as well as in role, but the job was a patronage plum for Sir this and Sir that.) He was a Duvillard de Durand whose time had come. His system of reporting and analysis of the incidence of birth, life and death became the model for the world. He was also the first functionary to install and deploy a computer on his premises, for the purpose of calculating and printing out annuity rates and the like.*[23]

Farr created a new kind of job and a new kind of office. No one could have foreseen its influence but it was known to be important. He established his credentials by his work on sickness, contributing to the debate on benevolent societies of the 1830s.[24] As well as particular analyses of sickness statistics, by 1837 Farr could produce, in one of the journals he edited, a tract on methodology providing an 'instrument capable of measuring the relative duration and danger of diseases' as well as their frequency.[25] In another paper he stated that 'the *force* of mortality, at any period of disease is measured by the deaths of a *given* number *sick* at a *given* time'. He then drew upon a century of hospital records. Two things were important: nosology (Farr helped revolutionize the classification of diseases) and counting according to the new nosology. Farr devised an apt word for what he was doing – nosometry, i.e. 'measuring' using a nosology. The very word reminds us that new classifications and new enumerations are inseparable. It also made counting sound more scientific,

---

* Babbage is much admired for conceiving a digital computer that did not work, while the Swedish inventor G. Scheutz is forgotten for having made one that did. Scheutz built his machine for calculating and printing out tables of five-figure logarithms. The original was purchased by an American visitor and presented to the Dudley Observatory, Albany, NY where it seldom worked and cost vast sums of money to repair. At the time of its sale it was exhibited at Somerset House, the site of the Registrar-General's office. Farr pirated the machine, having an engineer copy each of the 4,320 major pieces, 2,054 screws, 364 chains and 902 odds and ends (weight, 1,120 pounds). 'The idea had been as beautifully embodied in metal by Mr. Bryan Donkin as it had been conceived by the genius of its inventors, but it was untried. So its work had to be watched with anxiety, and its arithmetical music had to be elicited by frequent tuning and skillful handling, in the quiet most congenial to such production.' Scheutz fared poorly, as is indicated by sad letters that he and his son sent to Farr from Sweden, never complaining of Farr's theft, but anxious for financial help. The next generation of computers, using punch-cards adapted from the Jacquard loom of 1801, was devised by Hollerith for similar purposes, namely the work of the US census of 1890. Hollerith's company was one of the three parent companies of IBM.

for what, in those days, was more scientific than measuring? Farr could then conclude his paper with a stirring declaration of the new imperialism of statistical law:

The calculated relations of events agree as precisely with the results of direct observation as the calculated atomic weights agree with the results of very careful experiments. There is as much ground to believe the relations regular in one case as the other. If the whole field of life measurement, so successfully cultivated in this country, be taken into account, it will be found that calculation has been much more extensively applied to physiology in the wide sense of the word, than to chemical phenomena, and that while chemistry remains still confined to the 'horn-book of calculation', nosometry may, by the strenuous efforts of the present generation of medical men justly take its place among the sciences.[26]

7

The granary of science

London, 22 February 1832   Amongst those works of science which are too large and too laborious for individual efforts, and are therefore fit objects to be undertaken by united academies, I wish to point out one which seems eminently necessary at the present time, and which would be of the greatest advantage to all classes of the scientific world.

I would propose that its title should be '*The Constants of Nature and of Art*'. It ought to contain all those facts which can be expressed by numbers in the various sciences and arts.*[1]

Numerical regularities about disease, unknown in 1820, were commonplace by 1840. They were called laws, laws of the human body and its ailments. Similar statistical laws were gaining a hold over the human soul. The analogy was close, for laws of behaviour aimed at sick souls. Medical men were able to claim new expertise in matters moral and mental. Before proceeding, however, we should briefly ask an elementary question: what does a law of nature look like?

Our most familiar law is still Newton's. It says that the force of gravitational attraction between two bodies is equal to the product of their masses divided by the square of the distance between them – all multiplied by the gravitational *constant*. Newton did not write it that way, for he expressed his analysis in terms of ratios, so that the constant that we call '*G*' is invisible. His work did imply a value for *G*. A 1740 French expedition to Mt Chimborazo in Ecuador made a fair experimental determination of it, but the observers thought of themselves as determining the mass of the earth. In 1798 Henry Cavendish obtained a superlative laboratory measurement, and he actually computed *G*, but he still described himself as 'weighing the earth'. The idea of an abstract fundamental constant – as opposed to a stable measurable property of a physical object, such as the weight of the earth – was not fully articulated until the nineteenth century.

Our fundamental constants are quantities such as the velocity of light,

---

* Charles Babbage, writing to the eminent experimentalist David Brewster.

Planck's constant, the charge on the electron and the mass/charge ratio of
the electron, the Hubble constant, the rate of expansion of the universe –
and G. Among these, only the properties of the electron can be thought of
as properties of 'objects', and many philosophers would dispute even that.
The numbers are called fundamental because they occur as parameters in
the fundamental laws of nature. Many cosmologists of today entertain the
following picture. The universe is constituted first of all by certain deep
equations, the basic laws of everything. They are composed of variables
for measurable quantities, and free parameters whose values are fixed by
assigning constants – the velocity of light and so forth. Then various
boundary conditions are added, conditions not determined by the equations and the fundamental constants – the amount of mass and energy in
the universe, say.

Such a picture is implicitly hierarchical. First come the laws, then the
constants that fix their parameters, and then a set of boundary conditions.
It is not easy to combine such a cosmology with full blown positivism, for
the original laws of nature, with parameters not yet fixed by constants, do
not seem to 'describe' mere 'regularities'. They are constraints on
physically possible universes, suggesting a necessitarian attitude to laws of
nature. Such a cosmology is not far removed from Galileo's theism and his
picture of God writing the Book of Nature. The Author of Nature writes
down the equations, then fixes the fundamental constants, and finally
chooses a series of boundary conditions.

How did our ideas about constants evolve? Even before Descartes, the
celebrated algebrist Vieta did distinguish between variables and parameters of an equation. Despite this, geometrical rather than analytic ways
of thinking long persisted. They do not lend themselves to the idea of a
'constant' in an equation, because constant proportions are expressed by
ratios.[2] Lexicographers report that the French word *constant* was used for
fixed parameters by 1699. The English seem not to have adopted it during
the eighteenth century, doubtless because of the split between Newtonian
and continental mathematical traditions. The word 'variable' was nevertheless standard in the doctrine of fluxions almost from the beginning.
Thus even if 'constant' was not current, the idea was present. It is another
thing, however, to transfer the mathematical use to the description of the
world. The constants in algebra or analysis had to be identified with
constant numbers attached to things.

The 'weight of the earth' might do as a constant of nature for abstract
thinkers – as would, for example, the distances and periods of revolution
of the planets – but industrial manufacture made more difference to the
notion of a constant than facts about the solar system. In mundane matters
relatively few things are constant except what we make constant. 'Stan-

dards' begin with the coinage and other weights and measures of commerce. The US Bureau of Standards, now notable for its monitoring of many fundamental constants, was established only in 1901, even though, in my concluding chapter, we shall find C.S. Peirce begging for one in 1885. It was placed in the department of labor and commerce and was patterned on the English Board of Trade's standards department. That in turn replaced the chamberlains in the Exchequer, a type of office abolished in 1826. The chamberlains' first task had been the coinage, and then such units as pounds and feet, rods and chains. So many more things were being made and had to measure up, in 1826, that a need for vastly more comprehensive systems of standards was felt. The need was not to emulate the Napoleonic reform that had set the continent of Europe on the new and rational path of metric measurement, but merely to diminish English chaos in piecemeal ways.

Particular instances of what we *now* call fundamental constants had long been known: the velocity of light, for example. Yet that was just a number, of no universal or fundamental significance until the theory of relativity. Quite aside from an absence of thoughts about 'fundamental' constants, there was no category of physical constants or constants of nature until the 1820s. Babbage's letter to Brewster of 1832 was important not because it was influential (although Babbage was at his apogee in those years) but because it was representative.

Atomic weights had already been determined with some precision, especially by the Swedish analyst Berzelius. English chemists, distinctly less skilled, and moved by William Prout's guess in 1815 that the weights should be integral numbers, disagreed with European measurements. In 1831 one of the first acts of the newly formed British Association for the Advancement of Science was to direct Edward Turner to settle the matter. He concluded that Berzelius was right. There was, then, a conviction that there must be one true set of numbers for the elements, constants of nature. The issues were partly theoretical, partly practical. More straight-forwardly pragmatic was a handbook of tables for mechanical and civil engineers published the same year.[3] It provided numbers for tensile strengths and the like, and called them constants, even on its title page. The *OED* cites this as the earliest use of the word in this sense. Babbage owned the book.[4]

Babbage was not the first to want to compile lists of constants. His indefatigable contemporary, Johann Christian Poggendorf, editor of *Annalen der Physik und Chimie* (and later creator of the definitive nineteenth-century biographical and bibliographical science reference work) had just published tables of what Babbage calls 'the constant quantities belonging to our [solar] system'[5] Babbage, characteristically, had something far grander in mind, to be undertaken by 'the Royal Society, the Institute of France, and the Academy of Berlin'.[*6] His list had nineteen categories of constants, which were to be updated every two years, each academy taking its turn every six years.

The list began tamely enough, with (1) constants of the solar system (the distances of the planets, their period of revolution, and the force of gravity on the surface of each – G, the universal gravitational constant, was *not* included); (2) atomic weights; (3) metals (specific gravity, elasticity, specific heats, conducting power of electricity, etc.); (4) optics (refractive indices, double refraction angles, polarizing angles, etc.); (5) the numbers of known species of mammalia, molluscs, insects, etc., the numbers of these in fossil state, and the proportion of fossils that are from existing species as opposed to extinct ones. (If it seems odd to take the number of species as a constant, we should recall that that was precisely the issue of the gathering storm of evolutionary theory. Babbage was not close to the biologists, but he was quite intimate with Charles Lyell, who devised the new geology.)

We then proceed in (6) to the mammals, and catalogue the height, weight of skeleton, pulse rate and breath rate while at rest, period of sucking etc. In (7) we turn to people (tables of mortality in various places, proportions of the sexes born under various circumstances, quantity of air consumed per hour, proportion of sickness amongst the working classes).

(8) is about the power of men and animals: 'a man labouring ten hours a day will saw ( ) square feet of deal – ditto ( ) elm – ditto ( ) oak – ditto Portland stone – ditto Purbeck – Days labour in mowing, ploughing – &c. &c. every kind of labour – Raising water one foot high – horse do. – ox or cow do. – camel.' In the next sentence we get the Industrial Revolution: 'Power of steam engines in Cornwall'.

And so on: (9) vegetable kingdom (natural and cultivated, crop production and profitability); (10) geographical distribution of animals and plants (including 'the weight of potass [potash] produced from each kind of wood, and proportion of heat produced by burning a given weight of each'); (11) atmospheric phenomena; (12) materials (strength of, but also 'weight of coal to burn 10 bushels of lime', 'tallow to make soap' and 'constants of all trades'); (13) velocities (arrow, musket ball, sound, light,

---

* The reference to the Prussian Academy arose from Babbage's continental travels following a period of family sadness. They marked him and to some extent British science, for his experiences in Berlin motivated his sensational onslaught on the Royal Society. In 1828 he attended the Berlin session of the Deutsche Naturforscher Versammlung, which had been meeting annually in various cities since 1822. His 'Account of the Great Congress of Philosophers at Berlin on the 18th September 1828' was propitious for the founding of the British Association for the Advancement of Science in 1831. He, his close friend John Herschel and his editor Brewster drafted the constitution for the Association, with its plan of movable annual meetings patterned on the German society.

birds, average passage Liverpool to New York). That most universal of twentieth-century constants, the velocity of light, was put in exactly the same box as the speeds of the various kinds of birds.

There follow (14) geography (lengths of rivers, areas of seas, heights of mountains); (15) populations; (16) buildings ('height of all temples, pyramids, churches, towers, columns, &c.', obelisks, lengths of bridges, breadth of their piers); (17) weights and measures (conversion tables into English money, areas, weights); (18) 'tables of the frequency of occurrence of the various letters of the alphabet in different languages, – of the frequency of occurrence of the same letters at the beginnings and endings of words, – as the second or penultimate letters of words'; (19) numbers of books in great public libraries at given dates, numbers of students at various universities, observatories and their equipment.

This is not so far away from our modern handbooks, gazetteers, compendia and cyclopedias all rolled into one, except for the utterly motley array of numbers of disparate kinds of things. The motley is not a sign of madness but of eccentric enthusiasms. Aside from the 'respectable' sections that we find in our modern scientific handbooks – atomic weights or specific heats – many other numbers sought are signs of bees in Babbage's notorious bonnet.

For example, corresponding to (8) we find that fourteen days before his letter to Brewster Babbage had signed the preface to his marvellous inventory of recent British industrial invention, with careful studies of the efficiency of various modes of production.[7] Section (18) on the frequency of letters matches a communication to Quetelet, who published it in his journal, and recalled it affectionately in his eulogy of Babbage some 40 years later. Joseph Henry was moved to add, at that time, that if one were to protest that 'this question is never asked by the student of nature', we must recall that 'every item of knowledge is connected in some way with all other knowledge'.[8] Babbage's exercise, he suggested, would be useful when ordering type fonts. The letter frequencies had more to do with Babbage's ingenious but bizarre interests in cryptography.[9]

The 'sex ratios under various circumstances' in (7) referred to a letter to T.P. Courtenay, his Tory MP, and chairman of the Select Committee on Friendly Societies.[10] The letter was published by Brewster. Drawing primarily on Prussian statistics Babbage argued that the ratio of females to males among illegitimate births exceeded that for births in wedlock.*[11]

---

* Babbage was a witness before the Select Committee. In studying life tables, he had become fascinated by a phenomenon noted long ago by Laplace and others: there is always a proportional excess of male over female births, but this excess decreases for illegitimate births. Laplace showed that the excess is significant, and offered the following explanation: all children in foundling homes are registered as illegitimate, and parents have a tendency to abandon legitimate female but not male newborn, and in particular country families will

Section (6) on mammals harks back to a 'list of those facts relating to mammalia, which can be expressed by numbers [and which] was first printed in 1826. It was intended as an example of one chapter in a great collection of facts which the author suggested under the title of 'The Constants of Nature and of Art'.[12] Babbage proposed some 142 numbers measuring different parts of the bodies of mammals, followed by a more modest requirement for fishes.

The letter on constants of nature and of art is thus a more personal document than at first appears. Nevertheless this odd letter epitomizes the moment, 1832. The British Association printed Babbage's letter as a separate pamphlet. The first of the great Quetelet-organized statistical congresses republished it in 1853, as did the Smithsonian Institution in 1856. Joseph Henry, in his secretarial report to the Smithsonian as late as 1873, referred to Babbage's letter as the model for tables of specific gravities, boiling points and melting points.[13] Babbage's odder items were passed by. He remained a symbol of a new way to think about nature and our works: numerically.

Babbage's list is a powerful reminder that the numbering of the world was occurring in every branch of human inquiry, and not merely in population and health statistics. An early paper of T.S. Kuhn's has the rather startling title, 'The Function of Measurement in Modern Physical Science'.[14] Is not measurement so integral to physical science that one can hardly ask what its function is? Kuhn thinks not, but here I am concerned not with his argument but with an observation that is central to the paper. He begins with Kelvin's dictum that you know precious little about something if you cannot measure it.[15] That was commonplace at the end of the nineteenth century, but it became so, in general, and for all fields, only in that span of a hundred years. And it was as much a dogma for Francis Galton the biometrician as for Kelvin, the physicist.[16]

Kuhn's interest is in what he calls the Baconian sciences, what we now think of particularly as physics and chemistry, as opposed both to the life

abandon their daughters at city orphanages. Babbage added differential infanticide. During his stay in Berlin Babbage met with Hoffmann, the professor-director of the Prussian statistical bureau. He obtained the results of the Prussian census of 1828 and the ratios of male and female births for the preceding decade, cross-classified as illegitimate and legitimate. Among the legitimate, males exceed females by 10.6 births to 10, as opposed to less than 10.3 to 10 for the illegitimate. He may have had some eugenical thoughts, for he recalled a paper from the 1823 Paris Academy of Sciences, claiming that the sex ratio of ovine births can be immensely influenced by selection and diet of the parents. He also noted that in Prussia the Jewish birth rate exceeds the Christian one (5.35 live births per Jewish couple, as opposed to 4.78 for Christians). Moreover the disproportion of male over female births is substantially greater for Jewish families than for Christian ones (11.2 to 10 as opposed to 10.6 to 10). We shall return to the Prussian concern for Jewish numbers in chapter 22.

sciences and to the traditional mathematical sciences (e.g. astronomy, mechanics, geometrical optics, music). He puts the matter strongly: 'Sometime between 1800 and 1850 there was an important change in the character of research in many of the physical sciences, particularly in the cluster of research fields known as physics. That change is what makes me call the mathematization of Baconian physical science one facet of a second scientific revolution.'[17]

This revolution is thought of as second to the first, the scientific revolution of the seventeenth century. Kuhn is here speaking of a global event running across a large number of disciplines, at least those comprehended under physics, and including thermodynamics, electricity, magnetism, radiant heat and physical optics. He is not using the term 'scientific revolution' in the way he does in his famous book, *The Structure of Scientific Revolutions* (published a year after his paper on measurement). In that book a revolution occurs in a limited arena, a disciplinary matrix whose researchers might number fewer than 100. I have elsewhere stated some general characteristics of 'big' revolutions (such as the supposed second scientific revolution) as opposed to the little ones of Kuhn's *Structure*.*[18] Social and institutional determinants of such big revolutions are not hard to list, but more important is what Herbert Butterfield called the new feel that the ordinary person, living in those times, acquires for the world.[19] The first half of the nineteenth century generated a world becoming numerical and measured in every corner of its being. In our own 'information age' quirky Charles Babbage has become posthumously famous for elaborating the general principles of the digital computer. Instead I single him out as the self-conscious spokesman for what was happening in his times.

I described fundamental constants in terms of their role as fixing parameters in basic laws of nature. That is a conception more recent than Babbage. His constants were used in stating many a 'law'. He meant by law only a rule, a regularity, a uniformity, as when he wrote, for example, 'if the income of the voters follow a similar law [...]'.[20] Call him Baconian,

---

* New institutions are characteristic of 'big' revolutions. Just as in England the Royal Society and the scientific revolution went hand in hand, so in Britain the British Association and the supposed second scientific revolution were closely connected. I remarked above that Babbage played a great part in founding the British Association. The establishment often scoffed at it, with *The Times* thundering on about the 'British Ass', but it was a haven for the new generation of industrial technocrats and experimental scientists. Dickens's malicious accounts of it are fun: see his *Reports* of the meetings of the *Mudfog Association for the Advancement of Everything* in *Sketches by Boz*, complete with a section on 'Umbugology and Ditchwateristics', corresponding to the British Association's Section F, for statistics, founded in 1833 by Babbage, Quetelet and others. Babbage also was also a chief founder of the London Statistical Society in 1834.

positivist, in his conception of law. His was an attitude shared with the vast majority of French and English writers whom I shall mention. We have it in caricature with Quetelet's study of the law of blooming of lilacs in the springtime of Brussels. He discovered that Belgian lilacs burst into bloom when the sum of the squares of the mean daily temperature since the last frost adds up to $(4264°C)^2$.[21] That number is one which Babbage might cheerfully have included among his constants of nature and art. The number 4264 and the 'law' in which it occurs are about as nonfundamental as any that could be imagined but that did not diminish their interest for astronomer Quetelet.

Near the end of his essay on measurement, Kuhn emphasizes his 'paper's most persistent thesis: '*The road from scientific law to scientific measurement can rarely be traveled in the reverse direction.* To discover quantitative regularity one must normally know what regularity one is seeking and one's instruments must be designed accordingly.'[22] That applies excellently to many of the great triumphs of nineteenth-century physics: say Joule's determination of that new constant of nature, the mechanical equivalent of heat. But it quite misses the vast enthusiasm for measurement for its own sake that so marks Kuhn's period, 1800–50. Kuhn is a profound admirer of theory and has little use for positivists. But it was they, I propose, who made that second scientific revolution. In so saying, I in no way diminish the magnificent architecture erected at the same time by theoreticians. Nor need we pause to debate the point here. In the human and social arena, and more generally in the whole domain of the nascent concept of statistical law, it was the Baconian generalizers who did the work. They were ready and willing to produce 'laws' when they had no more theoretical understanding than Quetelet had of Belgian lilacs. Moreover they saw their task, in accumulating numerical data, in terms that conform to the most simple-minded and demeaning of readings of the original (and subtle) Francis Bacon. The more numbers that we have, the more inductions we shall be able to make. Babbage notes that not only is his list of nineteen categories incomplete, but also that

Whoever should undertake the first work of this kind [viz. 'A Collection of Numbers, the Constants of Nature and of Art'] would necessarily produce it imperfect ... partly from the many facts, which, although measured by number, have not yet been counted.

But this very deficiency furnishes an important argument in favour of this attempt. It would be desirable to insert the heads of many columns, although not a single number could be placed within them – for they would thus point out many an unreaped field within our reach, which requires but the arm of the labourer to gather its produce into the granary of science.[23]

What then are laws? Any equations with some constant numbers in them. They are positivist regularities, the intended harvest of science. Collect more numbers, and more regularities will appear. Now it is time to see how the empty silos of human behaviour began to overflow with laws of human nature.

8

Suicide is a kind of madness

London, 1 December 1815   It is clearly evident that, of late years at least, suicide has been immeasurably more frequent in Paris than in London. Whether this deplorable propensity be the consequence only of recent political events which, having annihilated religion have deprived the wretched of its resources and consolations in affliction, and by their *demoralizing* effects dissolved the social compact that alone makes life a blessing, is not easy to determine.[*][1]

Durkheim's *Suicide* of 1897 was the masterpiece of nineteenth-century statistical sociology. The choice of the most morbid of behaviours was no accident: there were mountains of suicide data upon which Durkheim could build. They came from the French fascination with deviants, especially those who were degenerate or could not contribute to the growth of the French population.

Durkheim invented his idea of *anomie*, of social and moral decline, of alienation or disintegration, in the context of suicide. That was his measure of communal pathology. In this way a medical notion (pathology) was transferred to the body politic on the back of statistics. As my epigraph illustrates, the connection between suicide and *anomie* was fixed much earlier. This little salvo fired in 1815 at the demoralized French – the French whose morals had been destroyed by revolution and Napoleon – inaugurates numerical sociology. I do not mean that suicides had not been counted before. The extraordinary records of suicide in Geneva from 1650 to 1798 have been carefully studied, and there are doubtless many more, in Switzerland alone, of comparable precision.[2]

I call the Anglo-French squabbling about suicide the beginning of numerical sociology because (a) there were numbers and (b) the numbers of suicide were seen as a moral indicator of the quality of life. The issue was immediately joined. Esquirol, the great student of mental imbalance, took

---

[*] George Burrows writing in the *London Medical Repository*, of which he was a co-founder and editor. In 1815 he was founding a small asylum in Chelsea, later enlarged to one named 'The Retreat' in Clapham. He was much concerned with bad laws about the mad: *Cursory Remarks on the Legislative Regulation of the Insane* (London, 1819).

up cudgels against the egregious Burrows who had dared to suggest that Parisians are more suicidal than Londoners.*[3] He was soon to be confirmed as the French suicide expert with his long article on suicide in the 60-volume French medical dictionary. He asserted that the very word 'suicide' in French is a new one: 'the term was created during the last century by the famous Desfontaines'.[4] (According to historical dictionaries, the first known occurrence of the word is in 1734; Voltaire used it in 1739. In English we have the word from at least 1651.)

There is a celebrated anticlerical tradition of defending suicide: Montaigne ('Life is slavery if freedom to die is wanting'); Donne's *Biathanatos*; Montesquieu, Voltaire and Hume. It made certain themes and examples famous: Montaigne, Montesquieu and above all Voltaire in the *Philosophical Dictionary* speak of the suicide of Cato the younger. There was an official classification of kinds of suicide, as seen through Enlightenment eyes, best represented by Cromaziono's *Storia critica filosofica del suicido ragionato* of 1759.[5] Esquirol was being deliberately disingenuous in stating that the idea of suicide was relatively new. He had a not very hidden agenda.

He was starting an argument to the effect that suicide is a new topic, one that has not been properly examined – and examination will show that suicide is a medical topic. Esquirol lived during one of the great periods of imperial expansion of his profession. He was implying that doctors have the right to guard, treat, control and judge suicides. They are no longer in the domain of moralists and priests, of Augustine and Aquinas. Self-murder has become, he writes, 'one of the most important subjects of clinical medicine'. This is claim-staking with a vengeance.

Esquirol had an implicit syllogism. (a) Madness is the province of the physician. (b) Suicide is a kind of madness. Therefore (c) suicide is in the province of the physician. For Esquirol, premise (a) was an established fact. Thus medicine can take suicide under its wing if only suicide can be shown to be a kind of madness. 'I believe that I have demonstrated', wrote Esquirol, 'that a man does not attempt to end his days except in delirium, and that suicides are insane.'[6] Such was the agenda of Esquirol and his

---

* Burrows's opposite number in France was the far more famous J.E.D. Esquirol. Around 1800 the French medical profession took over madness as its own special province. Three institutions are the chief sites of that transformation: the Paris asylums of Bicêtre, Salpêtrière and Charenton. One man is a convenient figurehead for the medicalizing of madness: Philippe Pinel, author of a *Traité médico-philosophique de l'aliénation mentale* (Paris, 1791). He became head physician of Bicêtre in 1792 and of Salpêtrière in 1794. Esquirol was his student and in 1810 his successor at the Salpêtrière, and head physician at Charenton in 1826. His achievements were architectural as well as conceptual. The very buildings of the new generation of provincial asylums at Rouen, Nantes and Montpellier were to his design. Their inmates were above all classified within his master category: monomania.

students: and there was an accompanying theory, that like most other madness, suicides were 'monomaniacs'. We shall soon find that it went hand in hand with the counting of suicides. First let us see how the French medical suicide establishment reacted to Burrows's allegations about the English being less prone to suicide than the French.

Burrows was not being especially anti-French. Throughout the Napoleonic wars scientific journals were at pains to report the work of their opposite numbers across the channel. Very often the theme was regret. War made traffic in knowledge so difficult. The periodicals of the national enemy were so hard to get hold of. This was bad, since the other side seemed to be arranging its science better than we were at home. Officialdom, awake! We shall be outdone by foreigners if funds and talent are not better employed.

The practice of recording weekly mortality and causes of death originated in London, and was made famous in Graunt's 1662 *Observations on the Bills of Mortality*. They had become the model for Europe, but had declined at home. Burrows lamented 'the annual barbarously ignorant Bill of Mortality of London'. Graunt's days were long gone. 'Too many are content with viewing effects only and search no further. From such cause, perhaps, the value of statistical enquiries has been under-rated.'

The French are something else, said Burrows. Indeed their ability to muster data for political economy may be the source of their prodigious war effort. Burrows had just obtained the French tables of mortality for 1813, summarized in the *Journal de médecine*. He admired them and noted the phenomenon familiar to statisticians since John Arbuthnot's 1710 proof of divine providence. More males are born every year in France than females. Burrows's caution with statistical regularity was well illustrated by his comment: 'Although 19 males are born to 18 females, yet the loss of males by their deaths is greater than the gain by births. How is it then, that the equilibrium of the sexes is preserved? This is a question I will not pretend to solve.' No Süssmilchian Divine Order for Burrows.

Burrows noted that in 1813 Paris had 141 suicides on land compared with 35 in London. There were 243 drownings in the Seine, compared with 101 in the Thames. 'It is well understood that those who are reported *drowned* in Paris are mostly considered to have met a voluntary death.'[7] French suicides were, then, far more common than English ones. Esquirol wanted none of that. Everyone knows (he urged) that the English are prone to suicide, so the statistics must be defective. In the previous generation, Sauvages had designated suicide as *melancolia anglica*. Nor was this a French slur (although it was one propagated by Montesquieu among others). Madness (and hence suicide, in Esquirol's concealed syllogism) was English. It was so characterized by a famous book of 1732:

The English Malady, or, a Treatise of Nervous Diseases of all Kinds, as Spleen, Vapours, Lowness of Spirits, Hypochondriacal and Hysterical Distempers.[8] That book had chiefly been a spirited defence of the lacto-vegetarian diet as a cure for insanity. The underlying theory was that the spleen is a source of madness. 'Tumours, swellings and ulcers are just a consequence of the basic disorder' of the spleen, and 'all nervous cases are but the several steps or stages in the same distemper'. The spleen will be improved by holistic treatment.

Authorities all agreed. In 1765 Dr Anne-Charles Lorry wrote that 'melancholy is a vice born with and endemical in the English'.[9] Madness was *morbis anglicus.* Everyone knew why: the defective English spleen, whose weakness was in turn caused by the terrible weather. The English penchant for scientific pursuits was a further cause of their endemic insanity. Esquirol largely rested his case upon tradition, and the reports of the English upon their own odd condition. Everyone knew that the English were the most suicidal of peoples; for Burrows to deny it was further proof of insular eccentricity. Esquirol also had justified suspicion of English suicide statistics. On Burrows's own testimony, London probably did not report as well as Paris. Esquirol assigned the problem to one of his students, J.-P. Falret. The result, published in 1822, was a dissertation on hypochondria and suicide.[10]

The immediate contretemps with Burrows involved only some niggling about numbers. Falret thought that 1813 was rather a bad year for Paris suicides, but not a typical one. Moreover, convinced that suicide is madness, he supposed that the way to overcome defective English statistics is to inquire after the number of mad people incarcerated in London. The English, as might be expected, have far more lunatics than the French, no fewer than 7,000 around the metropolis alone. Falret's book was instantly reviewed in Burrows's *Repository*, where it was called 'Excellent, even classical'.[11] Directly afterwards Burrows addressed the allegations about the English mad. The source of Falret's numbers can only be (he conjectured) remarks ascribed to a Mr Dempster, superintendent of St Luke's parish. Those data were founded on rumour. When one uses reliable authorities, one can identify only 4,041 confined lunatics in the whole of England and Wales.[12]

These debates are nebulous, but they did set the stage for the counting of suicides, and gave it a certain edge. Before we turn to the massive enumerations of the 1820s and 1830s, let us continue, in this chapter, to consider just what was being counted. 'Suicide', wrote Goethe, 'is an incident in human life which ... in every age must be dealt with anew.' Perhaps, in order to see the force of the aphorism, we need a list like the following:

heredity

temperament

age

sex

education

reading novels

music

theatrical performances

climate

seasons

masturbation

idleness

This is Falret's list of predisposing causes of suicide. Medicine had long
had four kinds of causes of disease and death: predisposing, direct (or
occasioning), indirect and general. Falret's occasioning causes of suicide
were more numerous than the predisposing ones. They included passion,
love, remorse, domestic problems, dreams of fortune that have been
frustrated, pride and humiliation, obsession with gambling, dishonour,
outrage at lost virtue, waves of passions, jealousy and conjugal tenderness.

Indirect causes included alcohol, syphilis (and mercury, its treatment),
opium, physical pain, scurvy and pellagra.[13] General causes included
governments, civilization, religious belief, sects and public morals.
General causes are precursors of Durkheim's *anomie*.

Many different things were going on in work like Falret's. It is hard to
keep an eye on all at once. They look unrelated, but they are not. Since the
story is complex I had better interject a list of some different strands.

1 The new counting of suicides, as part of the collection of data on
   deviancy.
2 The land-claim staked by physicians. Suicide is madness, and hence
   disease.
3 The organic theory of disease. Every disease is associated with an
   organ. Hence madness in general is associated with defective
   organs. Suicide as a kind of insanity must be the consequence of a
   defective organ.
4 The traditional taxonomy of medical causes as predisposing, direct,
   etc. This was retained through transformations in the conception
   of disease from humoral to organic. The list given by Falret,
   student of Esquirol, is a perfect example. We shall find that in

many of the statistical enumerations of our next chapter, suicides
were classified according to just these causes.

5 The idea that there are law-like regularities of a probabilistic sort.
These were obtained by generalization on the data of (1).

6 The theory, derived from the Gaussian theory of errors in astronomy
and geodesy, about the causal foundation for probabilistic laws. It
was imagined that the Gaussian law of error could be explained by
a concatenation of underlying little causes.

7 The putting together of (4) medical causes, (5) statistical laws of e.g.
suicide, and (6) the model of causation used in astronomy.

Strands (1) and (5)-(7) are developed in chapter 13. Here we are
concerned with (2)-(4). I have already mentioned a transition in the
treatment of the mad, which happened around 1800 when they were made
wards of doctors who directed asylums. A more basic change in the
practice and theories of physicians occurred at just the same time.
Physicians had regarded disease as imbalance in the whole body, but by
1800 disease was primarily to be located in an injured, defective or irritated
tissue or organ. To expand Esquirol's syllogism stated above: (a) madness
is medical. (b) Suicide is madness. So (c) suicide is medical. But (d) all
disease is organic. So (e) madness is associated with organic defects. So (f)
suicide is associated with organic defects.

This last item (f) sounds mad. Since it is so unfamiliar to us it is a place to
begin. The larger question is, 'Is suicide madness?' and the lesser one is, 'Is
suicide caused by a defective organ?' Note that if a student of Esquirol's
answered 'yes' to the former question, he was duty bound to answer 'yes'
to the second.

Thus a dissertation by Georget, an exact contemporary of Falret's and
another rising star in Esquirol's cosmos, announced: 'I consider madness
to be a disease of the brain, the organ of intelligence.'[*][14] Falret thought so
too. The head is the site of hypochondria and of suicide. So much for the
spleen, favoured organ of the humoral theory of disease. The doctrine
that the weather is responsible for the mad and suicidal proclivities of the
English was then instantly refuted. The Dutch climate, wrote Falret, is as
foul as the English one. Inhabitants of the low countries do not suffer from

---

* Georget was widely regarded as the most brilliant student of the phrenologist Gall. Books
by members of the Esquirol school call Georget's early death a tragedy for phrenology.
Possibly by way of advertisement, just as he was beginning to practise, he commissioned
the equally young Géricault to paint ten of his patients. After Georget's death his effects
were auctioned off. Five portraits were bought by a Breton doctor and have since been lost.
The remaining five remain a lasting testament to the mad of the day. All were 'monomaniacs'. It has been proposed that Géricault came to Georget for help in a mental crisis
during the controversy about his great 1819 *Raft of the Medusa*; the portraits may have
been recompense for services rendered.

the English Malady. The differentia between the English and the French must be more fundamental than climate.

The English were less keen on the organic theory of disease. Following Bichat's injunction, 'open up a few corpses', dissection was the rage in Paris. Burrows marvelled at the excessive 'zeal and labour' spent on cutting up cadavers in order to find out the proximate causes of suicide.[15] Esquirol and others had found (wrote Burrows) no difference between suicidal and nonsuicidal brains. The fact that there is no difference 'is almost constantly the case where the person has killed himself a short time after the propensity has declared itself ... This is additional testimony which leads to the inference that when the morbid changes are discovered in the brain, they are generally the consequence, and not the causes, of mental derangement.' Burrows finally lost his cool on the topic of dissecting the cadavers of suicides and scrutinizing their organs: 'It was as likely, in my opinion, to discover by that means why a lunatic imagines himself a deity or an emperor or a mushroom, as to detect the special physical cause of a man's killing himself.'

Burrows epitomized antitheoretical English medicine. Contrast F.-J.-V. Broussais, the great speculative French pathologist. We shall return to Broussais twice: in chapter 10 because he was the first physician to be roundly criticized on statistical grounds, and in chapter 19 because of his role in the invention of normalcy. Here, suffice to say that he believed that all illness had a local cause, in afflictions of particular tissues. He firmly believed in a 'stay-alive' instinct located in an organ whose absence led to suicide: 'Whatever opinion one would adopt about the reality of phrenology, it is necessary to recognize in mankind the existence of a propensity for staying alive. I do not know the seat of of this propensity, nor what its organ. I believe only that it exists. I believe that because I feel it in myself and see its effects in others'.[16] No one did find any defective stay-alive organs, but the idea lasted a long time. 'What organ [creates suicidal tendencies]?' asked Cazauvieilh in 1840. 'The organ', he replied, 'that presides over the intellectual and affective faculties ... It is necessary to seek this predisposition or organic modification. It exists in individuals, who, with no plausible motives or for trivial or imaginary causes, experience disgust for life and an irresistible propensity for suicide.'[17]

The grip of Esquirol's school was weakening. In 1844 Etoc-Demazy, in his book of statistical studies of suicide, was certain that commonly suicide does not rest on 'aberrations resembling those that are characteristic of madness'.[18] At most suicide is the consequence of insanity. It is not identical to it. Within months a counter-attack was mounted. Bourdin opened with the words, 'Suicide is a monomania.'[19] When one studies the 'real causes' of suicide, one is confronted by a 'veritable pathology'.

Bourdin asserted that 'We can prove that the act of suicide is always accompanied by or preceded by or followed by some explicitly mental problem.' Back and forth the battle went. In 1848 Leuret, who worked at Bicêtre, asserted three propositions. First, 'if it is true that madness depends upon an alteration in the encephalon, we are completely ignorant about what this alteration consists in'.[20] Secondly, 'the moral treatment practised by the generality of physicians is only considered as an auxiliary to physical treatment'. But thirdly, in the case of madness, this is an error. Leuret's book on the 'moral treatment of madness' reminds us that the analyst's couch and the therapist's consultation loom on the horizon.[21]

Leuret wrote that 'suicide is not always an instance of madness'. In the same year his friend Lisle quoted this sentence on the title page of his prizewinning essay on suicide statistics.[22] I have been describing what happened in the discourse of the time, but now we can witness the debate in the mind of a single person. Lisle began by saying that 'in many cases suicide is the result of a mental malady', while in others it is more like a deliberate action, similar to a crime, an error provoked by varying causes and dispositions. 'The doctrine according to which suicide is always the result of madness is a scientific error.' But by mid-book – the printers ran it off in segments – a frantic footnote was inserted. We should delete Leuret's word 'always' and write simply: '*Suicide is not an instance of madness.*'

I shall refer to these authors in several later connections. As a guide in keeping straight who is who, note that some of the titles cited mention statistics. As a crude generalization, the statistically minded doctors did not think that suicide was uniformly identical to or even uniformly associated with madness. Those who were more committed to the physiological way of thinking persisted in hoping for an organic solution to the problem of suicide. This difference of course persisted in topics where it has been noted by many scholars. For example the famous advocate of experimental medicine Claude Bernard abhorred statistical inquiries. He wanted to examine specific lesions and injuries to organs, not the average of many organs.

Why this long digression on suicide and the doctors? Partly because the steps (1)-(4) listed above lead on to (5)-(7): that is, not only did people discover statistical laws about suicide, crime, divorce, prostitution and other bad behaviour, but also they thought there was an explanation of the nature of statistical law that made it safe for determinism. This was a curious marriage of astronomical, mathematical and medical lore. It was a mythology of causation, of which, for example, Falret's strange list forms a part.

The present chapter is about suicide observed. Now we turn to suicide counted. We have noticed some inconsequential Anglo-French rivalry about the numbers of suicides. The protagonists knew full well that more statistical facts ought to be collected. These men were on the edge of a continent of statistics which was waiting to be explored. Burrows said it in 1820:

We coolly calculate the probability of life, to provide against the contingencies of mortality. Why, therefore, should we not examine and compute the risk of mental derangement? It is certain that in what degree we are exposed, the probability of [the occurrence of insanity] has been scarcely regarded.[23]

He had not long to wait: a year or two.

9

The experimental basis of the philosophy of legislation

Paris, 11 September 1831   Criminal statistics becomes as positive as
the other observational sciences; when one knows how to stick to
established facts, and groups them so as to separate out merely
accidental circumstances, the general results then present such a
great regularity that it becomes impossible to attribute them to
chance. Each year sees the same number of crimes of the same
degree reproduced in the same regions; each class of crimes has its
own particular distribution by sex, by age, by season ... We are
forced to recognize that in many respects judicial statistics represent
a complete certainty.
Inserted in 1832   We are forced to recognize that the *facts of the
moral order* are subject, *like those of the physical order*, to invariable
laws.[*][1]

By 1830 innumerable regularities about crime and suicide seemed visible to
the naked eye. There were 'invariable' laws about their relative frequency
by month, by method, by sex, by region, by nation. No one would have
imagined such statistical stabilities had it not been for an avalanche of
printed and public tables.

The model was set by the annual *Recherches statistiques sur la ville de
Paris et le département de la Seine*.[2] I say 'annual' – it took a while for the
administration to work smoothly, and the early volumes were usually late.
In due course the national ministries extended and made redundant most
of the statistical work of the capital. National volumes appeared regularly
and efficiently from justice, education and the like. Paris and Seine served
as their model.

The director of the *Recherches* was Joseph Fourier, famous for his work
on heat, and inventor of that fundamental mathematical tool, the Fourier
transform, but in old age connected with public commissions on insurance

---

[*] A.-M. Guerry, writing to Adolphe Quetelet. Quetelet read a paper on 9 July 1831, and
included this part of Guerry's letter in the published version. There was a little priority
dispute. Who first realized that criminal statistics present us with 'invariable laws?' Who
invented the study of 'moral statistics', who invented what was later called 'criminal
sociology'? Quetelet maintained that these were his ideas. Guerry has had his champions.

and social statistics.[3] He wrote most of the unsigned introductions to the volumes. They provide a solid informal exposition of the methods of probability and statistics. The principles stated therein received wide circulation. Adolphe Quetelet's little 1828 textbook of probabilities was similar in content and organization and often in actual wording.[*][4]

Fourier's methodological introductions are interesting, but it is the sheer scale of the enumerations that is important. The traditional tabulations of births, marriages and deaths are there, supplemented for example by massive pull-out pages dedicated to the great Parisian insane asylums. Admissions and releases were recorded; patients were classified by sex, marital status, age; deaths were sorted by causes, and lengths of stay by type of affliction. Nineteen physical causes were cited, including congenital idiocy, drunkenness, deformations of the skull, masturbation, pregnancy, libertine behaviour, and paresis. The mental causes of madness leading to confinement included exaggerated religion, ambition, political events, rage, love, and simulated madness.

We have read Burrows, in 1820, bemoaning the fact that although the statistics and probability of life and death were well studied, no one considered those of madness. By 1823 the facts for Paris in 1821 were available. In a decade he could have had pertinent information about all of France, while more cumbersome and less centralized data were becoming available in England.

Nor was there any longer a dearth of suicide statistics. The suicide tables for the city and the department had the same structure as those for insanity. Suicides were categorized by sex, age, marital status. Then came the method of suicide and its causes. Cross categories furnished proof of invariable laws. 'Any one little given to the study of these subjects would hardly imagine that the method by which a person destroys himself is almost as accurately and invariably defined by his age as the seasons by the revolutions of the sun.'[5] The means of suicide were hanging, firearms, jumping from a height, sharp weapons, poison, drowning and charcoal. Death by charcoal means carbon monoxide poisoning: most of the poorer classes cooked and heated by small charcoal fires in their tenements, so the brazier had the function of the modern gas oven.

These categories are perhaps 'natural' ways to classify suicides. They had been used in Paris for some time and are identical to those listed in a

---

[*] Quetelet was not a statistical novice. He had already studied the traditional kind of statistical law, that of birth and death. An innovation in that work was a sinusoidal law for the variation in rates of birth and death over the course of the year – an idea important to later discussions of suicide. But it was in France that he encountered the whole gamut of social statistics. He was in turn to become the greatest of international propagandists for the value of statistics. It was Fourier who gave Quetelet his introductions, presenting him to the Paris Academy and arranging for him to meet Villermé, the great reformist physician who studied the statistical connection between poverty, death and disease.

1792 treatise on insanity.[6] An administrative, legal or medical functionary was supposed to report the immediate cause of death. So drowning, say, was reported; in addition, the fact that a person had committed suicide. The admissible 'causes' were subject to ceaseless intervention from local, national and now international bodies. Thus for example it is virtually impossible to die of old age any more: that is not an officially acknowledged category.

The two most common methods of Parisian suicide were charcoal and drowning. The more statistics were collected, the more constant appeared the proportions between the methods that were used. The profile of London suicides was entirely different. There one either hung oneself or used a gun. But wherever one looked, 'One observes, year after year, within one or two units, the same number of suicides by drowning, by hanging, by firearms, by asphyxiation, by sharp instruments, by falling or by poisoning.'[7]

Not only were the methods of suicide deemed to be regular, but so was their seasonal variation. Everyone had assumed that winter was the cruellest time. National and climatic folklores intertwined. Since the English were, as everyone knew, the most suicidal, and the climate was partly the cause, then they must be most suicidal in the winter when the weather is worst. In fact, then as now, the citizens of England and Wales are the least suicidal of Europe (aside from the Irish). Then as now, Europeans of every nation were more suicidal in the summer than in the winter.

The methods of suicide are the causes of death, which were already required by the city or other administration. But in addition to methods the tables listed the causes of suicide, the reasons people kill themselves. These cannot be directly observed, but are a matter for common sense, popular psychology, or medicine. It was a medical thesis that every suicide is mad. Medicine provided a table of causes of madness. So medicine ought to provide a table of causes of suicide. It determined the causes according to which suicides should be classified in the tables.

The interrelations between the physicians and those in charge of the Parisian *Recherches statistiques* can be noted precisely. The volume for the year 1821, published in 1823, sorts suicides according to *motives*. That for 1822, published in 1826, sorts suicides according to *causes*. These were the years of Esquirol's doctrine on suicide and madness.

The switch from motives to causes does not make much difference to the sortings themselves. A motive in 1821 becomes a cause in 1822. There is love. There are *maladies* (not denoting sickness here, but corresponding to the defunct English 'malady': depraved, degenerate or morbid condition of mind or morality). There is disgust with life, domestic quarrelling, rage. There is bad conduct, such as gaming and loss therefrom. There is extreme poverty. There is fear of punishment. I emphasize that they were 'causes', because they fit in exactly with Falret's traditional structure of predisposing, direct, indirect and general causes. They provided a battery of independent interlocking causes of suicide. We shall find that these conceptions helped people to 'understand' how a statistical law could exist in a world of deterministic causes.

The Parisian series edited by Fourier was in large measure superseded by national annuals, for which in turn summary abstracts were produced. There were demarcation disputes. After 1826 the ministry of justice began publishing data about crime, prosecutions and convictions, generally following the model of the Paris *Investigations*. The volumes for 1827–30 set forth the material for what Guerry named moral analysis, insofar as it applied to suicide. But there was a question of whether suicide should be published by the ministry of justice – as if suicide were a crime, rather than a disease! After some wavering the justice ministry permanently assumed suicide under its wing in 1836. This may seem a slap in the face for the medical men: law, rather than medicine, claimed suicide. In fact, something more complex happened. A category of problems – pretty much what we now call 'social problems' – was created to be shared by joint experts, medical and legal. They founded the celebrated *Annals d'hygiène publique et de la médecine légale*, commenced in 1829. This was the chief organ for the doctors of alienation, suicide and demented crime. It was also a mine of health statistics. Sanitary statistics and legal medicine were part of the same apparatus, whose topics ranged from disease-ridden slums through crazed murders to prison design. As an example of the meshing together of these talents and sensibilities, there were pull-out illustrations with graphic drawings of prison suicides. Then followed suggestions on how to improve cells so as to prevent these grisly events.

The statistics of the Seine and those of the ministry of justice furnished the data for Guerry's 1832 essay on the 'moral statistics' of France. Like many other French books that I shall mention, it won the Prix Montyon, at that time awarded annually for work of a statistical nature. It is a superb object of noble dimensions with fine maps indicating the geographical distribution of crime. The hygienic movement gave us our present conception of graphical representation, the ancestor of today's computerized spreadsheets. The Academy of Sciences awarded Guerry a special prize for the publication in 1864 that represented the culmination of his work, a massive comparison between the moral statistics of England and France.[8] The award was not for the facts but for their display, their marvellous maps of crime and suicide. Guerry knew the importance of mechanizing this work and designed a calculator for handling his data. It is fitting that he called it an *ordonnateur statistique*. The present French name for the computer, the *ordinateur*, was reinvented in response to a request by IBM France to replace the franglais *computeur*.[9]

Amateurs loved Guerry's books.*[10] The results crossed the Channel well, fascinating both the statistical and the regional societies (e.g. summarized in the *West of England Journal* for 1836). Lytton Bulwer's 1834 book on French life proposed that an entirely new kind of history could be imagined. 'I am led to these reflections by a new statistical work by M. Guerry, a work remarkable on many accounts.' Guerry's tables, he wrote, 'afford sufficient matter for the most important work on history and legislation that has yet appeared'.[11] Buckle's celebrated 1857 *History of Civilization in England* fulfilled the prophecy – and, as we shall see in chapters 14 and 15, it emphasized statistical laws, to the point of exacerbating a debate about suicide and fatalism. Guerry's graphic materials were given pride of place by the British Association for the Advancement of Science at its meeting of 1851, associated with the Great Exhibition at the Crystal Palace. The 1864 book was demonstrated with a laudatory speech by William Farr at the statistical section of the British Association in 1865.[12]

Guerry called his work comparative statistics. That statistics should be comparative is part of their original mandate to measure the power and wealth of the state, as compared with other states. Burrows and Esquirol were bandying about comparative statistics of suicide for London and Paris. Guerry was able to be systematic where others were sketchy. He was a lawyer of independent means, well connected with officialdom. He worked with his cousin Guerry de Champneuf to help organize the statistical work of the ministry of justice. But he was very much a man from a previous generation, a man like Sir John Sinclair, although without the wealth. He was a public amateur giving advice to bureaucrats, but not one of their number.

In 1829 he had collaborated in a 'comparative statistics' of education and crime, whose conclusions were extended in his first major work, the 1832 moral statistics.[13] It had been generally assumed that education counters crime. Guerry presented what we now call rank-order statistics to refute this assumption. I can think of no earlier systematic and detailed use of this method. The educational level of each administrative unit was obtained from the records of the military draft boards, where the level of instruction professed by each conscript was noted. The crime rate for each

---

* The good Countess Flavigny, author of *L'Enfance chrétienne* and other improving works, 'never opened this work without a feeling of respect'. Toqueville is reported to have said, that were it not a dishonour to be cast into prison, he would like nothing better than to spend his years locked up, condemned to study *une pareille chiffrerie*.

unit was obtained from the tables of the justice ministry for the years 1827–30. Then units were rank-ordered in each of these two ways. It was shown that the higher the educational level of a district, the higher its crime rate.

Such a conclusion was sensational. Paris saw itself as being in the grip of a terrible crime wave. Ask a New Yorker of today about muggings, then double the fear: that was how Parisians felt. The police gazettes, rich in reports of crimes, were taken in weekly, and were the fertile sources of best selling novels like those of Eugène Sue.[14] Naturally one supposed that the degeneracy and ignorance of the working classes was the source of their criminal propensity, *penchant au crime* as the statisticians called it. Guerry seemed to prove the opposite. Assuredly he did not convince everyone. Wealth attracts criminals, wealth creates education, so Guerry's correlations were perhaps spurious.

What did Guerry himself think that he was doing? He told us explicitly. He thought that the old phrase *moral science* was outmoded; he was engaged in *moral analysis*.

What is the use of moral analysis? It aims above all, just like the physical sciences, to show the connections between phenomena, to give knowledge of intellectual realities considered in themselves outside of any idea of practical application. In the full rigorous use of the terms, science consists of knowledge, and not in deciding what to do.[15]

This was positive science, distinguishing fact and value. 'In stating rigorously the numerical facts bearing on society, moral analysis forms the experimental basis of the philosophy of legislation.' Condorcet's dream of social mathematics was thereby fulfilled in a positivist era of number and measurement. Lisle, a medical student of suicide quoted in chapter 8, wrote vividly about the methodology:

It is no longer permissible in our days to seek truth in pure theory, in vain abstractions or gratuitous hypothesis. The rigorous observation of facts has become, quite rightly, the starting point and the foundation of our knowledge. From this enlightened positivism is born the application of statistics to medicine and to the study of moral and political questions.[16]

'All the facts', wrote Lisle elsewhere of the material he had collected, 'demonstrate this remarkable proposition, already noticed by a certain number of writers, that moral facts, taken en masse, and considered in a general manner, obey, in their reproducibility, laws as positive as those that reign in the physical world.'[17] There is a double irony here. The word 'positivism' of the antistatistical Comte had been snatched and given our modern sense. Statisticians have been positivists ever since. Secondly, for all this talk of facts and patient pre-theoretical observation, the regularities so admired by a Guerry, a Lytton Bulwer or a Lisle hardly existed. Much later, German writers were to denounce the lot, and devise measures for showing that the stabilities were more imagined than real.

In Guerry's mind the paramount topic for moral statistics, after crime, was suicide. 'Among the subjects encompassed by moral statistics, suicide is one of those that has attracted the most attention, and that has been most discussed.' Writing in 1832, Guerry was annoyed that outside of Paris suicides were inadequately investigated. Even so, the records of the ministry of justice for 1826–30 did teach that 'During these four years, the proportional number of suicides committed in each region did not vary by more than 3 per cent about the mean. In the central region of Paris and the Seine it did not vary by more than 1 per cent.' More striking than the absolute suicide rate were the regularities among cross-classifications. In this preoccupation of Guerry's we find the roots of a need for the theory of correlation and regression. But in 1832 Guerry could do little, because outside of Paris he had only the gross unsorted numbers of suicides. He required data across the nation, and he did his bit to get them.

Until 1836, when at Guerry's instigation the ministry of justice began to compile more thorough suicide statistics, not even the easiest facts, namely the age and sex of suicides, were tabulated. So Guerry propounded a schedule in which constables should record, on the spot where the suicide was found: the sex, age and state of health; profession or social class; residence, birth place, marital status, number of children; finance: rich, comfortable, poor or miserable; education: literate, can read and write, illiterate; state of mind; morality (judicially condemned? adulterer? gambler? prostitute? concubine? drunkard?); religion.

Then there should be a record of the place, the medical circumstances, the date and hour, and the weather. How was it done? Why was it done? Was a letter left? Previous attempts? A parental history of madness or of suicide? What objects were found at the scene, or in the victim's pockets?

Some of this got into the requirements set by the ministry of justice; other aspects of Guerry's schedules were adopted only partially and regionally. Guerry himself outdid a phalanx of constables and clerks. 'He obtained from the police archives 85,564 individual records of suicides committed between 1836 and 1860, each one, so far as was possible, with an indication of the motives' that determined the suicide.[18] In his 1864 book comparing English and French moral statistics, there is an extraordinary categorization of 21,322 people accused of murder. These are analysed into 4,478 groups of individual motives, from which there emerged 97 classes of principal motives. One obituary notice related that the numerals in the cards on which Guerry kept his notes would, if written down in a line, stretch for 1,160 metres. Perhaps it was this that led me to the phrase 'an avalanche of numbers'.*

---

* Guerry won the 1833 and 1864 Montyon prizes for statistics. Subsequent winners included Civiale, Lisle and Le Play. Baron Montyon, the celebrated philanthropist, who had established many prizes before the revolution, lived chiefly in London after 1792, an FRS generously supporting fellow refugees. He returned to Paris only after the restoration. In 1820 he bequeathed a prodigious fortune to scholarship and charity. He published a number of 'statistical' works, none more curious than an *Exposé statistique du Tunkin, de la Cochinchine, du Camboge, du Tsiampa, du Laos, du Lac-Tho* (London, 1811), signed M. M—N, 'sur la relation de M. de La Bissachère missionnaire dans le Tunkin'. It was alleged that he had in effect stolen the work from a destitute missionary, fobbing him off with polite words and a few free copies and keeping the royalties for himself. The truth is more complex, but the story may illustrate Montyon's passion for statistics. Among the prizes that he left to be administered by the *Institut de France* was the interest on 10,000 francs, to be given to the best book of the year conducive to civic well-being. After much debate about how to administer this, the Institute announced an annual prize for statistics.

The successive competitors and winners well illustrate the growth of the statistical idea. In 1822 only departmental statistics were submitted. Guerry was the first to win with a piece of moral analysis. His rivals included a medical statistics of Avignon; a study of the cause of wealth and poverty among civilized peoples; biographies of remarkable men of Seine-et-Oise; occasional causes of the 1832 cholera outbreak at Salpêtrière; and in faubourg St Denis; a navigational map of the Rhine; and wine statistics of the Côte d'Or. Civiale (see next chapter) was the first medical winner. The story of the prize can be found in *Procès-verbaux des séances de l'Académie tenues depuis la fondation de l'Institut* (Paris, 1922), after vol. 7.

10

Facts without authenticity, without detail, without control, without value

Paris, 5 October 1835 In statistical affairs ... the first care before all else is to lose sight of the man taken in isolation in order to consider him only as a fraction of the species. It is necessary to strip him of his individuality to arrive at the elimination of all accidental effects that individuality can introduce into the question.[*][1]

Numbers were a fetish, numbers for their own sake. What could be done with them? They were supposed to be a guide to legislation. There was the nascent idea of statistical law, but hardly any statistical inference. Yes, one could conclude that the French are more prone to suicide than the English. Yes, Guerry could invent (almost without knowing it) rank-order statistics to argue that improved education does not counter crime rate. But hardly anyone sensed that a new style of reasoning was in the making.

Medicine is a good example. The statistics of Paris were full of tables reporting the great hospitals. Would not these batteries of numbers lead at once to tests of treatment and cures? Not at all. When the numbers were used, it was more out of professional jealousy than in a quest for objective knowledge.

The first use of statistical data to evaluate treatment was, it appears, in connection with the charismatic and polemical F.-J.-V. Broussais, whose belief in a 'stay-alive' organ I mentioned briefly in chapter 8. He will figure in chapter 19 because of the way that Comte transferred his physiological conception of the 'normal state' to society and politics. His speculations and his philosophy provoked controversy and resentment, but it was his practice that occasioned statistical assessment.

He was a radical proponent of the new organic 'physiological' theory of disease. Talk of revolutions in science has had its ups and downs among historians, but at least since 1953 – long before the Kuhnian fad – Broussais has been credited with a 'medical revolution'; 'the revolutionary break with the past and the new characteristic orientation with lesions and

---

[*] A committee of four mathematicians, including S.-D. Poisson, reporting to the Academy of Sciences on a statistical comparison of the success of two operations for gallstone.

localities'.[2] That is an overstatement, since it was not solely his revolution. Localization of disease had already become commonplace, but Broussais stands out as the most brazen populist spokesman for the movement.

All illness, he taught, has a local cause, and is the consequence of *irritation* or *asthénie* of the tissues – too many fluids or too few. Life is a matter of the excitation of tissues: one can see why such materialism would offend some. The task of physiological medicine is to determine how 'excitation can deviate from the normal state and constitute an abnormal or diseased state'.[3]

Broussais's enthusiasm for localization of disease in organs can only have been fortified by his career as a military doctor on active service throughout much of 1805–14. The wars of the nineteenth and twentieth centuries helped 'localize' medicine by serving up wounded soldiers whose injured organs could be directly correlated with specific mental or physical impairment. But what Broussais saw was not the man with shrapnel in his head surviving in relatively sanitary conditions – the standard of the First World War that did so much for neurology – but men with terrible fevers and suppurating wounds. He had seen irritants and inflammations aplenty. He saw typhus and phlebitis. The widespread French and British enthusiasm for 'irritation' and 'inflammation' as key medical concepts arose during the war years.

In 1814 Broussais resigned as a field doctor and took up a teaching position at the Val-de-Grâce military hospital. There he attracted throngs of students for his radical doctrines. His vituperative attack on the medical establishment of Paris roused its wrath and much invective.[4] Broussais went from strength to strength.[5] His topic? Above all, the organs and the tissues, their curious interdependencies, their pathological state and their 'normal state'.

The organ might be the site of the disease, but one could not work directly on the organ itself, deep in the body. Instead one treated the superficial part of the patient closest to the organ, or closest to the tissues related to the organ – and Broussais held that stomach and brain were intimately connected. The practical task was to relieve adjacent inflamed or irritated tissues of excess blood. Do you suffer from indigestion followed by a severe headache? Better that than a migraine. 'Moderate inflammations of the encephalon readily yield to leeching of the epigastrum, especially when the encephalitis has been preceded by gastritis; but violent sanguineous congestions of the brain require bleeding from the jugular veins, arteriotomy and leeches to the upper part of the neck ...'[6]

Blood-letting is an old remedy, but never was it so widely employed as in France between 1815 and 1835 – almost entirely thanks to Broussais. His name became a byword. Thus Balzac in *La Messe de l'athée*, 1830:

'this has cost more blood than all the battles of Napoleon and all the leeches of Broussais'.[*7] At the height of the influence of the 'physiological' school, denunciations of it in the French Parliament were in vain. The representative of a southern constituency made an oft-quoted plea on 19 April 1825:

armed with their pitiless leeches, [the doctors] drive to their graves our farmers in the Midi, who are exhausted by their labours during the fiery months of the year ... the leeches, perhaps useful for city-dwellers who take no exercise, quickly exhaust the blood that remains in their veins. One may say that this ingenious system, perhaps useful in itself, when followed by ignoramuses, has made more blood flow than the most pitiless conqueror.[8]

The novelist and the deputy alike loathed the dogmatic cruelty of the physiological school of medicine. It had other opponents, of which one kind was philosophical. Broussais was in many ways heir to the *idéo-logues*: he was a republican and above all a radical materialist. All mental events were events in the brain, caused by excitations. Victor Cousin, neo-Kantian, neo-Platonist, neo-royalist, restorationist, became by 1828 Brousssais's rival in the lecture halls, drawing hordes of students to his antimaterialist psychologism. Broussais was in philosophical trouble as the decade drew to an end.

More conservative or eclectic medicine, appalled both by his success and by his treatments, was also out to get him. A. Miquel wrote, in the mock-Pascalian form of 'letters' to a provincial doctor, a challenging critique of the entire doctrine of the 1821 edition of Broussais's main text book and its supplementary 1824 *Catéchisme*.[9] Much of it made highly philosophical points, but it also asked the question that we would now find relevant. Do the methods work? No, averred Miquel and a colleague. Broussais was defended by another physician, a former student and ally L.-C. Roche.[10]

Miquel noted that the number of deaths in Paris rose steadily with the advance of the new physiological medicine during 1816–23. This was attested by the statistical reports of Paris and the Seine. Roche retorted that the new doctrine made no headway until 1818, so the first few years don't count, and after that the increasing mortality corresponds only to the

---

* Balzac made a butt of Broussais in a dozen different works. In the 1830 *La Comédie du diable* a man in hell pleads for light punishment on the ground that on earth he has already been treated by Broussais for pneumonia. Broussais was the model for Dr Brisset in *La Peau de chagrin*. Brisset was an 'organicist' who used the word 'irritation' repeatedly and prescribed four treatments of leeches in as many pages. Most remarkable, however, is Balzac's *Physiologie du mariage* of 1826 and 1829, which begins with chapters on 'conjugal statistics' to which I shall return in chapter 16. This satire, whose very title is Broussaisist, has a chapter on marital hygiene that counsels the husband, 'Broussais shall be your idol. At your wife's least indisposition, and at the slightest pretext, make extensive use of leeches' – several dozen at a time, if possible.

increasing population. The antiphysiologists turned from generalities about Paris to the specifics of Val-de-Grâce. They asserted that in Broussais's hospital and those of his allies, the death rates were far higher than in other clinics. Roche retorted that the comparison class offered was for convalescent patients in spring and autumn, while Broussais was dealing with fevers at all times, including the heat of summer and the depths of winter. Moreover, urged Roche, look at the history of Val-de-Grâce itself. Take the four five-year periods starting in 1800, with Broussais in charge from 1815 to 1820. The success rate was lowest during 1805–14, a little better during 1800–4, and doubled during the administration of Broussais. 'Not surprising', retorted Miquel: 1800–14 was a period of war when one expects people to die in military hospitals!

These nebulous polemics should have put in place a mode of questioning. P.C.A. Louis is commonly said to be the founder of the 'numerical method' that had brief success in France and much more enduring consequences when transplanted to New England by his American students. (Perhaps his greatest effect was unknown to him, for one modest young man at his lectures was William Farr, later to create English vital statistics). From 1828 Louis undertook a series of statistical evaluations of blood-letting.[11] Bleeding, he found, was totally ineffective. This was so contrary to the current fad for leeches that it took him some while to dare to publish his results, or so he said.

Broussais, knowing that the best defence is attack, published a four-page pamphlet in 1832, under the heading, 'cholera vanquished: one death in 40'![12] But reports were circulating that the Paris hospitals released 30 per cent of their cholera patients alive; Broussais 'saved' only 19 per cent.[13] Magendie asserted that during a period of two days one of his Broussaisist colleagues lost 80 out of 86 patients, while he himself had saved 374 out of the 594 that he treated between 28 March and 23 April, 1832.[14]

Much shouting, little effect. I said that Broussais may have been the first physician to be destroyed by statistics. Yet in the strictly medical domain, he was more crushed not by a host of scurrilous numbers but by a single case, a famous friend who died of cholera. This was trumpeted as proof of the error of his methods. He was also the victim of the increasingly conservative and 'spiritual' political climate, evidenced by the success of Cousin's eclectic immaterialism. Broussais was not demolished, however. His theory of the brain as a set of organs led him to phrenology, of which he became a new champion. In the last few years of his life he once again packed the lecture halls. The issues were not merely medical, for phrenology was a refuge of materialism in an increasingly monarchical and spiritualist philosophical climate. Broussais quite literally died in its service, writing his part for an 1838 debate before the Academy of Sciences in the final throes of stomach cancer.[15]

There were, then, statistics galore, but few conclusive statistical inferences. They were tools of rhetoric, not science. For all the enthusiasm for numbers, they did not have the immediate effect that one would have expected. As William Coleman has observed, despite some pioneers that he himself investigated, 'the serious use of statistical methods in experimental physiology and medicine only began with the introduction of new techniques after 1900'.[16]

Lack of technique was not the whole story. There was a problem about the conception of medical facts. It is well illustrated by the one good piece of research that was both statistical and medical, winner of the Montyon prize in 1835, and published as a book in 1836: Jean Civiale's comparison between two highly disagreeable operations for stone, whose description we shall forbear.[17] Their names were *lithotomie* for a traditional method, and *lithotétrie* for a new technique developed and advocated by Civiale.

As early as 1828 Civiale requested the ministry of public education to obtain data on the effects of the two operations, and for his pains was sent the statistical reports of Paris and the Seine Department. Civiale persevered. In due course he reported that using the traditional method, 1,024 of 5,443 patients died, while using a new technique only seven out of 307 died from the operation, with a further three who apparently died from other causes.[18]

Civiale submitted his work for the Montyon prize. The referees appointed by the Academy of Sciences were the best. At their head was S.D. Poisson, who at this moment was stating the 'law of large numbers' to which I turn in chapter 12. The four men appointed to report on Civiale did not merely assess the work before them; they 'seized the occasion to speak on the application of probability to medicine'. We must assume that their target was precisely the debate about Broussais initiated by Miquel, and the subsequent numerical method of Louis. All such work, pontificated the jury of mathematicians, consisted 'of facts without authenticity, without detail, without control, and without value'.

Very well, but could there be authentic, controlled facts? There was something grudging about the report of the Olympian referees. They respected and admired Civiale's work; but they did not conclude that there should be more of the same. 'In practical medicine the facts are far too few for them to enter into the calculus of probabilities.' Should not the recommendation be, then, to enlarge the database? No, our reporters stated, because in applied medicine we are always concerned with the individual.

At this juncture comes the statement that I have used as my epigraph. In statistical reasoning we must 'lose sight of the man … strip him of his individuality'. Statistics can be applied only when we have classes that can be regarded as 'infinite masses'. 'It is altogether different in the domain of medicine.' In practical medicine the facts are too few to enter into the calculus of probabilities *not* because we cannot get more data, but because obtaining more data about different individuals is irrelevant to the particular case of the patient we wish to treat. It took some courage, perhaps, for a distinguished physicist in the audience to stand up and say that since 'medicine is just a science of observation like others, statistics and the probability calculus have a role in telling us what conclusions to draw, and with what degree of confidence'.[19] The mathematicians were haughtily indifferent to this modest observation.

It is well known that Claude Bernard, celebrated founder of experimental physiology, was antagonistic to the use of statistical inquiries. His reasons, however, were no different from those of Poisson, the most distinguished probability mathematician of the previous generation. How then could there be a use of statistics in human affairs? In the very institution designed to strip away the individuality of man, namely the court of law.

11

By what majority?

Paris, 14 August 1835   Gentlemen, what do you think is the
probability of a jury decision, in which the majority is seven against
five? Without a doubt, you will be shocked at the result. You will
find that the probability of error is about one in four.
Oh! Oh! Laughter from the left
I shall assert that in a large number of jury decisions, given by a
majority of eight to four, an eighth are marred by error – of eight
who mount the scaffold, there is on average one who is innocent.
Loud denials from the centre. Long agitation
Such, gentlemen, are the results furnished by the calculus of
probabilities, and provide the data needed to resolve our question.
*Renewed agitation ... the speaker is
interrupted ... private conversations break out on
every bench*[1]

Here is a way in which the new statistics seemed to matter. In 1785
Condorcet applied probability theory to judicial questions. In 1815
Laplace made some powerful *a priori* deductions about conviction rates.
Once judicial statistics were available, his protégé Poisson used statistical
inferences to overturn his conclusions. There is then a simple three-stage
story of probability arithmetic and the French jury. To repeat:

> 1785: no jury, no experience, no data. Condorcet deduced that the
> optimum twelve man jury will be one that can convict with a majority
> of ten or more members. But he preferred a jury of 30.[2]

> 1815: there were French juries, and some bad experiences, but no
> statistical data about conviction rates. The first French juries used
> Condorcet's rule, but later they decided by simple majority with one

---

* François Arago, the physicist, but also extreme-left member of the Chamber of Deputies.
The Bill before the Chamber amended the rules of the jury, which at that time required a
majority of at least eight to four. Simple majorities were called for, and the jury was not to
reveal the number of votes cast each way. This part of the bill was passed on 19 August, and
became law on 13 May 1836. Arago took the odds of error from Condorcet and Laplace.
He intervened on several occasions to clarify his position and his arithmetic, and was
disgusted by the yelling. 'If my calculation were easy to refute, I would not continually be
interrupted. Shouts are not reasons.'

complicated qualification. Laplace deduced that the simple majority was dangerous and that the qualification was worse than useless.[3]

1837: juries had been established on several different plans. There was some experience of each. There were published statistical data. Poisson deduced that juries should decide by simple majority.

The present chapter, centring on Laplace, and the next, built around Poisson, form a pair that parallels my before-and-after account of suicide statistics. There were crucial differences of course, for here we are concerned with a single set of tabulations, namely conviction rates, and a definite question, namely how to design the French jury. The problem was addressed by top mathematicians. But unlike the rambling talk about regularities of rates of deviancy, this work had almost no effect whatsoever. Why? Because it was the last gasp of Enlightenment moral science. It did use new statistical data in a brilliant way, but its conclusions were credible only to the mentality of a Condorcet.

Witnesses, assemblies and juries have played a significant role in the development of probability ideas. We tend to forget why they mattered. They were part of the notion so well surveyed by Daston, that there could be a 'reasonable calculus'.[4] In practical affairs we think that people would have wanted probabilities to compute financial advantage in trade, insurance or gaming. Daston shows that lore was more valued than rote, that familiarity with subject matter was more successful than abstract arithmetic. Probability was instead wanted for the life of reason. It was wanted to compute not profit but truth. Witnesses, assemblies and juries became its subject matter.

The empirical problem about a witness is: can this person be trusted? If so, to what degree? Perhaps we think that his credibility can be put on a numerical scale, say because he tells the truth 80 per cent of the time, or because we would bet 4:1 that he's now telling the truth. If these numbers make sense, one may proceed to matters of logic, of combining evidence. Three kinds of problem arise. How to combine the testimony of different witnesses to the same event? Then, how to combine the evidence of a witness with a different kind of evidence, say with a probability about the weather, the outcome of a roulette, or a voyage to the Indies?[5] Finally, how to combine a sequence of witnesses, one witness of a certain reliability reporting on the testimony of another witness also of imperfect credibility?

In the early annals of probability it is the third question, about a train of witnesses, that meets the eye. It seems the least important to us, partly because of the common law tradition that excludes hearsay. Why did it once matter? Because of the glorification of reason. Enlightened citizens were prepared to countenance a minimum of revelation, and no more. Superstition and miracles might entrance the populace, but rational people had to rely on natural theology. The literature on the credibility of alternative sources of revelation was extensive. Hume 'On Miracles' remains well known, and it has been argued that Thomas Bayes's famous essay, ancestor of modern 'Bayesian' statistical inference, was in part a response to Hume. The problem of miracles is for us a mere curiosity; once it was a pressing matter of life and after-death. Probability was the shield by which a rational man might guard himself against Enthusiasm. Likewise questions about voting systems still arouse the talents of the ingenious, but they grip few of us in the course of daily life. We concoct entertaining puzzles and paradoxes about voting, but what a contrast to the heady days when a people was about to set up its government and its jurisprudence on self-conscious rational principles.

A jury is a small body that decides by vote. How? There are three primary variables. First, how many choices are open to the jury? In the English system of criminal trials, there are two choices, guilty and not guilty. In the Scottish there are three, namely guilty, not guilty, and not proven. Secondly, what shall be the size of the jury? A traditional English jury is twelve in number. The Scots have fifteen jurors. Thirdly, by what majority shall the jury decide? The English jury had to reach a unanimous decision (today a majority of ten suffices).

Agitators in eighteenth-century France saw the jury as a weapon against arbitrary imprisonment. They knew of only one model to follow, England, but no ties of tradition or sentiment made it sacrosanct. Starting from nothing, how would a reasonable person design a jury system? Condorcet established the framework for discussion. There was an element of moral choice. How confident do we want to be that a jury has convicted rightly? How confident do we want to be that it has rightly acquitted? The two questions are materially different. It was argued that in troubled times, one wants to be sure not to acquit any malefactors, while in peaceful times, one can allow oneself moral scruples, and try to be sure that one does not convict any innocent. But given a moral decision fixing the probabilities of the two distinct kinds of error one can, urged Condorcet, proceed to moral mathematics, and compute the optimum jury system. Condorcet saw no absurdity in attacking the problem *a priori*.

The demand for a jury was foremost among the first articles of the *Convention* of 1789, and juries were incorporated in the constitution of 1791. As in England, there was to be a grand jury of accusation, in which eight citizens determined whether there was enough evidence to bring a case to court. This jury did not survive the Revolution. Then there was the petty jury, or jury of judgement, consisting of twelve citizens who heard the evidence and voted on guilt or innocence. A ten-vote majority was required for conviction.

This law owed much to Condorcet. He had argued that the English demand for unanimity among jurors was unreasonable. Almost never in the history of French law has anyone believed that you could count on twelve people agreeing. The apparent success of the English system was held to be factitious. The jury foreman might announce the unanimous decision, but in reality, the minority simply gave in. It was better, thought Condorcet, to be frank about the impossibility of unanimous decision, than to adopt English hypocrisy.

He thought that a majority vote of 10:2 was enough for conviction (although he preferred 30 jurors). But wrong convictions are inevitable, so the death penalty should be abolished. 'The penalty of death is the only one that makes an injustice absolutely irreparable; from which it follows that the existence of the death penalty implies that one is exposed to committing an irreparable injustice; from which it follows that it is unjust to establish it. This reasoning appears to us to have the force of a demonstration.'[6] Few paid any heed.

The jury did not fare well in troubled times. The twelve-man, majority of ten, jury came in 30 April 1790. It was amended more than once a year. The requisite majority was changed over and over again, with even a brief fling at unanimous juries. The method of voting was regularly changed, from completely open individual voting by each juror, who publicly cast a coloured ball into a coloured urn, to secret ballot, with the size of the majority kept secret. The method of empanelling jurors was frequently altered. And there were the people's courts during the Terror.

These changes were prompted by fluctuating ideologies. There were also practical difficulties: brigandage was rampant in the countryside, and gangsters terrorized the wretched jurors who had to cast their vote in such a public way. The problem of bandits was briskly solved in 1798. They were to be tried by a special tribunal. It had a president, two judges, and five special appointees, three of whom were military officers and two of whom were citizens of status; all were to be appointed by the First Consul.

So the problem of juries was pressing! England ceased to be the liberal model for the philosophers; she was the reactionary and ever perfidious foe.[*7] By 1799: 'The results of the jury may be judged from what takes

---

* A magistrate at Nîmes, contributing to the volumes of testimony that led to the Code of 1808, said of Great Britain: 'The changing picture of the crimes of that nation, which uses assassination and the plague to repulse an enemy which it has provoked into breaking a solemn treaty, ought not to induce us to adopt its system in criminal procedure. The jury has not rendered that people better; and if we recall what travellers have told us, there is no European country where robbery, especially upon the highways, is more frequent and better organized than in that island.'

place among the English – there is no country with a worse police and less individual safety.'[8]

The upshot of unrest and reform was the Code of 1808. Although the Code was durable, the jury was one of the least stable elements of French jurisprudence (and remains so today). In 1808 conviction was to be by simple majority, with one qualification to be discussed presently. Every political upheaval affected the jury. The law of 4 March 1831 required a majority of eight among twelve jurors for conviction. There were two more jury laws before the law of May 1836 reestablished the simple majority – after many a passionate word, like that of our epigraph.[9]

Laplace argued that the system of 1808 was defective. When a jury decided by a simple majority for conviction, seven against five, the chance of error was almost one in three: a 'terrifying' figure! (His computation made it $\frac{2}{7}$, not so bad as $\frac{1}{3}$, but worse than Arago's $\frac{1}{4}$). The code acknowledged the problem, for it had two levels of tribunal. There was a higher court of five judges. The jury gave its verdict. According to Article 351, the court of five judges could review the case when the jury split 7:5. One has to read the rule twice to understand it: if the opinion of the minority of the jurors was agreed by a majority of the judges in such a way that the votes for acquittal of all judges and jurors taken together exceeded that for conviction, then the jury was overruled.

Around 1815 these concerns prodded Laplace into serious reflection about juries.*[10] According to his analysis, the probability of testimony is a propensity of the witness – some are deceitful, others testify only when their opinion is well founded. The probability is independent of the nature of what is attested. He came to see that jurors may be more reliable in one case than another, for the quality of evidence may differ in different cases. Thus Laplace took the fact that a jury is unanimous as evidence *about* the case itself. It shows that the case is clear-cut and hence that well chosen jurors can be relied upon. On the other hand, the fact that a jury divides 7:5 is evidence that the case is a hard one, causing even impartial jurors to be unreliable. Thus Laplace thought of each juror as having a certain *a priori* reliability, measured by a probability. Then one had to assess the *a*

---

* None of this was obvious to Laplace. In section 50 of the *Théorie analytique* the decisions of tribunals were assimilated to the problems of combining witnesses. The first edition of the popular *Philosophical Essay on Probabilities* (1814) had no section on witnesses. In the second edition of the same year one such section was added, a summary of what went into section 50 of the *Théorie*, that 'the judgements of tribunals can be assimilated to testimony, by considering each judge as a witness who attests to the truth of his own opinion'. This concluding paragraph was soon recanted, and in the third edition of the *Essay* (1816) one finds the results I shall soon describe. The full argument was given in the first supplement to the *Théorie*, in 1816. It was immediately followed by an informal criticism of article 351, originally published in a pamphlet of 15 November, 1816. These results were made available to a wider public by Laplace's student and popularizer, Silvestre Lacroix.

posteriori reliability of the juror, given that the jury was unanimous or split 7:5 or whatever.

Laplace made three assumptions. First, the probability of guilt of an accused is $\frac{1}{2}$. Next, the *a priori* reliability of a juror lies between $\frac{1}{2}$ and 1. Why? If we thought it were less than $\frac{1}{2}$, we would rather toss a coin than use a juror. Laplace then postulated that the reliability of jurors is *a priori* uniformly distributed between $\frac{1}{2}$ and 1 (it's as likely to be any value in that interval as any other).

Finally, we need not analyse the reliability in terms of individual jurors, but can assume an average reliability. The calculations that follow from these assumptions are straightforward.[11] The conclusion is that a unanimous jury of n jurors has reliability $(\frac{1}{2})^{n+1}$. No tidier example of an *a priori* rabbit out of a hat can be imagined. Here is Laplace's table of conclusions:

For a jury that divides	the chance of error is:
12:0	$\frac{1}{8192}$
9:3	about $\frac{1}{22}$
8:4	about $\frac{1}{8}$
7:5	$\frac{2}{7}$
5:3	about $\frac{1}{4}$
9:0	$\frac{1}{1024}$
112:100	about $\frac{1}{5}$
501:500	about $\frac{1}{2}$

When a jury convicts by a split of 7:5, there is a $\frac{2}{7}$ probability that the person is innocent. That is too high: *effrayant*. Thus Laplace was against conviction by simple majority. A unanimous jury of twelve is safe, perhaps too safe. Laplace suggested that we strive for an error rate of one in a thousand, so that a unanimous jury of nine is suitable.

He also considered an eight-man jury: *viz* the special tribunal for bandits established by Napoleon. According to Laplace's method the accused has a better chance with a 144 person jury splitting 90:54 (error probability $\frac{1}{773}$) than with a unanimous eight-person special tribunal (error probability $\frac{1}{512}$). A mere majority of five among eight jurors will be wrong about a quarter of the time.

It followed from Laplace's calculations that Article 351 is terrible. Suppose that the jury decides to convict by a bare majority, 7:5. When the five judges just fail to override the jury three of them vote for acquittal, two for conviction. Then there has been a total of nine votes cast for conviction, and eight for acquittal, and the conviction stands.

On Laplace's analysis conviction by the double tier system is less to be trusted than the decision of the first court. A majority of one, in a group of seventeen, indicates more dissension, and a more difficult case, and hence a less reliable judgement, than a majority of two, in a jury of twelve.[12] Officialdom seems not to have been interested. Gergonne repeated all the arguments in his journal, which was the most important mathematics periodical of the day. He said that he had sent them to the ministry of justice months earlier, but had not even received an acknowledgement.[13] The ministry may have been unmoved for good reason. These deductions were pure reason, untrammelled by experience. Before passing to Poisson's use of empirical data I shall interject a curious incident.

During the apogee of Euler, there had been no greater mathematical centre than St Petersburg, but it fell into decline. Its revival owed much to M.V. Ostrogradsky, a minor figure but a mover and shaker who put in place the future glories of the Petersburg school of probability.[14] He was deeply perturbed at a feature of Laplace's reasoning that to us, now, seems entirely 'intuitive'.[15] A jury that divides 12:0 displays the same absolute majority as one that splits 112:100. Laplace found the former much more reliable, because the disagreement displayed by the second group of jurors shows it was confronted by poor evidence. Ostrogradsky dissented, maintaining that a 112:100 jury is exactly as reliable as a 12:0 majority. He mentioned the English House of Lords, that tries peers. In that case, the jury is some 600 peers trying one of its own, and Ostrogradsky held that when peers convict with a slim majority of twelve they are as reliable as commoners voting twelve to zero.*

It seems obvious to us that Ostrogradsky was wrong. But Laplace himself spent pages of the popular *Essay* arguing that a majority of 212:200 is much less reliable than one of 12:0. He cannot have thought that his readers would find it evident. This is only an 'intuition' that has become firm with the passage of years. Moreover Laplace had a little mathematical secret. I noted his innocent assumption – which sounds like a mere mathematical convenience – that all the jurors have an equal (unknown) *a priori* reliability. Ostrogradsky found that if you don't make that assumption, and follow approximately Laplace's course of reasoning, you deduce that a jury of 212:200 is exactly as reliable as one of 12:0!

* Ostrogradsky argued informally that a three-person jury splitting 2:1 is as good as a 'unanimous' one-person jury. For consider (a) a jury of three, voting 2:1; and (b) a jury in which an arbitrarily chosen juror votes first, for guilt, before the other two vote. In (b) there are three possibilities: (b1) the other two jurors agree with the first; (b2) they both disagree with the first; (b3) they disagree. The effect of (b3) is (a). But (b1) and (b2) are equally probable. Hence a vote of one juror for guilt is logically equivalent to a disjunction: three jurors voting by majority for guilt, or one or the other of two equally probable opposite events (which cancel out). Hence a conviction (2:1) is exactly as good as a conviction (1:0). And, by analogy, 12:0 is as good as 112:100. One hardly knows where to begin to reply! But on Laplacian principles, (b1) and (b2) are not equally probable given that the first juror voted for guilt; moreover Laplace's theory does not apply to a (1:0) 'jury'.

Ostrogradsky was the first mathematician, I believe, to represent a probability not as a number between 0 and 1, but as an 'upper and lower probability', as an interval r_*, r^*, with r_* as the lower limit of the probability and r^* as the upper limit.[16] Then, instead of assuming that there is an unknown *a priori* reliability r of all jurors, he allowed that each juror may have a different unknown *a priori* reliability, and insisted only that there is a common upper and lower reliability for all jurors.

Much to our astonishment, this assumption, far more plausible than that of Laplace, vindicates decision by simple majority. When the excess of the majority over the minority is d, and the reliability of an individual juror lies between $\frac{1}{2}$ and 1, the probability that a jury is correct is $(3^d + 1)$. *In figures:*[17]

For a jury that divides	the probability of error is
7:5	$\frac{1}{10}$
8:4	$\frac{1}{82}$
12:0 and 112:100	about 3^{-12}

Ostrogradsky sent his paper to Poisson in 1834. Poisson acknowledged receipt of the Russian paper, but we do not know what he thought of it. The next year he presented his own analysis of the jury system.

Laplace found 'terrifying' a system that executed people with almost a 30 per cent chance of error. Poisson was an old man who was too young to have felt the heady first breath of revolution (he was eight years old in 1789) and who began thinking about the jury after the Revolution of 1830. He didn't mind if two out of every seven people executed by majority decision were innocent. We can, he wrote, infer from the new justice ministry statistics that only 7 per cent of French juries divide by simple majority, so the net increase in error to the judicial system is very small, almost negligible. But that was just the beginning of the argument. Laplace had no judicial statistics; Poisson had. He deduced that the probabilities of error are not as great as Laplace supposed. The real empirical probability of error with a 7:5 decision is about the same as what Laplace computed for an 8:4 decision. So if you were happy with 8:4 juries on the basis of Laplace, you should be happy with 7:5 juries.

Thus by the end of 1835 Poisson had proved that the Chamber of Deputies had been wise when, on 19 August, it restored decision by simple majority. His book on the jury, published in 1837, was a mathematical vindication of conservative opinion. The elegance of Poisson's mathematics is uncontested. It was intended, however, to be an implement of information and control. It was as much a political tract as a mathematical one.

12

The law of large numbers

Paris, 16 November 1835 Things of every kind are subject to a universal law that we may call *the law of large numbers*. It consists in this: if one observes a very considerable number of events of the same kind, depending on causes that vary irregularly, that is to say, without any systematic variation in one direction, then one finds that the ratios between the numbers of events are very nearly constant.

Paris, 16 April 1842 The Law of Large Numbers does not exist. [*1]

The ministry of justice published annual data for the years following 1826. It highlighted summary figures for trials and convictions. They led Poisson to the great work of 1837 in which he proved a law of large numbers, and gave us the very phrase, 'law of large numbers', that still finds a place in every probability primer.[2] His book distinguished more clearly than any predecessor between 'relative frequency' and 'degree of belief' approaches to probability. It applied statistical tests and measures of reliability in a way that makes clear, as Stigler has shown, that Poisson understood their logic in an unequivocal way.[3] It provided the first sound mathematics for quite rare events, now called the Poisson distribution, work well reported by O.B. Sheynin.[4] The deductions from jury data have recently been analysed by Gelfand and Solomon, because of the 1967 decision of the United States Supreme Court, declaring it constitutional for juries to decide by majority and not unanimously.[5] In the same year England allowed conviction by a majority vote of ten against two. In 1967, for the first time ever, the common law had to address the question, 'By what majority?', that has perplexed the French since 1785.

Thus in many respects Poisson's book has been amply studied, but few

---

[*] S.-D. Poisson to the Paris Academy of Sciences and I.J. Bienaymé (recalling in 1855 what he said) to a Paris mathematical club. Poisson began work on the topic after noting that Laplace had two incompatible solutions to the problem of juries. 'This has long filled my mind with many doubts.' His admiration for Laplace constrained him from publishing, or so he said. Likewise Bienaymé in 1855: 'The state of M. Poisson's health did not allow me to give the required publicity to my remarks', referring to his conviction as early as 1839 that Poisson in turn had been wrong.

have noticed how timely it was in 1837. It addressed the burning issue of 1835: how should a jury vote? It was a work of moral science. Hence almost all its results were long misunderstood or ignored. It was a sport, ahead of its times and behind them. Poisson, Condorcet's heir and the end of the line, was able to employ the new statistics in ways that can still dazzle the knowledgeable, but he was engaging in what Daston has called 'the reasonable calculus: classical probability theory 1650–1840'.[6] The latter is the year that Poisson died, and with him, a great sociopolitical project.

The identification with moral science was made by Poisson himself at the start of his book. Laplace, he wrote, followed Condorcet when he took up the probability of judgements, 'one of the most delicate questions in the theory of probabilities'. Laplace used the principle originally given by 'Blayes'.[7] He made many happy uses of this principle, but 'it is only fair to say that the application of Blayes's rule to judgement is due to Condorcet'. We regard the majority vote of the jury as an observed effect, and the guilt or innocence of the accused as an unknown cause. Then we apply Bayes's rule to work out the probability of guilt or innocence.

The last book of moral science in the style of the Enlightenment was A.A. Cournot's 1843 work on chance and probability.[8] What are these chances *and* probabilities? Two kinds of thing, because Poisson and Cournot used the French words *chance* and *probabilité* to name two concepts. Probability would mean credibility, or degree of reasonable belief:

The *probability* of an event is the reason that we have for thinking that the event did or will take place.

But *chance* will denote an objective property of an event, the 'facility' with which it can occur:

Thus an event will have, by its very nature, a larger or smaller chance, known or unknown.[9]

It seems almost inevitable that such distinctions would be made in the 1830s. Old Poisson was poised between 'subjective' (*probabilité*) and 'objective' (*chance*) attitudes to probability. I claimed in *The Emergence of Probability* that our idea of probability is a Janus-faced mid-seventeenth-century mutation in the Renaissance idea of signs. It came into being with a frequency aspect and a degree-of-belief aspect. In the early days one could be indifferent as to the two directions in which probability might lead one. When Laplace was young probability greatly extended her purview, but there were to hand only the same old frequencies in games of chance, births, marriages and deaths, and errors of measurement. When he needed to talk of an objective frequency or propensity, Laplace cheerfully spoke of the *facilité* of various outcomes on chance set-ups, but he defined *probabilité* as a subjective notion, relative to our knowledge and to our ignorance. By the 1830s, however, the world teemed with frequencies, and the 'objective' notion would come to seem more important than the 'subjective' one for the rest of the century – simply because there were so many more frequencies to be known.

It is pointless to debate which of the two ideas is correct. We note only that one or the other may be more dominant at different times. Laplace made the subjective probability idea officially preeminent. When did the reversal of fortunes begin, with the objective idea swinging into favour? There is a very plausible answer. The avalanche of printed enumerations of social conditions began in the 1820s with the *Recherches statistiques* of Paris and the Seine directed by Joseph Fourier. His biographer Grattan-Guinness has observed that

during his directorship the bureau published four reports on the city of Paris, in which he presented in two papers the calculation of the mean and standard deviation of a large number of observations and the probability that a function under measurement lay within given limits. The study of statistics was then at a rudimentary stage of development and was dominated by Laplacian subjectivism concerning probability ... Fourier himself taught probability at the Ecole Polytechnique [shortly after Laplace in 1795] and ... his reports of the 1820s giving an *objective* account of statistical studies were a considerable novelty.[10]

Fourier by no means originated calculations of the probability that a quantity lay within certain limits – the theory is there in Laplace. But his application to mass social phenomena was largely new and in certain ways changed the feel of what one was doing. Perhaps Poisson learned more from Fourier than from Laplace. Be that as it may, he certainly continued the upswing of interest in objective probabilities. He wanted to estimate the (objective) rates of conviction by juries, and to know whether a change in the political tempo of the times had made an objective difference in the chance of conviction.

Laplace had two ways in which to address such questions. One is Bernoullian, and attends to relative frequencies; the other is Bayesian, and is usually now interpreted in terms of degrees of belief. Laplace almost invited his readers not to notice the difference.[11] Poisson, in contrast, was scrupulous in his attention to matters of reasoning. As Stephen Stigler reports,

Poisson's statement is as clear an application of Laplacian [Laplace in the frequentist mode] methods to the uncertainty of social data as we could hope to find. Even the arithmetic is correct. There is no reluctance, no equivocation, no qualification. The interpretation intended appears to be modeled after the informal fiducial arguments from the theory of errors in astronomical observations rather than being an ambiguously Bayesian statement about an unknown quantity.[*][12]

I suggest in chapter 23 that C.S. Peirce was the first to *explain* this logic unambiguously. Why this weird time-delay? Because the reasoning occurred in a work of moral science. No one paid any attention to it after 1843. Poisson's logic had to be rediscovered in other contexts, and Cournot did understand the logic and used it at least as well as Poisson, but he had to be rediscovered for work on economics, not probabilities.[13]

By the 1840s almost no one believed that there was a mathematical solution to the jury problem, and so all of Poisson's techniques fell by the wayside. Nobody gave a fig either for his exact computations or for his methods of reasoning. When you don't care, the best thing to do is to deny. Westerners, obsessed by phenomenal averages, denied. It was left to St Petersburg and Berlin to pick up the pieces. Today's textbooks teach the Poisson distribution, the limiting case of the binomial distribution for events that are very rare (a coin that almost always turns up heads). Many of the same textbooks still bear the unnoticed historical lesson on their face. They quote the comical (?) example that made the Poisson distribution famous: the rate with which Prussian officers of the 1890s were injured by being kicked by their horses.

To return to *chance* and *probabilité*: the fundamental distinction between 'objective' and 'subjective' in probability – so often put in terms of frequency *vs.* belief – is between modelling and inference. When we model processes in terms of probability, we suppose that there is some objective characteristic of things that behaves just like, say, an urn from which coloured balls are being drawn with stable relative frequency. When we infer using probabilities we are reaching conclusions about whose truth we are not quite certain. That is often thought of as subjective or at any rate

---

[*]   A fiducial measure of the reliability of an estimate is independent of the true unknown value of the quantity under estimate. I have one caution about Stigler's exemplary summary: the word 'astronomical'. Although we can discern Poisson using techniques that occur by rote in the observational astronomy of the time, Poisson's fiducial limits came out of Condorcet and Fourier. Long after the 1820s, the astronomers were loyal to Bessel's 'probable error' with its 50 per cent limits. Poisson, the moral scientist, computed all sorts of fiducial probabilities with very high limits, extremely close to 100 per cent. The astronomer needed only some standard for comparing the reliability of different observations, and the probable error is as good as any other. The moral scientist wanted to influence people, and to claim that he was 'morally certain' about his hypotheses. We have followed suit, abandoning the probable error in practical affairs. We now use fiducial limits and confidence intervals as spurs to action that we could not contemplate in astronomy (we can't change the stars, but we can change plant yields). So we use '95 per cent confidence limits' and the like. Despite what is said in textbooks, the numbers '95 per cent' or '99 per cent' don't mean much in themselves but are part of the rhetoric of standardization, legitimation and persuasion.

epistemic, knowledge-relative. Poisson was first *modelling* the behaviour of jurors in terms of probability. He supposed that the reliability of a juror is an objective fact about the juror; he gives right judgement in some definite proportion of times. Next he wanted to estimate the reliability of jurors. This was an *inference* to be drawn from the data of the ministry of justice. The inference could be drawn only with some degree of confidence, and Poisson set fiducial limits on his inferences. That might look like the probability of a probability. Poisson rightly distinguished: it is the ('subjective') probability of an ('objective') probability, or, better, the *probabilité* of a *chance*.[14]

Poisson wanted to know which is better: a jury that decides by simple majority, or a jury that decides by a majority of at least 8:4? Laplace had thought that simple majority decisions are viciously likely to be wrong. In 1831 the law was changed from a 7:5 majority to an 8:4 one, and this was reversed in 1835. Poisson aimed at showing that the conservative decision of 1835 was sound.[15] The ministry provided data for conviction of accused individuals in various kinds of trials after 1826. Between 1826 and 1830 convictions could be by simple majority. After 1831 and as far as Poisson's data were available, convictions were by a minimum of 8:4. The ministry divided cases into civil and criminal, into crimes against the person and crimes against property, and it reported the conviction rates for each year.

Conviction rates do not sound a promising basis for inferring the reliability of jurors. Well, Laplace had deduced reliability from no data whatsoever. Poisson's statistical model began by following Laplace. The behaviour of juries is governed by two underlying unknown parameters:

r: the average reliability of jurors.
k: the prior probability of guilt of the accused.

These numbers represent objective propensities of accused and jurors at a given time, and may change over the years. They may also be different for various kinds of trial: criminal and civil, and crimes against property and crimes against the person.

Poisson wanted not r and k, but the probability that the accused is guilty, given that he has been found guilty. In particular, he wanted the reliability of juries that may decide by simple majority, as opposed to those that must convict by at least 8:4.

$p_{g,i}$: The probability that the accused is guilty, given a conviction by exactly g to i.
$P_{g,i}$: The probability that the accused is guilty, given a conviction by at least g to i.

The ministry data show only, year by year, for various types of crime:

$C_{g,i}$: The proportion of the accused that are convicted by a majority of at least g to i.

We have this quantity for 7:5 in the years 1826–31, and for 8:4 in the years 1832 and after. How on earth could one derive the p's and P's from this? Since the actual proportion by which a jury split was secret, the ministry did not even know the value of

$c_{g,i}$: The proportion of the accused that are convicted by a majority of exactly g to i.

It is true that in the case of a 7:5 vote the decision was sent for review, but the data reported only the number of trials sent for review. As trials of groups and of conspiracies were common at the time, the data fell significantly short of telling Poisson the number of individuals found guilty by a 7:5 vote.

Even if one did know the proportion of juries that convict by exactly 7:5, we would be far from the p's and r's. That is where Condorcet's magic enters, for he had been able to write down an equation connecting all these quantities.[16] It had the consequence that if we obtain the proportion of convictions at exactly 7:5, and we estimate k, the probability of guilt, by the actual conviction rate, then we can actually solve the equation to find r, the reliability of jurors, and hence (by more Condorcet-style prestidigitation) the probability that a person convicted 7:5 is actually guilty.* We can also determine the relative chances of error for juries that can convict by simple majority and those that require a majority of 8 to 4.

Hence the unknown $c_{7,5}$ is the key to solving Poisson's problem. Now suppose the following is true: the reliability of jurors is the same from year to year. Then we can use the results after 1832 to estimate $C_{8,4}$, and those before to estimate $C_{7,5}$; and of course

$$c_{7,5} = C_{8,4} - C_{7,5}.$$

Thus the question arises as to whether the conviction rates for the various sorts of crime were constant. In the model being used, this is a question of whether the reliability of the jurors was constant. There will be some random variation even with constant average reliabilities. Are the differences between successive years significant? Poisson was able to compute

---

* Laplace, it will be recalled, set $k = \frac{1}{2}$. That may sound innocent, but it is very handy for making a certain integration in solving Laplace's problem. Poisson was scathing. Surely we think that the probability of guilt of an accused exceeds $\frac{1}{2}$? Surely we have more confidence in our judicial process, than to imagine that it is a mere toss-up as to whether the accused is rightly accused? In fact, Laplace well agrees with modern experience. In recent judicial practice in England and Wales, where since 1967 juries may decide by a majority of 10:2, the conviction rate in trials that proceed to a jury decision is almost exactly 0.5. Indeed Laplace's totally *a priori* model fits the English situation curiously well, I believe.

that, with high (subjective) probability, the variations in the years 1826–9 were due to chance. But the deviation for 1830 was significant. The conviction rate in that year is markedly less than in preceding years. Poisson provided a numerical measure of the significance of the difference. He had, he thought, detected a real change in court behaviour. 1830 was a year of revolution. Either the court was bringing too many criminals to trial in a draconian attempt to maintain order, or jurors were, in revolutionary spirit, declining to bring in convictions. At any rate the 1830 figures are to be discounted in computing $c_{7,5}$. The consequence? In the case of a jury that divides by exactly 7 to 5, the probability of error

for crimes against property: 0.0382
for crimes against the person: 0.1627.

The second figure is not much larger than $\frac{1}{8}$. Recall that Laplace had deduced that a jury dividing 7:5 erred about $\frac{2}{7}$ of the time, while one dividing 8:4 erred one time in eight. Thus: anyone who argued, according to Laplace's reasoning, that the 1831 (8:4 minimum) law should be restored, should be content with the 1835 law (simple majority). And who was Poisson addressing here, if not Arago and his ilk?

I have been discussing the second half of Poisson's researches. Let us now turn to the first, and to the celebrated law of large numbers. The connection is that 'r', the 'average' reliability of a juror. Poisson's mathematical problem was well understood for situations which could be modelled with each juror having the same reliability as every other. But this, as Ostrogradsky had observed, is preposterous. Some jurors are more reliable than others. *Poisson's law of large numbers was devised in order to solve just this problem.* He studied as a model the situation in which reliability varies from juror to juror, but in which there is some law (Poisson's word) or probability distribution (our phrase) for reliability among French jurors.

Abstractly, the situation was this. Jacques Bernoulli's famous theorem, published posthumously in 1713, applied to repeated drawings, with replacement, of balls from an urn with black and white balls. Let the proportion of black balls in the urn be p. We take this to be the probability of drawing a black ball. Draw a ball, note its colour, replace it and shake the contents. We can consider a sequence of many such draws, and the relative frequency with which black is drawn on such a sequence. We can ask, what is the probability that the relative frequency is within some small 'error' e of p? Bernoulli could answer, and that answer became well known. But suppose one is considering a population of urns in which the proportion of black balls varies from urn to urn? We choose an urn at random, and then draw a ball at random. Once again, in repeated urn/ball draws, there will be a relative frequency with which black is drawn. Let q be the overall proportion of black balls in the urns. Can we make any statement about the probability that the relative frequency of drawing black, in urn/ball selections, is within some small 'error' of q? Yes. The precise statement is what Poisson called the law of large numbers.

Nowadays a philosopher reading Poisson would say that he had in mind two different things with his catchy phrase, 'law of large numbers': an empirical phenomenon, and a mathematical theorem. But his attitude was that of the mathematical physicist – less the physicist of 1835, than the student of the 'rational mechanics' of 1785. On the one hand, experience would verify facts, and on the other, mathematics would demonstrate the very same facts. Poisson was untroubled by any distinctions between the analytic and the synthetic, between the *a priori* and the *a posteriori*, between the necessary and the contingent. Facts are facts.

Thus he thought that the law of large numbers is 'a fact of experience that never goes wrong'.[17] It was verified in moral affairs and in physical science. In 1835 he used as examples the stability of rates of shipwreck, of mortality, and of conviction on trials of various kinds – but, as we have seen in chapter 10, he did not favour using rates of cure by physicians or surgeons. 'These examples, of every kind, can leave no doubt about the generality and exactitude [of the law], but it was desirable that it should be demonstrated *a priori*, for it is the basis of those applications of the probability calculus that are of the greatest interest to us.'[18]

One can see him working his way towards the idea in his occasional lectures to the Academy. Thus on 11 April 1836 he recalled that he previously 'considered the law of large numbers to be a fact that we observe in things of every kind'.[19] But, he continued, we must make a distinction. Suppose we are tossing a five-franc piece and note that in 2,000 tosses it comes up heads 1,100 times. We infer that there is a single constant unknown chance of getting heads, namely $\frac{11}{20}$. This chance is the consequence of a common cause, of the way the coin and tossing device are made. But now suppose we toss 2,000 different coins, and get 1,100 heads. We cannot imagine that the coins have identical constitutions. The causes and hence the chance of heads will vary from case to case.

Most matters of jurisprudence, practical affairs, moral and even natural science are like the many-coin case, and not like the Bernoullian one-coin-many-times case. Likewise each voyage to the Indies is different. One is beset by a typhoon, one has an incompetent master, and another is beset by pirates off the straits of Malacca. There is no constant cause acting upon the mariners, but there is (Poisson asserted, speciously) a constant effect, a constant proportion of wrecks. Likewise for juries, whose jurors vary in wisdom and prejudice, but manifest a stable overall effect in the tabulations of the ministry of justice.

Having convinced himself *a posteriori*, Poisson proceeded to establish *a priori* that one could expect statistical stability when considering a sequence of events. Each could be determined by its own causes, so long as there were a law of the distribution of the causes. One corollary surprises the novice. Let us call drawings with replacement from a single urn Bernoulli trials, and drawings with replacement from a multitude of urns Poisson trials. How quickly do relative frequencies tend to stabilize in Bernoulli trials? In Poisson trials? There's more variability and hence less speedy convergence in Poisson trials, isn't there? No. In a certain sense Poisson trials tend to converge more quickly than Bernoulli ones.[20]

According to an old tradition, associated with students of Newton such as De Moivre, the stability of relative frequencies was a sign of Divine Providence. Poisson thought that his theorem put paid to that:

> One would be tempted to attribute [statistical stability] to the intervention of an occult power, distinct from the physical or moral causes of events, and acting in some way to keep order; but theory shows us that this permanence takes place necessarily so long as the law of the probability of the causes, relative to each class of events, does not change.[21]

His law of large numbers was not, however, well received. Weekly during April 1836 – recall that the change in the jury rules was not made law until May of that year – a highbrow battle raged at the meetings of the Academy.*[22] Yet the interest was brief, and, behind Poisson's back, highly critical. One young mathematician, I.J. Bienaymé, was utterly sceptical, as is indicated by my epigraph. Heyde and Seneta have described how, on the mathematical side, Bienaymé denied that Poisson had added anything to Bernoulli.[23] As early as 1839 he had argued that one could obtain Poisson's conclusions by using a theorem of Laplace, an opinion with which one cannot entirely agree.[24] On the experiential side,

> when one engages in genuinely serious scientific research, not limited to a small number of observations, and in which one compares facts over a number of years, it is hard not to notice that the variations exceed those of the limits set by Bernoulli's theorem.[25]

'I hope that the term I have been discussing' – the law of large numbers – 'will not be retained in scientific usage.'[26] Bienaymé's hope has not been fulfilled. But in a sense he should have felt gratified, because Poisson's kind

---

* One critic recalled that at the time of the Terror, revolutionary tribunals acquitted only 5 per cent of the accused. Poisson was able to enjoy a mathematical joke in reply. His analysis provides two solutions for the reliability of jurors (there is a quadratic equation involved), one greater than and one less than $\frac{1}{2}$. We deduce that in revolutionary times, the

of moral science died out. There was a small cottage industry of studies of the jury problem, using alternative models of juries. Cournot took up the matter with great clarity and little inspiration.[27] He was not alone, but the entire programme was short-lived.[28] It became an amusement for mathematical dilettantes, and if we wish to pursue it we shall have to turn, say, to the worthy but hardly central Devonshire Association for the Advancement of Science.[29] In short, what was left of moral science became genteel. The likes of Guerry and even Quetelet had nothing like the mastery of the judicial statistics evinced by Poisson. But they were the voice of the future, for moral science was replaced by moral analysis and then by quantitative sociology.

Poisson's book was translated into German, but under a new title – as a *Treatise on probability theory and some of its most important applications*. That is, by changing the title it became a different kind of book. Even in 1838 the astronomer Bessel referred to the law of large numbers with more respect than it was to receive in France for many a decade. But it was left to P.L. Chebyshev to create a proper understanding. In a youthful work he made clear what the theorem is about.[30] The law of large numbers, or rather the central limit theorem, became part of the standard syllabus at St Petersburg.[31]

As for France: despite Bienaymé, the term 'law of large numbers' became entrenched, and it was taken to denote a profound fact about the world. Against the advice of sceptics, statistical law was enthroned. When there are enough events, they display regularities. This law passed beyond a mere fact of experience. It was not something to be checked against experience; it was the way things had to be. Not because there was a mathematical demonstration of the law – no one paid much heed to what Poisson had proved. The law of large numbers became a metaphysical truth. No matter that hardly anyone in France understood Poisson's mathematics, nor that the empirical phenomena are a great deal more irregular (to our eyes) than was popularly urged. Thanks to superstition, laziness, equivocation, befuddlement with tables of numbers, dreams of social control, and propaganda from utilitarians, the law of large numbers – not Poisson's theorem but a proposition about the stability of mass phenomena – became, for the next generation or two, a synthetic *a priori* truth.

reliability of jurors was represented by a number less than $\frac{1}{2}$. Jurors were less reliable than tossing coins.

13

Regimental chests

Brussels, 21 February 1844 Another question of the highest importance presents itself here. One may ask if there exists, in a people, *un homme type*, a man who represents this people by height, and in relation to which all the other men of the same nation must be considered as offering deviations that are more or less large. The numbers that one would have, on measuring the latter, would be grouped around the mean, in the same way as the numbers that one would obtain, if the same typical man had been measured a large number of times by more or less imprecise methods.*[1]

The powerhouse of the statistical movement was Adolphe Quetelet, the greatest regularity salesman of the nineteenth century. As soon as Parisian judicial statistics were published he noticed 'the terrifying exactitude with which crimes reproduce themselves'.[2] The number of criminals is constant; the relative proportions of different sorts of crime remains the same. 'We know in advance how many individuals will dirty their hands with the blood of others, how many will be forgers, how many poisoners, nearly as well as one can enumerate in advance the births and deaths that must take place.'[3] He described the phenomenon as a 'kind of budget for the scaffold, the galleys and the prisons, achieved by the French nation with greater regularity, without doubt, than the financial budget'.[4]

Evidently Quetelet felt the same awe, in the face of statistical stability, that Guerry experienced. But where Guerry was a man of meticulous fact, Quetelet was a man of vision, an astronomer who saw in the behaviour of his myriads of fellow citizens regularities worthy of the stars. Heavenly bodies are governed by specific and known laws. What specific laws govern people? Poisson's law of large numbers provides no answer. Understood as a theorem of mathematics it is not a law of behaviour.

---

* Adolphe Quetelet, from a long essay for the Belgian statistical commission, which he also issued separately, dedicating it to his distinguished students. The occasion was a party held on 10 March, commemorating his 30th year in the professorate. On his nineteenth birthday, 22 February 1815, he had been appointed professor at the newly-established royal college at Ghent (which replaced the Napoleonic imperial lycée). This reverse *Festschrift* for his students was a birthday present to himself.

Erroneously understood as a universal empirical generalization that series tend to stabilize, it may show that social laws will reveal themselves in statistics, but it is not itself a social law.

What then, in moral science, could compare to the differential equations of physics? 63.5 per cent of jury trials may yield convictions, but that is a mere constancy nothing like a law of astronomy.[5] What is? The question did not arise for Guerry, trained as an advocate, but was inevitable for Quetelet, the Astronomer-Royal of Belgium. He was just the man to find sociological laws worthy of the name. He was fond of numbers, and happy to jump to conclusions. It is astonishing how profoundly Quetelet's jumping to conclusions affected the twentieth-century conceptual scheme of truths and possibilities to which we still subscribe.

By the start of the nineteenth century a 'law of errors' had been developed for observational astronomy and other sciences of measurement such as photometry and geodesy. Generous, astonished, and, I venture, credulous Quetelet announced in 1844 that a great many human attributes have a graph, or distribution, just like that which had long been associated with coin tossing, and which had been elaborated for mathematicians as the 'curve of error'. Stephen Stigler has given a masterly description of what he calls the 'Gauss-Laplace synthesis', achieved by 1827, the year that Laplace died.

It brought together two well-developed lines – one the combination of observations through the aggregation of linearized equations of condition, the other the use of mathematical probability to assess uncertainty and make inferences – into a coherent whole. In many respects it was one of the major success stories in the history of science.[6]

The familiar graphical representation of the idea is the 'bell-shaped curve', the Normal distribution or Gaussian distribution that peaks about the mean. There were two routes to this curve. The oldest, written down by De Moivre as early as 1708, obtained it as the limit of a coin-tossing or binomial distribution. We think of a coin being tossed n times, and note the proportion k of heads. After many k-fold trials we obtain a graph showing the number of occasions on which we got 0 heads, 1 head, 2 heads ... n heads. The curve will peak around the probability of getting heads with the coin. As n grows without bound, a Normal distribution results.

The second route was that of the observational astronomers. Under plausible assumptions the distribution of errors will follow the same curve.[7] Now the curve is defined by two quantities: the mean, and some measure of dispersion. Dispersion is important to the measurer: if all the measurements cluster about the mean, we think of the average as reliable. If they are spread out, we think it is not. A Normal distribution is defined by its mean and standard deviation. Any measure of dispersion would do. Throughout the nineteenth century, 'probable error' was used.[8] This term was introduced by the great observational astronomer F.W. Bessel around 1815, and for long was the only measure of dispersion that was widely used.[9] The core idea is that the probable error divides measurements into two equally probable classes: in the long run half the measurements will err in excess of the probable error, and half will be more exact.

Now whether we think of the Normal distribution as an error curve or as the limit of a binomial coin-tossing game, we are concerned with what we think of as real quantities. The coin has a real objective propensity (so we suppose) to fall heads in a certain proportion of tosses. The celestial position being measured is a real point in space, and the distribution of errors, we suppose, is an objective feature of the measuring device and the measurer. Quetelet changed the game. He applied the same curve to biological and social phenomena where the mean is not a real quantity at all, or rather: *he transformed the mean into a real quantity*.

It began innocently enough. In a series of works of the early 1830s he gave us 'the average man'. This did not of itself turn averages – mere arithmetical constructions – into real quantities like the position of a star. But it was a first step. One much-read site of 'the average man' was his *Treatise on Man* of 1835.[10] In England the *Athenaeum* considered 'the appearance of these volumes as forming an epoch in the literary history of civilization'.[11] It has been argued that this review was an important stage in Darwin's travels towards evolutionary theory, just as it has been urged that an 1850 essay by John Herschel on Quetelet set Maxwell on the road to statistical mechanics.[12] However slight or profound those influences and filiations may have been, there is no doubt that 'the average man' stuck, even though almost no one had favourable things to say about the concept when taken literally.

There's a steady chorus: but there isn't really an average man! To which there is a commonsense reply: no one says that there is a man who is the average man, divorced 0.17 times and with 2.2 children. 'Average man' is a handy shorthand only. But for Quetelet the *homme type* was importantly more than shorthand. It was an early codification of two fundamental nineteenth-century transitions.

First, we see from the epigraph that Quetelet was not talking about an average for the human species. He was talking about the characteristics of a people or a nation, as a racial type. Where before one thought of a people in terms of its culture or its geography or its language or its rulers or its religion, Quetelet introduced a new objective measurable conception of a people. A race would be characterized by its measurements of physical and moral qualities, summed up in the average man of that race. This is half of the beginning of eugenics, the other half being the reflection that one can introduce social policies that will either preserve or alter the average qualities of a race. In short, the average man led to both a new kind of information about populations and a new conception of how to control them.

There is a second, more academic aspect of Quetelet's *homme type* that had extraordinary conceptual consequences. We can think of average height as an abstract – the convenient result of an arithmetical operation – but we can also begin to think of it as a 'real' feature of a population. In 1988, it was noted that the longevity of Japanese has been increasing every year, to the point where the Japanese are now the most long-lived nation on earth. We find it hard not to think of this as being a real feature of Japanese life and culture, just as 'real' as the fact that Japanese corporate entities have among them the world's largest accumulation of disposable capital for investment.

It was Quetelet's less-noticed next step, of 1844, that counted far more than the average man. He transformed the theory of measuring unknown physical quantities, with a definite probable error, into the theory of measuring ideal or abstract properties of a population. Because these could be subjected to the same formal techniques they became real quantities. This is a crucial step in the taming of chance. It began to turn statistical laws that were merely descriptive of large-scale regularities into laws of nature and society that dealt in underlying truths and causes.

His 1844 monograph went far in four quick steps. Step 1: 'Let us suppose that I measure the height of some individual several times, with great care.' The measurements won't be identical. If the causes of error work equally towards measuring high and low, there will be a distribution with values clustering around the average height. There will also be a dispersion measured by probable error. Step 2: Quetelet compared this situation with repeated observations of a single astronomical quantity, made over four years at the Greenwich Observatory. There we have mean, probable error, and the whole Gaussian analysis. This established practice is exactly analogous, he said, to measuring the height of one man over and over again.

Step 3: 'In the preceding examples, we knew, despite the fluctuation in figures, that there really did exist a number for which we were looking, be it the height of an individual or the right polar ascension.' What if we don't know whether there was one real quantity being measured? Given a lot of measurements of heights, are these the measurements of the same individual? Or are they the measurements of different individuals? If and only if they are sufficiently like the distribution of figures derived from measurements on a single individual. That suggests a way to tell whether a collection of statistics is derived from a single homogeneous population defined by a real quantity, or several distinct but mixed populations.[13]

Step 4: at this exact point[14] there occurred one of the fundamental transitions in thought, which was to determine the entire future of statistics. Up to here the monograph considered quantities that exist in nature. Here we pass from a real physical unknown, the height of one person, to a postulated reality, an objective property of a population at a time, its mean height or longevity or whatever. This postulated truth unknown value of the mean was thought of not as an arithmetical abstract of real heights, but as itself a number that objectively describes the population.

What could legitimate this move? We shall say that it objectively describes the population if the distribution of heights or whatever is what it would be if a single individual were being measured inaccurately. In step 3 we looked at a bunch of measurements and asked if there was one man. Now we use the same technique when we know we are talking about different men, and if there is a satisfactory Normal curve, we say that there is one true value, a property not of a person but of a collective.

Quetelet had precious few examples of Gaussian distributions. 'Male height is still almost unknown even in the most civilized countries of Europe.'[15] And why *should* one collect such information? It is interesting only if one believes, with Quetelet, that it signifies some underlying real characteristic of a population. He did find one unlikely source for an example: in 1817 the *Edinburgh Medical Journal* had published the height and chest measurements of over 5,000 soldiers in eleven Scottish regiments.[16]

What Quetelet read was a classification of soldiers by regiment, by height, and by chest circumference in inches.* He ignored heights,

---

* Or did he read only an abstract prepared by an assistant? The *Journal* published a table for each of eleven regiments of militia, based on data furnished by a contractor, 'a gentleman of great observation and singular accuracy'. The point of the tables was *not* to show the uniformity of the militiamen, but instead to illustrate regional differences 'in different counties of Scotland, from which inferences may be drawn as to the influence of the nature of the county and climate, food and occupation, upon the growth of man'. There was a difference of 1.3 inches in chest measurement between the stout lads of Kirkcudbrightshire and the hollow-chested youths of Lanark. The latter were also on average 1.2 inches shorter. If Quetelet had actually seen these pages, how could he have averaged away the whole point of the data?

It was also 'ascertained by actual Measurement, upon an extensive scale, in Retail Hat-shops in London and Edinburgh' that Scottish heads are on average a size larger than English ones (21¾ inches compared with 21⅝). The median was the same, but there were many more large heads in Edinburgh than London, as one might expect, considering the relative levels of culture of the two cities at the time. The distributions, incidentally, were definitely not Normal.

combined the girth distributions for the different regiments, made some trifling errors in sums,[17] and obtained a distribution for 5,738 chests, with maxima at 1,073 soldiers at 39 inches and 1079 at 40 inches.

He concluded that this was just as if you measured a single Scot with a chest almost 40 inches in circumference. In metric terms the probable error was about 33.34 millimetres. As he put it next year in a popular work, if 'a person little practised in measuring the human body' were repeatedly to measure one typical soldier, '5,738 measurements made on one individual would certainly not group themselves with more regularity ... than the 5,738 measurements made on the Scotch soldiers; and if the two series were given to us without their being particularly designated, we should be much embarrassed to state which series was taken from 5,738 different soldiers, and which was obtained from one individual with less skill and ruder means of appreciation'.[18] Such was the rhetoric with which Quetelet gave us the mean and the bell-shaped curve as fundamental indices of the human condition.

The law of errors applies as a matter of fact to this human attribute, chest circumference, or so Quetelet alleged. And to almost all others: Quetelet had immediately applied his distribution to heights of French conscripts. It did not quite fit, which he blamed on fraud, i.e. draft-dodging by feigning shortness. Much later Quetelet took his doctrine to be positively proven during the American Civil War, by data from 25,878 volunteers.[19]

Nowadays our first question is: how well do Quetelet's data fit the curve of error? There was no standard test of goodness of fit. Poisson's fiducial limits weren't part of Quetelet's repertoire. He took a theoretical binomial curve for results of tossing a coin 1,000 times, divided it into segments, and compared it with corresponding segments of the curve for Scottish chests. He found them sufficiently similar.

Within weeks (it seems) the floodgates had been opened. Every sort of physical attribute of humans and then of all the animal and vegetable kingdom was investigated and plotted as if according to the law of error. Next came the moral attributes, for example, the ability to write poetry. One might have expected that Quetelet, an astronomer by profession, would have taken the Gaussian 'error of observation' approach to his bell-shaped curve. It is significant that he took instead the binomial route. It enabled him to understand, or to think that he understood, why natural phenomena should be Normally distributed. For how was one to understand the amazing (alleged) fact that human traits are Normally distributed? The metaphor of the tailor is illustrative, but serves only to aggravate the problem. A man's chest is not chosen by an incompetent tailor. How then can the collectivity of chests be just as if it had been produced by one?

There never was an answer, but a gentle analgesic balm could be applied to soothe conceptual discomfort. The Scottish chests could become part of a story about statistical stability. How was one to understand statistical stability in a Laplacian universe, a universe in which an adequately informed mind would be able to compute each and every future event, from one complete momentary account of the state of affairs in the universe? Laplace had said that probability is in part the result of our knowledge, in part, of our ignorance. But there was a more structured response than that, couched in terms of minute causes that led to the production of an event. The response seems incoherent to many of us today, but it did not wear its difficulties on its face. I shall present the response in a very schematic way, using a sequence of five steps: the coin; the binomial distribution for repeated coin-tossing; errors of measurement; suicide and crime; chests. The following five paragraphs are intended to present not ideas that I think are coherent, but ideas that were by many people found sufficiently satisfying.

1   A coin falls either heads or tails. Which way it falls is determined by the initial conditions of tossing, and by Newtonian mechanics. There is a very large number of variables within the initial conditions. These can be thought of as a large number of possible 'causes', some of which favour heads, and others of which favour tails. On any given toss, the causes that pertain at that toss will determine the outcome of that toss. The probability of getting heads can be pictured as the ratio of favourable causes, to the total number of causes. Our ignorance of the underlying minute causes forces us to talk of probability, and to use observation to determine the ratio of favourable to total causes.

2   In repeated tossing we obtain the binomial distribution whose limit has the form of the curve of errors. We can 'explain' the statistical stability of a coin, and the fact that most often in a sequence of tosses the relative frequency is the same as the probability, by our story of chances for a single toss, plus a mathematical deduction. Quetelet said he had found that the chest curve for soldiers was binomial, and thereby carried with it, in his mind, the idea of a large number of independent trials. This assimilation of the chests to coin-tossing meant that each chest is the product of a large number of minute independent causes.

3   When we are trying to measure the position of an object, or the degree of intensity of light, we are by no means tossing a coin. But the errors made in each measurement are themselves the product of minute causes acting on the instrument, the observer, the signal passing from object to instrument and the like. This helps us understand why the error curve and

the binomial distribution have the same shape. Such 'reasoning' was no part of the work of Gauss or his illustrious predecessors. It was a way for the reflective but less gifted to understand something conceptually embarrassing.

4   We turn to the statistical stability of the moral sciences. Here too we can have the picture of lots of minute and varying causes determining an individual human action. The causes vary from person to person, some people being inclined to murder and some not at all. How can statistical stability result in such a situation? Poisson knew the answer when there is a probability distribution or law of 'causes'. But just what are the myriad minute causes that determine our decisions for good or ill? To answer, the medical model of chapter 8 above was invaluable. Medicine already had a vast categorization of causes under the several heads of predisposing, occasioning, indirect or general. They were causes of illness. Suicide was the perfect bridge between medicine and crime. On the one hand, we had the conclusion of the syllogism with the two premises, 'suicide is a kind of madness', and 'madness is a disease'. Suicide was, albeit briefly, held to be a disease, and hence subject to the panoply of medical causes. Yet suicide was the most heinous crime of all, the most mortal of sins. So we could think of something like that list of causes applying to other vicious acts. Guerry's late work was particularly obliging. Recall his cross-classification of 21,322 murders into 97 principal motives and 4,478 subsidiary motives. A fine array of little independent causes! Thus it was by Poisson that the mathematics of Bernoullian statistical stability was transferred to crime, but it was by medicine that the underlying metaphysics of probability, namely the picture of minute causes, was assimilated.

5   Finally we pass to Quetelet's inspired conjecture that human attributes, mental and physical, are distributed just like the law of errors. We are far removed from (1), the toss of a single coin. Yet the rhetoric of (1)–(4) turns Quetelet's proposal, which ought to have been unintelligible, into a startling empirical fact. Doubtless some causes determine the chest circumference of each soldier. The size of the parents has something to do with it but plainly there are many other factors. We 'know' that a multitude of interacting independent causes tends in a large number of cases to produce a Gaussian curve. The mathematics of probability and the metaphysics of underlying cause were cobbled together by loose argument to bring an 'understanding' of the statistical stability of all phenomena.

Francis Galton was, I think, the first to see that the story about 'independent petty influences', as he called them, won't do at all for inheritance.[20] But, as I shall argue in chapter 21, that required a new way of thinking about statistical law. Galton also expostulated against the term 'probable error': 'the term Probable Error is absurd when applied to the subjects now in hand, such as Stature, Eye-colour, Artistic Faculty, of Disease'.[21] The point is that 'error' makes no sense when one is speaking of mean eye-colour or whatever. Quetelet had *made* mean stature, eye-colour, artistic faculty and disease into real quantities. Once he had done that (and it is never recorded that in 1844 he had constructed this entirely new kind of reality) deviation from the means was just natural deviation, deviation made by nature, and that could not be conceived of as error.

Or was nature creating such distributions after all? Did phenomena really fit Quetelet's curves? For a great many years, any empirical distribution that came up in a hump was Gaussian *because that was all it could be*. That was all it could be because of the story of little independent causes, which had, for a while, created another synthetic *a priori* truth. No one devised routine tests of goodness of fit, because the question did not arise. The first tests were not proposed for another 30 years, and then by German writers such as Lexis who were altogether sceptical of what they called *Queteletismus*, and indeed of the very idea of statistical law.[22] Porter has admirably reported Lexis's struggles with tests of dispersion.[23] Lexis was not explicitly testing the hypothesis that distributions are Gaussian, but he did conclude, in effect, that about the only thing that was distributed in that way was the distribution of births – a happily binomial type of event.

The law of error had chiefly mattered to astronomers. Quetelet exported it to the human sciences, wrapping it in an obscure metaphysics of minute underlying causes. He added a more respectable element of astronomical causation to the package. The motions of the planets obey strict laws, but may be perturbed by the presence of a body that passes too close. When the body moves away, the old stable pattern is restored. Quetelet gladly used this idea to explain departure of statistical data from regularities. Like Poisson, he noted that French conviction rates were unusual in 1832. They were even more erratic in his own land 1830–3, traumatic time for the low countries and for the Belgian Astronomer-Royal. (Among other things, Quetelet's new observatory, then under construction, was a battle site). Those disturbances were perturbations – in an astronomer's sense of the word – due to the passage of heavy political events. They were what Quetelet called variable causes intervening in crime rates. He thought that the 'measure of civilization of a nation can be found in the way in which it makes revolutions' – the less brusque the transition, the less the displacement of statistical constants, and the more civilized the event.[*24]

---

* After the troubles of 1848, Quetelet told Albert, Victoria's consort, that the instabilities of the moment would be replaced by a return to normalcy when the disturbance had passed. The revolutions and rebellions of 1848 were 'veritable moral cholera', however 'it is at least

What I have been describing is, in my opinion, not very coherent. One can see the attraction of Quetelet's analogy between the curve of errors and the distribution of girths. But the explanation in terms of little independent causes does not hang together. It is an historiographic maxim that when a body of ideas seems incoherent to us, we fail to understand the ideas. I suggest that events of this chapter furnish a counter-example. These ideas about causation made no more clear sense then than now. There is a simplistic explanation for the resilient incoherence. A deterministic world view was threatened on many fronts by the phenomena suggested by the new statistics, and there *was* no coherent way to understand the burgeoning phenomena. The talk about underlying causes was only one element in the papering over of conceptual cracks. There were many signs of malaise, to be discussed in chapter 18, but first let us examine the strange case of statistical fatalism. Long before Quetelet had turned his attention to Scottish chests, he wrote, in 1832, to Villermé:

> It is society that prepares the crime; the guilty person is only the instrument who executes it. The victim on the scaffold is in a certain way the expiatory victim of society. His crime is the fruit of the circumstances in which he finds himself.[25]

If statistics teaches us about a budget of crime, and that lesson has as a consequence that the criminal is merely an instrument, then where is his free will? Why is he responsible for what he did? What future for morality?

consoling to think that they cannot in any way alter the external laws that guide us. Their action is transitory . . .' Quetelet, who wanted to use statistics as a tool for reform in 1830, found solace in statistics, in 1848, as a preventative against revolution.

14

Society prepares the crimes

London, 16 July 1860 The statistical discoveries of one nation are the lights of all nations.

Despite the accidents of conflagrations, the unstableness of winds, the uncertainties of life and the variations in men's minds and circumstances, on which fires, wrecks and deaths depend, they are subject to laws as invariable as gravitation and fluctuate to within certain limits, which the calculus of probabilities can determine beforehand.

This holds of crimes, and other acts of the will, so that violation itself is subject to law.

Shall a system of fatalism be built upon this foundation?

No, for statistics has revealed also a law of variation.

Introduce a system of ventilation into unventilated mines, and you substitute one law of accidents for another.

These events are under control.

Some races, however, commit crimes of violence in greater proportion to other races.

Some classes are more dangerous.

[But] as men have the power to modify their race, they have the power to change the current of human actions within definite limits, which statistics can determine.*[1]

Words like these signal the connection between information and control. Statistical information leads to the discovery of statistical laws. We who collect the information change the boundary conditions and thereby change the laws of society. Such control of a human population seems to diminish its freedom. This thought did not foment issues about the moral dimensions of political action. Those were the self-confident days of that hymn in praise of industry and empire, the Great Exhibition at Crystal Palace. Instead of engendering political self-doubt, the connections

---

* William Farr, the effective head of the office of the Registrar-General for England and Wales, in his welcoming speech to the fourth International Statistical Congress. The presidential address was given by Albert, the Prince Consort, who also devoted much of his speech to allegations of fatalism.

between information, control and statistical law created a metaphysical quandary, which was called statistical fatalism.

'Society prepares the crimes and the guilty person is only the instrument.' Thus ran Quetelet's excited letter to Villermé published in 1832. The idea created a crisis. By 1836: 'The moral order falls in the domain of statistics . . . a discouraging fact for those who believe in the perfectibility of human nature. *It seems as if free will exists only in theory.*' But: 'by modifying the institutions or the administrative practices one can diminish the criminality of a country'. These words of d'Angeville are representative.[2]

We are more familiar with an entirely different connection between free will and statistical probabilities. The second wave of quantum mechanics, which commenced in 1926, established that the fundamental laws of microphysics are irreducibly probabilistic. In 1936 John von Neumann proved the first 'no hidden variables' theorem: no necessitarian, purely deterministic laws can underlie quantum physics. Some physicists and many kibitzers inferred that physics proves the reality of human freedom. Even today some say this solves the problem of free will.

The contrast between the sensibility of the 1830s and the 1930s seems paradoxical. In the 1930s, the conviction that the laws of nature are probabilistic was thought to make the world safe for freedom. The incoherence went in the opposite direction in the 1830s: if there were statistical laws of crime and suicide, then criminals could not help themselves. In 1930, probability made room for free will; in 1830, it precluded it.

This contrast only seems paradoxical. In the 1930s the laws of physics, which had long been the model of impersonal and irrevocable necessity, were shorn of their magisterial power. They had once ordained the slightest motion of the lightest atom and hence the fall of every sparrow, perhaps the Fall itself. By 1936 they described only the probabilities of the future course of any individual particle. At most the collective behaviour of an enormous collection of entities or events was determined. Hence individuals within the ensemble might act freely. In the 1830s, in contrast, human behaviour was lumped under new probabilistic laws that were constantly compared to the law of gravity. Physics was still inexorable. Laws of society were like laws of physics and hence could not be violated. The 1930s pulled physics, and hence all law, away from determinism. The 1830s pulled laws of society towards physics, and hence towards determinism. That's why probability seemed to create space for freedom in 1936, and seemed to rule it out in 1836.

But that's not the whole story. Why, in the 1930s, did statistical probability support free will? It must have been thought that if an event falls under a (merely) probabilistic law, then the event could well be a free act. But in the 1830s many (such as d'Angeville, quoted above) thought that if a human action falls under a probabilistic law, then it cannot be free. Most analytic philosophers would say, without hesitation, that the d'Angevilles of those days were plain wrong. Maybe that is what reason teaches, but uncanny feelings to the contrary are not unknown. I am slightly unnerved in a strange city when I go out to buy the morning's newspaper. The vendor or dispenser has a paper waiting just for me. When I return home I ask at the kiosk if there was a spare unsold paper a couple of days ago. There never was. Someone else was there to buy mine.

We need no official crime statistics to start thinking like this, but we do need a technology of distribution. The first tentative discussions of statistical fatalism were about the almost constant number of letters to residents of Paris that ended up at the dead letter office. The phenomenon, noted by Laplace, was discussed by polymath Thomas Young in 1819. He assured his readers that it implied no 'mysterious fatality', but the example was used for decades.[3]

The cool-headed analytic view says that a statistical law may apply to a population, but members of the population remain free to do as they please. The law applies only to the ensemble of individuals. No law constrains *me* to buy a newspaper, even if there is a law about my neighbourhood. Despite this glib and comfortable opinion, we have not made our peace with statistical laws about people. They jostle far too roughly with our ideas about personal responsibility.

We are not clear, for example, about extenuating circumstances. The casual reader of court cases knows the problem confronted by judges and juries. As I write a man of 23 is found guilty of murdering the three year old daughter of his mistress; before the murder he sodomized the child; he then threw her out of a car window in a garbage bag. The judge, not noted for leniency, almost apologizes: 'I know that the circumstances of your life have been absolutely appalling, but even so you are sentenced to life imprisonment without possibility of parole for eight years.' The defence had entered a strong plea for clemency on the grounds of the man's past, as if he could not help doing something heinous. Alleged statistical laws ('A person physically and sexually abused as a child by both parents becomes an abuser with probability 87 per cent, etc.) are entered as part of the plea. The person was not really responsible. Even judges who devote their lives to such matters are far from sure about extenuating circumstances of a statistical sort.

We owe the cruellest parody to Dickens. *Hard Times* is a notable antiutilitarian and antistatistical tract. Cissy couldn't even utter the word 'statistics'. The best she could come out with in Mr Gradgrind's class is

'S-s-s-s-tutterers'. Gradgrind firmly taught the inviolability of statistical law. By the end of the novel his horrid son Tom was exposed as a thief.

'If a thunderbolt had fallen upon me,' said the father, 'it would have shocked me less than this.'

'I don't see why,' grumbled the son. 'So many people are employed in situations of trust; so many people, out of so many, will be dishonest. I have heard you talk, a hundred times, of its being a law. How can *I* help laws? You have condemned others to such things, Father. Comfort yourself.'[4]

Dickens was deeply distrustful of utilitarian statistics. There is a strong sense in which he did not believe in the validity of statistical generalizations. Today, they are inescapable, but we have not yet worked out how to deal with statistical extenuation and its effect on responsibility. We should therefore look with some charity on the likes of d'Angeville confronting the problem for the first time.

One thing is clear. Had there not been that avalanche of numbers in 1820–40, and the accompanying conception of statistical law, we would have no such problem. The judge would not have had to apologize to the murderer; he would gladly have called him a monster and put him away for life. Another connection between statistical law and freedom is still with us. Farr's speech suggests the idea. People are not fated to follow a statistical law, because the conditions of application of the law can be changed. There are laws about fires in the city, but fire marshals, building codes and city planning can alter the risks. The same can be done for classes of the population. We, the administrators, alter the cityscape and so change the hazards of fire. Likewise *we*, the governing classes, can alter the laws that apply to *them*, the governed.

That is a remarkable response to the allegation that statistics implies fatalism. It seems to grant the point! Farr said he was rejecting fatalism, but he was maintaining a strict social determinism. The members of the governed class remained bound by a statistical law, albeit one that was chosen by a well-meaning bureaucracy.

Quetelet and Farr alike represent the philanthropic and utilitarian aspect of nineteenth-century statistics. That is its dominant side. Both men appear to have had the most worthy of instincts. They wanted to improve the lot of the labouring classes, and they thought that they could do so by exercising a new kind of control. Discover what are the statistical laws that govern crime, disease, vice, unrest. Then find ways to alter the conditions under which those laws apply. Guerry was positivist: moral analysis must obtain the data upon which legislators should decide, but it can make no suggestion to the legislator. The distinction between fact and value remained sacred. Quetelet, at least in his youth, was reformist. The annual crime rates are a 'necessary result' of our social order, so the legislator must introduce changes to modify them. Farr saw himself not only as colligating statistical facts, but as obliged to make recommendations.*[5]

Readers sympathetic to the great movements of reform will want only to praise the generous instincts of a Farr, but they should not ignore the way in which functionaries such as he created the infrastructure of one of the kinds of power by which our society operates. We obtain data about a governed class whose deportment is offensive, and then attempt to alter what we guess are relevant conditions of that class in order to change the laws of statistics that the class obeys. This is the essence of the style of government that in the United States is called 'liberal'. There are graphic examples. The compulsory integration of American schools by bussing is a famous one. As in the nineteenth century, the intentions of such legislation are benevolent. The *we* who know best change the statistical laws that affect *them*. That is one of the points of Dickens's satire.

I do not decry the extraordinary changes in the quality of life that were effected by the utilitarian activists. None were more successful than the sanitary reformers, who radically revised the expected life-span of everyone on the face of the earth. Clean water and washing did wonders long before there was a widely held or well-founded germ theory of disease. A majority of activists held strongly to a 'bad air' (malaria) or miasma theory of contagion. In the beginning they wanted to clean up putrid water not because it was itself the fount of contagion but because it smelt bad and created the foul air that spread disease. Despite their having the wrong basis for action, their reforms inaugurated what we now call the population explosion. Sanitation marched across the world with empire, radically increasing life expectancy.†[6]

The aim was to improve health, but let us not forget morality. Late in the century landlords and employers were urged to install running water toilets in their tenements or factories. The sales pitch was aimed less at the health of the labouring classes than at morality. The water closet was,

* Farr's annual *Letter to the Registrar-General*, published at the end of the *Annual Report of the Registrar-General of England and Wales*, was always fascinating. For example, childbed or puerperal fever was a major cause of infant deaths. The final solution – that the midwife and doctor should wash their hands and sterilize their instruments – is usually attributed to Semmelweis. Many years earlier Farr had included in his annual letter Robert Storrs's investigations and identical recommendations. Farr went on to the training of women in sanitary midwifery. This would also remedy the fact that women 'have now so few fields of profitable employment'. In combining two such disparate social issues, Farr was the embodiment of rational utilitarianism. The persistence of puerperal fever in England shows the limitations of its influence.

† For Farr and his fellows, health and wealth went hand in hand. 'It may be affirmed, without great risk of exaggeration, that it is possible to reduce the annual deaths in England and Wales by 30,000, and to increase the vigour (may I not add the industry and wealth?) of the population in equal proportion; for diseases are the iron index of misery, which recedes before strength, health and happiness as the mortality declines.'

among other things, intended as an architectural structure that would ensure the privacy of bodily functions, a natural extension of the walls to separate the sleeping quarters of parents and children, a final material codification of the rules of the nuclear family. When combined with safe water disposal, however, it was also a significant health measure. It is hardly an exaggeration to say that morality and health were always combined in the utilitarian mind.

My words may suggest that the combination of health and morality is a structural device by which the rich were able to regulate the behaviour of the poor. However much reform was cloaked in philanthropic zeal, its real function was to preserve the established order, or so some will say. Perhaps, but regimes that scarcely distinguish health from morality are applied to the prosperous too: 'moral causes, and the regulation of the mind, have perhaps more influence on the educated classes, but all must derive benefit from outdoor exercise'. Here it was madness and suicide which good air and athletic activity were intended to prevent.[7]

Nevertheless statistical laws do apply to classes. It is the laws about 'them', about the other, that are to be determined, to be analysed, and to be the basis for legislation. The classes in question are not abstract entities but social realities. Inevitably it is the labouring or criminal or colonial classes that are the chief objects to be changed, for their own good. We know *Les Misérables* as Victor Hugo's magnificent novel, even if only as transformed into a musical. His title, distant and vaguely romantic to us, was standard technical terminology of the day, much used by statisticians.[8] *Les misérables* included brigands, beggars, vagabonds, abandoned children, prostitutes.

It is evident that the statistics of this class (the prostitutes), if followed and made precise according to age, family condition, and movement will be found very useful to the statesman in determining the first motives for bad morals, the lifestyle, the probability of culpability, and the organization of surveillance.[9]

The prostitute and the statesman: I need not further emphasize the *them* that is watched and the *we* who engage in the necessary surveillance.

Aside from the classes within a society, there are also the larger classes that we call races. The primary connotation of race to us is skin colour. When Farr in his speech spoke of race, he meant any national, tribal or even family group linked by inheritance and with a commonality entrenched in custom. 'Men have the power to modify their race', he wrote. Thus began eugenics.

In recent years Daniel Kevles and others have made us very conscious of the eugenics movement, pioneered by Francis Galton and continued by his protégé Karl Pearson.[10] I shall not elaborate on this theme except to make two remarks. First, the movement has deservedly had a bad press; yet it is too often forgotten that it was motivated by very much the same philanthropic utilitarian considerations that underlie all 'liberal' attempts to modify a population. Secondly, the roots of eugenics are found earlier than is commonly supposed. They lie in the Queteletian idea of statistical law determining the features of a population. Farr's speech to the statisticians of the world testifies to this. In a few moments he moved from the management of fires to the management of classes to the management of races.

His explicit topic was none of these. It was statistical fatalism. According to that doctrine, if a statistical law applied to a group of people, then the freedom of individuals in that group was constrained. It is easy to regard this as an epiphenomenon, an oddity accompanying the early days of statistical thinking. In fact it betrays an initial perplexity about the control of populations on the basis of statistical information. Statistical fatalism was the symptom of a collective malaise. We read a metaphysical worry about human freedom, at times well nigh hysterical. We can hardly credit it as a specimen of rational thought. Exactly. The knot was not metaphysical but political. The issue that was hidden was not the power of the soul to choose, but the power of the state to control what kind of person one is.

There were, nevertheless, metaphysical as well as political disquiets. This fatalism was only one of many signs of a transition in the ideas of causality, necessity and determinism in general. This assertion gains force in chapter 18, where I examine the strange discussions of determinism during this period. Here I can be brief about statistical fatalism, for Porter has well described the course of events, and Lottin has a superb analysis of Quetelet's own views on the topic.[11]

Free will and determinism have always been debated, but not statistical fatalism. It was new, for there never had been statistical laws before. Let it be a statistical law that a certain proportion of the people in such and such a district will commit suicide next year. Then (it seemed to follow) it is not true of each inhabitant that he or she was free not to commit suicide. For if each person were free to do so, then it might have happened that none did so, and hence it was not after all a statistical law about the population.

This problem could hardly have arisen before 1820. Yet there is truth in the saying that there is nothing new under the sun. Phrenology had already faced many of the logical issues. 'This new type of research has not only interested scientists and several men of letters; it has passed from the philosophical retreat and the academy into the salons, indeed into the milieu of the most frivolous people; it has been, and it is, the subject of all conversations, the object of an active curiosity.'[12] We now think of phrenology as a silly game for telling a person's character by the bumps on the head. Indeed maps of the head, with 'faculties' indicated are comical, with their bumps for character traits such as 'amativeness or philoprogenitiveness'.[13] We can be entertained by the model according to which neighbouring organs and their associated faculties influence each other.*[14] But Robert Young and others have shown convincingly that phrenology, which we think of as pure error, was part of a larger reform that made diseases have their seat in specific organs.[15]

'The essential point is – whether there really exists such an uniform correspondence between certain forms of the head, skull or brain, and certain characters of mind'.[16] Gall and Spurzheim claimed that there was. They were wrong. But aside from the medical and psychological questions about phrenology, there was a moral one. Suppose that character traits are determined by organs in the brain. Suppose further that some of these traits are vicious. Then a person could not help being lecherous, proud, sly, avaricious, could he? Was he then free? Was he responsible for mayhem, if that were his disposition?

The organs were supposed to be associated with 'propensities' for crime or creativity. That is the English word, revived by Karl Popper, who invented a 'propensity' theory of probability in the 1950s. 'Propensity' was a term of art in phrenology, but the connection with statistical fatalism was closer than that. The French word was *penchant*. Quetelet's statistical expression was identical: *penchant au crime*. Spurzheim employed propensities to rebut the accusation of fatalism. First, some of our attributes are settled at birth. One cannot choose to be the oldest or youngest sibling. We are also given certain mental and moral characteristics, as we are given other physical traits at birth. Why should we think that implies fatalism? 'The faculties of the will, and the motives which determine the will, are given and innate', but so what?[17]

Some of Spurzheim's considerations usefully turn our expectations upside down. Materialist wisdom says that the laws of physics govern everything; for Spurzheim it was the opposite. 'Physical laws are submitted to chemical laws: gravity, for instance, is a physical law; and it is modified by chemical affinity.'[18] Physical and chemical laws are subord-

---

* A phrenologist in 1815:

> Mr Hume has asserted that we know nothing of cause and effect, but by an observance of the uniform conjunction of Phenomena. We admit that the regular succession of phenomena suggests the notions that they are connected by cotenation [*sic*] of causes, by exciting a particular faculty, but the conception of causation thus excited is the result of a particular organ; we have some reason to believe that this is wanting in animals. It is marked on each side by the organ of Comparison. This organ, says Dr. Spurzheim, asks Why? It produces Inquisitiveness into causes, and is a necessary ingredient in the character of a philosopher.

A few years later Georget tried to identify the categories of Kant's transcendental analytic – cause, substance, and the like – with organs in the brain, but he recanted on his deathbed.

inate to organic ones, which in the end are subordinate to laws of the human faculty. 'Liberty consists in the possibility of doing or not doing anything, and in the faculty of knowing the motives and of determining one's self according to them.' Thus the free person knows his propensities, knows his motives, reflects upon them and decides upon his course of action. The will begins with the knowing and reflecting faculties. Morality begins with the faculty of duty and of justice. Moral liberty is will applied to absolute conscience.[19]

The good doctors did not agree on everything. Gall admitted wicked propensities; Spurzheim denied them, holding that moral evil 'consists in actions which are not conformable to the whole of the faculties proper to man'. That harks back to ancient debates about fatalism and freedom. The element in phrenological theory that mattered to statistics was that it created an argument to separate a *penchant* from a determining factor. The old slogan of Leibniz, 'inclines without necessitating' was given new application.

The statisticians wrote in a similar vein. There is a *penchant au crime*, yes, but each individual man has a *force morale* that will help him. That is reminiscent of Spurzheim's hierarchy. But there were additional, statistical, elements as befits the shift in problem. Free choices were seen as little individual causes (as described in chapter 13) that even out in the big picture. 'The larger the number of individuals, the more individual will fades out, and allows the series of general facts to predominate, the facts which depend on general causes, and in virtue of which society exists and is conserved.'[20]

Thus for Quetelet free acts are minuscule causes that cancel out and allow of the larger regularities. Conversely, those larger regularities do not preclude individual free will. But may not they imply a grand fatalism, about humankind itself? Quetelet asserted the theme of utilitarian improvement of the race. To avoid global fatalism, we must believe in the perfectibility of man. The progress of civilization results from changing the conditions of mortality, and the same can be said for our moral condition.[21]

It was not, however, to the statisticians or their opponents that we owe the most intense and widespread debates about statistical determinism. James Clerk Maxwell observed that 'The statistical method of investigating social questions has Laplace for its most scientific and Buckle for its most popular expounder.'[22] Upon the publication of his *History of Civilization in England* in 1857, T.H. Buckle became the lion of the London season. Could a nineteenth-century history of civilization be based on statistical fatalism? Yes, and one whose fatalism was confirmed by our old friends, the statistics of suicide:

In a given state of society, a certain number of persons must put an end to their own life. This is the general law; and the special question as to who shall commit the crime depends of course upon special laws; which, however, in their total action, must obey the large social law to which they are all subordinate. And the power of the larger law is so irresistible, that neither the love of life nor the fear of another world can avail anything towards even checking its operation.[23]

15

The astronomical conception of society

Leipzig, 29 April 1871 The French school, always absorbed in the astronomical preoccupations of its founder, sees in man, who lacks freedom of the will, only a being who is subjected to some sort of external and independent force, one which has the remarkable knack of making man, who is not conscious of this force, yet feel responsible for his actions.

The German school ... finds this French interpretation perverse and untenable, for it turns a proposition, that in itself is sound, upside down. One need not deny that if there were such a powerful external law at work, then there would be a regular repetition of crimes, marriages, suicides etc. But it is a mistake to say that existing regularities can be explained only by such external laws. The regularities establish for the careful thinker only the existence of some powerful causes, whether they be external to the agent or internal.*[1]

Buckle published the first volume of his *History of Civilization in England* in 1857. He was 36, a familiar Victorian figure – the shy bachelor, neurasthenic, constantly beset by nervous and gastric disorders, working obsessively, prodigously erudite, filled with a vision of some unspoken grandeur, and, in a brief moment of total success, lionized. His book won instant fame all over Europe. He was dead at 40. A line in Dostoyevsky's St Petersburg notebook, written about 1862: 'Read and reread Buckle and Moleschott!'[2] But he was not received in the same way in all parts of Europe. For example, the contrast between German and English reactions to Buckle reflects not only different ideas about probability and deter-

---

* G.F. Knapp, lecturing just after the defeat of France, and during the Paris Commune (18 March–28 May, 1871). Knapp set up the Leipzig statistical office in 1867, and in 1869 became professor at Leipzig University. In his reminiscences he shows himself as having been always ambivalent about French thought. The ambivalence is ironically displayed in his own career. He was called to the newly German University at Strassburg, 1874, and left when it became French again in 1918. At the end of his lecture of 29 April 1871, he implied that one evil result of 'Buckle's *Queteletismus*' was the reaction that it produced, 'nihilistic rejection of the state and its duties, and the release of the individual from all bonds of society ... which at present leads, on French soil, to the greatest catastrophe of our time [the Commune]'.

minism but also fundamentally opposed ways of understanding law, society, and the nature of the person.

Buckle intended his book as a prologomenon to a world history of civilization. From statistical fatalism, so vividly illustrated by suicide, he moved to a rigid historical determinism, in which climates and land masses determine the course of history more than the apparent free choices of political actors. His larger themes were discussed in their day, but it is remarkable how his use of the statistics of suicide and crime fascinated the reading public. The great reviews and literary magazines were deluged by discussions of fatalism.[3] Buckle founded his doctrine on Quetelet, who returned the favour, quoting him at length in *Physique sociale*, his 1869 rewriting of the 1835 *Sur l'homme*.[4] When John Herschel complained that Buckle's mad fatalism was giving statistics a bad name, Quetelet was complacent.[5]

The debate raged in England for more than a decade. No topic was more intensely discussed before it faded into oblivion. A philosophical logician like myself may find the 'last word' in John Venn's *The Logic of Chance*, first published in 1866. He quoted Buckle's words with which I ended the last chapter: 'The above passage as it stands seems very absurd and would I think, taken by itself, convey an extremely unfair impression of the author's ability. But the views which it expresses are very prevalent, and are probably increasing with the spread of statistical information and study.'[6]

Venn had a diagnosis of the attractions of statistical fatalism, but someone bitten by statistical fatalism would not be cured by Dr Venn. He proceeded by logic-chopping. Analyses and distinctions were to eliminate philosophical confusion. He could deploy a thorough set of well-articulated distinctions between probability ideas. He is often said to have invented one of the two basic theories about probability, namely the frequency account. The 'fundamental conception', he wrote, is that of a series which 'combines individual regularity with aggregate regularity'.[7] Probability has no meaning except in connection with such a series. Any probability must be referred to a series. The probability of an event is its relative frequency in the series.

The chief competing view had been set forth a generation earlier by Augustus de Morgan: 'Probability is the feeling of the mind, not the inherent property of a set of circumstances.'[8] De Morgan held that 'Probability is a sort of sister science to Formal Logic.' It 'investigates the rules according to which the amount of our belief of one proposition varies with the amount of our belief of other propositions with which it is connected'.[9] This was derived from Laplace's notion, but made plain that it was not a question of subjective or personal degrees of opinion, but a logical relation between evidence and reasonable degrees of belief.

Neither Venn nor De Morgan originated their opposed ideas.*[10] Each was a careful analyst employing a sophisticated set of conceptual distinctions about probability. In Germany at the time of Buckle there was no comparably delineated set of probability concepts. Needless to say no such sweeping generalization is exactly true. In 1842 Fries, a Kantian, severely criticized the 'subjective' and 'French' ideas of Laplace and his ilk.[11]

The fact that before Venn, Ellis in England (1842), and to some extent although in different ways Cournot in France (1843) and even Fries in Germany (1842) were going down the road to a frequency approach needs no explaining. Theirs was an era when statistical regularities were rampant. Despite this tendency it remains true that German thinkers had not yet elaborated conceptual frameworks of the sort available in France and England, something which was in part due to a great resistance to the very idea of statistical law. We have noticed in chapter 3 the large number of definitions of the science of statistics, so that Rumelin could catalogue 63 and then add another. In contrast, the competing distinctions between conceptions of probability made little headway among most German writers. This is a partial explanation of the contrast between German and English receptions of Buckle.

In 1860 Buckle was translated into German by a young Hegelian, who remarked that it would be wrong to read his author as a materialist: he was only an Englishman.[12] The book provoked an astounding flurry of assaults on statistical fatalism and *Queteletismus*. It had gone through seven German editions by 1901, and there was also a definitive edition in five volumes, in English, issued by the German publishers Brockhaus in 1865.

The translation was greeted by all manner of reactions. Within a year

---

* As remarked in chapter 12 above, an avowed preference for objective over subjective probabilities may begin with Fourier in the 1820s. Nevertheless one favoured predecessor for Venn as 'founder' of the frequency theory is Leslie Ellis, an almost exact contemporary of Buckle's, who had an equally short lifespan and who was even more grievously afflicted by nervous disorders. He was a polymath who undertook the translation of Francis Bacon, wrote about the shape of cells in the beehive, and tried to design a Chinese dictionary; he was much admired as a mathematician at Cambridge, where he had been Senior Wrangler, but wanted the chair of jurisprudence. He was involved in an important British controversy about the method of least squares, involving Herschel (on the basis of the latter's report on Quetelet) and others. On 14 February 1842:

> For myself, after giving a painful degree of attention to the point, I have been unable to sever the judgement that one event is more likely to happen than another, or that it is to be expected in preference to it, from the belief, that on the long run it will occur more frequently.

the quantitative psychologist Wilhelm Wundt, in the course of exaggerated praise of statistical thinking, damned Buckle. The man had conflated the natural history of the human race and its (social) history.[13] There was a good deal more such shooting from the hip, but running through the reactions there was one standard objection.

Regularities (*Gesetzmässigkeiten*), it was urged, are not laws (*Gesetze*) nor even rules (*Regeln*). Yes, there are statistical regularities, but it is a solecism to speak of statistical laws. Laws of nature are determined by real causes, which act on individual events and necessarily produce their effects. The myriad little French causes of Laplace or Quetelet, which generate the statistical distributions, do not cause those distributions; so the distributions are not laws. But only a law could constrain human freedom.

Thus did Kant's heirs confront Quetelet. In the West the spirit of positivism made out that all laws were mere regularities. A belief in causes over and above regularities was an illegitimate residue of the metaphysical age. Hence it was quite in order to speak of statistical laws. In the East, the shade of Königsberg provided a philosophy that rode well with the communitarian approach to statistics to which I have so often referred.

Quetelet's supposed fatalism was not entirely unknown in Germany before Buckle. Ernst Engel had addressed it a few years before the *History of Civilization in England*, and urged the objection that was to become routine: statistical regularities are not law. In the history of official statistics, Engel was in a certain sense the successor of Farr. For decades Farr, at the helm in the Registrar-General's office, set up an organization and methods that provided a template for all nations. Engel, whose career I have described at length elsewhere, ran the Prussian Statistical Bureau from 1860 to 1882, and gave the world a model of a centralized statistical bureaucracy.[14]

He started his statistical career in his native Saxony, where in 1854 he became head of the Saxon bureau and founder of its statistical periodicals. Pure essence of mandarin bureaucrat, he seldom restricted himself to figures. He had visited Quetelet during his *Wanderjahr*, 1847, and written about statistical determinism in 1851. He repeated the conclusions in an 1852 monograph on Saxon population trends.[15] People marry, breed and move of their own free will. Why then are there regularities? Quetelet had used marriage rates as proof of statistical law in the domain of morals. So Engel embarked on a discussion of free choice. A decade later, after he had accepted the call to Berlin, he returned to the topic. Buckle had just appeared in Germany; Engel had attended the conference in London at which Farr and Albert had discussed fatalism. In his own official journal, the Prussian Bureau's monthly, he gave a bluff working statistician's view of the free will debate.[16]

Thanks to Buckle, his focus was suicide. That does not go without saying, for suicide was not perceived as a German 'problem', even though no nation was more suicidal than Engel's native Saxony.[17] The first extended German survey of European suicide rates was published only in 1864, and then as the second half of a work that elaborated statistical fatalism. The author was Quetelet's admirer Adolph Wagner, to whom I soon return.[18] The first thoroughgoing official study of Prussian suicide to be made public had to wait until 1871. It must have been encouraged by the statistical fatalism controversy.[19]

Yes, wrote Engel, it is true that 'in a given population almost the same number of people commit suicide each year'. But that is a mere rule, for we cannot assign a cause of precisely this effect. Hence it is not a law. But if it is not a law of nature or of society, then it cannot impinge on freedom of the will. For Engel, that ends the question. You are never entitled to call something a law unless a cause is known, so you are not entitled to speak of laws of suicide. Engel was ever an admirer of Quetelet, but to him Quetelet was a man who, however he hedged his words, was 'at bottom, a determinist', a man who held that in a large number of observations of individual acts 'the law that constrains freedom manifests itself with the most complete clarity'.[20]

Now why should an administrator worry about fatalism? To answer that, one needs to comprehend Engel's philosophy, which can hardly be distinguished from his career. Like many of his contemporaries he was deeply distressed by the squalor of the poor engendered by the new German capitalism. He wrote about the horrors of the increasing throngs of homeless, about the explosions of steam boilers, the maiming of workers. His solution was the traditional one for eastern Europe, whether it be Saxon or Prussian, in Pest or in Petersburg. It was the opposite of the invisible hand, the laissez-faire *Manchesterthum*. The prosperous segments of society must create paternalistic institutions of self-help for the workers. That would resolve the tensions between labour and capital. Engel did his part by inventing savings banks, mortgage insurance and other institutions that became part of the standard stabilizing apparatus of industrial democracies.

In 1871 he was a founding member of the *Verein für Sozialpolitik*, an economic ginger group. Its members were nicknamed *Kathedersozialisten*, professor-socialists. Every German statistician to be mentioned in this chapter was a member or associate (so were most of the men of influence in the field whom I don't mention). In a later parliamentary debate the minister of education took the opportunity to continue the bad joke, calling these men *Kathederunsozialisten* – a sentiment echoed by the great socialist leader Franz Mehring.[21] They were not socialists but preservers of traditional order in new economic conditions. Engel and his colleagues created the knowledge and the systems of bureaucracy that enabled Prussia to inaugurate workmen's compensation, the old age pension and the other trademarks of the 'social net'. Mehring remarked that reactionaries who complained about their work resembled a cancer-ridden patient terrified of the knife, denouncing his surgeons. Mehring was not displeased, for he hoped that the disease was fatal. The less the social-professorial surgery, the sooner the patient would die.

The politics of the *Kathedersozialisten* differed from those of Mehring's socialists, but they shared a presupposition, a vision of society. The state, they argued, is not formed by individuals who collaborate in choosing the way that they govern themselves. The state is prior. Without it there cannot be a person. It is therefore the responsibility of the state to mould itself and its institutions so that individuals can form themselves into good people. The Prussian statistical bureau under Engel's guidance became a self-conscious exponent of this holistic political philosophy.

It was, of course, not shared by every German scholar. It is instructive that the one writer who went out of his way to agree with *Queteletismus*, i.e. to accept statistical fatalism, was precisely a laissez-faire atomistic adherent of the Manchester school. This was the economist Adolph Wagner, whose book of 1864 achieved some notoriety.[22] But Wagner experienced a radical politico-economic conversion about 1870, in time to become, with Engel, a founding member of the *Verein für Sozialpolitik*, the professor-socialists. By 1880 he had recanted his fatalism, or at least concluded that his earlier advocacy was grossly exaggerated.[23] Wagner is thus a valuable illustration. When he subscribed to a 'Western' atomistic and individualist vision of society, he believed in statistical law to the extent of favouring fatalism. As his conceptions became more collectivist, his enthusiasm for statistical fatalism declined.

In 1862 Engel had argued: we have statistical regularity, but not law, hence no causes acting on individuals to determine suicides, hence no constraint on free will. In 1864 Wagner argued: we have statistical regularity and although this is not in itself a 'law', it shows that deterministic laws are at work. Hence causes are in play and hence there are constraints on freedom.

But why, we may wonder, was Wagner so sure that regularities diminish freedom? Surely the law of large numbers suffices to get the large scale regularity without invoking constraints on freedom? Wagner did not evade the issue. He held that the law of large numbers was a sham. Statistical homogeneity cannot be derived by a mathematical trick; it can result only from causation. No law can apply to an ensemble unless there is a set of (deterministic) laws applying to the individuals. Hence 'the idea of an absolute and arbitrary will, governed neither by rules nor by law', collapses in the face of the data furnished by moral statistics.[24]

The larger part of Wagner's book classified the suicides of Europe according to every available scale: sex, income, current price of grain, season, method, civil state etc. The result was a table or schedule of autodestruction worthy of Guerry. He enjoined his readers to imagine a land in which the constitution decrees the number of persons who will kill themselves as per the schedule. No dictator could enforce such laws, he wrote, but society itself does so by a causality that we do not yet grasp.

German reaction to Wagner was almost uniformly hostile. People urged different conclusions. Wilhelm Drobisch, who had been alerted to statistical determinism as early as 1848,[25] inferred that there must be laws peculiar to the minds of suicides and criminals.[26] There was, however, a central core to the opposition, which chiefly issued from economists who were members of or associated with the *Verein für Sozialpolitik*. 'Law' was the word to watch. Gustav Rumelin, running the statistical bureau in Württemberg, challenged the semantics of phrases such as 'statistical law' and 'law of large numbers'. Those propositions are not *laws* at all.[27] As for the alleged regularities about suicide, Rumelin, like his colleagues in the official bureaucracy such as Engel, was more interested in plotting changes in relative frequencies of social deviancy than in dressing up numerals as signs of stability.[28]

G.F. Knapp, author of my epigraph, provided the most satisfying 'eastern' analysis of Quetelet.[29] He rightly expressed himself in national terms, writing of the 'German school' (in which he kindly gave pride of place to Drobisch) against the 'French school'(which included Buckle). He had a diagnosis and a cure leading to 'true *Queteletismus*'.

The diagnosis had two parts. One was obvious: Quetelet was a victim of his education, and thought that social laws, if they existed, had to be like laws of physics. That led to an 'astronomical conception of society', in which the forces acting on people were like cosmic forces or gravity. But there had to be a diagnosis of the disease that went deeper. After all, Quetelet was the only astronomer in the crowd.

Knapp then went to the heart of the matter. Quetelet confused social science with *Anthropologie* (not what, in English, we now call anthropology or ethnography, but the science of Man). That was a science of individuals. It was atomistic. It had its place. But social science was a science of culture, a culture in terms of which individuals had their being and found their nature. True *Queteletismus* was the use of statistical regularities as a guide to the state of a culture. It was not the case that individual people were constrained in their freedom by belonging to a culture. For they had no essence, they had no atomic individualistic self to be constrained, until they were human beings within a culture. That historicist, holistic vision of a people, whose application to statistics was best expressed by Knapp, is the reason that the western conception of statistical law could gain little foothold in nineteenth-century Germany.

Knapp's characterization of Quetelet's 'astronomical conceptions of society' reads curiously like passages from Durkheim's *Suicide*, where 'cosmic forces' acting on a population are invoked. It is a commonplace that the two great schools of social science stem from Durkheim and from Weber. Weber, precisely because his methodology was nonstatistical, is not my topic; Durkheim is. Conservative utopian that he was, he could not evade his immersion in western, atomistic, individualist conceptions of a person and the world. Given the character of several generations of French statistics, the seed that he gave the rest of the world was almost inevitably expressed in terms of suicide statistics. Knapp's diagnosis of Quetelet can be transferred to Durkheim, founder of statistical sociology, whose *Suicide*, as we shall see, epitomizes the astronomical conception of society.

Durkheim and Weber serve to remind us of a statistical/antistatistical polarity. In the next two chapters we examine the antistatistical backlash, a doubt more radical than any we have seen. In the case of sociology, both the statisticians and the antistatisticians are alive and well today, heirs respectively of Durkheim and Weber. Buckle's philosophy, in contrast, is dead. But in the case of historical determinism, the poles exactly parallel to those of Durkheim and Weber are those of Buckle and Marx. Buckle read the statistics and purveyed a purely statistical fatalism. Marx read the statistics of Engel or Quetelet or Farr with indifference, divining with their aid the underlying laws of society that bind it in a totally nonstatistical necessity.

16

The mineralogical conception of society

I applied to the observation of human societies rules analogous to those used in the study of plants and minerals; in other words I created a method that allowed me to know personally all the nuances of peace and discord, of prosperity and suffering, which are found in contemporary European society.[*1]

The dusty collection of numbers invited parody as soon as public statistics were under way in the 1820s. The jokes were feeble and are best forgotten, with one exception. Balzac's *Physiology of Marriage* began with meditations headed 'conjugal statistics'.[2] The first printing of 1826 had 20 octavo pages on this unpromising topic. The second and standard version of 1829 had 62. What began as a spoof ended by making Balzac think hard. 'In 1826 the notion of conjugal statistics furnished Balzac only with an amusing idea' writes Bardèche, first modern editor of the obscure printing of 1826; 'the additions of 1829 show us that Balzac's mind had become oriented towards very different reflections. What in 1826 had been a matter for simple calculation, became in 1829 a general view of society, a sort of panorama of the French bourgeoisie.'[3] Statistics directed him towards the human comedy.

The *Physiology* had lots of targets other than statistics. Its very title and a chapter on hygiene made fun of Broussais's 'physiological' school of medicine. Balzac may have had in mind another title (it is written in his notes): 'the marital code, or the art of keeping one's wife faithful'. In the end the piece was subtitled 'Eclectic philosophical meditations on conjugal happiness and unhappiness'.[4] The 'meditation' headed 'conjugal statistics' noted how in the past 20 years the bureaux have determined the number of hectares of forests and meadows in the country, and the number of kilos of beef, of litres of wine, of eggs and apples consumed in Paris. It can tell us 'how many armed men, how many spies, how many employees, how many students; but as to virtuous women? – Nothing.'

* Frédéric Le Play, summing up his life's work, 1829–79, in a series of monographs about the 'domestic life and the moral condition of the working populations of Europe'.

Balzac set out to deduce the number of virtuous women. The tone of this sophomorish and, as we would now say, chauvinist parody modulated over the next couple of years. As income, wealth and possessions were 'introduced into the statistics, it furnishes new classifications ... the "honest woman" and the man *comme il faut* which in 1826 are only abstractions, are [in 1829] designated by perfectly clear characteristics'. In 1826 the honest woman 'has a carriage, that is all. In 1829, one specifies the income of her husband, the level of his education, the location of his lodgings, his station and style of life.'[5]

This increasingly precise classifying of people mirrored the official statistics of the day. The years 1826–9 exemplify a shift in that era of enthusiasm from mere counting to increasingly minute classifications of the people counted. Balzac was familiar with this. His father had been fascinated with the Malthusian debate, and made statistical reformers such as Benoiston de Châteauneuf known to his son, who in turn put them into the 1829 *Physiology*.

Bardèche implies that attention to the published statistics set Balzac on the road to the *Comédie humaine*. That overstates the case, but it is true that Balzac, for all his mockery, was leaving simplistic satire, and moving to the conviction that governed his genius: society is divided into genres of people just as distinct as the species of zoology. There is a tidy before-and-after picture, that is, before his life's work had been properly commenced, and after it was almost completed. It can be nicely framed by two sentences.

In 1829, in a passage added to the meditation on 'conjugal statistics': 'The naturalists think of man only as a unique species in the order *Biman* established by Duméril in his analytic Zoology; if for the naturalists, there exist no other species than those that are introduced by the influence of climate, which have furnished the nomenclature of fifteen species ... the physiologist must also have the right to establish the genuses and sub-genuses according to certain degrees of intelligence and certain moral and pecuniary conditions of existence'.[6]

More succinctly in 1842, in the preface to the *Comédie humaine*, 'There exist at all times certain social species just as there are zoological species'. And why cannot the student of humanity put all the species into one volume, as Buffon did for zoology? The answer, in a word, is particularity, an answer that occupied Balzac for 20 volumes.

The comparison to zoology was added to the *Physiology* between 1826 and 1829. One may then advance a thesis about one surprising influence of late 1820s number fetishism, with its increasingly fine classifications published in the burgeoning tabulations of the various bureaucracies. It suggested to Balzac, in specific detail, the idea of a sequence of monographs portraying, in the form of the novel, every type of the French bourgeoisie, classified according to region, status, wealth and occupation, and constituting an ambivalent combination of satire, observation and story-telling.

How true is that thesis to Balzac? We need not stay for an answer. What is true is that the idea suggested itself to many of his contemporaries and juniors. The panoramic novel of the types of humanity was, if not invented, confirmed. And there is more than one type of author: for example Fréderic Le Play, the mining engineer from whom I take my epigraph. A man no less ambitious than Balzac, his vision of his life's work was formed exactly when Balzac's was. He dated it 1829. Like Balzac's *Comédie humaine* it started with the idea of classifying the various types of humanity, sorted first according to their conjugal situation, their families, and then according to their location, their work, and above all the domestic budget. It was directed not at the prospering classes of France but at the labourers of Europe. It was cast not in the form of novella but as quantitative studies of individual household expenses. It was numerical but, like Balzac's masterpiece, antistatistical. It did not study Quetelet's averages but used representative individuals to display the chief features of their type, as a rock or plant might serve the natural historian as a paradigm.

Le Play portrayed nomads in the Urals and cutlers in Sheffield, Swedish smiths and tenant farmers in Castille – with Moroccan carpenters and villagers in (modern-day) Syria thrown in for good measure.[7] The family, Le Play held, is the basis of every society, and hence is the proper focus of social science. We must proceed not by averaging families but by studying the family of this typesetter (Brussels) or that weaver (Godesberg).

Le Play did not systematically publish his results until 1855, when he put 36 families on view (he had many more in storage). He called the whole method one of writing *monographies*. These studies are different in kind from any statistical work that I have hitherto described. Yet they were numerical. How? The core of each monograph was a household budget, be it that of a Basque fisherman or of a master bleacher in the Clichy suburb of Paris. Every item of a year's income in cash and kind was faithfully recorded. Likewise each sort of annual expense was tabulated, not just rent and food, but candles and cabbages.

Like many other books to which I have referred, Le Play's *Ouvriers européens* won the Montyon prize. The reporters, among whom was Bienaymé, encouraged the author to publish additional monographs, noting that he said he had data on some 300 more families in reserve. The large, elegant and expensive volume was soon exhausted. 'We recommend a new popular edition [*à petit format et sans luxe*] that would put at the disposal of all its purchasers a work of statistics that touches on such numerous and wide interests'.[8] Only in 1878 did Le Play complete an extended version, containing the original 36 monographs and 21 new ones. The prize was awarded in 1856, the year of publication of Lisle's *Suicide* (see pp. 71, 78 above), which had won the Montyon prize in 1848. Today we pause before recognizing both books as works of 'statistics' but the reporters of the day had no such difficulty. I shall however be anachronistic, and refer to the numerical work of Lisle or Quetelet or whomever as statistical, and contrast it with Le Play's method of representative monographs.

Le Play was a mining engineer. The School of Mines in Paris demanded an extended field trip, undertaken in the Hartz mines by Le Play and a comrade at the school.[*][9] The Hartz silver mines have prompted more philosophy than any others: there Leibniz acted as technical adviser, and Montesquieu used them as a model for the organization of labour.[10] It was there that Le Play formed the project of interviewing the family of a working man. The Hartz mountains served for his first and most fondly remembered monograph. That was in 1829. In 1830 he was severely injured in an explosion, and could not use his hands for a year. It was a year of revolution which turned Le Play into a traditionalist. Much later he said that it filled him with a patriotic desire to work for reform and stability, but his immediate reaction, while still unable to do much physical work, was to restart the publication of the *Annales des mines*, suspended in 1830, and to commence a new periodical, *Statistique de l'industrie minérale*. He assumed charge of the statistical department of the central administration of mines. Le Play was not 'antistatistical' thus far; he was one more boulder in the cascading avalanche of printed numbers.[11]

In 1840 he produced a small brochure on the uses of statistics. Statistics is 'the observation and coordination of facts that interest the social body from the point of view of government ... Politics must unceasingly use statistics as the means by which to regulate its administrative activities.'[12] Le Play was being a good functionary. The pamphlet was chiefly a plea for a central French statistical office (granted only in 1885). Quetelet had been urging that every nation should establish such a master bureau, but Le Play never referred to Quetelet nor any other statistician. The experience in the Hartz mountains had been indelible. Statistics furnishes data for routine

---

* Energetic young men. They had five tasks: (1) study of the mines and working environment, with reports on the authorities, and miners' families; (2) excursions in the immediate vicinity of the mines; (3) geological exploration; (4) more general study of particular localities; (5) quick trips to form a summary knowledge of the region. Except when they travelled with a native, all travel was cross-country, on foot, using a map and compass. In the 200 days the two young men walked 6,800 km. On the 20 days dedicated to quick trips, they did 60 km a day. Is it possible to walk 60 km a day cross-country in the Hartz mountains?

administration, but to understand society, look to representative individuals, not average men, mere husks of reality.

He never wrote of a conversion away from the statistical practices of his contemporaries. He vacated them. The word 'statistics' is not among a careful list of definitions of 'the 300 words that constitute the language proper to the science of society'.[13] As for the 'science of society' itself: 'The name "social science" is novel, but the thing itself is ancient ... it teaches men the art of being happy.'[14] In an odd way Le Play was in the tradition of Sir John Sinclair, whose ministers had described the nuances of each parish in order that he might determine the quantum of happiness.

Le Play saw himself as Comte's true heir. But Comte, he added, had made one egregious error, a consequence of being under the sway of Condorcet and hence of revolution. Comte had foreseen knowledge and civilization passing into a phase of positive science, in which the metaphysical and theological ideas disappeared. Comte had succumbed to the fundamental error of modernity. Without doubt the new physics and chemistry had replaced that of Aristotle. It does not follow that newfangled moral science should replace the Ten Commandments: to assimilate moral to natural science 'is the first among the errors of our epoch.'[15] We suffer, he wrote, from two aberrations, 'the false dogmas of science and labour'. 'According to the first of these aberrations, experimental sciences ... are called in to destroy the fundamentals of the moral order. These pretended savants ... methodically class man with the animals ... use anatomy and physiology ... but ignore morality.'[16]

Le Play had a much more radical vision of French degeneracy than the utilitarian statisticians. We have seen how French writers were obsessed by the declining birth rate, and connected this with deviancy, be it madness, vagrancy, crime, drunkenness, prostitution or suicide. Le Play put his finger on vice, not deviancy: the wickedness and corruption of the ruling classes. The decay of France had begun with the luxury of the Sun King. The court of Louis XIV, holding the Ten Commandments in contempt, had begun a cycle of cynicism whose inevitable upshot was the sequence of revolutions and rebellions that had destroyed the fibre of the nation. A parallel and collaborating cause was (what he took to be) the French system of inheritance, in which property was divided among all the male children. This weakened families and encouraged a low birth rate, said he. France had once been fecund and able to send emigrants to Canada, but 'the compulsory division of inheritance destroyed the stem-family which sent out our ancient emigrants, whilst it has doomed our race to sterility'.[17]

Le Play respected what he called the patriarchal family, in which all property resided in the male leader of the clan, and was passed on to a next male leader. But that, he recognized, suited only earlier forms of social organization such as those he found in Bulgaria or across the Urals. His reports on non-European families in North Africa and the Near East were fostered by a curiosity about patriarchy.

What he admired in Europe was the stem-family, the *famille-souche* (a word patterned after the German *Stammfamilie*). The property was kept intact, passed from senior son or chosen child to senior son or chosen child, while the other children, supported by defined pecuniary inheritances or dowries, were put forth in the world to try to make a new fortune. All other types of family were called unstable, meaning that each generation of children established new families. Unstable families were divided into shaky (*ébranlées*) and disorganized (*désorganisées*). Every reported family of the Rhine, Belgium or England was unstable; so too were all those of France except in Brittany or the Midi, where the stem-family was still maintained.

Le Play saw his work as manifestly political. In addition to founding a society for the elaboration of his method, which by 1878 had produced ten volumes of collective monographs, he himself had published numerous tracts.[18] The earlier among these found favour with Napoleon III at his most autocratic. The titles show why.[19] Germany and England were held up as models. The Hartz mountains had been chosen for his youthful field trip because he had read a book of 1814 by an Englishman who said that the future lay in northern Germany. Despair caused by the revolutions in France reinforced admiration of the British system, and then, from a distance, of the American.*[20]

He was not keen on stating a set of explicit rules for his method. Do it! Follow examples.[21] He had chapters on method but these always turned at once from practical instructions to generalization and moralizing. We are concerned with 'places, people, subsistence and societies. These grand phenomena of nature and of the social life, observed without preconceived ideas, interpreted without bias have been for me the true origins of the method.'[22] Anthony Oberschall says that Le Play's monographs were 'based on participant observation'.[23] The interviews were indeed conducted after Le Play had been some time in a community, usually on government business, but his observations were more a matter of partici-

---

* But he feared that a spirit of scepticism and lack of respect for the decalogue were increasing in England and America. The civilized world had a last hope: British North America, and in particular Lower Canada. Québec had the best of all worlds: it had a British constitution and the traditions of France before they had been sullied by Louis XIV, and it was unpolluted by revolution. The ancient system of inheritance was preserved. 'Thanks to the severity of the climate, the absence of great wealth and to the distance from great commercial highways which have aided in preserving its faith and public peace better than they have ever before been maintained under the regimes of constraint of antiquity or of the middle ages', there was on earth one society that lived up to Le Play's standards.

pating in the power structure. Le Play determined from the foremen, manufacturers, school teachers, clerics or chiefs of the district which was the most representative family that would collaborate with him. To say this is not to denigrate his method, only to avoid anachronism.

The monographs were divided into three, with the household budgets as the core. The first part was a thorough account of the location and practices of the family in its site (history, rank, religion, health habits, clothing, dwelling, recreation, together with the state of manufacture and agriculture in the region). The third part contained social and moral reflections on the immediate causes of the condition of the family as reported. In the middle was the *monographie* proper, namely the description of the family summed up in its domestic budget.[24] These budgets remain extraordinary documents, full of surprises for the browser, and rich in fact for the interested historian, demographer or student of classes and populations. But are they science? Aren't they just anecdote, dominated by Le Play's peculiar political obsessions and utopian fantasies? He thought not. After 1856, when his work became known, when for a few years Napoleon III was to some extent his patron, and when he had founded a society to propagate his method, 'The chances of error emanating from preconceived ideas were fended off more than ever by the intervention and the control of numerous collaborators.'[25] The most important heir to the monographic method was Emile Cheysson, who carried it on until the end of the century.[26] It is possible to see Le Play as the preeminent figure in an influential antistatistical movement.[27] He is more truly represented as a man whom Napoleon III made *conseiller d'état*, in short, a convenient toy for the forces of reaction, soon to be consigned to the faded toybox of history's nursery. Or should we, as Lorraine Daston has cautiously suggested to me, see Weber's theory of ideal types as the true successor to Le Play's method of monographs?

Le Play left us a legacy less speculative than that. The idea of using the household budget was powerful in itself. As always with the Comtian antistatistical tradition to which Le Play was heir, it was the statisticians who preempted it. The budget is the source of today's technology of cost of living indices and the like. The line of filiation back to Le Play is plain. It passes through Ernst Engel. I've used the director of the Prussian statistical office as a foil against the French statisticians, to effect an East/West contrast. But here he has another role. Le Play was no 'western' statistician in the mould of Quetelet. Engel, like Le Play, admired the authoritarian second empire and the quaint plans for industrial peace encouraged by Napoleon III.[28] He picked up from Le Play the idea of using household budgets. And simultaneous with Le Play's first collection of monographs about European workers, Ducpetiaux had produced some household budgets which he discussed at the International Statistical Congress in Paris, 1855. Engel was there.

Le Play thought that the annual schedule of incomings and outgoings provided a summary account of the life of a family, representative of the manner and quality of life in a region. Engel argued at once, in 1857, that a statistical average of household budgets would be a fundamental tool of economics, since it could be used as an objective measure of the prosperity of a class or of a nation. This would require rigorous classification of kinds of expense that can be used for cross-cultural comparison: Le Play's impressionistic monographs do not lend themselves to the right kind of quantitative analysis (Engel implied).

What is consumption? What is production? Engel laughed at those who say that only the production of material goods counts as production. For that would mean that the barber is not a producer, but becomes one when he makes a wig out of your hair. Engel was on to the concept of a service industry. All cultural contributors, teachers and preachers, must count as producers. Likewise consumption must cover spiritual goods as well as material ones. A football match is a material production, because, for the players, it counts, like a spa, as health care. A night at the opera is cultural consumption and a morning at church is ethical consumption.[29]

Engel proposed that the proportion of outgoings spent on food, other things being equal, is the best measure of the material standard of living of a population. For intercultural comparison of subsistence we need a standard unit of 'consumption need'. It would be like the ohm, the amp or the volt of electricity. Just as those units were named after great men, let us call the standard unit of subsistence the 'quet'.* The point was to provide a way to compare the proportion of expenses dedicated to subsistence. Engel moved along to his last work, a comparison of Belgian prosperity over 40 years. We have forgotten quets, but our contemporary terminology had arrived: cost of living (*lebenskosten*), for example, has a central place in Engel's text.

A law has been named after Engel in the light of this work. Engel's law states that 'the poorer the individual, the family or a people, the greater must be the percentage of the income needed for the maintenance of physical sustenance, and of this a greater proportion must be allowed for food'. It is odd to find this as a law, since Engel had used the proportion of outgoings on food as the *measure* of material standard of living. To the innocent Engel's law looks like a tautology. Perhaps that is as it should be,

---

* Assumptions: males past the age of 25 have equal subsistence needs, as do females past 20. Define the subsistence needs of an infant as 1 quet. For immature people of age n, the need shall be $(1 + \frac{n}{10})$. So the needs of an adult male are 3.5 quets, and those of a female are 3 quets. (Farr, noted Engel, had suggested a smaller discrepancy between the needs of males and females, $\frac{13}{12}$.)

given Engel's own scepticism about the very concept of statistical laws. Anything that did get called a law would be the consequence of a definition, not an inductive regularity.

Engel's law was picked up in the United States as early as 1875, and given a little content: 'An increasing income among the workers is associated with the following types of distribution of expenditures. (a) The proportion of expenditure for food becomes less. (b) The proportion of expenditure for clothing stays the same. (c) The proportion of expenditure for rent, fuel, and light stays the same. (d) The proportion of expenditure for sundries increases.'[30] Engel's law has remained part of the American statistical technology, a tool about which one does not think. One should.[31]

Le Play's household budgets were descriptions of individual families that were representative of the workers of a region. They say a lot about how the family lived, its needs, its pleasures, its possibilities. Le Play thought that he could deduce from the budget the state of the family and its prospects. Engel's budgets were something entirely different. They were measures of populations, not of 'social species' in the style of Balzac or Le Play.

The taming of chance seems irresistible. Let a man propose an antistatistical idea to reflect individuality and to resist the probabilification of the universe; the next generation effortlessly coopts it so that it becomes part of the standard statistical machinery of information and control. But could not a more articulate, wilder, euphoric backlash preserve some of the ancient freedoms of chance?

17

The most ancient nobility

Paris, 16 May 1861
Magis: Statistics, madam, is a modern and positive science. It sheds light on the most obscure facts. Thus lately, thanks to laborious research, we have come to know the exact number of widows who crossed the Pont Neuf in the course of the year 1860.
Horace (rising): Ah, bah.
Désambois: That's prodigious. And how many?
Magis: Thirteen thousand four hundred and ninety eight ... and one doubtful.*[1]

The self-important statisticians with their ponderous tables were figures of fun. Thus Célestine Magis, secretary of the Statistical Society of Vierzon. A little later, in a play that ran at the Palais Royal, a statistician tried to find the number of married people per kilometre in his *département*. Result: $16\frac{1}{2}$ married men, and $17\frac{3}{4}$ married women.[2] Bad jokes abounded. We have seen that Balzac, in the era of enthusiasm for statistics, came to take them seriously. What began as a parody, the 'conjugal statistics' of *The Physiology of Marriage*, became a reflection on the very nature of classifying human beings. That was 1829. An era of optimism about the possible uses of statistics ended in 1848, prompting many kinds of backlash.

One was political. The statisticians were typically advocates of liberal utilitarian reform. People who had no truck with their philosophy, or with its pretensions to resolving current social issues, held them in contempt slightly mingled with fear. The numbers, to use Poisson's prescient words,

* *Les Vivacités du Capitaine Tic*, by Eugène Labiche and Edouard Martin, opening at the Vaudeville Theatre. Horace says of the statistician, 'That's not a man, that's a tirade.' Désambois to Lucille, daughter of Mme de Guy: 'He has published a work ... printed.' Magis: 'I would not dare take the liberty, but, since you allow me, I will be happy to bring you my slim volume, *Monographie de statistique comparée*.' Magis also informs his audience, on another occasion: 'In seven minutes twelve weevils in a hectolitre of wheat produce 75,000 individuals, of which each can devour three grains a year, hence 225,000 grains in all.' Horace: 'And have you found out how to destroy your weevils?' Magis: 'Oh, that's none of my business.'

did strip human beings of their individuality. The utilitarians, seemingly so concerned with the welfare of humanity, became, like Dickens's Gradgrind, indifferent to people. Ephemera such as Captain Tic spoke for a less reflective version of this resentment.

The body of conservative opinion in London, Paris and the provinces was hostile to argument based solely on statistical data. This did not prevent grudging recognition of a need for bureaucracies such as the Board of Trade or the office of the Registrar-General of England and Wales. A great many of the British 'Blue Books' – parliamentary papers – were compilations of statistical data. In the French system, the statistical departments of ministries such as justice, mines and education were insatiable. National vainglory helped. If Sweden had better health statistics, or the Austro-Hungarian Empire better railway statistics, then everyone else had to follow suit. Administrators took pride in their public numbers. Their reams of tables showed that a job was being done, one that required a larger staff.

Statistics became integral to political debate, but there were a good many influential potential consumers of numbers who seldom really wanted them as a basis for action. Whether or not Disraeli actually said, 'There are three kinds of lies: lies, damned lies, and statistics', the story that he did so conveys a real truth.[3] Here I deliberately speak of the statisticians in or under the sway of Paris and London, where the inclinations of the enumerators were to find laws underlying the numbers, social laws that would then be used as bases for legislation. Prussian statisticians had no illusions that they were revealing laws, and the relationship of the Prussian statistical office to centres of power was different from that in the West. One does not find claimed for Bismarck an aphorism like that attributed to Disraeli.

A second type of backlash was more philosophical. We know Comte was bitter about probability theory. People were enthusiastic only because they lacked 'philosophical discipline':

The irrational approval given to the so-called Calculus of Chances is enough to convince all men of sense how injurious to science has been this absence of control. *Strange indeed would be the degeneration if the science of Calculation, the field in which the fundamental dogma of the invariability of Law first took its rise, were it to end its long course of progress in speculations that involve the hypotheses of the entire absence of Law.*[4]

Strange indeed! I have added emphasis to Comte's statement for that is precisely the wonder of the taming of chance, that indeterminism should be brought into the world on the back of calculation, originally created to handle the deterministic. Comte was almost fully apprised of what was going on. Indeterminism was barely conceived when he wrote, but he, who loathed the very thought, foresaw its future empire. He saw also that the new indeterminism would not be, as he put it, 'brought back to the ancient hypothesis of arbitrary wills'. It was something new, and worse. Comte was unspeakably bitter. 'The idlest discussions of mediaeval schoolmen' he continued, 'contain probably nothing so hollow, or indeed so absurd, as the accepted notions of the modern algebraists upon the measurement of probabilities, nay of expectations.' Yet one phrase of his prophetic cry of dismay unpacks the riddle: 'the hypothesis of the entire absence of law'. For that was not, in the end, to be the hypothesis. Instead there was the hypothesis of a new kind of law. It was statistical laws that installed indeterminism, but Comte was as opposed to the statistical conception of society as he was to the calculus of chances.

Comte is the most ironic figure in my entire story, because he understood what was happening better than anyone, and detested it. He flung forth names, such as 'social physics' and then 'sociology' itself. They were picked up by his statistical enemies and made their own, just as 'positivism' bizarrely became the name for antihistoricism in philosophy. Here was the man who named his school positivist and invented the word, the man who denied any metaphysical underpinning for our idea of laws of nature because there are only universal regularities. Yet (like Hume before him) he was completely convinced, without reason, that the understructure of the world had to be described in terms of universally applicable laws. Statistical regularities collected by the number fetishists were contemptible. The mathematics of the probabilists were 'childish speculations and erroneous principles'. Alas poor 'sociology'! Before the end of the century, in France at any rate, a pretty standard course in sociology would begin with words like these:

It is above all with statistics that we shall try to nourish our studies. True eloquence in sociology is the eloquence of figures. By statistics sociology can foresee and forecast: the law of large numbers gives them an almost infallible character. Do not fear that such confidence in the results of statistics is an implicit negation of free will, for whoever says liberty says reason, just the opposite of caprice and arbitrariness.[5]

That was published in a journal dedicated to 'criminal anthropology' and to 'normal and pathological psychology'. Criminal anthropology will recur in chapter 20, and in chapter 19 we shall continue the Comtian irony with 'normal'. We owe to Comte the transfer of the ideas of the normal and the pathological from physiology to society. Yet his intention was always that of the physiologists, to speak of the normal individual and the deviations from the norm that we call ill-health. By transference, he wrote of the individual society as normal or perturbed. He never thought of the normal as a statistical concept at all, and yet it came to denote the premier statistical idea of the late nineteenth century.

Physiology itself did generate a third kind of statistical backlash, well described by Georges Canguilhem, William Coleman and others.[6] Its most distinguished spokesman was Claude Bernard, the founder of experimental physiology. The physician's task, he said, is to determine exactly what causes disease, and what cures it. The statistician may report that 80 per cent of the victims treated in a certain way will recover, but the patient wants to know, 'Will *I* survive?' Only a fully deterministic science of medicine can answer. Bernard's experiments were directed at the tissues, organs or secretions of this or that individual. This was not to preclude generalization, for when the conditions that caused the failure of one particular pancreas were fully understood, we would see how they would destroy any other pancreas. We would know why they were lethal, and would envisage steps towards intervention, prevention and cure. In contrast, what could a mere average teach us? The case was put graphically at a time when the chemical analysis of urine was a significant tool for the physiologist and even the physician. If the statistician wants to know about average European urine, sneered the physiologists, let him go to the lavatories of a Paris railroad station.

Bernard was fully in the tradition of Bichat; he was a more sophisticated (and more agreeable) Broussais; he was a man well versed in his Comte, although not free of ambivalence. He was antistatistical because of his faith in the possibility of finding out the deterministic causes of disease. He studied individuals in the clinics and the laboratory, rather than populations in hospitals or provinces, for only in the material flesh and blood and pus and urine could he investigate causality. Certainly the individual patients and excretions that he examined and treated were representative of the race and its diseases, but that was a straightforward consequence of the uniformity of nature.

The physiologist and the mineralogist turned sociologist – Bernard and Le Play – are two representatives of the same antagonism to statistics. Both complained that it abstracts from reality, leaving meaningless averages. We don't want averages; we want individuals, representative individuals. From the rich and full study of a carefully chosen individual case we can learn far more about the class that it represents than we can derive from mechanical tabulations of facts about the masses. Down with the number-crunchers! But this slogan did not mean down with numbers. Le Play's budgets were unalloyed numerals; Bernard's experiments were pure measurement.

Dickens and Disraeli, Comte and Bernard, Labiche and Le Play: each in his own way was angry at the statisticians. A fourth and far more radical type of backlash denounced the statistician as producing a science of human beings that eliminates their humanity. Dostoyevsky's 'Underground Man' jeered at the utilitarians who 'deduce the whole range of human satisfactions as averages from statistical figures and scientifico-economic formulas'.[7] He mocked 'The Palace of Crystal, eternally inviolate' which the nineteenth century would erect, not just at the Great Exhibition of 1851, but, metaphorically, over everything.[8] 'There's our nineteenth century – and it was Buckle's century too.'[9] Two years before publishing the *Notes from Underground*, we recall, Dostoyevsky enjoined himself to read and reread Buckle. Dostoyevsky's notebook for 1864 (the year the *Notes* were published) shows that he took seriously, if sceptically, Buckle's contention that the course of human life is determined towards statistical stability by such overarching causes as climate.[10] He wanted to know what would change the overall condition of his fellows, and hence their collective behaviour. But it is the next move, made by his interlocutor, that repelled him: 'since all volition and all reasoning may be tabulated, because the laws of our so-called free will may indeed be discovered, it follows, quite seriously, that some sort of table may be drawn up and that we shall exercise our wills in accordance to that table'.[11] Reply:

But there is one very puzzling thing: how does it come about that all the statisticians and experts and lovers of humanity, when they enumerate the good things of life, always omit one particular one?

One's own free and unfettered volition, one's own caprice, however wild, one's own fancy, inflamed sometimes to the point of madness – that is the best and greatest good, which is never taken into consideration because it will not fit any classification, and the omission of which always sends all systems and theories to the devil.[12]

This cry for untrammelled freedom was not a demand for absolute lawlessness. Dostoyevsky's revulsion against the utilitarians was part of a greater *angst* than that which prompted Dickens's loathing. He was steadfast in preaching not just freedom, but also caprice. It was as if the utilitarians and statisticians had stolen words such as 'freedom' and 'chance' for their idle debates on statistical fatalism. Dostoyevsky virtually said: Let them abscond with those great ideas: we shall always have caprice. They'll not dare to steal that!

That leads on to a fifth type of backlash: the invention, or at any rate restoration, of pure chance. I chose my title, *The Taming of Chance*, because of the way in which the nineteenth century captured chances within a structure of statistical law. That result had not been fully achieved by 1860. Quetelet's extraordinary hypothesis about the law of errors – that it is the standard curve for the physical and moral attributes of people – was a foisting of law on to humanity and free choice. But it was conceptually bolstered by the fiction of myriad underlying deterministic causes giving rise to a Normal distribution.

Thus statistical laws in the hands of Quetelet were on the road to autonomy, but they had not arrived. Only later would they be treated like laws in their own right, with no need of subservience to minute necessitating causes. I describe that further erosion of determinism in chapters 21 and 23. People and the world became not less governed but more controlled, for a new kind of law came into play. That is why I speak of chance being tamed.

Well before these events were completed, an opposite idea of chance came into circulation. That was the ultimate backlash, a sort of statistical nihilism. The ancient and divine prerogatives of *pure chance* must be restored! The well organized and rational God of the Enlightenment had been invoked by eighteenth-century Newtonians in England to explain statistical stability, but there lingered the spark of older and more fickle gods who relished pure chance, the very stuff that the enlightened Hume had said is a word that signifies nothing. That spark was rekindled by Romanticism, and was fanned by Nietzsche.

The poet Novalis had written in 1797 that chance manifests the miraculous. The individual is 'individualized by one single chance event alone, that is, his birth.'[13] In Zarathustra this idea blazed forth in a famous blessing:

To stand over every single thing as its own round roof, its azure bell ... Over all things stand the heaven accident, the heaven innocence, the heaven chance, the heaven prankishness.

'By chance' – that is the most ancient nobility of the world, and this I restored to all things: I delivered them from their bondage under purpose.[14]

Heaven is turned in to a 'dance floor for divine accidents', 'a divine table for divine dice and dice players'. How then did rationality arrive in the world? 'Irrationally, as might be expected: by a chance accident.'[15] There are a number of important ways in which Nietzsche and Peirce were the two great complementary philosophers of the end of the nineteenth century. Their conception of chance and creation and necessity was curiously similar. Both believed that our world, which others find orderly, is a product of chance. Neither thought that the presence of law in the universe makes it any less chancy.

Gilles Deleuze has a succinct summary of one of Nietzsche's thoughts here. The dice of creation 'thrown once are the affirmation of *chance*, the combination which they form on falling is the affirmation of *necessity* ... What Nietzsche calls *necessity* (destiny) is thus never the abolition but rather the combination of chance itself.'[16] There are all sorts of plays here. Chance, Nietszche asserted, makes sense only when we have a concept of purpose. But we get this idea of purpose and reason in part from being in what looks like an orderly world. Those who know that the universe is a matter of blind chance are untroubled by simulacra of purpose. 'Those iron hands of necessity that shake the dice box of chance play this game for an infinite length of time: so that there *have* to be throws which exactly resemble purposiveness and rationality of every degree.'[17]

Nietzsche grasped the most difficult philosophical lesson about chance to which we have thus far been exposed. Necessity and chance are twinned, and neither can exist without the other. Neither explains the other, no more than heads explains tails.

The bad player is the one who tries to calculate and play with the odds, as if his game, his life, were one of a large number of games. To do so is at best to succumb to another necessity, the necessity of the law of large numbers. The good player does not fool himself, and accepts that there is exactly one chance, which produces by chance the necessity and even the purpose that he experiences. Not even a long run of universes would annul the chance that brought into being our world, and only the false consciousness of a bad gambler could make it seem otherwise.

Where Nietzsche wrote that 'there *have* to be throws which exactly resemble purposiveness and rationality of every degree' he may sound like some who object to the argument from design for the existence of God. They say: if the universe is sufficiently ancient, then by chance the particles that make it up would have arranged themselves in the orderly way that we see at present. There would be no need for a creator to plan things this way. Hence the best explanation of what Hume called 'the fine adjustment of means to ends', or of what modern cosmologists call the 'fine-tuning' of the universe, is that we live in a very old universe – or in one member of a long sequence of successive universes. We should infer to the best explanation: our universe is ancient, or one of many, in which case the regularities found in our world are not so surprising after all. I believe that this inference is fallacious. All we can say is that either an extremely improbable event has occurred (our finely-tuned universe came into being) or ours is a designed universe. If you don't like the hypothesis of divine design, then opt for pure inexplicable chance. To reason otherwise is to commit what I have named the 'inverse gambler's fallacy'.[18] It is also to have what Nietzsche would have dismissed as false consciousness in matters of chance and necessity. Nietzsche did not *infer* that we live in an ancient, chancy universe. He experienced it. It was for him a given, just as for Peirce, in my epigraph to chapter 23, 'chance pours in at every avenue of sense'.

Nietzsche's reflections on chance had an ambivalence worthy of the subject. He enjoyed what he called 'the empire of chance', one of the two realms in which we dwell, the other being that of purpose.[19] He also called chance crassly stupid. He was obsessed by two enemies, sanity and insanity. 'Not only the reason of millennia, but their madness too, breaks out in us. It is dangerous to be an heir. Still we fight step by step with the giant, chance, and over the whole of humanity there has ruled, thus far, only non-sense, un-sense.'[20] But this very chance is also the pushing apart of creativity.[21] I see Nietzsche not as getting away from necessity but as seeing always that chance and necessity are inextricable: the deepest lesson of the taming of chance.

The lesson has been played out again and again by unwitting actors. Think of Paul Eluard, king of Dada, composing and publishing poems that consist simply of words, first written on slips of paper, and then drawn from a hat. We've really escaped necessity here, publishing purely random words! Yet in exactly the same decade L.J.C. Tippett first collected and finally published tables of random sampling numbers under the auspices of Karl Pearson's journal, *Biometrika*.[22] These were systematically random numbers, taken from the digits of dates of births and deaths in parish registers. These cradle and tombstone digits of pure chance were intended to increase the efficacy of data analysis, to bring order into chaos, to derive firm bounds for any error that might be produced by chance fluctuations. Dada and *Biometrika*: two sides, we might say, of the same coin.

18

Cassirer's thesis

Leipzig, 14 August 1872   A mind which knew for a given very small period of time the position, direction and velocity of all the atoms in the universe, would be able ... by an appropriate treatment of its world-formula, to tell us who was the Iron Mask, or how the 'President' came to grief. As the astronomer predicts the day on which, after many years, a comet again appears in the vault of heaven from the depths of space, so this 'mind' would read in its equations the day when the Greek cross will glitter from the mosque of Sofia, or when England will burn her last lump of coal.[*][1]

In the light of so trenchant a statement of the doctrine of necessity can we seriously speak of the erosion of determinism by 1872? Ernst Cassirer raised a more unexpected question. He took the above passage as evidence of the *invention* of determinism! He acknowledged the all-too well-known deterministic aphorisms of Laplace but said that in their day such words were 'hardly more than an ingenious metaphor':

The idea that the metaphor should be endowed with a wider meaning and validity, that it should be the expression of a general epistemological principle, occurred in a much later period, and its date can be established quite definitely.[2]

Namely 1872, the occasion of the speech by Du Bois-Reymond. Why should Cassirer say that is when determinism began? A feeble answer: there are many kinds of determinism, and Cassirer was drawing attention to some novelty added to the idea of determinism around 1870. That is plausible enough. I respect a jibe attributed to the late J.L. Austin. He was asked, 'There is more than one distinct idea of determinism, is there not,

[*] From a speech by Emil Du Bois-Reymond delivered to the annual meeting of the Versammlung Deutscher Naturforscher und Aertze. By 1872 he was celebrated as a physicist, chemist and above all neurophysiologist of stature. In 1847 he had, with Brücke, Ludwig and Helmholz, founded a Berlin ginger group that aimed at proving that the workings of the brain are to be understood in terms of electricity. Twenty-five years later he was an elder statesman of science entitled to address the deep questions of metaphysics. A speech by Du Bois-Reymond was something. In one talk he created a sensation by asserting both that Goethe was not quite the literary giant that is commonly assumed, and that he was simply muddle-headed in his famous contributions to the theory of colour and vision.

Professor Austin?' 'No', he replied, 'less than one.' Cassirer might have been saying that around 1870 a well-defined version of determinism emerged out of previously obscure notions. He himself was thinking chiefly about microphysics in 1936, and might have been asserting that a determinism, clearly enough stated to be incompatible with the new quantum mechanics, was itself of fairly recent origin. But I shall take Cassirer at his word, as proposing that determinism as a serious idea came into being only around 1870.

That flies in the face of all conventional historiography. The shock of Cassirer's paradox makes us examine truisms about determinism that we tend uncritically to accept. I think that Cassirer was wrong, but that he hints at surprising truths. Something dramatic was happening to the doctrine of necessity around 1870. I put it down to an underlying malaise about determinism. One of the side-effects was a silly season in the philosophies of freedom and necessity. The intense worries about statistical fatalism were only a fragment of a larger battiness.

We should first check out the very word 'determinism'. Cassirer did not make a philological excursion, but he might have predicted that the word did not have its present philosophical meaning until the 1870s or so. He would have been right. That does not prove that our present *idea* of determinism did not previously exist under another name – 'necessity' for example. But presence or absence of a word or a meaning is instructive. So I shall first give a little history of our word 'determinism'.

The Dictionary of the History of Ideas begins by saying that 'the English word "determinism," like its French, German and Italian counterparts, is of seventeenth- and eighteenth-century coinage'.[3] That is a mistake, although a surprising one, for most people instinctively agree in expecting 'determinism' to be an old word. The author goes on to distinguish 'two different, but related, doctrines. One, the doctrine that choice between different courses of action can, in all cases, be fully accounted for by psychological and other conditions ... The other ... is the doctrine that everything that happens constitutes a chain of causation.'

The earlier doctrine was called 'determinism' only at the end of the eighteenth century, and then only in German. The second came to be called 'determinism' only in the 1850s to 1870s. It was this second doctrine that was so trenchantly expressed by Du Bois-Reymond. Cassirer was right to this extent: the kind of determinism he meant was so called only around the time of the famous speech.

Our word first appears as *Determinismus* in German. It was sufficiently well understood to serve in 1789 as the title of a book in the phrase 'determinism and moral freedom'.[4] Kant first used the word in his 1793 book on religion. There he jeered at this new coinage as a mere *Blendwerk*, that is, eyewash, a sham, a confidence trick, a piece of intellectual juggling.[5] If the (unnamed) users of this word want a label, wrote Kant, let them take *Praedeterminismus*. This name makes the idea clear: our choices are predetermined by our motives, desires and beliefs. Predeterminism would be a fitting name today for most philosophical versions of decision theory and of rational choice theory, the fantasy according to which a utility or preference function, plus a probability function over beliefs, determines what a person will do. That concept has nothing to do with what Du Bois-Reymond – or Laplace – had in mind.

For 'determinism' in English the *OED* cites the Scottish metaphysician, Sir William Hamilton, writing in 1846. He explicitly contrasted determinism, which, he said, has to do with motives and purposes, with necessitation by efficient causes, which he called blind fate.[6] Thus he used 'determinism' to mean something expressly contrasted with the Du Bois-Reymond/Laplace/Cassirer idea. Hamilton was Kantian and pro-German. His usage faithfully reflected German practices, such as might be illustrated by H.C.W. Sigwart, or given in a German philosophical dictionary of the day.[7]

The *OED* is not strictly correct in assigning the first usage to Hamilton. Here is an exposition of Kant for English readers of 1798: 'Determinism is the principle of determining the will from sufficient internal (subjective) reasons. To obtain this principle with that of freedom, i.e., absolute spontaneity, occasions no difficulty.'[8] As for French, the words, imported from German, do occur in an 1811 French version of Gall and Spurzheim's phrenology.[9] In 1836 the Académie Française published this acerbic pair of entries in an appendix to its dictionary of the French language:

Determinist: Name of a little known German sect, of little influence here.
Determinism: System, principles, doctrine of the determinists.[10]

French readers will immediately associate the word *déterminisme* with Claude Bernard. His immensely successful *Introduction* to experimental medicine had a running discussion of what he calls 'determinism'. His usage was a little different from English, and paralleled our word 'mechanism'. The mechanism of a watch is that which actually produces the movement of the hands. Likewise Bernard's *déterminisme* meant that which actually does the determining. 'The experimental doctor successively exercises his influence on diseases when he knows their experimental determinism, that is to say, their proximate cause.'[11] He also used the word *déterminisme* for his doctrine that something material determines every physiological event. 'Experimental critique puts everything in doubt, except the principle of scientific determinism.'[12] One thing was quite manifest: determinism excluded statistical law. The influence of

Comte upon Bernard was variable, but sometimes it shone through: 'I do not know why one gives the name *law* to results obtained by statistics. According to me, a scientific law can only be founded on certainty and on an absolute determinism – not on a probability.'[13]

The word *déterminisme* was being used by a philosopher just when Bernard was writing on experimental medicine. The energetic neo-Kantian Charles Renouvier used it much in a work of 1859 whose title manages to mention man, reason, passion, liberty, certainty and moral probability.[14] The word occurs less frequently in an earlier volume of 1854, but there we do find a mention, in so many words, of the 'famous problem of free will and determinism'.[15] Renouvier explicitly cited and quoted Laplace; we must therefore qualify Cassirer's assertion that Laplace was understood at most 'metaphorically' until 1870.[16]

So we must antedate the philological version of Cassirer's thesis. The word 'determinism' did not come to denote the doctrine of necessity in 1872, in Germany, but in the 1850s, in France. We cannot dismiss Renouvier on the ground that he was not influential, or on the ground that his readership was limited to France. William James began his famous lecture 'The Dilemma of Determinism' by saying, 'We see in the writings of Renouvier, Fouillée and Delboeuf how completely changed is the form of all the old disputes about freedom.'[17] In his 1904 presidential address to the American Psychological Association, he candidly and with some emotion stated his debt: 'I owe all my doctrine on this subject [Effort and the Will] to Renouvier.'[18] James's last and not quite finished book, *Some Problems of Philosophy*, is dedicated to the French philosopher, 'feeling endlessly thankful as I do'.[19] One of James's first publications was a review, in 1876, of Renouvier's philosophy.[20] He there used the word determinism in the sense of causation.*

The *OED* gives 1876 – but not William James – as the first occasion of the modern (doctrine of necessity) use of the word 'determinism' in English. The definition is 'the doctrine that everything that happens is determined by a necessary chain of causation'. But the word was already in circulation with this meaning. For example, James Clerk Maxwell gave a talk in 1873 to the Eranus club, a club composed of former members of the better-known Cambridge secret society, the Apostles. The title: 'Does the progress of Physical Science tend to give any advantage to the opinion of

---

* Renouvier favoured Kant purged of noumena. His *La Critique philosophique* appeared almost weekly for a decade after 1871 before settling down to a more sedate pace. In the beginning it was largely written by himself. The effusive tenderness expressed by the dying James for Renouvier – who died in 1903 – must reflect James's memories of youthful crisis. Living in a boarding-house as a student in Germany, he endured dreadful depression, feelings of lassitude and indifference that he described as loss of will. He recalled himself as having pulled through by reading Renouvier.

Necessity (or determinism) over that of the Contingency of events and the Freedom of the Will?'[21]

So much for the word. Let us not overemphasize its novelty. The verb 'to determine' has a more than casual connection with the doctrine of necessity. In chapter 2 I quoted Hume: 'Every object is determin'd by absolute fate to a certain degree and direction of its motion.' He was talking not about fate but about causal determination. Leibniz's own index to the *Theodicy* had an entry for the French word *détermination*, with numerous references.[22] He also used expressions like *inevitabilem determinationem supralapsorium*.[23] Pierre Bayle's *Dictionary*, in the article on Jansenism, used the verb 'to determine', and Leibniz drew attention to this very passage in his *Theodicy*. *Determinare* and *determinatus* occur often in Spinoza.[24] Finally, the distinction between the *idea* of determinism in extended substance, and the *idea* of determinism or predeterminism in the mind, was well discussed early in the nineteenth century, as a difference between 'the relation between motive and action and that of cause and effect'.[25]

So let us turn from the word to the idea. Was Cassirer right to say that efficient cause determinism – the doctrine of necessity – became a serious universal proposition only in 1872? I do not think so. Common wisdom is correct. Laplace was not writing metaphors. Hume and Kant were necessitarians about the phenomenal world of objects. Sometimes determinists were called mechanists, as was Lamettrie, after he had observed in his book on the soul how a disease and high fever affected the workings of his own mind. His Parisian peers were so shocked that he moved to Leiden and in 1747 published the even bolder *L'Homme machine*.[26] More commonly a man would be called a materialist, as was Baron d'Holbach. We must accept that although there is no one canonical timeless version of determinism, in the sense of the doctrine of necessity, there is a persistent thread of such determinism running through all post-Cartesian European history.

What then is the interest of Cassirer's thesis? The first is that the word 'determinism' attached itself to causal necessity between the late 1850s and the early 1870s. Secondly, it did so in a particular connection. Bernard in France and Du Bois-Reymond in Germany were physiologists. They denied vitalism, and held that all living processes are subject to the workings of chemistry and electricity (or the like). The Berlin workers extended these physical sciences to the brain itself. Laplace, Kant and Hume were remarkably cautious about anything to do with the brain. You can read Laplace (but not Lamettrie!) as speaking of necessity only in the realm of extended, spatial, material substance. In his public statements we read nothing of mental events. Du Bois-Reymond devoted his life to brain events and held a correspondence theory verging on identity theory: brain events correspond to and may even simply be the same as, mental events. That was the project of his 1872 lecture, to understand consciousness and free will in such a metaphysics. He stated that we shall never comprehend. We are at the border of possible scientific knowledge, a border that science cannot transgress. Thus Cassirer is correct on a more than verbal point. The newly styled determinism was more imperial than Laplace. It was intended to hold sway over the brain, the locale of mental events.

That was not, however, the only thing happening to determinism in those days. There was an enormous range of zany discussions. The problem of free will itself is universal, and it can be readily introduced into cultures that have nothing like our Western views of causality. It is never remarkable to find people discussing freedom. What is extraordinary about mid-nineteenth-century Europe is a frantic constructing of new and certainly very odd arguments about freedom. Our much discussed statistical fatalism provides one example; another, to be developed in chapter 20 below, arose from Cesare Lombroso's criminal anthropology of 1876. The entire tradition of European jurisprudence must be rejected, because criminals are born, not made; they are atavistic throwbacks. Punishment as retribution is folly; the death penalty is immoral because murderers, born to kill, are not responsible for their acts. That at any rate was the great issue of the first great Congress of Criminal Anthropology, held in Rome in the autumn of 1885.[27]

Much more modestly, but not obviously more coherently, James Clerk Maxwell's discussion of free will focussed on the work of two French mathematicians. The concern was lasting. Karl Pearson wrote, 'I hold a letter of Clerk Maxwell in which he states that the work of Saint-Venant and Boussinesq on Singular Solutions is epoch-making ... the great solution to the problem of free will.'[28] What work was this, that solved the problem of free will? It was a contribution to the mathematical theory of elasticity. Elasticity no longer matters much, but in the latter half of the nineteenth century it was *the* problem of cosmology. All standard models of the aether had internal contradictions or hopelessly violated experience, yet electromagnetic transmission without an elastic aether seemed unthinkable. Many believed that Saint-Venant's breakthroughs on elasticity would yield the correct solution.

One of his investigations, continued by Boussinesq, concerned 'singular solutions'. The two men were fascinated by equations with singular points a, such that by substituting values arbitrarily close to and less than a, one got solutions wildly different from those of values arbitrarily close to but larger than a. There is more than a whiff of modern catastrophe theory and chaos theory in this research. Then (as now) such authors thought that their work had profound extramathematical significance. It would explain free will in a mechanistic world. Most of the time what we do is routinely foreordained. But occasionally we are in the presence of a physical singular point, when by a choice of one of two acts, arbitrarily close together, we can achieve totally different effects. Free will operates, as it were, through the infinitesimal interstices of singular solutions. Maxwell compared the situation to the pointsman on a nineteenth century English railway, who did nothing most of the day, but could direct the train on one of two divergent lines at certain junctions. Maxwell wrote that 'Singular points are by their nature very isolated, and form no appreciable fraction of the continuous source of existence.'[29] He may well have been thinking of a singular point in his own life. It was long unclear which of two women he would marry, and that decision was indeterminate. Once it had been made, however, one of the possible courses of his life unravelled in a routine way; the other was permanently closed off. It is a symptom of the state of determinism in the 1860s and 1870s that this idea could have been so warmly embraced by minds as powerful as that of Saint-Venant or as profound as that of Maxwell.

Maxwell's enthusiasm may offend a certain philosophical sensibility. Topics change when we turn to the philosophers of his day, but they do not improve. Renouvier used the law of large numbers as part of a bizarre strategy.[30] The plan was to create post-Kantian antinomies. For example, any argument for determinism can be turned into one for free will, and vice versa. Renouvier gave many examples, but I will discuss only one. The determinist asserts that the world operates by fixed causal laws of nature. The indeterminist replies that these might be only the consequences of the law of large numbers applied to a great many events. Viewed externally, a free act is indistinguishable from a ticket in a lottery. The law of large numbers declares that absolute regularity emerges in a long run of draws, so deterministic regularity can be explained in terms of freedom. Renouvier's determinist retorts that each allegedly free act must have an underlying deterministic explanation. Recalling Laplace's dictum that all probability is subjective, Renouvier wrote:

Laplace's exposition of principles entirely conforms to the spirit of science, or, perhaps better, to the spirit of scientists, all or almost all of whom are quite ready to avow or reproduce this principle. You find a clear and concise notion of probability here also (the same one that I develop in my chapters on the categories), but disfigured by a profession of faith in necessity, which seems to me, at the very least, useless and in consequence arbitrary.[31]

The neo-Kantian Renouvier then made a positivistic move, stating that just as final causes have been eliminated from science, we have now reached the stage of eliminating efficient causes, and, with them, the idea of universal determinism.

Thus far Renouvier seems like an agent in the erosion of determinism. He did foreshadow Peirce, but Peirce concluded that the doctrine of necessity is plainly false. Thus they differ in two ways. First, Renouvier matches his denial of determinism with a denial of freedom, leaving us with an antinomy to be resolved by transcendental analysis. Peirce had a firm one-sided thesis. Secondly, Peirce (unlike James) was rightly very cautious in connecting his antideterminism with 'free will', whereas Renouvier's arguments arose only in the context of human freedom.

We must not discount the importance of Renouvier for Peirce. We have noticed the ties and obligations of Peirce's sometime friend and patron, William James, to Renouvier. Nor is Renouvier the only relevant French writer. In 1874 Emile Boutroux published his remarkable dissertation on the contingency of laws of nature. The fundamental tenet is emergentism and a hierarchy of structures. On the stages of development of the world, we may begin with elemental atoms. Then there is a structure of molecules, but, conjectured Boutroux, the laws of atoms may not determine the laws of compounds. The laws of those compounds, even the organic ones, may not fix the laws of plant and animal life. The biological laws may not determine the psychological laws of reasoning creatures. The biological and the psychological laws may not determine the laws of society. Thus at each step of the hierarchy we have contingency, and the evolution of new laws undetermined by simpler structures.

In the universe there can be distinguished several worlds, forming, as it were, stages superposed on one another. These are – above the world of pure necessity, of quantity without quality, which is identical with nonentity – the world of causes, the world of notions, the mathematical world, the living world, and lastly the thinking world.

Each of these worlds appears, at first, to depend strictly on the lower worlds, as on some external fatality, and to receive from them its existence and laws ... Nevertheless, if we examine and compare the concepts of the principal forms of being, we see that it is impossible to connect the higher forms with the lower ones by a link of necessity.[32]

There is a dark saying of Boutroux: 'Determinism, as it contracts, becomes more and more impenetrable to necessity.'[33] He was using the word 'determinism' in the sense fixed by Bernard – he means the ability of one thing to bring about another thing. On the one hand Boutroux was speaking of contraction: less and less should be regarded as determined. On the other he was speaking of necessity: within modified ideas of determinism, the notion of necessity has less and less of a place. The end-product of this contraction is Peirce's world of absolute chance: a world in which laws emerge in an evolutionary process that is entirely contingent. I do not know that Peirce had much close contact with Boutroux. James certainly did, and there is said to be a substantial unpublished James-Boutroux correspondence. Peirce had at least professional contacts with Renouvier, who published the French versions of two of Peirce's most celebrated essays.

We may query whether the relationship between Boutroux and Renouvier in France, and James and Peirce in Cambridge, was one of influence or of parallel development. In the case of another figure in the taming of chance, the filiation is manifest. The most famous student of Boutroux was Emile Durkheim. He is important to our analysis for several reasons. His 1897 *Suicide* was the culmination of a century of French fascination with suicide statistics. He rejected the idea that stable distributions of crime or suicide were to be explained by myriad petty underlying independent causes. Instead there were 'suicidogenetic currents of a certain strength' that ran through a given society.[34] 'Collective tendencies or passions' are 'forces *sui generis*' which dominate the consciousness of a single individual. This 'is brilliantly shown by the statistics of suicide', although, in a footnote, 'such statistics are not the only ones to do so. All the facts of moral statistics imply this conclusion.'[35] 'Collective tendencies have an existence of their own; they are forces as real as cosmic forces.'[36]

Durkheim envisaged a new kind of law, investigated by statisticians and established by statistical data. It would be completely autonomous of underlying little independent causes. This was one by no means coherent strategy for taming chance. Chance was to be brought under the sway of a new kind of law said to be analogous to those of electricity and gravitational theory.

This move was unexceptionable for a student of Boutroux. *Suicide* urged that society as a whole is not simply the sum of the individuals. The whole is greater than the parts. 'It is from Renouvier that the axiom came to us: a whole is not equal to the sum of its parts.'[37] The laws of society, analogous to cosmic or electrical forces, arose from principles greater than those deducible from properties of individual psychology. Emergentism was one way to absorb statistical law without creating a confrontation between the laws of society and the deterministic underpinning of the merely physical world. In 1907, when Durkheim was an established figure, he wrote that 'My teacher M. Boutroux ... at the Ecole Normale Supérieure often repeated to us that each science must explain by "its own principles" ... Very much impressed by this idea I applied it to sociology. I was confirmed in this method by reading Comte ...'[38] Twenty-two years earlier, as a young man in search of a tenured academic post, he had already affirmed the teachings of Boutroux. Sociology 'is a science that is independent and *sui generis*. There are three worlds in nature: above physical phenomena, above psychical phenomena there are sociological phenomena.'[39] That was in 1885. In his inaugural lecture for his 1888 course on sociology, he asserted that 'for Comte, society was a *sui generis* being.'[40] In 1897, collective forces that generate suicide stability were equally called *sui generis*.

We seem to have come some distance from the epoch of zany ideas about determinism and free will. We are now at the edge of sociology, and that (we like to think) is real knowledge. We can be done with those old holists and get on with things; we can ignore free will, can we not? No, not Durkheim. His idea of the grand cosmic-like forces acting on individuals from 'outside' solved the problem of free will! His paragraph stating this is no less strange than those of his predecessors whom I have quoted.

Without wishing to raise a question of metaphysics outside our province, we must note that this theory of statistics does not deny men every sort of freedom. On the contrary, it leaves the question of free will much more untouched than if one made the individual the source of social phenomena. Actually, whatever the causes of the regularity of collective manifestations, they are forced to produce their effects wherever they occur, because otherwise these effects would vary at random, whereas they are uniform. If they are inherent in individuals, they must therefore inevitably determine their possessors. Consequently, on this hypothesis, no way is found to avoid the strictest determinism. But it is not so if the stability of demographic data results from a force external to the individual. Such a force does not determine one individual rather than another. It exacts a definite number of certain kinds of actions, but not that they should be performed by this or that person. It may be granted that some people resist the force and that it has its way with others. Actually our conception merely adds social forces to physical, chemical, biological and psychological forces, which act upon men from without. If the latter do not preclude human freedom, the former need not. The question assumes the same terms for both. When an epidemic centre appears, its intensity predetermines the rate of mortality it will cause, but those who will be infected are not designated by this fact. Such is the situation of victims of suicide with reference to suicidogenetic currents.[41]

19

The normal state

> Until Broussais, the pathological state obeyed laws completely
> different from those governing the normal state, so that observation
> of one could decide nothing for the other. Broussais established that
> the phenomena of disease are of essentially the same kind as those
> of health, from which they differed only in intensity.
>
> The collective organism, because of its greater degree of
> complexity, is liable to problems more serious, varied and frequent
> than those of the individual organism. I do not hesitate to state that
> Broussais's principle must be extended in that direction, and I have
> often applied it there to confirm or perfect sociological laws. But
> those who would apply the analysis of Revolutions to the Positive
> study of Society must pass through the logical training given by the
> simpler phenomena of Biology.*[1]

Normality is like determinism, both timeless and dated, an idea that in
some sense has been with us always, but which can in a moment adopt a
completely new form of life. As a word, 'determinism' came into use in the
1780s, and assumed its present most common meaning in the 1850s. As a
word, 'normal' is much older, but it acquired its present most common
meaning only in the 1820s. Now although the two words are conspirators
in the taming of chance, they enter in very different ways. The normal was
one of a pair. Its opposite was the pathological and for a short time its
domain was chiefly medical. Then it moved into the sphere of – almost
everything. People, behaviour, states of affairs, diplomatic relations,
molecules: all these may be normal or abnormal. The word became
indispensable because it created a way to be 'objective' about human
beings. The word is also like a faithful retainer, a voice from the past. It
uses a power as old as Aristotle to bridge the fact/value distinction,
whispering in your ear that what is normal is also all right. But also, in the

---

* Auguste Comte, in the first volume of his *Système de politique positive* (1851). Broussais
  was used in chapter 10 to illustrate the first statistical tests of medical treatment. Georges
  Canguilhem, to whom the present discussion is indebted, calls Broussais's principle (and
  its physiological trappings) a 'thesis whose fortune certainly owed more to the personality
  of the author than to the coherence of his text'.

events to be described, it became a soothsayer, teller of the future, of progress and ends. Normality is a vastly more important idea than determinism, but they are not unrelated. A story of the erosion of determinism is also an account of the invention of normalcy.

'Normal' bears the stamp of the nineteenth century and its conception of progress, just as 'human nature' is engraved with the hallmark of the Enlightenment. We no longer ask, in all seriousness, what is human nature? Instead we talk about normal people. We ask, is this behaviour normal? Is it normal for an eight-year-old girl to ...? Research foundations are awash with funds for finding out what is normal. Rare is the patron who wants someone to investigate human nature. We have almost forgotten how to take human nature seriously. When a man is corrupt or careless, we say, 'Oh, that's human nature.' 'You can't go against human nature,' we mutter, indifferently.

When was the last great debate involving human nature? 1829. In those days a controversy in part about human nature could thrust a young man into prominence, create his career at a stroke, seat him in a powerful legislature, and leave him in a position to be one of the handful of most widely known intellectuals for the rest of his prodigious life. I refer to Macaulay's celebrated assault on James Mill. Of course I exaggerate. Macaulay had a lot going for him, and his opinions about human nature were only one of his vehicles. My point is that they could be such a vehicle at all.

Mill and Macaulay faced off, Macaulay in the pages of the *Edinburgh Review*, Mill in the *Westminster Review*.[2] Macaulay thundered at Mill because he ventured to speak about human nature without ever considering what people actually do. Mill's *Essay on Government* for the *Supplement* to the fifth edition of the *Encyclopaedia Britannica* was published repeatedly in various pamphlets and books in the early 1820s.[3] This utilitarian tract was met by fiery eloquence:

Mr Mill [wrote Macaulay] is an Aristotelian of the fifteenth century, born out of due season. We have here an elaborate treatise on Government, from which, but for two or three passing allusions, it would not appear that any governments actually existed among men. Certain propensities of Human Nature are assumed; and from these premises the whole science of Politics is synthetically deduced![4]

Mill: 'from what else [but human nature] *should* it be deduced?'[5]

This debate, conducted in the great reviews of the day, was a focus of opinion for a decade. It is almost inconceivable that the same thing should happen today. Or is it? One thinks of E.O. Wilson *On Human Nature*.[6] The great sociobiology debate also began in one of the great reviews.[7] Some idea of human nature is deep, not in human nature, but in our memories, a spark ready to kindle yet another new morality or metaphysics. I cannot so blithely say that it has been smothered by the idea of normality.

But despite Wilson's ironic title, the phrase 'human nature' was not integral to the sociology debate, whereas normal behaviour regularly appeared as a key concept. It was quite the opposite in 1829–30. Macaulay observed that 'it is the grossest ignorance of human nature to suppose that another man calculates the chances differently from us, merely because he does what, in his place, we should not do'.[8] He then recited the most extravagant choices. Mill responded by quoting Macaulay in full. He urged that strange tastes may be corrected by education. 'A given Greenlander may not be persuaded out of his train oil; but it might be possible to lay the foundations for persuading some future Greenlander, that claret is the better of the two.'[9] We have no difficulty understanding the issues, nor in recognizing Mill's bland utilitarian self-confidence in his own values, but something was absent. Today someone would at once start talking about normal tastes and deviant excesses, a conception that simply did not occur in this debate, filled as it was with monsters such as Caligula rather than deviations from the mean. That was hardly possible then, for the word 'normal' had not yet acquired its present sense. It did that exactly when these final fireworks of 'human nature' splashed across the sky. The first meaning of 'normal' given in any current English dictionary is something like 'usual, regular, common, typical'. The *OED* says that this usage became current after 1840, and gives 1828 for its first citation of 'normal or typical'. That was in a work of natural history alluding to French writers.[10]

It is indeed to the French that we must look. Americans know the odd expression 'normal school' for a teachers' college. The first Ecole normale was established by a decree of 7 brumaire, year III of the Revolution. The neologism was explained in a speech 5 days before, on 28 October 1794: such schools should be 'le type et règle de toutes les autres'. The speaker was Joseph Lakanal, the man who, between 1793 and 1795, had the power to enact many of the plans for education conceived by Condorcet. It was not education, however, that furnished the modern sense of the word 'normal', but the study of life, as the *OED* citation suggests. Biology and medicine did the trick, abetted by Auguste Comte's radical extension of the idea, and Balzac's popularization of the word in satirizing the doctors. The original site of the modern sense of the word 'normal' was, as in my epigraph, the phrase 'normal state' (of an organism, paired with 'pathological state').

But let us start with older senses of 'normal'. The word entered modern European languages as soon as geometry was expressed in the vernacular. It meant perpendicular, at right angles, orthogonal. *Norma* is Latin, meaning a T-square. Normal and orthogonal are synonyms in geometry; normal and ortho- go together as Latin to Greek. Norm/ortho has thereby a great power. On the one hand the words are descriptive. A line may be orthogonal or normal (at right angles to the tangent of a circle, say) or not. That is a description of the line. But the evaluative 'right' lurks in the background of right angles. It is just a fact that an angle is a right angle, but it is also a 'right' angle, a good one. Orthodontists straighten the teeth of children; they make the crooked straight. But they also put the teeth right, make them better. Orthopaedic surgeons straighten bones. Orthopsychiatry is the study of mental disorders chiefly in children. It aims at making the child – normal. The orthodox conform to certain standards, which used to be a good thing.

One can, then, use the word 'normal' to say how things are, but also to say how they ought to be. The magic of the word is that we can use it to do both things at once. The norm may be what is usual or typical, yet our most powerful ethical constraints are also called norms. According to the *Dictionary*, the word 'norm' in this sense of the stern moralists is even more recent than the use of 'normal' to mean usual or typical.

Nothing is more commonplace than the distinction between fact and value. From the beginning of our language the word 'normal' has been dancing and prancing all over it. Moralists seldom notice that. The word 'normal' is like that baneful Californian shrub, poison oak, which assumes whatever form resembles the environment. Now it is a creeper, crawling close to the earth, now a pleasant round bush five metres high, now a vine encircling a madrone and then trailing from a branch 40 metres above the ground; now it is red, now it is green, now it is leafless but the sap is running and itching to attack. It has been said of Emile Durkheim, whose idea of normal and pathological societies is the topic of my next chapter, that he tried to achieve 'the closure between the "is" and the "ought" . . . in terms of his distinction between the "normal" and the "pathological".' 'No aspect of Durkheim's writings has been more universally rejected than his notion of normality and pathology, and rightly so.'[11] Rejected in specifics, yes. But for much of the century before Durkheim, and ever since, we have regularly used 'normal' to close the gap between 'is' and 'ought'. Wrongly so, perhaps, but that is what the concept of normality does for us.

The normal is average. We also use the word 'mean' for the average of a Normal distribution. What in English became the average man is in French *l'homme moyen*, institutionalized by Quetelet. Doesn't this idea of the mean go back to Aristotle? Yes, but beware. The mean is almost as playful as the normal. The idea of a mean or intermediate (that's a description) which is excellent (an evaluation) is one of the most familiar of Aristotle's teachings. He did not have the is/ought hangups inculcated by Hume. The golden mean (as the phrase is commonly understood) is golden (good) and lies (as a matter of fact) between extremes. Aristotle was subtle and careful. He wrote, 'Virtue is a mean between two vices, one of excess and one of deficiency.'[12] Then something less easy to construe: 'As far as its substance and the account stating its essence are concerned, virtue is a mean; but as far as the best and the good are concerned, it is an extremity.'

Aristotle explicitly restricted the application of the concept of a mean, because it is an excellence that contrasts with excess or deficiency. Not all mid-points are means. Spite and adultery, he taught, are in themselves base, and not base because of excess or deficiency. Hence they admit of no mean. The same is true for excellences such as temperance and courage. As I read Aristotle, intellectual powers such as intelligence cannot be characterized by a mean, precisely because they are virtues. His conception of the mean is thus radically different from that of a century that defines degree of intelligence by a Normal distribution with a mean scaled at 100.

That does not imply that Greek notions have had no effect on the idea of the normal. They have, and nowhere is this more plain than in the case of medicine. It is an old idea that health is a mean between excesses and deficiencies, between heat and cold, for example. Health as the mean – no mere average, but not unconnected to the modes and medians distinguished by later statisticians – was part of the old medicine. On it was superimposed the idea of pathological organs. The concept of the pathological sounds, at first hearing, as old as illness itself, but it underwent a substantial mutation a little before 1800. Disease became an attribute not of the whole body but of individual organs. Pathology became the study of unhealthy organs rather than sick people. One could investigate them in part by the chemistry of the secretions of living beings – urine, for example. For the pathologist the normal came into being as the inverse of this concept. Something was normal when it was not associated with a pathological organ. Thus far the normal would be secondary, defined as the opposite of the primary notion, the pathological. But then what Comte called the great 'principle' of Broussais turned this around. The pathological was defined as deviation from the normal. All variation was characterized in terms of variation from the normal state. In Comte's opinion, Broussais's principle was the completion of a principle of continuity that Comte attributed to d'Alembert (he might better have chosen Leibniz). Note the two parts of this 'principle': (a) pathology is not different in kind from the normal; 'nature makes no jumps' but passes from the normal to the pathological continuously. (b) The normal is the centre from which deviation departs.

Of course there were ever so many nonmedical routes to the normal.

The industrializing world demanded standardization. We recall Babbage and the constants of nature and art, as enumerated in chapter 7. He hardly distinguished standards of art that are imposed by engineers from constants and norms that are to be recorded from nature. Nor is the role of quartermasters during the Napoleonic campaigns to be forgotten. They ordered and moved vast quantities of stores in order to feed and equip prodigious numbers of men and animals. They needed standardized units of everything to run their shows efficiently. Modules had not yet been invented, but were a twinkle in the eye of every keen staff officer. Nor need one wait for revolution or Napoleon. Canguilhem remarks that 'The article on "gun-carriage" in the *Encyclopédie* of Diderot and d'Alembert, revised by the Royal Artillery Corps, admirably sets forth the motifs of normalization of work in arsenals ... Here we have the thing without the word.'[13]

The new martial arts and crafts made warfare increasingly a matter of machines that cried out for standards. Finlaison, the National Actuary of chapter 6 who doubted that there was a quantum of sickness, made his mark running naval dockyards. He turned them from financial catastrophes into cost-efficient enterprises. He imposed standardization, normalization – and wrongly thought that you could not do that with sickness. He failed to see what the next generation, that of William Farr and the like, would do with disease. Do I seem to be hopping haphazardly from ships of the line to the sickness of labourers? It was Finlaison himself who changed jobs by way of promotion from manager of HM Dockyards to directing the national health and its correlate, the national debt acquired by improvidently selling annuities.

The idea of norms and standards must have been irresistible, but our modern usage of the very word 'normal' evolved in a medical context. This mattered. Standards are standards, and are met or not met. There is no continuous passage away from the norm – or if there is, it is to be corrected, the contractor reprimanded, the workman dismissed. The idea of continuous deviation from the normal came from pathology, as interpreted by Auguste Comte. His biomedical hero was F.-J.-V. Broussais, to whom he attributed what he called 'the law of variability'.[14] He made it a basis for social science and it became part of his political agenda.

As we have seen in chapter 10, Broussais was the 'physiologist', the radical proponent of the new organic theory of disease. The task of physiological medicine is to determine how 'excitation can deviate from the normal state and constitute an abnormal or diseased state'.[15] But a diseased state simply is an irritated tissue or organ, which is nothing other than 'a normal excitation that has been transformed by an excess.'[16] When one is sick, some irritant has made natural 'phenomena more or less pronounced than they are in the normal state'.[17] Broussais's sentences here sound ordinary enough (unlike some strange ones I quoted in chapter 10). We do not notice that the word 'normal' is being used here, in this way, for pretty well the first time.

Balzac often made fun of Broussais.[18] I believe that it may be through Balzac that Broussais's technical term 'normal state' – denoting the noninflamed, nonirritated state of an organ or a tissue – entered common language. Historical dictionaries of the French language commonly attribute the first general usage of 'normal' meaning 'typical' to Balzac or to Comte, always embedded in the phrase 'normal state'. Thus, in *Eugénie Grandet* of 1833, Mlle d'Aubrion had a nose that was too long, big at the end, and which was 'yellowish in the normal state, but completely red after dinner, a sort of plant-like phenomenon'.[19] A nose, an organ, was *flavescent* (the medical-sounding adjective that Balzac appears to have invented for just this sentence). The symptoms are precisely of the sort studied by Broussais. In due course, for example in *La Cousine Bette* of 1847, the 'normal state' would be given a more general usage, as when laziness is called the normal state of artists.[20]

Broussais's 'normal state' might have made its way into language unattended, but it was the enthusiasm of Comte that gave it elevation and status. The idea that the pathological is not radically different from the normal, but only an extension of the variation proper to a 'normal organism', was, he wrote, an 'eminently philosophical principle whose definitive establishment we owe to the bold and persevering genius of our illustrious fellow citizen, Broussais'.[21] The important point was that all the characteristics of a thing were defined relative to the normal state. Explicitly: 'The law of Broussais subordinates all modifications to the normal state.'[22] Broussais wrote of physiology, but his principle must be extended to 'intellectual and moral functions' – and then, as my epigraph continues, to the whole study of society.

Those sentences, with their rapt admiration for Broussais, were published in 1851, by which time, if the doctor was remembered at all by the public, it was as a conceited curmudgeon. Comte did not know Broussais specially well; his good friend in the physiological school of medicine was the much more reputable and far less mercurial Blainville, protégé of Cuvier and successor to Lamarck.[23] (We need hardly mention that the Lamarckian model of evolution by continuous variation also hovers in the background of Broussais's principle.)

Why was Comte so loyal to Broussais? It is well known how on 2 April 1826 he commenced, with some fanfare, the course of lectures intended to be the exposition of all knowledge preparatory to the new positive age: the lectures that became the *Cours de philosophie positive*. He broke down.

The lecture for 12 April was cancelled. In uncontrollable depression, he consigned himself to the care of Esquirol, who released him on 2 December with a docket, 'Not cured'. He got better, despite concerted attempts by his family and friends.*[24] The lectures resumed on 4 January 1829, and the learned world did not spite him. In attendance were Broussais, Blainville, Fourier, Navier and Poinsot, not to mention his alienist, Esquirol.[25]

The one intellectual achievement of his convalescence was a short review of Broussais's *De l'irritation et de la folie*, published in mid-August 1828.[26] When Comte reprinted it in 1853, he noted that it had been written while recovering from his 'cerebral attack' (an attack on an organ, not the mind), saying that 'the insight gained through my personal experience was utilized in this review of the memorable work in which Broussais worthily combatted the metaphysical influence'.[27]

Comte valued Broussais for several reasons. One was as ally against the 'metaphysical influence', i.e. Germanic importations with claims to a spiritual psychology. A powerful force for evil (as seen by Comte) was Victor Cousin, neo-Kantian, neo-Platonist, neo-royalist, a man all in favour of things spiritual. In May 1828 Cousin had completed a threateningly successful course of lectures on the new philosophy, and Broussais's book was in part an onslaught upon it.

The opposition to Cousin was a curious alliance of materialists who might, in 1828, have been characterized by their enemies as the mad Comte, the sadistic Broussais and the last of the doddering *idéologues* – none other than Daunou, who began my chapter 5 inaugurating moral science, who had preached the sermon for those who died attacking the Bastille. In 1828 he was denouncing Cousin as a theosophical gnostic, who would corrupt the republic into reaction and would 'plunge the human race into darkness'.[28] After the Revolution of 1830, he was, with that same splendid oratory, denouncing the young professors who had 'seconded the violence' of 'despotic governments'.[29]

A more personal element in Comte's lifelong dedication to Broussais was the explanation of his own breakdown in material terms. He had been sometimes violent, sometimes silent in the slough of despond, but all that

---

* Once again, a standard tale may be repeated on grounds of verisimilitude rather than proven truth. The populist theocratic priest Félicité de Lamennais convinced Comte's mother that her son should endure a religious marriage ceremony to his wretched first wife. This farce was duly performed, although the groom was 'raving mad' at the time. Not that Esquirol's asylum was better: Comte wrote that had Broussais studied asylums himself,

  he would have been convinced that, despite the promises of their directors, the entire intellectual and moral portion of the treatment is in fact abandoned to the arbitrary action of subordinates and rough agents, whose conduct almost always aggravates the malady that they should be trying to cure.

was just variation from his normal state produced by irritation and infla-
mation of the tissues. It was not his *fault*. We use variation from the
normal today in order to relieve a sense of responsibility. Comte seized
upon normality because it possessed that saving virtue.

Cured, he translated normality to the social sphere. Hitherto pathology
'had persisted in representing the majority of important diseases as
independent of any change in the normal state of the organs'. Broussais
made it a matter of degree. What was true of Comte's depression – it was a
deviation from the norm caused by perturbation – would henceforth be
true of social illness too. But when Comte moved normality to the political
sphere, he effected another twist. The normal ceased to be the ordinary
healthy state; it became the purified state to which we should strive, and to
which our energies are tending. In short, progress and the normal state
became inextricably linked. Consider that eminently political science,
biology. Impressed by Bichat's physiology, and deploring recent trends,
Comte wrote around 1850 that 'Biology is now less close to its normal
state than it was at the beginning of the century.'[30] The normal state of
biology was what it ought to be, and what with enough progress it would
achieve. 'Progress is nothing but the development of order: it is an analysis
of the normal state.'

Positivism did not, in Comte's late years, direct us to an existing norm,
and certainly not to an average. It was the only politically viable road to
the 'true normal state'. 'The positive spirit [is] the only possible basis for a
resolution of the intellectual and moral anarchy that above all characterizes
the great crisis of our time ... The positive school was gradually prepared,
during the revolutionary struggle of the past three centuries, to constitute
as much as is possible the true normal state of all the classes and elements'
of knowledge and of society.[31]

Comte thus expressed and to some extent invented a fundamental
tension in the idea of the normal – the normal as existing average, and the
normal as figure of perfection to which we may progress. This is an even
richer source of hidden power than the fact/value ambiguity that had
always been present in the idea of the normal. The tension makes itself felt
in different ways. If we think ahead to sociology and to statistics, in the
modern comprehension of those terms – that is, if we think ahead to the
work encrusted around names such as Durkheim and Galton – we feel the
tension acutely.

On the one hand there is the thought that the normal is what is right, so
that talk of the normal is a splendid way of preserving or returning to the
status quo. That's 'Durkheim'. On the other hand is the idea that the
normal is only average, and so is something to be improved upon. That's

'Galton'. Durkheim called deviation from the norm pathology, while Galton saw excellence at one extreme of the Normal distribution.

'Galton' stands for improving averages, by whatever standards of value can be taken for granted. When it is a matter of living beings, that translates into eugenics. There we first focus on the Queteletian mean and then surpass it. 'Durkheim' harks back to the Aristotelian mean, for it is the ideal state of good health. For the conservative Durkheim, writing of normal and pathological states of society, the normal tends to be something from which we have fallen. For Comte's revolutionary positivism, it was something for which we should strive.

The tension in these aspects of the normal will not dissolve just by noting that there are two ideas, one of preservation, one of amelioration. The former carries within it fondness for origins, youthful good health, an ideal condition to which we should be restored. The latter lusts after teleology, of ends that we may choose for the perfection of ourselves or of the race. Two kinds of progress. Words have profound memories that oil our shrill and squeaky rhetoric. The normal stands indifferently for what is typical, the unenthusiastic objective average, but it also stands for what has been, good health, and for what shall be, our chosen destiny. That is why the benign and sterile-sounding word 'normal' has become one of the most powerful ideological tools of the twentieth century.

20

As real as cosmic forces

> To tell the truth, we do not possess a criterion that allows us to measure exactly the degree of happiness of a society. But it is possible to estimate comparatively the state of health or disease in which it finds itself, for we have at our disposal a well known fact that translates social malaise into figures: namely the relative number of suicides ... In order that these abnormal acts should increase, it is necessary that the occasions of suffering should also increase, and that at the same time the force of resistance of the organism should be decreased. One can thus be assured that societies where suicides are most frequent are less healthy than those where they are more rare.*[1]

This switch from health to disease had been prefigured in the early days. In 1799 Sir John Sinclair had wanted to measure the 'quantum of happiness', but by 1825 legislators were trying to determine the 'quantum of sickness'. Durkheim's first study of suicide neatly draws together these and later strands: happiness/health, normal/abnormal, and the medical model of suicide. Condorcet's moral science had been turned into empirical investigation, but the adjective 'moral' had not yet been hidden from view. The paper was subtitled 'a study of moral statistics'. Five years later, Durkheim's first book announced, on its first page, that it was 'an attempt to study the facts of moral life according to the method of the positive sciences ... We do not wish to extract a morality from science, but to practise the science of morality.'[2]

The present chapter is not an exposition of the roots of Durkheim's early sociology, any more than the next one is a systematic account of Galton's contributions to statistics. The aims are fourfold. First, to confirm that Durkheim's conception of the normal state of society is part of the discourse of Comte and physiology. Secondly, to locate it in another

* From Emile Durkheim's first published research paper, on suicide and the birth rate, published in 1888. During the preceding three years he had been writing an important series of review essays surveying the state of work in sociology, mostly published in Pierre Janet's *Revue Philosophique*. In 1887 he had been called to Bordeaux to teach sociology. The topic of his 1889–90 course was suicide.

discussion, criminal anthropology. Thirdly, to show how a new layer of 'reality' was being added to statistical facts. Finally I shall develop the essential tension in the idea of normality, a tension between the figure whom we call 'Durkheim' and the one we call 'Galton'. Rather than thinking that it is just an accident that both Durkheim and Galton made much use of the word 'normal' seemingly in different senses, I argue that it illustrates the core of our conception of the normal.

Durkheim was keen on using statistical data as indices of happiness and abnormality. That culminated nicely in the theory of *anomie* pressed in *Suicide* of 1897. But the development was not as straightforward as might be suggested by my epigraph. For two ideas were intertwined in Durkheim's early work: normality and functionalism. To ignore the latter is to fail to grasp what he was doing to the normal itself. Durkheim advocated and perhaps invented functional explanation of social phenomena, in which one explains a social practice by showing that, unknown to those who engage in it, it helps keep the society in existence.[3] Durkheim's first book, the 1893 *Division of Labour*, proposed a functional explanation for the division of labour in industrial society.

Functional explanations commonly explain the 'obvious'. The division of labour seems to arise naturally enough, and to need no explanation. The manufacturer who owns the mills, and the insurance company that directs its clerks and its collectors of premiums, have plenty of inducements for specializing their labour force. Economists from Adam Smith onwards had explained how division increases wealth. Isn't that enough? Not for Durkheim. He argued that a modern society would disintegrate without the division of labour. That is why it persists. Without it the centrifugal forces present in modern society would make it fly apart. Unknown to us, this very practice creates the bonds that join us together. A fundamental ethical problem was thereby solved: 'since the division of labour becomes the chief source of social solidarity, it becomes at the same time the foundation of the moral order'.[4]

I would like to disentangle not only the political resonances of Durkheim's thesis but also the functional explanation from the normal/ pathological part of Durkheim's early work. I can't. The introduction to the first edition of *Division* was an essay on the normal, rich in allusion to physiology. Why should so bold an attempt at functional explanation start by talk of physiology? Because Durkheim had to show that the division of labour is normal. How can one tell whether a social phenomenon is normal or morbid? 'The question does not differ essentially from the one the biologist asks when he seeks to separate the sphere of normal physiology from that of pathological physiology.'[5]

In expanding the idea, Durkheim revealed how much of the Queteletian average had been incorporated (over Comte's dead body) into the Comte-Broussais theory of the normal. The physiologist, wrote Durkheim, calls normal what is found in the average of the species. The average is to be understood as 'the central dense mass' that may be represented by a single number 'because all those in the average region may be represented by the one around which they gravitate'.* After ascribing this technique to physiology, Durkheim continued: 'The same method must be followed in ethics. A moral fact is normal for a determined social type when it is observed in the average of that species; it is pathological in antithetical circumstances.'

The 1888 connection between suicide rate, birth rate and happiness was of a piece with most biopolitics of the past two centuries. Durkheim took it for granted that France's relatively low birth rate was bad for France. He had absorbed the connection between infecundity and degeneracy. But he noted a gap in reasoning. Utilitarian economists judged the success of an economic policy in terms of the production of happiness for a large number of people. They also modelled the effects of population growth on the state of the economy. They assumed that an increase in the population of France – especially vis-à-vis Germany and England – would produce greater wealth and hence greater happiness for the French people. This placid prejudice demanded argument, or so Durkheim thought. But how could one measure the happiness of a people?

Not by wealth but by health. We can 'be assured that societies in which suicide is more frequent are less healthy than those where it is more rare'. So runs my epigraph; the passage continued: 'We thus have a method for dealing with the controversial problem of population.' The inverse correlation between fecundity and suicide was not spurious. 'Married people are less exposed to suicide than celibates, and likewise the fathers of families than husbands without children'.[6] Where the family is strong, where domestic traditions are rich, suicide is less frequent. Note that suicide is like a disease: people are 'exposed' to it, like the smallpox. 'All weakening of the birth rate implies a weakening in domestic sentiment; we have just seen that this last gives rise to suicide.' Suicide, then, is 'an index of the state of health of societies'.[7]

There was also the idea that what is normal in a society is indicated by an average, which in turn is a mark of what is right. This thought rides

* Should one bother unpacking Durkheim's awful metaphors? Maybe this one is instructive. If we take the talk of mass and gravity seriously, then the mean is the point about which *all* the mass gravitates, not just that in the average dense region. At this juncture Durkheim was trying to fight Comte and to fight Broussais's principle, by holding that only elements in the average region (the normal region) gravitated around the mean, leaving room for pathological states, or outliers, which are discontinuous with the normal – contrary to Broussais (and to mechanics!). Durkheim changed his mind in 1893–4; he deleted this Introduction from the second printing of *Division*.

poorly with the previous one. Suicide rates are averages, and thus ought to indicate what is normal, and hence good conduct. Medical comparisons may clarify the matter. Something may be an index of evil but at the same time may have a function. 'Pain is commonly regarded by laymen as the index of morbidity', but pain is essential.[8] It is not a morbid phenomenon properly speaking. Is suicide? If not, could the solution urged in the 1888 'Suicide and the Birth Rate' be allowed to stand? How could one combine suicide as the mark of morbidity with averages as defining normality?

The problem was made pressing by Durkheim's reflections on crime, the topic for his lectures at Bordeaux 1892/3 and 1893/4.[9] In the course of them he changed his mind about whether crime is normal: that is, he changed his mind between the 1893 *Division of Labour* and the 1894 *Rules of Sociological Method*. In the former he began a chapter on the anomic division of labour by saying that 'the study of deviant forms permits us to better determine the conditions for the existence of the normal'.[10] But do not think that we should include in 'the division of labour the profession of the criminal and the other noxious professions. They are the negation of solidarity ... this is not a case of the division of labour, but one of differentiation pure and simple.' 'The differentiation that disintegrates (cancer, microbe, criminal) is altogether different from that which concentrates the vital forces (division of labour).'[11] Crime, in short, was pathological, disintegrating, while the division of labour was normal, concentrating the vital forces. Notice that this contravened Broussais's principle: the pathological was not here a modification of the normal but something different in kind from it.

Next year he observed that 'if there is any fact whose pathological character appears incontestable, that fact is crime' – but that is only appearance.[12] Less crime would be a sign of trouble. 'There is no occasion for self-congratulation when the crime rate drops noticeably below the average level, for we may be certain that this apparent progress is associated with some social disorder.'[13] We must understand the function of crime. It is whatever offends against the fundamental principles of conduct. A community of saints would always have crime, because in human nature there would always be some variation from conformity, and such variation would constitute infraction of saintly custom, and hence crime. 'Criminality disappearing under one form, reappears in another. From which it follows that it is a contradiction to conceive of a society without crime.'[14] Exactly: this was a conceptual, not an empirical assertion. A society requires fundamental principles in order to be coherent, in order not to fall apart. A principle of conduct will stay in place only if it is offended against. Without infractions principles would lose their force and society would lose its bonds. Thus crime – understood not as what we call crime, but simply as whatever is repressed in a society -- is essential for the preservation of society. Thus the claim that crime is normal was part of a functional explanation of crime.

Here we see two quite distinct ways in which Durkheim understood the normal. One was functional, one not. In the former a normal phenomenon 'is bound up with the general conditions of collective life of the social type'.[15] The nonfunctional version regarded a phenomenon as normal for a society of a given kind 'when it is present in the average society of that species at the corresponding phase of its evolution'.[16] He enjoined us to apply the functional criterion for normality to a 'social species' that has not yet reached the full course of its evolution.[17]

Was crime normal? No in 1893, yes in 1894. The 'error', said Durkheim, had resulted from not applying the rules of sociological method.[18] That was his explanation of a change of mind. But we can hardly understand Durkheim's switch without recalling one of the greatest debates of the day. The discourse in which to locate his use of the word 'normal' is that of criminal anthropology. The criminal anthropologists of the Italian school held that criminals are different in kind from normal people. Few French writers agreed by the 1890s, but there remained the question whether crime could be part of a normal society. That was what vexed Durkheim in the course of his lectures during 1892–4.

Criminal anthropology had many roots, including both phrenology and the work of Paul Broca, but it was established or reestablished with vigour in 1876, with the publication of Cesare Lombroso's book on 'criminal man'.[19] It was a self-proclaimed positive science – which in Italy mostly meant strict adherence to Charles Darwin and Herbert Spencer. It was built around the concepts of the normal and the abnormal. Lombroso began with a vivid conjecture that came to him while doing a post-mortem on a notorious bandit with an ape-like skull. 'At the sight of the skull, I seemed to see all of a sudden lighted up as a vast plain under a flaming sky, the problem of the nature of the criminal – an atavistic being who reproduces in his person the ferocious instincts of primitive humanity and the inferior animals.'[20]

Flushed with Darwin, Lombroso concluded that criminals are born, not made. They are throwbacks to our caveman or monkey past. This fact was proven by anthropometry practised in jails. The state gladly provided the results of beheadings.[21] To these empirical studies Lombroso added the observation that criminals are often epileptic. He deduced that epilepsy is also atavistic. This is confirmed by the fact that criminals are epileptoid. Abnormality had a scientific basis. Criminals were a race apart.

The topic took hold in France. By and large the French authors favoured sociological over anthropological theories of crime. The first

Congress of Criminal Anthropology was held in Rome in 1885, the second
in Paris in 1889. A mighty battle was waged. Such was the hostility that
met the Italian school in Paris that it boycotted the third Congress in Brussels in 1892. This had the consequence, as the French summary innocently put it, that 'the success of of the Congress at Brussels exceeded all
expectations', and included among its results 'the complete disappearance
of the criminal type, [viz.] Lombroso's born criminal'.[22] Now the criminal
man, the atavistic throwback, had been completely discontinuous with
normal people. To abolish him was to restore Broussais's principle, and to
make crime a mere deviation from normalcy. This 'result' of the congress
parallels Durkheim's change of opinion about the phenomenon of crime.

It is difficult for us to grasp the wild fluctuations in opinion that were
then possible. It may help to have a map of criminology contemporary
with Durkheim's lectures. In 1896 Enrico Ferri, follower of Lombroso
and later head of the Italian socialist party, drew up a typology of theories
about crime, built around the poles of normality and abnormality.[23]
Durkheim had just published the *Rules*. It will be seen that he is slotted in
at (1b). Using just the surnames in this chart, one can reconstruct a bibliography for a course of lectures on criminal sociology.[24]

Crime is a:
1   normal phenomenon that is (a) biological (Albrecht)
                      or (b) social (Durkheim)
2   a biological abnormality due to
      (a) atavism, which is (i) organic and psychic (Lombroso)
                      or (ii) psychic only (Colajanni)
      (b) pathology in the form of
          (i) Neurosis (Dally, Minzloff, Maudsley, Virgilio, Jelgersma,
          Bleuler)
          (ii) neurasthenia (Benedikt, Liszt, Vargha)
          (iii) epilepsy (Lombroso, Lewis, Roncaroni)
      (c) a defect of nutrition in the central nervous system (Marro)
      (d) a defect of development of the inhibitory centres (Bonfigli)
      (e) moral anomaly (Despine, Garofalo)
3   a social abnormality due to,
      (a) economic influences (Turati, Bataglia, Loria)
      (b) juridical unadaptability (Vaccaro)
      (c) complex social influences (Lacassagne, Colajanni, Prins, Tarde,
      Topinard, Manouvrier, Raux, Baer, Kirn, Gumplowicz)

The idea of normality was central to the classification and to the texts; it
was not rare even in titles: an example is an 1893 essay of Lombroso's,
Delinquent, Prostitute and Normal Women. This is the ferment in which

Durkheim's idea of the normal and the pathological was brewed. Did Durkheim argue in 1894 that crime had a function in maintaining a society? Lombroso followed up that lead immediately, with an essay on the benefits of crime.[25]

This is not to say that Durkheim willingly played any part in criminal anthropology. He made a few scathing references to Lombroso. He also noted sardonically that although 'there is no society where the rule does not exist that the punishment must be proportional to the offence; yet, for the Italian school, this principle is but an invention of jurists ... the entire penal system, as it has functioned until the present day among all known peoples, is a phenomenon contrary to nature'.[26] He here referred to Raffaele Garofalo (2e), whose book on criminology had been published in French translation in 1891.

Garofalo's work was entirely structured around the normal/abnormal poles. Durkheim noted that he 'has tried to distinguish the morbid from the abnormal', contrary to Durkheim's physiological model, which identified the abnormal with the pathological.[27] Garofalo's position (ill-stated in Durkheim's rebuttal) was that there are two types of criminals, comparable to the colour-blind person and the blind person. Truly violent criminals are blind. The rest, (a trio composed of the murderers and those who assault persons, the thieves and those who take property, and the 'cynics' whose crimes are sexual in nature) are like the colour blind; they suffer from 'moral Daltonism'. They can't tell the difference between good and bad, and hence suffer from moral anomaly. But this anomaly, Garofalo argued, is not a pathology or type of infirmity or morbidity; it is an ethical regression through retrogressive selection.

Durkheim's change of mind about the normality of crime was part of the reaction of French sociologists to Italian criminal anthropology. It was also a return to Comtian origins. The pathology of crime was only a modification, which came in degrees, of the normal state of a society. It thereby became possible to use an index of modification as an index of the health or morbidity of a society. The original programme of the 1888 'Suicide and the birth rate' was once again made legitimate. Thus Durkheim, in wrestling with crime while lecturing on criminal sociology, was not only producing 'rules of sociological method': he was also resolving his doubts about his original research programme, and thus gearing himself up to write *Suicide*.

Suicide, like crime, was quickly declared part of the normal state. 'At any rate, it is certain that suicidogenetic currents of different intensity, depending on the historical period, have always existed among the peoples of Europe; statistics had proved this ever since the last century, and juridical monuments prove it for earlier periods. Suicide is therefore an element of their social constitution and even, probably, of any social constitution.'[28] (There followed an especially feeble functionalist discussion. Would Durkheim really have thought that if, as with crime, people stopped killing themselves, this would be a sign of some incipient breakdown in society?)

Suicide is normal, but increases in the suicide rate can indicate morbidity. Now we can proceed to the issue of causation. What produces stable averages, be they the norm for a society of a given type, or pathologically deviant averages such as excessive suicide rates? It would be something collective, something greater than Quetelet's little independent causes operating at the level of individual psychology. We've noticed Durkheim's penchant for mixing metaphors. There was cosmology: the social forces acting on individuals were comparable to cosmic forces like gravity. There was medicine: suicide is a disease striking, epidemic-like, at a community, better resisted by some than by others. There was electricity (or fluid dynamics?): 'suicidogenetic currents'.

The cause of suicide rates would be collective. I concluded chapter 18 with Durkheim's debt to Boutroux and Renouvier. From them he learned well that the whole is greater than the part. The laws of sociology must be *sui generis*, a tag that I there quoted three times in a paragraph. It is wrong completely to separate out the 'functionalist' parts of this opinion, but Durkheim's idea of autonomous laws that produce statistical regularities can often be read in a nonfunctional way.

Collective tendencies have a reality of their own; they are forces as real as cosmic forces, though of another sort; they, likewise, affect the individual from without, though through other channels. The proof that the reality of collective tendencies is no less than that of cosmic forces is that this reality is demonstrated in the same way, by the uniformity of effects.[29]

Durkheim's collective forces were untainted by indeterminism or even chance: they were agents that necessarily produced stable chance phenomena. They were nevertheless described by a new kind of law of collective phenomena, a law endowed with its own 'reality'. Quetelet had made the mean of a population as 'real' as the position of an island or a star. At the time of Durkheim, the laws of deviation from the normal themselves became part of reality. But unlike Galton he did not think that the laws were themselves statistical. It was Galton who led us to the autonomy of statistical laws, in a sense that I shall define precisely in terms of explanatory power.

Galton could not accept the view of Quetelet and others that the Normal curve was the product of myriad independent petty causes. Nor could Durkheim, although he had nothing like Galton's savvy about the failure of that idea.[*][30] He did criticize Quetelet's idea of the average man.[31] The average man could not be the intervening variable that somehow accounted for statistical stability. It is commonly said that Durkheim refuted Quetelet and surpassed him. Not at all – for all his bitter critique he stayed in the Queteletian mould. (Galton had no need to be bitter about Quetelet because he did surpass him.) The reason why there must be cosmic forces acting upon the population and producing the tendencies to suicide is that there can be no other explanation of the statistical stabilities. Durkheim was truly a member of the French school of statistics. What could be closer to what Knapp ridiculed as the astronomical conception of society than Durkheim saying that social statistics are the product of forces that can be compared only to the powers of the cosmos acting on us from without?

Galton and Durkheim each had an idea of the normal and the abnormal that they intimately connected with the reality of a new kind of law. Of course Durkheim's emergentist philosophy was alien to Galton, and their central and obsessive visions of the normal were by no means the same. The Normal distribution describing a group, which Galton treated as a real and autonomous law, is a law of a different kind from that governing Durkheim's 'cosmic' forces acting upon the collective. Throughout this book I have capitalized the initial letter when writing of the Normal distribution.[32] That was surely to show that a very special meaning of normality was involved? It may seem a mere play on words, to connect Galton's use of the word 'normal' with that of Durkheim.

Another test confirms this conclusion. What is the opposite of the normal? The abnormal, certainly. But for Galton the normal was characterized by the Normal curve; the abnormal was what strongly deviated from its mean. For Durkheim, the abnormal was called the pathological. In the end the abnormal is sick. For Galton, the abnormal is exceptional, and may be the healthiest stock of the race. As a very poor first approximation, Durkheim identified the moral with the normal. For Galton the normal was not good but mediocre. Some extremes were not pathological but superb. The right and the good are to be found at the right hand end of the Normal curve of talent or virtue.

These then were two visions of the normal. Galton's idea of normality is embedded in our culture, not only in the IQ test but in an unending array

[*] Durkheim did read Galton's theory of regression in the 1889 *Natural Inheritance*. He described what he read with admiration. But he pretty much misunderstood Galton's point, for, rather in the spirit of Quetelet, he thought the theory of regression established that pathological conditions would gradually revert to the mean: 'the deviations produced are never more than short-lived, and succeed in being maintained for a time only in very imperfect fashion'.

of standards of normal behaviour. His is a success story; in specific details, Durkheim's is not. Nevertheless they are both part of that fundamental transition that links the erosion of determinism, the emergence of a new kind of indeterministic law, the taming of chance, and the displacement of human nature by the idea of normality.

21

The autonomy of statistical law

London, 9 February 1877   The typical laws are those which most
nearly express what takes place in nature generally; they may never
be exactly correct in any one case, but at the same time they will
always be approximately true and always serviceable for explanation
... They show us that natural selection does not act by carving out
each new generation according to a definite pattern on a
Procrustean bed, irrespective of waste. They also explain how small
a contribution is made to future generations by those who deviate
widely from the mean, either in excess or deficiency, and they
enable us to discover the precise sources whence the deficiencies in
the produce of exceptional types are supplied, and their relative
contributions. We see by them that the ordinary genealogical course
of a race consists in a constant outgrowth from its centre, a constant
dying away at its margins, and a tendency of the scanty remnants of
all exceptional members to revert to that mediocrity, whence the
majority of their ancestors originally sprang.[*][1]

The silly season in determinism had no bounds. 'Given an hour of a man's
life, and an anthropometric seraph could calculate all that he ever has been,
and all that he ever will be.'[2] Thus, in 1871, did the social sciences emulate
the Laplacian maxim of universal determinism. Laplace spoke of the
lightest atom; in this sentence, the novelist speaks of a man. Laplace spoke
of knowledge at an instant; the novelist speaks of measurements taken
over an hour. Francis Galton set up anthropometric booths in public
places to determine the measurements of passers-by. No seraph he, but he
shared and popularized the idea that physical and mental measurements
were the key to human nature.
   It was in this context of optimistic anthropometry that there occurred a

---

[*] Francis Galton lecturing to the Royal Institution. On this occasion he was able to
supplement his modest mathematics with an analogue simulating the Normal distribution.
He called it the 'quincunx' (a quincunx is five points, four at the corners of a square and one
at the centre). Lead shot is dropped through a series of pins with this arrangement, and
piles up to exhibit the Normal curve. He had a simple one made in 1873, but the idea of the
1877 model is a two-stage arrangement to illustrate heredity. Coincidentally, C.S. Peirce
developed his quincuncial projection for map-making during the same decade.

fundamental transition in the conception of statistical laws. Galton at the time of my quotation was well on his way to devising the theory of correlation and regression. That story has been well told by others.[3] We now say regression towards the mean rather than reversion towards mediocrity, but Galton's terminology reveals his fascination with the exceptional, the very opposite of Quetelet's preoccupation with mediocre averages.

In this chapter I shall draw attention to the way in which laws of a statistical sort become 'serviceable for explanation', as my epigraph puts it. I believe this marks an important passage in the taming of chance. One can explain something by using a statistical law only if it is in some way autonomous, and not reducible to some set of underlying causes. A difficulty of exposition arises here, for there is much philosophical debate about statistical laws, about explanation, and about statistical explanation. I believe my concerns are quite different from any of those that are commonly aired, but I shall be misunderstood if I do not state the problems, if only to distance myself from them.

I shall not be arguing that Galton or any contemporary seriously thought that statistical laws were irreducible to underlying deterministic principles. To say that such laws are irreducible is to say that the universe does not have any set of deeper and nonprobabilistic laws that entail the statistical behaviour. Only with the advent of quantum mechanics and its elaboration in the 1930s did the idea of irreducibility become widely entertained. An important event was John von Neumann's 'no hidden variables' theorem of 1936, of which in recent years there have been many careful and sophisticated developments. The phrase 'no hidden variables' indicates a precise way of stating that quantum mechanics as at present understood cannot be reduced to an underlying deterministic theory.

Despite the widespread acceptance of 'no hidden variables' results, some authors find the question of reducibility of deep importance, partly because it is a way of preserving determinist metaphysics. There have been repeated and often brilliant attempts to produce explanations of how large-scale statistical homogeneity can be the result of underlying deterministic processes. They began with Poisson's law of large numbers. The most famous deliberately pro-determinist attempt is Boltzmann's *H*-theorem. More generally, such a programme includes, from a variety of philosophical perspectives, work by Henri Poincaré, and much ergodic theory.[4] I shall avoid such matters entirely.

I am concerned with a conception that falls short of irreducibility; indeed it is less a conception than a practice. I shall speak of autonomy as opposed to irreducibility. Someone who claims, perhaps in the light of work by von Neumann, that some statistical laws are not reducible to underlying causal and determinist structures, holds that such laws are irreducible. What then is autonomy? It can be usefully illustrated by one of the signs of a difference between prediction and explanation. *Statistical laws became autonomous when they could be used not only for the prediction of phenomena but also for their explanation.* Statistical explanation has been much discussed by philosophers in recent years, but they have focussed on the explanation of individual events. An event may be very probable, or be of a type that happens very frequently, but does that explain its occurrence on a particular occasion? How does one explain the occurrence of events of a type that seldom occur? Is explanation provided by data that increase the probability of the event?[5] These are not the issues that concern us here, but rather what scientists commonly call explanation, namely the explanation of a phenomenon. Galton wanted to explain what he believed were curious phenomena of a thoroughly regular and law-like sort, about the distribution of hereditary genius in gifted families.

Galton based his views about inheritance on detailed genealogies, and on a classification of talent fitting his own scale of values. His anthropometric booths were a tiny fraction of his studies of physical characteristics, and how they too are distributed and inherited. He established the anthropometric laboratory at University College, London, which in due course became the first modern department of statistics. Karl Pearson, Galton's profound admirer, who gave us the chi-squared test of goodness of fit and much else, held the chair in that site, endowed by Galton. Pearson founded the great statistical journal, *Biometrika*, as well as *Annals of Eugenics*. The second was as much an organ of applied statistics as the first, and both were conceived in the spirit of Pearson's practical positivism: apply 'value-neutral' science and statistical techniques to the issues of the day.

Anthropometry was presented benignly as the science of measuring the human body and the proportions between its parts, but my quotation about the anthropometric seraph reveals its innermost dreams. It had strong connections with the control of populations. That remains the meaning of the old French term *anthropométrie judicaire*, a method of identifying criminals by measurement. The system was invented in 1880 by Alphonse Bertillon. Rivalry between Bertillon and Galton spurred the invention of the theory of correlation, as described below. The most extreme version of these ideas was being developed in Italy, as the criminal anthropology briefly mentioned in the preceding chapter.

Like the British physicists of his day, Galton was a genius at transforming abstract representations into physical modelling. His quincunx for making the random fall of shot pile up as a Normal curve is well known in science museums today. He devised a way of literally photographing the average man. By a rather original technique a sequence of individuals was successively exposed on a photographic plate.[6] Then you could actually see the slightly blurred 'type' before your very eyes. Thus fundamentally different types could be displayed: army officers, private soldiers, criminals convicted of murder or crimes of violence, nonviolent felons, and Jews.[*7] He was an authoritarian person: only one such could invent the silent dog whistle for guard dogs, and be central in the introduction of finger-printing as the world's standard of identifying criminals.

His advocacy of eugenics, its antecedents in criminal anthropology, and its consequences for measuring intelligence have been well described by, for example, Donald MacKenzie, Daniel Kevles and Stephen Jay Gould.[8] Galton's fascination with natural inheritance has become better known, in our days, for its vices than for its virtues. His work on regression was an immediate outcome of a problem about inheritance. His invention of the theory of correlation arose from his problems about identifying criminals.

There is a pretty obvious puzzle about inheritance. Exceptionally tall people do have tall children. Brilliant men and women have gifted children. But except during decades of sharp dietary improvement, by and large tallness does not go on regenerating itself in yet greater tallness. Certainly the children born to parents of true genius are seldom as gifted. Galton had a problem. He thought that unusual qualities, be they moral, mental or physical, do breed true, to a large extent, while at the same time there is an inevitable reversion towards mediocrity, ordinariness and the commonplace.

If you really believed that exceptional and desirable qualities would consistently be repeated and improved on in the progeny, you would be hard pressed not to ascribe some merit to some simplistic version of eugenics. And the existence of sperm banks established by a few conceited men of talent shows that some do succumb to such ideas. But Galton was no fool. His intellectual problem arose from the following fact: he instinctively believed in the idea that the best breed the best and the worst breed the worst, and at the same time took so much data on the question, by following the genealogy of extraordinary families, that he saw that this is not exactly true. Moreover the phenomenon of reversion to mediocrity applies to people who are exceptional by any criterion: the fat and the skinny, the couch potatoes and the scalers of Everest, the sensitive and the brutal, the flashdancers and the clumsy.

Galton's difficulties did not end there. He subscribed to Quetelet's

* What did the subjects of these photographs think of Galton? 'The individual photographs were taken with hardly any selection from among the boys in the Jews' Free School, Bell Lane. They were the children of poor parents. As I drove to the school through the adjacent Jewish quarter, the expression of the people that most struck me was their cold scanning gaze, and this was equally characteristic of the schoolboys.'

doctrine that most of the interesting traits of people and living species have a Normal distribution – they follow what Galton himself was soon to describe in just those words: 'the Normal curve'.[*][9] I do not claim any direct connection with the Comte-Broussais use of the word 'normal' – by the time that Galton attached the word to the curve, the word just meant typical, and carried all the Comtian baggage with it. The match between the word and the curve was waiting to be consummated.

Although Galton became acquainted with the Gaussian law of error from a geologist, his chief introduction to the idea was John Herschel's detailed review of Quetelet's exposition of the theory of probability.[10] Galton made the Gaussian law the basis of his studies in *Hereditary Genius* in 1869.[11] He too was much taken by the famous 5,738 Scottish chests, and with Quetelet's marking off the curve into bar graphs indicating where the various percentages of girths were to be found.

Galton, unlike Quetelet, was not impressed by averages. It was distributions and deviations from the mean that interested him. From Quetelet he had learned a way to think about deviation from the mean, by using the curve of error. That focussed his perplexity about inheritance. If we look at a species over time, we will see slight drifts in the mean and dispersion of a trait under study. But basically (in his opinion, long before the theory of genetic drift had occurred to anyone) the curve is constant. New exceptional beings are thrust up from less outstanding families, and more ordinary people are the progeny of exceptional parents. That's what keeps the curve of the population pretty constant, but with a curious slow interchange among the families on the tails of the curve, furthest away, for better or worse, from the mean.

So here we have a *phenomenon* to explain (reversion towards mediocrity in the course of generations) and a fundamental statistical *assumption*, that traits of interest commonly conformed, pretty well, to the Normal curve. The phenomenon is very hard to understand, but it becomes unintelligible when added to the account of the Normal distribution from the time of Quetelet: that it was the product of a lot of little independent causes, as in the limiting case of the binomial distribution. This struck Galton very firmly:

First let me point out a fact which Quetelet and all writers who have followed in his path have unaccountably overlooked, and which has an intimate bearing on our work tonight. It is that, although characteristics of plants and animals conform to

---

[*] He was using the expression 'Normal Curve', with capital letters, regularly by 1888. Galton was less wedded to the Normal curve, or law of error, or Gaussian distribution, however it be named, than one might expect. In 1877 he advised H.P. Bowditch to force his anthropometrical results 'to the Procrustean bed of the "law of error"'. But he did think that the law was roughly right most of the time. He was curiously attracted to Procrustean beds at this time; he spoke of another in my epigraph, also of 1877.

the law, the reason for their doing so is totally unexplained. The essence of the law is that differences should be wholly due to the collective actions of a host of *petty* influences in various combinations.

Now the processes of heredity are not petty influences, but very important ones ... The conclusion is that the processes of heredity must work harmoniously with the law of deviation, and be themselves in some sense conformable to it.[12]

If one asks the question, why did Galton and not Quetelet invent the theory of regression and correlation, it is important, as Victor Hilts has remarked, that in such discussions Galton spoke of the Normal curve as a 'law of deviation'. Thus where Quetelet was thinking of a central tendency, and hence of the mean, Galton, always preoccupied by the exception, was thinking of the tails of the distribution, and of the dispersion. Mathematically speaking, the mean and the dispersion are necessary and sufficient for describing the curve – co-equals as defining properties, we might say. But Quetelet and Galton attended to them very differently. The concentration on dispersion led to correlation coefficients, or so Hilts argues.[13]

To refer to the two men's differing attitudes to the parameters of the Normal curve is to make a useful conjecture about the working of their minds. But something more obvious was also in play. Galton was interested in heredity. Without having any idea about the precise mechanism, he was sure that it had to work by the transmission of bearers of hereditary traits, which he named germs or 'gemmules'. He thought that the blood might be the carrier of genetic material. In 1870 he was trying out experiments on blood transfusion between black and white rabbits. Silver grey does, into which some white rabbit blood had been transfused, were crossed with silver grey bucks into which an almost complete transfusion of blood from white rabbits had been made. (Galton thought the transfusions were successful. One hardly credits this, but then where did the blood go?) The rabbits supposedly bearing white blood did indeed give birth to some offspring with whitish toes. Galton was briefly elated, until it was pointed out that what breeders called 'orphan feet' was quite common.[14] Galton's fascinating experiments and conjectures did not pan out, but they show how fixed in his mind was the thought that traits were transmitted by lumps of hereditary material, and not by 'a host of petty independent influences'.

I have said much about the 'petty independent influence' understanding of the binomial law (to use Quetelet's phrase) or the Normal curve (to use Galton's). I have called it comfortable but conceptually incoherent. Galton was the first to find it distinctly uncomfortable, and hence to rethink the meaning of the curve. I do not say he gave up his belief in some underlying determinism, nor even that he gave up the model of petty independent influences. He did something quite different.

He saw that reversion towards mediocrity was a mathematical consequence of the Normal curve. That is, if a population is Normally distributed, it can be deduced that in a second generation there will be a Normal distribution of about the same mean and dispersion, but one in which the exceptional members will typically not be descended from exceptional members of the previous generation. I say that this can be deduced. Galton did not strictly deduce it, but rather demonstrated it by the device of his shot-dropping machine, the quincunx, in which an analogy of this effect could be observed. That led him to the remarkable thought: the phenomenon that puzzled him could be deduced from the fact (or assumption) that traits were distributed according to the standard statistical law, the law of errors.

Galton was quite self-conscious about his explanations. My epigraph speaks of being 'serviceable for explanation' and uses the verb 'to explain' for precisely the phenomenon I have been discussing. I do not suppose that this is the first time that anyone explained a fascinating but puzzling phenomenon by showing that it followed deductively from the statistical properties of a distribution. I do suppose that Galton saw very clearly what he was doing. In one stroke he was (a) explaining and (b) leaving out the 'host of petty independent causes' story. He was regarding the Normal distribution of many traits as an autonomous statistical law. Statistical law had come into the world fully-fledged. Galton saw that chance had been tamed.

Is this too strong a statement? Have I merely taken an impressive-sounding phrase, 'the taming of chance', and pinned it on a protesting Galton? Galton, when he let himself go, was no slouch at turning a pretty phrase. Here he is, on 26 January 1886, giving a Presidential Address to the Anthropological Institute:

I know of scarcely anything so apt to impress the imagination as the wonderful form of cosmic order expressed by 'the law of error'. A savage, if he could understand it, would worship it as a god. It reigns with severity in complete self-effacement amidst the wildest confusion. The huger the mob and the greater the anarchy the more perfect is its sway. Let a large sample of chaotic elements be taken and marshalled in order of their magnitudes, and then, however wildly irregular they appeared, an unexpected and most beautiful form of regularity proves to have been present all along.[15]

A couple of years later the savages of this paragraph were upgraded: 'The law would have been personified by the Greeks and deified, if they had known of it.'[16]

Did anyone but Galton see how chance was being tamed? To answer it is convenient to pass on a stage, from regression to correlation. I said both were invented by Galton – barely. Galton's contribution to correlation was merely to strike the spark, almost inadvertently. If the man of so many and various labours had a leading concern, it was anthropometry. He thought this had many applications, including the identification of criminals.

His great competitor in the matter of identification was Alphonse Bertillon.[17] Now Bertillon proposed that a set of mug-shots of every criminal should be made, both facing and sideways showing the ear. The system has been widely adopted. Newcomers to the United States may wonder, when they are photographed for their 'green cards' which make them resident aliens, why the photographer for the immigration service insists that the right ear be clearly visible. The answer is, in a word: Bertillon. He had the theory that a person could be identified by the ear, and produced an extraordinary *Bulletin signalétique* of ear types, showing the whorls of every possible ear for purposes of identification. As Carlo Ginzburg has shown in a marvellous essay, the fact was not lost on art historians, or on Sherlock Holmes.[18]

In addition to ears, Bertillon constructed a list of body measurements to be recorded along with the mug-shots. This was important when numbers could be transmitted telegraphically to any police force in the world, but photographs could not, and the ear system called for much mastery before it could be used. Bertillon proposed that height, and lengths of foot, arm and finger should be recorded. He seems to have thought that these four measures were, in some undefined way, independent. Galton saw at once that there was much redundancy in this system, for tall people tend to have big feet, long arms and long fingers. They were, in short, correlated. To prove this he began working graphically from a Normal distribution of people from whom he had collected hundreds of such anthropometric measurements. He very quickly began to see that a measure of correlation could be derived empirically, and was closely connected to his lines of regression. He then moved to the mathematical problem of characterizing correlation and, with some assistance, solved it. Once again he thought that he had suddenly explained something: that from certain statistical laws about the distribution of traits one would deduce general phenomena about how traits are correlated.

This story is interesting for those interested in the mathematical angle of the story, but Galton himself, after his initial idea about correlation, was quickly overtaken by mathematicians such as Karl Pearson or F.Y. Edgeworth. Pearson later noted that the formulae used in the theory of correlation had been used much earlier in the Gaussian tradition, for determining the error curves when two coordinates were determined by a single method (so that their errors would be 'correlated').[19] And there was at least one other predecessor, later and clearer.[20] About these there are two things to say. First, as MacKenzie writes, 'the point is that for neither of [those earlier workers] was statistical dependence in itself the focus of attention, as it was for Galton'.[21] Secondly, the predecessors were working in the Gaussian tradition of estimating 'real' positions given independently of any method of estimating. I have emphasized that Quetelet made the average height into something 'real'; Galton now added another tier of reality. It made correlations as real as causes. In fact, in Karl Pearson's opinion, it destroyed causes.

Pearson was the positivist author of *The Grammar of Science*, and not unprejudiced about causes. Cause, in the canons of positivism, was a metaphysical notion. A good way to surpass metaphysics was to annul causation. The passage I am about to quote was written long after Galton's death, after a career in which Pearson had advanced the theory of correlation as much as anyone. He doubtless paid more attention to the discovery of correlation theory than it deserves. Nevertheless he is a splendid witness to the consequences of the taming of chance, and to the effect of the autonomy of statistical law on the very notion of causality. Or, as he would have preferred to put it, he testified to the correlation between the taming of chance and *the elimination of ordinary causality*.

He remarked that everyone before Galton had missed the analysis of correlation. Most of the attempts to apply quantitative analysis to psychological, medical and sociological research – be it by Condorcet or Quetelet, or even Laplace – had been 'sterile' for lack of grasp of the concept.

Galton turning over two different problems in his mind reached the conception of correlation: *A* is not the sole cause of *B*, but it contributes to the production of *B*; there may be other, many or few, causes at work, some of which we do not know and may never know … This measure of partial causation was the germ of the broad category – that of correlation, which was to replace not only in the minds of many of us the old category of causation, but deeply to influence our outlook on the universe. The conception of causation – unlimitedly profitable to the physicist – began to crumble to pieces. In no case was *B* simply and wholly caused by *A*, nor indeed by *C*, *D*, *E*, and *F* as well! It was really possible to go on increasing the number of contributory causes until they might involve all the factors of the universe … Henceforward the philosophical view of the universe was to be that of a correlated system of variates, approaching but by no means reaching perfect correlation, i.e. absolute causality.[22]

22

A chapter from Prussian statistics

Berlin, 22 July 1880   The incompetent statistics that are the
product of this agitation force us once again to recall the first
commandment for a statistician: thou shalt not bear false witness
against thy neighbour.[*][1]

My chapters have become successively more removed from daily affairs.
The early numbers printed by enthusiasts and bureaux generated the idea
of statistical laws. Ideas about causation were revised. New content was
given to the notion of normalcy. I have increasingly moved from practical
matters to abstract ones. I shall conclude with the statistical epistemology
and metaphysics of C.S. Peirce, a high-powered speculative philosopher if
ever there was one. But the numbers that set these steps in motion were
intended to be administrative tools. Lest we forget that, let us return to an
example. I began this book with two anodyne moments in Prussian
statistics: here is a third and more problematic one.

The 'agitation' of the epigraph was the wave of antisemitism that peaked
in the new German Empire during 1879–81. We are here concerned with
only one tiny aspect of it: the use or abuse of statistical data. As Salomon
Neumann went on to complain ' "the mass immigration of Jews across the
Eastern frontier of the German Empire" has been quite simply erected
into a statistical axiom. For the masses it summons up a nightmare, but it is
no less effective in higher society, even in the learned world, where it is
dressed up in economic or ethnological clothing, or some similar garb.'
Neumann subtitled his pamphlet 'a chapter from Prussian statistics'.
Prussian statistics between 1860 and 1882 meant, above all, Ernst Engel,
the gifted administrator who appears in the background of several
previous chapters. Neumann and Engel parted company pretty radically
by 1881: Engel's bureau commented magisterially on Neumann's first
edition of the 'fable' and Neumann angrily replied in the third.[2] But their
conception of the role of statistics was very much the same: it was what I

---

[*] Salomon Neumann, writing at the height of the Berlin wave of antisemitism, 1879–81, in a
pamphlet, 'the fable of massive Jewish immigration: a chapter from Prussian statistics'.

have, in caricature, been calling the eastern view of numbers and of laws. Aside from the old time Manchester school Liberals, who advocated the invisible hand across the board (a group including a majority of Berlin Jewish business, intellectual and political leaders in mid-century, but not Neumann) this attitude to numbers ran across conventional party lines.[3]

Neumann learned medicine on the student tour: Halle, Berlin, Vienna, Venice, Paris. He was admitted as a doctor in Berlin in 1845.*[4] Much of his daily work was administrative, but his publications were chiefly aimed at analysing health statistics. An essay of his on Berlin mortality rates appeared in an issue of *Der Arbeiterfreund* almost immediately before a paper of Engel's on 'industrial partnerships'.[5] Their concerns overlapped: *The Working Man's Friend* was the organ of the *Central Verein für das Wohl der Arbeitenden Klassen*. Society for the welfare of the working classes: the name of the organization and of its publication make plain its reform-from-above nature. Neumann was a founding member of the society and its delegate to the second, third and fourth International Statistical Congresses, 1855, 1856, and 1860. Engel attended in his official capacities. He was conspicuous in in 1860, in London, ensuring that the next Congress would be held in Berlin.

Neumann can usefully be put beside his famous contemporary and fellow Pomeranian, Rudolf Virchow (1821–1902). Scientifically, Virchow transformed pathological anatomy – but let it not be forgotten that he also was a founder of the German anthropological society, and did detailed, almost Galtonian, studies on physical anthropometry. Curious as to racial characteristics, he organized a census to determine the distribution of blonde and dark-haired Germans (most aren't blonde). And he went with Schliemann to Troy in 1879. A strong Liberal in the Prussian House of Representatives, after 1880 he was elected to the Reichstag and became leader of the opposition. But he was if anything more active in Berlin politics, largely concerning himself with health and social welfare. His very theory of the cell was individualistic, as his theory of the state wanted to be republican. His philosophy was the very opposite of that conservative holism that I have called 'eastern', but even he was so part of his milieu that he could write in 1859 that 'as in the lives of nations, so in the lives of individuals the state of health of the whole is determined by the well-being and close interrelation of the individual parts; disease appears when

---

* The *curriculum vitae* of his dissertation are signed *ego Salomon Neumann Judaeus*. It had been obligatory for a Jewish physician to take an oath of office in the synagogue. Doctors of other faiths had long been allowed a civil oath. Neumann was the first Jewish doctor in Berlin successfully to petition for the parallel right. Thereafter all Jewish doctors opted for the civil oath. From the year of the founding of the Alliance Israélite Universelle (1869), he was an active member, presiding over various local committees. At the time that he published his 'fable', he had just become president of the Hochschule für die Wissenschaft des Judenthums in Berlin, of which he was a founding member.

individual members begin to sink into a state of inactivity disadvantageous to the commonwealth, or to lead parasitic existences at the expense of the whole'.[6]

Neumann was already a holist and never had to make these moves. Differences between the two men in point of philosophy were no hindrance to their collaboration. Neumann became a Berlin city councillor in 1859 and remained so until 1905. Such men pioneered many of the sanitary reforms that turned Berlin from one the most disease-ridden capitals of Europe to its healthiest. Virchow also considered Neumann to have settled many issues about Jewish immigration, citing the 'fable' in the *Abgeordnetshaus* directly after its publication. But that is to anticipate.

In 1851 Neumann published a characteristic study in Virchow's medical journal. It had a ponderous enough title, 'On medical statistics of the Prussian state according to the report of the statistical bureau for 1846'.[7] The opening proposition was striking. In bold letters it stated: 'Public health care is the duty of the state.' In our day we base ourselves upon the rights of man and of equal membership in the human race. The only purpose of a state is the welfare of its members, for it is founded upon the organic union of equally entitled human beings. The true content and aim of political science is prosperity of the people, grounded upon the normal development of mankind according to the laws of its physical and mental nature. This understanding produces a 'new ethical world view'.

Good health, Neumann continued, is essential to the full development of each person. It follows from this and the above premises that the state is obliged to provide medical care for its citizens. *'Medical science is a social science.'* Society has contented itself with a lot of talk about new learning, but it ignores the real fruits of medical knowledge. It can use these only when medicine is viewed as a social science.

There was a corollary about madness. There are different kinds of insanity, and statistics show that their prevalence varies both in history and in different parts of Europe. That is because insanity is essentially connected with the culture and social conditions in which it occurs. Madness is doubly a social construct. Not only do different kinds of society induce different forms of madness, but also, what counts as insane varies from one social group to another. In chapter 8 we noted Esquirol and others of the 1820s declaring that madness is the province of the physician; now in the 1850s the German medical reformers were amending that. Yes, madness is the province of the medical man, but only because the medical man is a social scientist.

So much for Neumann's philosophical stance. His immediate worry in his paper of 1851 was the uneven distribution of health care across the kingdom. He had a very practical objection to Quetelet's notion of taking averages. The theoreticians may have protested against Quetelet that the deviation from the mean on the curve of errors is just as important as the mean. Did that matter to ordinary people? Yes! 'A picture is illusory when it tries to create an abstraction from real life ... the datum that there is one doctor per square mile throughout the state gives absolutely no indication of the real possibilities of medical assistance.' He ranked the 26 provincial jurisdictions in Prussia by the number of medical personnel per inhabitant per square mile. The western provinces were rich in doctors, while the eastern ones had appalling doctor/patient ratios. Neumann confirmed that mortality and disease are inversely proportional to the availability of medical care. Wasn't this a spurious correlation? Money draws doctors then as now, and money keeps people healthier because they are cleaner and better fed. But Neumann's picture of the doctor was not the physician at the bedside; it was the sanitary reformer who could change whole districts.

Neumann's data were taken from the Prussian statistical bureau whose former director, Hoffmann, had asserted that 'prosperity and culture express themselves numerically in the laws of mortality'. On that doctrine England is more cultured than France, and France than Germany: in 1850 the ratios were 45:40:27. Well, said Neumann, there are better measures of culture and prosperity, namely the availability of medical care. We can do something about that now. And as for the usual stuff about laws of mortality: that, Neumann angrily asserted, is nonsense. It is not a law that Germans die sooner than the English, and by a great margin. The phenomena are a product of society that can be altered.

For example: the 20 per cent death rate for newborn infants is not a fact of nature but a consequence of the power (*Macht*) of civilization. Virchow had returned from Upper Silesia reporting the statistics of the terrible typhus epidemic:

No one would have thought such a state of affairs possible in Prussia, which took so much pride in the excellence of its institutions ... we now see the endless rows of figures, every single one of which denotes untold wretched misery ... we must not hesitate to draw all those conclusions that can be drawn from such a horrible experience. I myself had drawn the consequences when I returned from Upper Silesia, and was determined, in view of the new French Republic, to help in the demolition of the old edifice of our state.[8]

Thus the radical of 1848. Young Neumann agreed. We should, he wrote, see the horror not as rampant disease but as a 'social epidemic'.[9] The miserable workers of the region have nothing left for them but sex and brandy. Thus 'the population increases as rapidly as it loses its physical strength and moral fibre'. (Contrast German biopolitics with that of the French. Degeneracy, which made the French infertile, made Silesians fecund).

Neumann quoted an ironic remark of Dieterici, current director of the Prussian statistical bureau. The inhabitants of Silesia have transcended the conditions of human life – just like the Christian ascetics of the first century, except in the opposite direction. Dieterici had urged that the birth rate is not directly affected by population density, but only indirectly, by the availability of food. That is still an Enlightenment doctrine, reminiscent of Malthus and the physiocrats before him. Neumann brushed it aside. The highest birth rates were in the east, in Posen, Danzig and so on, where the people starved. The lowest ones were in the west, in cities such as Munster and Dusseldorf.

Neumann's own paper of 1851 had the fervour of youth and the spirit of '48. He was 24. There is every evidence that he remained true to his statistical and medical principles. What would such a man do when, as a mature and influential citizen of Berlin, a city councillor and at the same time newly elected president of the Hochschule für die Wissenschaft des Judenthums, he saw statistics turned into fuel for antisemitism? There was a moment of incredulity in his entire community. The second edition of Neumann's 'fable' appeared in 1880. An additional preface ended not by recalling the prohibition against bearing false witness but by quoting a sentence from a speech of Theodor Mommsen's, on 18 March of that year. 'Is the empire of Kaiser Wilhelm really the country of Frederick the Great, the country of enlightenment and tolerance, the country in which one asked about character and quality of mind, rather than religious confession and nationality?'*[10]

There had been a great Jew-hate – *Judenhetze* – in Berlin in 1819 but nothing further of comparable proportions until 1879. It built up during the 1870s. I restrain comment to a few well-known facts. On the pamphleteering side, Wilhelm Marr (already author of an ignored piece of hate literature, his *Judenspiegel* of 1862) led the way with his tract declaring and denouncing the victory of Judaism over Germanism. On the financial side a stock-market crash in May 1874 was blamed on Jewish financial manipulations, with facts based upon a celebrated stop-the-disaster-before-it-happens speech to the Reichstag, on 7 February 1873, by Eduard Lasker, himself a prominent member of the Jewish community. Jewish businessmen had been prominent Liberals and advocates of *Manchesterismus*. People with an opposite view of economics and of society were glad to call that both a Jewish and an antiGerman doctrine. Bismarck's anticlerical *Kulturkampf* had been supported by Jewish writers and businessmen. Priests and pastors were glad to counter-attack.

---

* Hermann Cohen's eulogy called Neumann 'a good German *Burger*... whose style had the direct sturdiness, the high seriousness and the fundamental matter of factness which used to be taken as characteristic of the German type of mind'.

These antagonisms were fuelled by the spectre of massive Jewish immigration from the east. Inflammatory pamphlets urged that there was a terrifying influx from northern parts of the Austro-Hungarian empire, such as Galicia, and from Russia. They entered the eastern provinces, Silesia, Posen and East Prussia. Then there was a corresponding flow to the rest of Germany. The character of the German people was being altered. Most of the pamphlets were written by vicious nobodies, but one sequence came from Berlin's most eminent historian, the vitriolic scholar-politician Heinrich von Treitschke.[11] Neumann addressed himself to the minimal 'fact' common to all these rantings, the 'statistical axiom' about the massive immigration of Jews into Germany.

Was this immigration a fact? One might have expected the excellent statistics of Prussia to provide an immediate and unreflective answer. I noted in chapter 3 that complete tables, known as *General-Judentabellen* or *Provinzial-Judenfamilie-Listen* became a routine part of the Prussian system of counting people by 1769.*[12] These tables became merged with standard enumerations of people by religious conviction. *Israeliten* replaced *Juden* as the head of one column alongside thirteen kinds of Christians. The desire to know statistical facts about Jews did not thereby disappear. In chapter 7 we noted in passing that Charles Babbage, during his 1828 visit to Berlin, had obtained from Hoffmann, director of the Prussian statistical bureau, numerous Prussian numbers. Babbage passed on two items of information that had been drawn to his attention. The excess of male over female births among Jews was larger than in the total population, and the Jewish birth rate itself was greater than the average. The number and distribution of Jews was a regular topic, for example in the 1840s paper *On the Jewish Question: A Statistical Discussion*: a 'statistical overview and comparison of the increase of the Jewish and Christian population in the periods 1816–1825, 1825–1834, 1835–1843 and 1843–46 in the individual administrative districts of the Prussian state'.[13] Christian and Jewish 'biostatistics' were regularly compared.[14]

Yet Jewish immigration had not been so systematically studied. Why? Partly inertia. The statistical bureau had for decades concerned itself less with immigration than emigration. Were young men leaving the country

* In 1823 Leopold Zunz proposed a systematic study of Jewish statistics by the Jewish community. His 'Basis of a future Jewish statistics' called for 39 different types of information. In some ways reminiscent of Achenwallian or academic reporting on the state, it was written at the beginning of the avalanche of printed numbers, and so includes many newer ideas. In 1862 Neumann was a founder of the Zunz foundation in Berlin, and later he was its president. His 1884 essay on the statistics of Jews in Prussia from 1816 to 1880 was dedicated to Zunz on the occasion of the latter's 90th birthday. It quoted Zunz who, in 1823, urged that false statistics and no statistics are equally bad bases for action. English readers' most direct knowledge of Zunz will come from George Eliot's *Daniel Deronda*.

to avoid military service? The bureau was required to study emigration to keep track of draft-dodging. Then there was the post-1848 emigration to America of small artisans and tradesmen. They had favoured the liberal or republican causes of the failed revolution of 1848 and were disgusted with the upshot. Missouri's gain, Germany's loss. By chance there were data for a 'controlled experiment': an immigration/emigration study published in 1847, just before the insurrections. It found that there were only half as many immigrants as emigrants, but that on average each immigrant brought 409 thalers into the country, while each emigrant took out only 182, leaving a positive cash balance for the nation.[15] For some time after 1848 the balance was in the opposite direction.

The confessional or racial make-up of immigrants and emigrants was thus of little interest: one wanted sex and age, to detect draft dodgers, and secondly net worth, to see what was happening to the funds of the nation. Thus in the census of 1864–5, we find immigrants classified by sex, social class, profession before immigration, and place of former residence. Race and religion were not noted.[16] But there remained lots of indicators. For example: was there a vast increase in the population of the eastern provinces, explicable by the influx of those bearded oriental hordes? Neumann noted that in one table of population published by the Bureau in 1867, showing population increases by administrative district, Posen had the second lowest rate of increase and Gumbinnen, a few miles from the Russian border, the fifth. He had to reason like this because the 'confessional' information in public documents diminished year by year. The Central Statistical Commission, with Engel in the chair, decided not to do a systematic confessional question for the census of 1875. Engel was out of step with the times: that was the very year in which the marriages of Jews with gentiles had to be separately registered.[17] So just at the time of the antisemitic agitation, there were fewer data about the Jewish population. Thus it became increasingly easy to invent 'statistical axioms' about the mass-immigration of Jews.

Just before 1880 an unsigned essay in the bureau's statistical yearbook spoke of 'the striking increase in the number of Jews', which it attributed to a lower mortality rate and to immigration. The essay was not too consistent, saying both that the main cause was immigration from the Austro-Hungarian Empire (Galicia, just south of what we now think of as Poland, is intended), and that the main cause was Jewish longevity.[18]

Neumann was well placed to comment because the 'balance' among segments of the population had been something of a hobby of his.[19] Two apparent facts had been noticed throughout the century. Jews in Germany lived longer, and had proportionally more children surviving beyond the age of five, than their neighbours. Neumann argued that the change in the proportion of Jews in Prussia or in the new German Empire was due only to the higher birth rate and lower mortality of Jews. In fact the proportional increase of Jews was lower than one would predict from these 'natural' sources of growth, because more Jews emigrated than immigrated.

The tone of Neumann's refutation was measured, although the appendices in successive editions became more heated. For example, at the end of the first edition, Neumann criticized Adolph Wagner's book on political economy – the same Wagner whose 1864 tract on statistical fatalism was discussed in chapter 15 above. Wagner then denounced Neumann from the Abgeordnetshaus and in a review. The sum total of his irritated judgement: there is some Jewish immigration, so how on earth could the proportion of Jews in Germany remain the same? Neumann could scarcely contain himself. Jews don't just immigrate, they emigrate. Even if only the same proportion of Jews emigrate, as the proportion of Germans as a whole, that would suffice to keep the proportion of Jews. And American Jewish sources report a quarter of a million German Jewish immigrants in the United States, which indicates that the proportion of Jews who emigrate is greater than that of other Germans.

The bureau printed a disdainful dismissal of Neumann's book as an unsigned essay on 'Foreign-born inhabitants of the Prussian state'.[20] We are deluged by questions about Jews, it began, but we will do our best to provide some information. Then follow a number of paragraphs extracted from the reports from eastern administrative districts. Thus a loyal Prussian reporting from Oletzko despaired: his village simply 'looks' Polish, because all the evangelical parents have their children confirmed by Polish Catholic priests, so that the children can go to the best schools in town. From Stargard we learn of migrant labourers from Bohemia, 'itinerant roofers and vagabonds' known as *vängtuner* who fleece the locals at blackjack (vingt-et-un). After many more such relevant details, a line was drawn across the page.

The author then reported that he had read Neumann's 'fable'. He ignored Neumann's careful deductions. He drew attention only to Neumann's animadversions on the yearbook article. Had not Neumann noticed that this piece was not strictly an official statement of the bureau, but a contribution from outside? And had not Neumann noticed that Dr Engel praised von Fircks, the author of the essay? Thus did the Prussian statistical bureau respond to the 'fable'. Little wonder that in an appendix to his third edition, Neumann said in disgust that none of his substantive points had been debated.

Not every official scorned Neumann. The statistical office of the city of Berlin was independent of the Prussian Bureau, and by 1880 it was increasingly more up-to-date than the Prussian one. Engel had a curious disregard for the age structure of the population, which is essential for computing long-term trends.[21] In contrast the Berlin office handled age structure at least as well as any of its peers in Europe or America. Its director was Richard Boeckh, nephew of a great humanist and philologist, and thus nurtured in the Hamann-Herder-Humboldt tradition that a people is determined by its culture, and its culture is determined by its language. As a young man he had thought much about questions of ethnicity and language. An 1866 essay urged the statistical significance of everyday language as a distinguishing mark of nationality, as did a later book on German population and language regions.[22]

In these works Boeckh repeatedly asserted that nationality has nothing to do with how you look, your religion or your ancestry. What matters is the tongue in which you express yourself. Boeckh did have numerous political conclusions. He denounced the French for not allowing the people of Strasbourg their German university. According to Boeckh, writing the year before the Franco-Prussian war, the French were practising cultural genocide. He thought that every confession should conduct its religious services in the vernacular. His target, on both Herderian and Lutheran principles, was plainly Latin, not Hebrew. On Boeckh's criterion most East Prussian Jews were German (Yiddish being counted a German dialect in the statistical reports) even if they shared with Catholics the vice of religious instruction in a foreign tongue.[23]

The reaction of Boeckh's office to the antisemitic furore was completely different from that of Engel's. Boeckh's own 1880 yearbook was full of gibes at the ignoramuses babbling in the newspapers about Jewish immigration. It wrote of 'the abuse and demoralisation of statistics through the antisemitic agitation'.[24] Neumann expressed thanks for this 'good sense' in his third edition.

Engel was furious. An unsigned review in his *Zeitschrift* discussed Boeckh's Berlin yearbook and a new yearbook coming out of the new imperial statistical office (i.e. for the entire *Reich*, as opposed to Engel's province, Prussia). The objectivity of the imperial yearbook was described as a model for all. Boeckh got a dressing-down for deigning to address the daily press. Journalists deal with current events; a statistical office must record information for administrators, legislators and commercial men, as well as for posterity. Let all statisticians in the future stay away from politics, and be Olympian. (As if Engel stayed away from politics; he was retired in 1882, probably for outspoken disagreement with Bismarck's grain policies.[25])

In consequence statistical practice tried to come full circle. In chapter 3 we saw the establishment of public bureaux that made the number-collecting amateurs redundant. Now one needed a fund of amateur information to prevent abuse of numbers by the establishment. The Berlin Jewish community formed a statistical society. At first it operated in conjunction with organizations for the promotion of knowledge of Jewish culture, such as the Zunz Foundation or the Lehranstalt für die Wissenschaft des Judenthums. One of the most active members in the Jewish statistical movement was Alfred Nossig, who in 1887 had published on 'the statistics of the Jewish race'.[26] An autonomous Verein für jüdische Statistik was established in Berlin. In 1904 it became a fully-fledged Buros für Statistik der Juden under the direction of Nossig.[27] Its fate needs little commentary.[*28]

Antisemitism was hardly peculiar to Berlin. Paris was to be ripped apart by the Dreyfuss affair, which started in 1894. Thou shalt not bear false witness against thy neighbour: Neumann had said that was the first statistical commandment. False testimony, it seemed, had to be met by facts. There was a wave of collection of Jewish statistics in Europe and in the United States. The present chapter has been grim enough, and teaches more about the reality of statistics than the taming of chance. So I shall conclude on another note, a curious instance of Jewish statistics that returns us to Galton and the Anthropometric Institute.

Australian-born Joseph Jacobs, scholar of myth and folk tales, translator of Aesop, addressed 'the purity of the Jewish race', and concluded in the affirmative.[29] Galton's approach was mimicked. Corresponding to 'Mr. Galton's classical experiments at the International Health Exhibition, 1885', at which Galton took anthropometric measurements of passers by, Jacobs and a colleague took measurements 'in the first instance at the Jewish Working Men's Club, Great Alie Street E.'.[30] Following 'Mr. Galton's hypothesis, that talent is distributed round an average mediocrity like shots are distributed around the bull's eye of a target', he estimated 'the comparative ability of Englishmen, Scotchmen and Jews'.[31] Normal curves were constructed according to Galton's method, relying on biographical dictionaries and some judgement calls to pick out able men. Jews have a greater proportion of able men than English, with Scots in between. The Normal curve is symmetric, so we expect the same result on the opposite side: lunatics are, according to Jacobs, more common among Jews than among the English; once again, the Scots are in between. The

---

* Nossig was a man of many parts – sculptor, musician, historian, statistician and 'practical Zionist', i.e. one who favoured finding a Jewish national home not necessarily in Palestine. In 1917 he led negotiations with Germany, Austro-Hungary and Turkey to establish a home in Turkey. In 1943, when he was 79, he was in Warsaw negotiating (he thought) with the occupying forces for safe emigration from the ghetto. The Jewish resistance believed he was collaborating with the Nazis, and shot him. A happier story is that of a co-founder of the Jewish statistical bureau, his exact contemporary Arthur Ruppin, who also died in 1943, fêted in Jerusalem as a great scholar.

rule of the Normal law is not quite *a priori*. For a moment Jacobs considered a counter-example which 'deterred' him; he found 'that the United States has the smallest proportion of lunatics among civilized states. But instead of disproving our position, we have here a remarkable confirmation of it. For the United States has not produced a single man of the first class, except Washington and perhaps Emerson, in the last century.' Nor does the sway of this mighty law stop at generalities, such as genius and madness. Its writ runs everywhere:

The curve serves to distribute musical or linguistic ability as well as general ability. If Jews have, as we shall see they have, more musicians and philologists at the top of the scale, they should have more deaf mutes at the lower end of it: we know they have.[32]

23

A universe of chance

Chance itself pours in at every avenue of sense: it is of all things the most obtrusive. That it is absolute is the most manifest of all intellectual perceptions. That it is a being, living and conscious, is what all the dullness that belongs to ratiocination's self can scarce muster the hardihood to deny.[*][1]

The Age of Reason, of ratiocination, had seen things differently. Peirce reversed Hume's dictum, 'that chance, when strictly examined, is a mere negative word, and means not any real power which has anywhere a being in nature'.[2] It wasn't easy. Peirce had tried to settle on half measures.

For a long time I myself strove to make chance that diversity in the universe which laws leave room for, instead of a violation of law, or lawlessness. That was truly believing in chance that was not absolute chance. It was recognizing that chance does play a part in the real world, apart from what we may know or be ignorant of. But it was a transitional belief which I have passed through.[3]

Peirce denied determinism. He also doubted that the world is a determinate given. He laboured in a community seeking to establish the true values of Babbage's constants of nature; he said there aren't any, over and above those numbers upon which we increasingly settle. He explained inductive learning and reasoning in terms of merely statistical stability. At the level of technique, he made the first self-conscious use of randomization in the design of experiments: that is, he used the law-like character of artificial chances in order to pose sharper questions and to elicit more informative answers. He provided one of the standard rationalia for statistical inference – one that, named after other and later workers, is still with us. He had an objective, frequentist approach to probability, but also

---

[*] C.S. Peirce, writing in early 1893 a 'Reply to the Necessitarians'. Peirce had 'attacked the doctrine that every event is determined by law ... At the end of my second paper, the partisans of the doctrine of necessity were courteously challenged and besought to answer my arguments. This, so far as I can learn, Dr. Carus alone, in *The Monist* of July and October 1892, has publicly vouchsafed to do.' Peirce's papers did provoke one other immediate response: in the April 1893 issue we read John Dewey on 'The Superstition of Necessity'.

pioneered a measure of the subjective weight of evidence (the log odds). In epistemology and metaphysics, his pragmatic conception of reality made truth a matter of what we find out in the long run. But above all, he conceived of a universe that is irreducibly stochastic.

I end with Peirce because he believed in absolute chance, but that is not my focus. His denial of the doctrine of necessity was incidental to a life permeated by statistics and probabilities. Somebody had to make a first leap to indeterminism. Maybe it was Peirce, perhaps a predecessor. It does not matter. He 'rejoiced to find' himself in the company of others, including Renouvier.[4] He did argue against the doctrine of necessity, but it was not an argument that convinced him that chance is an irreducible element of reality. *He opened his eyes, and chance poured in* – from a world which, in all its small details, he was seeing in a probabilistic way. In this respect, although he was very much a nineteenth-century man, he was already living in a twentieth-century environment. His working days of experimental routine, and his voyages of the mind, took place in a new kind of world that his century had been manufacturing: a world made of probabilities.

Peirce is the strongest possible indicator that certain things which could not be expressed at the end of the eighteenth century were said at the end of the nineteenth. I do not use him here because he is the happy upshot of preceding chapters, the point at which groping events finally led to the truth as we now see it. Not at all: some of what he wrote strikes me as false and much of it is obscure. I use him instead to exemplify a new field of possibilities, the one that we still inhabit. Chance poured in at every avenue of sense because he was living in a new probabilistic world. One can't grasp that just by reading him on the romantic subject of absolute chance. You have to glimpse the almost innumerable ways in which his world had become constructed out of probabilities, just like ours.

This chapter is twice as long as preceding ones, and differs in other ways as well. It breaks down into sections:

1 A measurer at the Coast Survey (biographical)
2 Necessity examined
3 Errors of observation
4 Psychophysics and randomization
5 Induction and hypothesis
6 Disposition and relative frequency
7 The truth-preserving virtue
8 Probable error
9 Induction and the weight of evidence
10 Community

1   A MEASURER AT THE COAST SURVEY

Philosophers know some rough and ready facts about Peirce's career, often presented as an endless sequence of hackwork. It is noted that he applied for but failed to gain or retain regular university work, that late in life he eked out a living writing 182 longish entries in Baldwin's philosophical *Dictionary*, doing translations for the Smithsonian, or producing 348 more or less weekly reviews for *The Nation*. Hence it has been less emphasized that for the 30 most vigorous years of his life he was employed by the US Government in the Coast Survey. This is not a mere biographical detail. His job was measurement and the improvement of measuring devices and it was there that he formed his philosophy of chance.[5] Peirce was a transitional figure, a public employee who for most of his years in office was able to do pretty much what he wanted. When the Coast Survey fell under the fiscal scrutiny of Congress, he was on his way out.*[6]

Peirce grew up in Cambridge, of solid New England stock. His father Benjamin Peirce ('universally acknowledged to be by far the strongest mathematician in the country'[7]) worked the boy mercilessly but could provide patronage because in addition to being a professor at Harvard he was a dominant figure in the Observatory and a power in the Coast Survey. C.S. Peirce was taken on by the Survey in mid–1861, when he was 21, and promoted to the rank of assistant in 1867, when his father became Superintendent. His father died in 1880. After the survey was reorganized on the lines of a more modern bureaucracy, Peirce was obliged to resign.

He had not been very constrained by his job but he performed his duties with passion.[8] He was a measurer, an observer and a designer of instruments. He was much occupied with measuring gravity, using

---

* It was found 'that for several years beginning in 1873 C.S. Peirce, assistant, has been making experimental researches with pendulums without restriction as to times or places; that since 1879 expenditures on account of those experiments, aside from salaries of chiefs and assistants, amount to about $31,000; that the meager value of those experiments to the bureau has been substantially destroyed'. That is the *Washington Post* of 7 August 1885 reporting on the findings of a Joint Commission of Congress looking into the Coast Survey. Peirce got off lightly, as may be seen from the headline: 'Intoxicated and Demoralized/A Terrible Arraignment of the Coast Survey Officials/Prof. Hilgard and Others Charged with Being Drunk in Office Hours/Full Text of the Investigating Committee's Report'. Peirce was accused only of overdedication to worthless science. He retorted that the costs were one third of those alleged, that his instructions were all on file, that no records had been destroyed, and 'I maintain the value of determinations of gravity in general, and the excellence of mine in particular.'

pendulums of his own design. His researches in photometry were intense. He managed to match wavelengths of light to the length of a rod, an achievement that would make the standard metre obsolete. His father thought that his greatest achievement.

2 NECESSITY EXAMINED

'The Doctrine of Necessity Examined' might seem a fine conclusion to a study of the erosion of determinism. But now that we have arrived it is perfunctory. Peirce could not take seriously any determinist antagonist. Could such a one not open his eyes or any other sense and see? In brief, Peirce noted that necessity is a not a universal doctrine, not even in the European tradition: we've had Epicurus (and Lucretius) on 'spontaneous chance'.[9] Observation can't establish 'mechanical causation'. We observe only 'that there is an element of regularity in nature'. That has 'no bearing whatever upon the question of whether such regularity is exact and uniform'.[10] Arguments *a priori* or based on inconceivability can (thanks to J.S. Mill) be given no credence. But most important, the diversity and specificity of the universe is evolving, together with laws of the universe. There is spontaneity in the world, of which our sense of free choice is a minor element.

Such was Peirce's sequence of commonplaces; he himself concluded by not explaining 'the chief of my reasons'. He asserted that the 'hypothesis of chance-spontaneity is one whose inevitable consequences are capable of being traced out with mathematical precision into considerable detail'. He doubted that other mathematicians would follow him, 'so that the strongest reason for my belief must for the present remain a private reason of my own', although one that will for future mathematicians prove to be a 'veritable gold mine'.[11]

3 ERRORS OF OBSERVATION

Peirce spoke of 'that law of the distribution of errors which Quetelet, Galton, and others, have applied with so much success to the study of biological and social matters'.[12] He respected their work, but because he was an observer, the error law was first of all about error and about judgements, not biometrics.

His 1870 study 'On the Theory of Errors of Observations' began with casual remarks on the logic of relations and the nature of induction, which must have puzzled virtually all of its few readers with the exception of Peirce's own father – but then it appeared as an appendix to the *Report* of the newly-appointed Superintendent of the Coast Survey, namely his father.[13] The paper had a plain derivation of the theory of observations. Care must be taken in application. The right sorts of approximations must be used. Peirce was scrupulous in commending procedures set out by Encke in Berlin 30 years earlier, but the point of the paper came at the end.[14] He wanted to see how training could improve the 'personal equation' of an observer.

Observatories routinely determined the instant at which a planet or a star crossed the meridian. Observers differ systematically in their measurements. Bessel represented this by the 'personal equation', a correction factor to be added to the measurement taken by an individual.[15] Peirce asked: could one improve an observer's personal equation? For someone versed in the error curve, this does not mean: could one be trained to make less error? It means: could the variation in one's errors be diminished by practice?

Peirce reported on an untrained boy, who for a month made 500 judgements of time every weekday. He had to press a key each time he heard a sharp rap. His errors (delays) made on each day were plotted and the curve smoothed. On the first day 'the observations were scattered to such an extent' that no serious curve-smoothing was possible, but soon the familiar bell-shaped curve emerged. The 'personal equation' changed, first reducing to the point at which the lad was only a seventh of a second late, then increasing a little. But the 'probable error or range of errors was constantly decreasing after the twelfth day'. By the end of the month this measure of variation was only about $\frac{1}{80}$th of a second. This meant that one or two of his observations were as good as a great many by someone less on his toes. Draconian Peirce 'would therefore recommend that transit-observers be kept in constant training by means of some observations of an artificial event which can be repeated with great rapidity, so that several hundred can be taken daily without great labor'. One could train a person to make judgements that fit the Normal curve. We have seen the curve become a biological and social reality. For Peirce it became a psychological reality.

4   PSYCHOPHYSICS AND RANDOMIZATION

The personal equation arose in astronomy, but is a matter for psychology. Psychophysics was founded in the 1850s by the brilliant but strange Gustav Fechner. He asked, how well can people distinguish objects of slightly different weights? He used 'a method of right and wrong cases'. A subject, typically the experimenter Fechner himself, was given two boxes, one heavier than the other, and asked on a series of trials to pick the heavier. The difference in weight, and the proportion of right judgements, indicated sensitivity to that difference in weight. But was there a general law for a person's ability to discriminate?

Yes: the Gaussian curve once again. The variance measured the sensitivity of an individual.[16] Here was more autonomy for statistical laws: they presented a psychological reality of which we are not even conscious, but which is nonetheless part of our system of sensation and judgement. Fechner, like Galton, found the probability curve wonderful. He compared it to Proteus who 'seems to avoid every answer through the charming forms he assumes, but one thing suffices: remain undeterred, hold him constantly to the same point – and a reliable answer will be forced out of him'.[17] Michael Heidelberger argues that Fechner was quite literally the first thoroughgoing indeterminist of modern times.[18] It is unclear how closely he connected indeterminism and stochastic variation. If one judges that he assimilated the two, then he must have conceived of the Gaussian distribution as autonomous well before Galton came on the scene.

Fechner had held that there is a threshold below which one cannot discern small differences. The Normal distribution of sensitivity becomes invalid for a small enough difference in weight. Peirce made the next step by insisting on the 'reality' of the curve even below the threshold of conscious perception: if forced to judge which of two weights is the heaviest, the observer will make subliminal distinctions, whose accuracy will continue to fall off according to the curve of error. How to investigate this hypothesis? The experiment conducted in 1884 by Peirce and a student, Joseph Jastrow, later a distinguished professor of psychology, embodied a number of innovations that we now take for granted in work of this sort.[19] For example the subject was 'blind' – elaborate devices ensured that he did not know whether he was presented first with a heavier or a lighter weight. More important, this was the first experiment in which the sequence of trials was chosen by an artificial randomizer, and in which the use of the randomizer was built into the analysis of the data.[20]

Here we witness two small steps in the taming of chance. First, one's psychological curve of error became an inferred, theoretical curve, which one cannot judge by introspection. It became a reality underneath the phenomena of consciousness. Secondly, Peirce deliberately used the properties of chance devices to introduce a new level of control into his experimentation. Control not by getting rid of chance fluctuations, but by adding some more![21] Peirce thought that his discovery, that there is no minimum threshold,

has highly important practical bearings, since it gives new reason for believing that we gather what is passing in one another's minds in large measure from sensations so faint that we are not fully aware of them, and can give no account of how we reach our conclusions from such matters. The insight of females as well as certain 'telepathic' phenomena may be explained in this way. Such faint sensations ought to be fully studied by the psychologist and assiduously cultivated by every man.[22]

Some will read the 'insight of females' and 'every man' in the light of the fact that Peirce had just endured a painful divorce and successful remarriage. The remark about telepathy is relevant. The word 'telepathy' was two years old. The Society for Psychical Research had been founded in London in 1882. Its members wanted to replace vulgar and popular enthusiasm for mediums by a scientific study; instead of communication from the dead at séances, they supposed that there was a phenomenon of thought transference between living people. The first project of the society was to conduct a census of examples of telepathy, and then to engage in experiments. An American Society for Psychical Research was founded in Boston in 1884, with the same ends. (The aura of those psychic times can be gleaned from Henry James's novel *The Bostonians*). The 1884 American society was short-lived, folding in 1889 out of scepticism. The English society continues to this day. Experiments on telepathy not surprisingly led to a long tradition of randomized experimental design, although the full rationale was poorly understood until the work of R.A. Fisher in the 1920s. But that is another story.[23]

5   INDUCTION AND HYPOTHESIS

Randomization in the design of experiments is a technique for drawing statistical inferences. It has become part of the logic of induction, reminding us that induction is not just a matter of thinking but of doing. Peirce's own theory of probable inference is closest to that of Jerzy Neyman and E.S. Pearson. That is, it is a theory of inductive behaviour, of doing. But Peirce did not dismiss the philosophers' problem of induction. He took it with high seriousness.

How is it that a man can observe one fact and straightway pronounce judgment concerning another different fact not involved in the first? Such reasoning, as we have seen, has, at least in the usual sense of the phrase, no definite probability; how then can it add to our knowledge? This is a strange paradox; the Abbé Gratry says it is a miracle, and that every true induction is an immediate inspiration from on high. I respect this explanation far more than many a pedantic attempt to solve the question by some juggle with probabilities, with the forms of syllogism, or whatnot. I respect it because it shows an adequate cause, and because it is intimately connected – as the true account should be – with a general philosophy of the universe.*[24]

* When the Vatican Council of 1870 sanctioned the doctrine of papal infallibility, Gratry became its best known critic. Peirce's 'Four methods of Settling Opinion' was penned in 1872, directly after the Council. It was an early version of Peirce's most widely read essay,

Peirce connected induction and probability in a novel way, connected with his own general philosophy of the universe. But before we get to that, some preparatory explanation is in order. From the time of his Harvard lectures of 1865 Peirce consistently distinguished 'three kinds of inference': deduction, induction and hypothesis.[25] What's hypothesis?

I once landed at a seaport in a Turkish province [while scouting for the 1870 solar eclipse expedition]; and, as I was walking up to the house which I was to visit, I met a man upon horseback, surrounded by four horsemen holding a canopy over his head. As the governor of the province was the only personage I could think of who would be so greatly honored, I inferred that this was he. This was an hypothesis.[26]

The method of hypothesis proposes a conjecture that explains a puzzling or interesting phenomenon. For a while he renamed this method 'abduction'. (He also used 'retroduction' in a related sense.[27]) He said he wanted this 'peculiar name' to make clear that the conjecturing of a preferred hypothesis was not induction at all.[28] A few philosophers have adopted Peirce's peculiar word, and others follow Gilbert Harman's attractive phrase 'inference to the best explanation'. I shall continue with the standard nineteenth-century word of Peirce and his predecessors such as Whewell: hypothesis.[29]

Peirce only briefly toyed with the thought that some kind of probability attaches to an inference made by the method of hypothesis. He gave that up. One difference between the foundations of induction and of hypothesis is this: probability has *nothing* to do with hypothesis. Probability has *something* to do with induction. Peirce's innovation lay in saying what that something is.

6 DISPOSITION AND RELATIVE FREQUENCY

Told that probability has something to do with induction, most people suppose that if the proposition A is the conclusion of an inductive inference, then we infer something of the form, 'The probability of A is p.' No!

It may be conceived, and often is conceived, that induction lends a probability to its conclusion. Now that is not the way in which induction leads to the truth. It lends no definite probability to its conclusion.[30]

To see why, we need to examine both Peirce's conception of probability and his conception of inference.

'The Fixation of Belief'. What the final version calls 'the method of authority' Peirce called, in 1872, 'the method of despotism'. The references are undoubtedly to the Vatican Council and Gratry's onslaught. Peirce often spoke of Gratry with respect: 'the modern theories of Boole, Apelt, Herschel, Gratry, Whewell, Mill'. Much later he said that Gratry was like the more famous Babbage and Boole, 'off the main lines of intellectual traffic' but 'still read'.

Peirce's central ideas about probability were commonplace. He regularly and rightly honoured Boole's 1854 *Laws of Thought*.[31] From Boole he learned the idea of a logical algebra. More important, he realized that his youthful unreflective degree-of-belief approach to probabilities and combining evidence was badly wrong.[*][32]

He was soon convinced that probability applies not to an individual event, but to a series. He first thought that a probability is a relative frequency in an actual series. That was Venn's idea. When he reviewed Venn's book in 1867, the year after it appeared, he wrote: 'Here is a book which should be read by every thinking man'.[33] (Years later he was less enthusiastic: a 'blundering little book'.[34]) Originality is not at issue. As I said in chapter 15, most writers younger than De Morgan had a frequentist theory, which was almost inevitable in an era of enthusiasm for statistical laws.

Peirce came to call this approach nominalist. He said his own thought evolved towards the realism of Duns Scotus. He remarked that every young man should be a nominalist, but every mature one a realist. His own ideas about probability followed this pattern. By the 1890s he was proposing a dispositional or propensity theory of probability: the probability of throwing a six with a die is the relative frequency with which the die would fall six in tosses of a certain sort, were they possible. He spoke of the 'would be' of a die. Arthur Burks has documented this evolution from frequency to propensity and suggested reasons for Peirce's development.[35]

The dispositional 'would-be' idea is new only in explicitness. What did Laplace mean by the *facilité* of obtaining heads with a coin – the ease of throwing heads – if he did not mean Peirce's 'would be'?[36] At most we may say of Peirce what he said of Venn in 1878:

The conception of probability here set forth is substantially that first developed by Mr Venn, in his *Logic of Chance*. Of course, a vague apprehension of the idea had always existed, but the problem was to make it perfectly clear, and to him belongs the credit of first doing this.[37]

7 THE TRUTH-PRESERVING VIRTUE

What is remarkable is not Peirce's conception of probability but the way that he connected it with the soundness of arguments. The idea was already present in a Boston lecture delivered on 31 October 1866: 'A piece

---

* Before reading Boole he wrote rubbish about probability. In 1861: 'If a premiss rests on a thousand data each of which has one chance in ten of being worthless, the chance of the premiss itself being false is one out of twenty octillion nonillion vigintillion vigintillion vigintillion vigintillion vigintillion vigintillion vigintillion vigintillion vigintillion vigintillion vigintillion vigintillion vigintillion vigintillion.' Compare an older Peirce lashing out at the probabilities derived by the hapless leaders of the Society for Psychical

of evidence which yields a likelihood always yields that likelihood by a process which would more often yield truth than the reverse; and every process which is known to yield truth more often than the reverse gives likelihood'.[38]

'More often yielding truth than the reverse': that is the core of Peirce's understanding of deductive and inductive logic. '*Logic* is the science needed in order to test argument.' It does so not by examining individual arguments but by considering the 'genus' of an argument. If the genus is such that the conclusion of the argument is true whenever the premises are true, the argument is *demonstrative*. If it is such that the conclusion is usually true when the premises are true, it is merely *probable*.[39] In either case, a valid argument has 'the truth-producing virtue'.[40]

When the premises are quantitative, we may be able to replace the 'usually' by a numerical probability. That does not mean that conclusion has a probability of such and such. Rather: the conclusion is reached by an argument that, with such and such a probability, gives true conclusions from true premises.

8 PROBABLE ERROR

Peirce had a model for this kind of argument, based on the standard practice of astronomers, the 'probable error'. The probable error divides measurements into two equal classes. If the errors are Normally distributed, then in the long run half the measurements will err in excess of the probable error, and half will be more exact. But what does this amount to?

Then, as now, most consumers of statistics used 'cookbooks' to make calculations without caring much what they meant. Most seem to have thought: 'I am measuring a position x. I average my measurements to obtain the mean m. I compute the probable error e. The probability, that m is within e of x, is a half.' That is a mistake – but not far from the truth.

Think of estimation on the basis of measurements as a kind of inference. Inductive inference pertains to a genus of arguments. Arguments have premises. In this case, arguments of the genus will have two premises (a) the actual set of measurements of which the mean is m and the probable error is e, and (b) the proposition that errors are Normally distributed. The inference to be drawn is 'x is within e of m'. The inference is *not* 'the probability is $\frac{1}{2}$ that x is within e of m'. If we wish to use a probability-related concept, we ought to say, 'this conclusion is reached by a

Research: 'these numbers, which captivate the ignorant, but which repel thinking men, who know that no human certitude reaches such figures of trillions, or even billions, to one'.

genus of arguments which lead from true premises to true conclusions as often as not'.

Peirce is original in understanding the logic of the situation. Readers familiar with the logic of statistical inference will have noticed that Peirce was providing the core of the rationale of the theory of confidence intervals and of hypothesis-testing advanced by Jerzy Neyman and E.S. Pearson in the 1930s, which is still, for many, the preferred route in statistics.[41] As usual, I am unconcerned with Peirce the precursor. Neyman did not learn anything from Peirce. Still, there is a certain line of filiation. The first modern statement of the rationale of confidence intervals was given not by Neyman but by the Harvard statistician E.B. Wilson. Wilson had been a pupil of Peirce's cousin B.O. Peirce, and was a lifelong admirer of the family. He was one of the few readers of C.S. Peirce on errors of observation, and wrote a paper about it.[42] He had the right perspective as regards predecessors. What he had done, he wrote very late in life, was merely to correct the 'logic' of reasoning that employs standard deviations.[43] E.L. Lehmann has pointed out that as far as computation (as opposed to logic) is concerned there is a long tradition of constructing confidence intervals involving Laplace and Poisson, followed by Lexis and one may add Cournot.[44] But it appears that only Peirce, Wilson and then Neyman got clear about the logical principles of this type of reasoning.

9 INDUCTION AND THE WEIGHT OF EVIDENCE

Have we lost the problem of induction in the niceties of statistical inference? Peirce thought that the matters just examined are at the heart of induction:

the general nature of induction is everywhere the same, and is completely typified by the following example. From a bag of mixed black and white beans I take out a handful, and count the number of black and the number of white beans, and I assume that the black and white are nearly in the same ratio throughout the bag.[45]

Sampling, then, was Peirce's model for induction. The rationale can always be cast into the same logical form as the beanbag. 'Now the scientific conduct of this kind of reasoning is highly complex', he wrote, but the logical principle is always the same.

Peirce became clear about the relation between induction and hypothesis. We frame hypotheses, and test them by induction. Thus we reject hypotheses by a method that errs only a small proportion of the time. My emphasis on rejection is faithful to Peirce: a scientific person 'ardently desires to have his present provisional beliefs (and all his beliefs are merely provisional) swept away, and will work hard to accomplish that object'.[46]

Peirce's theory of probable inference applies only when the premises are quantitative enough to validate probability calculation. He did distinguish – rather too late in his life to satisfy some critics – what he called crude, qualitative and quantitative induction.[47] His account of qualitative induction was poor. He thought that in science one should strive for hypotheses that can be tested quantitatively. He was a man of his time, assenting to Kelvin's dictum that one does not understand a thing until one is able to measure it. That was to be expected of a professional measurer, a student of geodesy.

Peirce was well aware that there are personal judgements of probability and that a psychologist might measure them. Stigler has conjectured that in the psychophysics experiments described above, Peirce was the first experimenter 'to elicit subjective or personal probabilities, determining that these probabilities varied approximately linearly with the log odds'.[48] If the probability of an event is p, the odds are the ratio $p/(1-p)$. The log odds are the logarithm of that ratio. Peirce also had the idea that a logarithm of odds helps explain an intuitive idea of the weight of evidence, a theme which has been extensively developed by I.J. Good.[49]

10 COMMUNITY

'But there remains', wrote Peirce after urging his ideas about induction, 'an important point to be cleared up.'[50] I want to know how reliable my *next* inference is, not that my method of inferring leads to the truth more often than not.

An individual inference must be either true or false, and can show no effect of probability; and, therefore, in reference to a single case considered in itself, probability can have no meaning. Yet if a man had to choose between drawing a card from a pack containing twenty-five red cards and a black one, or from a pack containing twenty-five black cards and a red one, and if the drawing of a red card were destined to transport him to eternal felicity, and that of a black one to consign him to everlasting woe, it would be folly to deny that he ought to prefer the pack containing the larger proportion of red cards, although from the nature of the risk it could not be repeated. It is not easy to reconcile this with our analysis of the conception of chance.[51]

Peirce's response was remarkable.

It seems to me that we are driven to this, that logicality inexorably requires that our interests shall *not* be limited. They must not stop at our own fate, but must embrace the whole community. This community, again, must not be limited, but must extend to all races of beings with whom we can come into immediate or mediate intellectual relation ... There is nothing in the facts to forbid our having a *hope*, or calm and cheerful wish, that the community may last beyond any assignable date.

That leads to 'that famous trio of Charity, Faith and Hope'.[52] Cantankerous solitary Peirce held that 'social sentiment [is] presupposed in reasoning'. In Peirce's first major series of papers we read that 'the very origin of the conception of reality shows that this conception essentially involves the notion of COMMUNITY, without definite limits, and capable of an indefinite increase in knowledge'.[53] This is the exact opposite of the Cartesian foundation of reality on the introspective individual ego. 'Most modern philosophers', Peirce wrote in the same essay, 'have been in effect Cartesians. Now without wishing to return to scholasticism, it seems to me that modern science and modern logic require us to stand upon a very different platform from this.'[54] The frequent references to community were written at the Coast Survey, where it had real emotional content. His community of inquirers was the community of geodesists, the people in Boston, Berlin, London, Paris, Brussels and even some in Washington.

11 TRUTH AND SELF-CORRECTION

Peirce seldom discussed truth. He did teach that truth is the opinion that people would settle down on if they settle down on anything. Early and nominalistically he wrote that truth is what we are fated to believe. Later, 'if truth consists in satisfaction, it cannot be any *actual* satisfaction but must be the satisfaction that *would* ultimately be found if the inquiry were pushed to its ultimate and indefeasible issue'.[55] This is the general form of the transition from nominalism to realism, already noted in connection with chance: it corresponds to the switch from probability relative frequency in an actual series to a 'would-be'. Note the 'ifs' in his minimalist account of truth. Peirce was well aware that

> we cannot be quite sure that the community ever will settle down to an unalterable conclusion upon any given question. Even if they do so for the most part, we have no reason to think the unanimity will be quite complete, nor can we rationally presume any overwhelming *consensus* of opinion will be reached upon every question. All that we are entitled to assume is in the form of a *hope* that such conclusion may be substantially reached concerning the particular questions with which our inquiries are busied'.[56]

This hope is identical to the hope already voiced when he wrote that probability logic is founded on faith, hope and charity.

Peirce is thought to have had a justification of induction, namely, that it is a self-correcting method that leads to the truth. He has even been praised for inventing the idea. Larry Laudan has observed that the praise is misplaced, for this was no innovation in the nineteenth century. It was commonplace and if anything Peirce 'trivialized' it.[57] But an even stronger statement is to be made. It is a simple tautology to say that induction is a self-correcting method that necessarily leads to the truth. Peirce did not think that first of all there is the truth, and then there is a method for reaching it. The truth is what induction gives. His theory of probable inference is a way of producing stable estimates of relative frequencies. But on the other hand the real world just *is* a set of stabilized relative frequencies whose formal properties are precisely those of Peirce's estimators. Method and reality do not fit by good fortune or preestablished harmony. Each defines the other.

This is not an 'interpretation' of Peirce. He said as much himself, even as early as 1869. An inductive form of argument should lead to conclusions that 'would be more apt to be true in the long run ... than a random assertion would be'. In a footnote:

This sufficiently sets forth the essential elements of an argument; but does not define it, since in introducing the conception of truth it commits a diallele.[58]

'Diallele'? The right word (if such there be) was 'diallelon', invented by Sir William Hamilton in 1860. In the *Century* dictionary, Peirce defined it thus:

diallelon: In *logic*, a tautological definition, a definition which contains the word defined, the definition of a term by means of another which is itself defined by means of the first; definition in a circle.

12 EVOLUTIONARY LOVE

It seems empty hocus-pocus to think of truth and scientific method as linked by circular definition. Truth is a matter of how the world is, we protest, and method is what we do. Hence there is a fundamental question about a method: is it any good? That means, does it effectively lead us to find out the way the world is?

Peirce's answer is extraordinary to us, but not to his contemporaries. Many took for granted a striking and necessary parallel between the evolution of mind and of matter. Idealism, of a sort that we have long forgotten, was rampant. 'Matter is effete mind' is a far more striking saying in 1989 than in 1898. Peirce's father Benjamin, in a textbook of mechanics: 'Every portion of the material universe is pervaded by the same laws of mechanical action, which are incorporated into the very constitution of the human mind.'[59] Pragmaticism is a hyperbolic version of this: *the universe reaches its successive states by processes formally and materially analogous to those by which sound method reaches its conclusions.* The connection between 'the way the world is' and 'how we find out about it' is one of identity of organic structure.

At the end of chapter 18 I mentioned Emile Boutroux's doctrine of contingently evolving natural law. William James and to some extent Peirce were close to the Boutroux circle and to Renouvier. Laws of nature, they held, were not given from the beginning of the universe, as most modern cosmology has it. Laws of complex forms were not determined by laws of simpler forms, but came into being as those complex forms emerged in the history of the universe. That's Boutroux in 1875.

Peirce wrote that a philosophy of induction should be embedded in metaphysics. For him, that meant evolutionary metaphysics. It was a metaphysics rich in corollaries for a professional measurer like Peirce. Laws of nature are commonly presented as equations with some fixed parameters, none other than Babbage's constants of nature. But if laws are evolving from chance, we need not imagine that the constants are anything more than limiting values that will be reached in some indefinite future. The ultimate 'reality' of our measurements and what they measure has the form of the Gaussian law of error. It is bank balances and credit ledgers that are exact, said Peirce, not the constants of nature. Stop trying to model the world, as we have done since the time of Descartes, on the transactions of shopkeepers. The 'constants' are only chance variables that have settled down in the course of the evolution of laws.

Peirce combined evolving laws with an evolutionary epistemology. Why are our instinctive ways of classifying things so well suited to simple induction? It is often suggested that natural selection adapts species so that they make discriminations that match the functionally relevant aspects of their environment. If we distinguish colours early, it is because telling things apart by their colour helps us survive. Even if this were true, it would not explain why people are able to explore the cosmos and the microcosmos. There is no discernible evolutionary advantage in our ability to formulate the concept of gravitational force, to go through the steps from Kepler to Newton, and finally to be a 'pendulum-swinger' like Peirce determining the gravitational constant. Peirce morosely remarked that the talent for such thoughts and activities makes one poor company and impedes survival.

Our ability for inquiry of an abstract sort is a product of evolution, but it is at best of indifferent value for our survival. We should think instead of mental abilities as evolving parallel to the evolution of the laws of the universe. We can discover the latter because they and our minds have evolved in the same way. Peirce called this 'evolutionary love'.[60]

13   CHANCE IS FIRST

I have not been presenting an interpretation of Peirce, an attempt to explain or to highlight what he really meant. I have aimed only at describing a man whose professional life as a measurer was immersed in the technologies of chance and probability, and who, in consequence of that daily experience, finally surrendered to the idea that there is absolute chance in the universe. He poured this experience of chance into most aspects of his philosophy, including those that we now find esoteric. Peirce was the first philosopher completely to internalize the way in which chance had been tamed in the course of the nineteenth century. It is fitting that the further reaches of his metaphysics could also be summed up in my title, 'the taming of chance'. But where my title was metaphorical, in a Peircian summation it would be literal. For Peirce's history of the universe, in which blind Chance stabilizes into approximate Law, is nothing other than the taming of chance.

Is Reason comforted then, does that giantess, metaphysical chance, no longer threaten or offer untold delights? Do we live in a world made safe by statistical laws, the laws of averages writ small upon the tiniest particles of matter? Of course not. Peirce was fond of trios, which he called Firsts, Seconds and Thirds. 'Chance is First, Law is Second, the tendency to take habits is Third.'[61] That did not mean that chance is annulled by statistical law, or that the successive throws of the dice engender a world in which we can resume or reassume Hume's comfortable habits. What was First is always so. Even when the dice are cast in circumstances of eternity, as when we contemplate the constellations of the cosmos, or cast in circumstances of complete and personal particularity, as when we seal our own fate, chance pours in at every avenue of sense. We cannot suppose that Peirce saw the 1897 copy of *Cosmopolis* containing the poem by Mallarmé, three years his junior.[62] But he was at one with the thought, 'A throw of the dice never will annul chance.'

NOTES

Translations in the text are my responsibility unless otherwise noted.

1 The argument

1 F. Galton, *Natural Inheritance* (London, 1889): 66.
2 W. Wundt, *Beiträge zur Theorie der Sinneswahrnehmung* (Berlin, 1862): xxvi.
3 I have begun to discuss them in 'Making up People' in T. Heller *et al.* (eds.), *Reconstructing Individualism* (Stanford, 1986): 222–36. See also my 'Biopower and the Avalanche of Printed Numbers', *Humanities in Society* 5 (1982): 279–95. For much more detailed work from a different perspective, see Alain Desrosières and Laurent Thevenot, *Les Catégories socioprofessionelles* (Paris, 1988); S.R.S. Stretzer, 'The Genesis of the Registrar-General's Social Classification of Occupations', *The British Journal of Sociology* 35 (1986): 522–45.
4 T.S. Kuhn, 'The Function of Measurement in Modern Physical Science' (1961), in *The Essential Tension* (Chicago, 1977): 220.
5 Ian Hacking, 'Styles of Reasoning', in J. Rajchman and C. West (eds.), *Postanalytic Philosophy* (New York, 1985): 145–64; this is an expanded version of 'Language, Truth and Reason', in M. Hollis and S. Lukes (eds.), *Rationality and Relativism* (Oxford, 1983): 48–66. I read the draft of A.C. Crombie's *Styles of Scientific Thinking in the European Tradition* in 1980, and have been referring to it ever since. I hope to see the published version soon.
6 This list is from A.C. Crombie, 'Philosophical Presuppositions and Shifting Interpretations of Galileo', in J. Hintikka *et al.* (eds.), *Theory Change, Ancient Axiomatics and Galileo's Methodology* (Dordrecht, 1981): 284.
7 William H. Kruskal and Frederick Mosteller, 'Representative Sampling. I. Non-scientific Literature', *International Statistical Review* 47 (1979): 13–24; 'II. Scientific Literature, Excluding Statistics', *ibid.*, 111–27; 'III. The Current Statistical Literature', *ibid.*, 245–65; 'IV. The History of the Concept in Statistics', *ibid.*, 48 (1980): 169–95.
8 Alain Desrosières, 'The Part in Relation to the Whole: How to Generalize? The Prehistory of Representative Sampling', in M. Bulmer *et al.* (eds.), *The Social Survey in Historical Perspective* (Cambridge, 1989).
9 I.J. Good, 'Changing Concepts of Chance', a review of L. Krüger *et al.* (eds.), *The Probabilistic Revolution* (2 vols., Cambridge, Mass., 1987), in *Nature* 332 (1988): 406.
10 Ian Hacking, *The Emergence of Probability* (Cambridge, 1975). 'The person whom we call Hume' was the topic of the last chapter of that book, but his role

was completely different from that of Peirce in the present one. Leibniz was my witness then, and Peirce is my witness now.

11 D. Garber and S. Zabell, 'On the Emergence of Probability', *Archive for History of Exact Sciences* **21** (1979): 33–53. See also chapter 1 of Daston's *Classical Probability* (note 13 below).

12 Ian Hacking, 'From the Emergence of Probability to the Erosion of Determinism', in J. Hintikka *et al.* (eds.), *Probability, Thermodynamics and the History of Science* (Dordrecht, 1981): 105–23, made plainer my debt to Michel Foucault which was already so obvious in *The Emergence of Probability*. My debt to later work by Foucault is equally evident in the present book. The third part of 'Five Parables' in R. Rorty, J. Schneewind and Q. Skinner (eds.), *Philosophy in its Context* (Cambridge, 1984): 103–24 states the overall programme of *Emergence*. To some extent 'Two Ways for the Philosopher to Use the History of Knowledge' in *New Literary History* (forthcoming 1990) does the same for the present work. For an earlier and blunter statement, see 'How should we do the History of Statistics?' *I&C* **8** (1981): 15–26.

13 William Coleman, *Death as a Social Disease* (Madison, Wis., 1981); Lorraine Daston, *Classical Probability in the Enlightenment* (Princeton, 1988); L. Krüger *et al.*, *The Probabilistic Revolution*; Donald MacKenzie, *Statistics in Britain, 1865–1930: The Social Construction of Scientific Knowledge* (Edinburgh, 1981); Theodore M. Porter, *The Rise of Statistical Thinking 1820–1900* (Princeton, 1986); Stephen M. Stigler, *The History of Statistics: The Measurement of Uncertainty before 1900* (Cambridge, Mass., 1986).

14 Gerd Gigerenzer *et al.* (eds.), *The Empire of Chance: How Probability Changed Science and Everyday Life* (Cambridge, 1989).

15 Mallarmé's *Un Coup de dés jamais n'abolira le hasard* was published in *Cosmopolis* in 1897, but his typographical instructions were not exactly followed until a printing of 1926. Where I have used translated phrases from this piece, they are from Brian Coffley (trans.), *Dice Thrown Never Will Annul Chance* (Dublin, 1965).

2 The doctrine of necessity

1 C.S. Peirce, 'The Doctrine of Necessity Examined', *The Monist* **2** (1892); *Collected Papers of Charles Sanders Peirce* (Cambridge, Mass., 1931–58), **6**, 28.

2 *Ibid.*, 45.

3 P.S. de Laplace, *Essai philosophique sur les probabilités* (Paris, 1814), trans. F.W. Truscott and F.L. Emory, *A Philosophical Essay on Probabilities* (New York, 1951): 3.

4 C.C. Gillispie, 'Mémoires inédits ou anonymes de Laplace sur la théorie des erreurs, les polynômes de Legendre, et la philosophie des probabilités', *Revue d'histoire des sciences* **32** (1979): 223–79.

5 Laplace, *Essay*, 4.

6 I. Kant, *Grundlegung zur Metaphysik der Sitten* (1785), ed. P. Menzer, *Kants Gesammelte Schriften* (Berlin, 1903): *Erste Abteilung* **4**, 449.

7 M. Julienne Junkersfeld, *The Aristotelian Thomistic Concept of Chance* (Notre Dame, Ind., 1945).

8 A. De Moivre, *The Doctrine of Chances* (London, 1738): 241.

9 D. Hume, *A Treatise of Human Nature* (London, 1739), ed. L.A. Selby-Bigge (Oxford, 1888): 130.

10 D. Hume, *Enquiries Concerning Human Understanding* (originally *Philosophical Essays* of 1748), ed. L.A. Selby-Bigge, (Oxford, 1902): 95.

11 Hume, *Treatise*, 399f.

12 D. Hume, *The History of Great Britain* (London, 1757): **2**, 452. (chapter LXII; the last two volumes of what is commonly called or reprinted as Hume's *History of England* were entitled *History of Great Britain* as they dealt with the nation after the Act of Union).

13 Laplace, *Essay*, 3.

14 X. Bichat, *Anatomie générale appliquée à la médecine*, (Paris, 1801): xxxv.

15 *Ibid.*, liii.

16 J.G. Herder, *Ideen zur Philosophie der Geschichte der Menschheit* (Riga, 1784).

17 I. Kant, 'Idee zu einer allgemeinen Geschichte in Weltbürgerlicher Absicht' (1784), trans. L.W. Beck, 'Idea for a Universal History from a Cosmopolitan Point of View', in Kant, *On History*, (Indianapolis, 1963): 11.

3   Public amateurs, secretive bureaucrats

1 J.W. Goethe, *Italian Journey (1786–1788)*, trans. W.H. Auden and E. Mayer (New York, 1962): 21. J. Sinclair, *A Statistical Account of Scotland* (Edinburgh, 1791–9): **20**, liii.

2 For a study of the consequences of this obsession, see Robert A. Nye, *Crime, Madness and Politics in Modern France: The Medical Concept of National Decline* (Princeton, 1984).

3 *Cf.* Gerald N. Grob, *Edward Jarvis and the Medical World of Nineteenth-century America* (Knoxville, 1978).

4 W. Petty, *The Petty Papers*, ed. the Marquis of Lansdowne (London, 1927): **1**, 171.

5 O. Klopp (ed.), *Die Werke von Leibniz* (11 vols., Hanover, 1864–8): **5**, 303–15.

6 Otto Behre, 'Uber den Anteil germanischer Völker an der Entwicklung der Statistik', *Allgemeine Statistisches Archiv* **7** (1907): 75.

7 Otto Behre, *Geschichte der Statistik in Brandenburg-Preussen bis zur Grundung des königlich Statistisches Bureaus* (Berlin, 1905).

8 *Magazin für die neue Historie und Geographie* (23 vols., 1762–93). *Wochentlich Nachrichten* (1773–87). For a thorough discussion of the 'amateurs' and their weeklies or monthlies, see W. Schöne, *Zeitungswesen und Statistik: Eine Untersuchung über den Einfluss der periodischen Presse auf die Entstehung und Entwicklung der Staatswissenschaftlichen Literatur, speziell der Statistik* (Jena, 1924).

9 C.G.A. Knies, *Die Statistik als selbständige Wissenschaft: zur Lösung des Wirrfals in der Theorie und Praxis dieser Wissenschaft* (Kassel, 1850): 3.

10 Johann Bernoulli, *Reisen durch Brandenburg, Pommern, Preussen, Curland, Russland und Pohlen* (4 vols., Leipzig, 1779–80): **2**, 197.

11 *Ibid.*, **4**, 86.

12 J.P. Süssmilch, *Die gottliche Ordnung in der Veränderung des menschlichen*

Geschlechts, aus der Geburt, dem Tode und der Fortpflanzung desselben erwiesen (Berlin, 1741).

13 *Ibid.*, 18.

14 J.P.Süssmilch, *Versuch eines Beweis dass die erste Sprache ihren Ursprung nicht von Menschen, sondern allein vom Schöpfer erhalten habe* (Berlin, 1766). For the influence of this work, see Bruce Kieffer, 'Herder's Treatment of Süssmilch', *The Germanic Review* **53** (1978): 96–295.

15 For references and discussion see Hacking, *The Emergence of Probability*, 166–71.

16 William Derham, *Physico-Theology: or a Demonstration of the Attributes of God from His Works of Creation* (London, 1713).

17 Michel Foucault, *The History of Sexuality*, (New York, 1980): 138.

18 I take the phrase 'risk portfolio' from Mary Douglas and Aaron Wildavsky, *Risk and Culture: An Essay on the Selection of Environmental Dangers* (Berkeley, 1982).

19 Richard Boeckh, *Die geschichtliche Entwicklung der amtlichen Statistik des preussischen Staates: Eine Festgabe für den internationalen statistischen Congress in Berlin* (Berlin, 1863).

20 For a bibliography, see W. Sachse, *Bibliographie zur preussischen Gewerbestatistik 1750–1850* (Göttingen, 1981).

21 Behre, 'Uber den Anteil germanischer Völker', 77. M. Schmeitzel's book and lecture summary is *Einleitung zur Staatswissenschaft* (Halle, 1732).

22 For a thorough history of this entire period, up to 1835, see Vincenz John, *Geschichte der Statistik: Ein Quellenmässiges Handbuch für den akademischen Gebrauch wie für den Selbstunterricht* (Stuttgart, 1884), **1**.

23 A.L. Schlozer, *Staats-Gelehrtheit nach ihren Haupt-Theilen, im Auszug und Zusammenhang*. Part 2. *Allgemeine Statistik*. **1**, *Theorie der Statistik: Nebst Ideen über das Studium der Politik überhaupt* (Göttingen, 1804): 47.

24 G. Rumelin, 'Statistik', *Tübinger Zeitschrift für Staatswissenschaft* **4** (1863): 645.

25 *Cf.* note 10.

26 H. Westergaard. *Contributions to the History of Statistics* (London, 1932): l4.

27 Sinclair, *Statistical Account*, **16**, 16–18.

28 Ernest Gray (ed.), *Man Midwife: The Further Experiences of John Knyveton, M.D., Late Surgeon in the British Fleet, During the Years 1763–1809* (London, 1946): 135.

4 Bureaux

1 'Zur Geschichte des königlich preussischen statistischen Bureaus', *Zeitschrift des königlich preussischen Statistischen Bureau* **1** (1860): 4.

2 His own account of its early years is J. Sinclair, *Account of the Origin of the Board of Agriculture and its Purposes for Three Years after its Establishment* (London, 1796).

3 The first fruits, serving as exemplar and promise of the future, were in J. Sinclair, *Specimen of the Statistical Account of Scotland, Drawn up form the Communications of the Ministers of the Different Parishes* (Edinburgh, 1791).

4 J. Sinclair, in a circular letter dated 1 November 1794; *The Statistical Account of Scotland* (Edinburgh, 1799): **20**, xvii.

5 11 July 1797; *Ibid.*, liii.

6 L. Krug, *Topographische-statistische-geographisches Wörterbuch, der sämmtlichen preussischen Staaten oder Beschreibung aller Provinzen, Kreise, Distrikte, Städte etc. in den preussischen Staaten* (13 vols., Halle, 1796–1803).

7 Krug's first ill-fated journal was *Preussischer Anzeiger*; the second was *Annalen der preussischer Staatswirtschaft und Statistik*.

8 This is suggested in the essay on Krug in the *Allgemeine Deutsche Bibliographie* (Leipzig, 1878–99): **17**, 216. For further biography, see Otto Schwarz, *Leopold Krug als Nationalökonomie: Ein Beitrag zur deutschen Sozial und Wirtschaftsgeschichte im 19. Jahrhundert* (Frankfurt a.M., 1904).

9 L. Krug, *Betrachtungen über den National-Reichtum des preussischen Staate und über den Wohlstand seiner Bewohner* (2 vols., Berlin, 1805).

10 'Zur Geschichte' (note 1 above), 3.

11 A letter from Stein of 7 May – three weeks before the royal decree – initially proposing a statistical office is mentioned in Hermann Loening, *Johann Gottfried Hoffmann und sein Anteilen der staatswirtschaftlichen Gesetzgebung Preussens. Erster Teil: 1765–1813* (Halle, 1914): 47. I am grateful to Ernst P. Hamm for help in studying the Prussian bureau, and especially the work of Hoffmann.

12 Richard Boeckh, *Die geschichtliche Entwicklung der amtlichen Statistik des preussischen Staates* (Berlin, 1863): 28.

13 The chair of 'cameralism'; his predecessor, Kant's colleague Kraus, was the man who brought the ideas of Adam Smith to the German public; see Loening, *Hoffmann*, 26.

14 'Zur Geschichte'(note 1 above), 4.

15 *Ibid.*, 6.

16 On this and other aspects of Engel, see Ian Hacking, 'Prussian Numbers 1860–1882', in Krüger *et al.*, *The Probabilistic Revolution*, **1**, 377–94.

17 *Mittheilung des preussisches statistisches Bureaus*, 1851–60.

18 'Verzeichnis der von der königlich Regierung auf dem laufenden erhalten statistischen Nachrichten', *Zeitschrift des königlich preussischen statistischen Bureau* **3** (1863): 287–308.

19 Ernst Engel, 'Die Volkzählung, ihrer Stellung zur Wissenschaft und ihre Aufgabe in der Geschichte', *ibid.* **2** (1862): 31.

5   The sweet despotism of reason

1 *Gazette nationale ou Le Moniteur universelle* no. 203 (23 germ. l'an IV: 12 April 1796). The report of the meeting is continued in the next two issues.

2 Norton Wise, 'How do Sums Count? On the Cultural Origins of Statistical Causality' in Krüger *et al.*, *Probabilistic Revolution* **1**, 395–426.

3 'Eloge de M. Buquet', in *Œuvres de Condorcet*, ed. A. Condorcet-O'Connor and F. Arago, (Paris, 1847): **2**, 410.

4 *Discours prononcés dans l'académie françoise le jeudi février MDCLXXXII à la réception de M. le Marquis de Condorcet* (Paris, 1782). Many key writings are translated in *Condorcet: Selected Writings*, ed. K.M. Baker (Indianapolis,

1976). The reception speech, with Condorcet's subsequent unpublished revisions is on pp. 3–32. The definitive study of Condorcet's moral science is K. M. Baker, *Condorcet: From Natural Philosophy to Social Mathematics* (Chicago, 1975).

5 *Selected Writings*, 18f.

6 *Ibid.*, 184. K.M. Baker, 'The Early History of the Term, "Social Science"', *Annals of Science* **20** (1964): 211–26, revised in his *Condorcet*, 391–5.

7 For an account of the name-battles, see J. Lottin, *Quetelet: statisticien et sociologue* (Louvain, 1912): 331–66.

8 K. Pearson, *The History of Statistics in the 17th and 18th Centuries against the Changing Background of Intellectual Scientific and Religious Thought. Lectures Given by Karl Pearson at University College London during the Academic Years 1921–1933* (London, 1975): 448, 495. Pearson's description of Condorcet is in part a description of Pearson himself. *Cf.* Ian Hacking, 'Karl Pearson's History of Statistics', *British Journal for the Philosophy of Science* **32** (1981): 177–82.

9 For a graphic overview of socio-statistical materials and their availability, see Bertrand Gille, *Les Sources statistiques de l'histoire de France. Des enquêtes du XVIIe siècle à 1870* (Paris, 1964).

10 L. Daston, *Classical Probability in the Enlightenment* (Princeton, 1988), chapter 3.

11 J.H. Lambert, 'Anmerkung über die Sterblichkeit, Todtenlisten, Geburten und Ehen', Part IX of *Beyträge zum Gebrauche der Mathematique und deren Anwendung* (Berlin, 1765). Lambert's analysis is criticized in H. Westergaard, *Die Lehre von der Mortalität*, (2nd edn, Berlin, 1889): 200. Westergaard's *Contributions to the History of Statistics* (London, 1932) provides numerous other examples of 'laws of mortality' and also discusses in some detail the issues about mortality raised by inoculation and then vaccination against smallpox. His information is very greatly supplemented by Daston, although the emphasis is different. Westergaard was looking for past laws of mortality, while Daston explains why they had so little practical significance.

12 His *Gesetz der Sterblichkeit* goes as follows. Let y be the number of survivors at year x from a population at birth of N people. Then if t is the age at death of the oldest survivor, and k, m and n are adjustable parameters, he proposed:

$$y = N[(t-x)/t]^2 - k(e-x/m - e-x/n)$$

Using a table of Süssmilch's, he took the values

$t = 96$
$k = 6176$
$m = 31.651$
$n = 2.43114.$

The places of decimals are spurious, and the equation greatly overestimates mortality at age 2 and underestimates it everywhere else.

13 E.-E. Duvillard de Durand, *Recherches sur les rentes, les emprunts et les remboursemens* (Geneva, 1787).

14 A comment by F. Garnier in *Correspondance mathématique et physique* **1** (1825): 18.

15 Mme de Stäel, *De l'influence des passions sur le bonheur des individus et des nations* (Lausanne, 1796); *Œuvres* (Paris, 1820): **3**, 10.

16 Condorcet, *Œuvres*, **10**, 75.

17 Condorcet, *Essai sur l'application de l'analyse à la probabilité des décisions rendue à la pluralité des voix* (Paris, 1785).

18 For a retrospective view with references, see K. Arrow, *The Economics of Information* (Cambridge, Mass., 1984): 179.

19 C. C. Gillispie, 'Probability and Politics: Laplace, Condorcet and Turgot', *Proceedings of the American Philosophical Society* **116** (1972): 1–20.

20 The lectures late in life were published as P.C.F. Daunou, *Cours d'études historiques* (Paris, 1842–9). The final volume has an attack on a work by Broussais that I mention several times in later chapters; see J.-F. Braunstein, *Broussais et le matérialisme: médecine et philosophie au XIXe siècle* (Paris, 1896): 111-l6.

21 See Baker, *Condorcet*, 272–85, esp. p. 280.

22 Published by the Institut in 1796.

23 E.-E. Duvillard de Durand, *Analyse et tableaux de l'influence de la petite vérôle sur la mortalité à chaque âge et de celle qu'un préservatif tel que la vaccine peut avoir sur la population* (Paris, 1806). See also his *Rapport du Collège des médecins de Londres, sur la vaccination, suivi d'une analyse de son influence sur la mortalité* (Paris, 1807).

24 Published by the Institut in 1813.

25 Marie-Noëlle Bourguet, 'Décrire, Compter, Calculer: The Debate over Statistics during the Napoleonic Period', in L. Krüger *et al.*, *Probabilistic Revolution*, 307.

26 For a thorough study of Napoleonic statistics, see Marie-Noëlle Bourguet, *Déchiffrer la France: la statistique départementale à l'époque Napoléonienne* (Paris, 1989).

27 Bourguet, 'Décrire', 312.

28 *Ibid.*, 313.

6   The quantum of sickness

1 'Report of the Select Committee to Consider the Laws Respecting the Friendly Societies', *Parliamentary Papers* (1825 [522] IV 321): 44.

2 *Ibid.*, 14.

3 *Ibid.*, 152.

4 'Report by John Finlaison, Actuary of the National Debt, on the Elementary Facts on which the Tables of Life Annuities are Founded', *Parliamentary Papers* (1829 [122] III 287).

5 'Report' on Friendly Societies, 6.

6 'Resolutions of the Select Committee (of 1824) appointed to Inquire into the State of the Law of the United Kingdom [etc.] so far as relates to the Combination of Workmen and others, to Raise Wages, or to Regulate the Hours of Working', *Parliamentary Papers* (1825 [437] IV 499): 64 Appendix No. 22.

7 H. Westergaard, *Contributions to the History of Statistics* (London, 1932): 53–60, on A. Berch, E. Salander, Th. Wassenius, P. Elvius, E. Carleson and particularly Per Wargentin (1717–83).

8 A. Deparcieux, *Essai sur les probabilités de la durée de la vie humaine*,(Paris, 1746).

9 Until age 32, he reasoned, we should expect one adult labourer in 45 to be too sick to work on any given day. Up to 42 we should add a quarter more [$\frac{1}{48}$ + $(\frac{1}{4})(\frac{1}{45}) = \frac{5}{192}$]. And so on, with $\frac{6}{192}$ ill between 43 and 51, $\frac{7}{192}$ between 52 and 55, and $\frac{8}{192}$ between 58 and 64, or one man in 24 incapacitated at any time during these last eight years of working life. Why these figures? About half the people alive at 30 survive another 28 years, while about half those alive at 60 survive another thirteen years. Thus the probable duration of life at 30 is about twice that at 60. So the vital forces are twice as strong at 30 as at 60. Hence the proportion ill at 30 should be half the proportion ill at 60, a ratio to which Price's fractions $\frac{1}{48}$ and $\frac{1}{24}$ conform.

10 'Report' on Friendly Societies, 40.

11 *Ibid.*, 162.

12 'Report of the Committee of the Highland Society of Scotland appointed in 1820 to inquire into the State of Friendly Societies', *Prize Essays and Transactions of the Highland Society of Scotland* 6 (1824): 271–560.

13 *Ibid.*, 312.

14 For the rules, see *Prize Essays and Transactions* 5 (1820): 569–71.

15 *Ibid.*, 420; summarized by the Select Committee in its 1825 Report on p. 137.

16 1825 'Report' on Friendly Societies, 39.

17 *Ibid.*, 58.

18 *Ibid.*, 75.

19 *Ibid.*, 140.

20 'Report from the Select Committee appointed to consider the Laws respecting the Friendly Societies and to whom was referred the Report of 5th July 1825', *Parliamentary Papers* (1826–7 [588]): 3, 869.

21 M. Mitchell, 'Factories Inquiry: A Supplementary Report',[Supplementary to Dr F. Bissett-Hawkins's main report], in J. R. McCulloch, *A Statistical Account of the British Empire* (London, 1837): 48.

22 For biography, see John M. Eyler, *Victorian Social Medicine: The Ideas and Methods of William Farr* (Baltimore, 1979).

23 The quotation is from W. Farr, *Tables of Lifetime Annuities and Premiums with an Introduction by William Farr* (London, 1861): cxxix; for further description see Farr's essay in *Philosophical Transactions of the Royal Society* 149 (1859): 837–78. For Scheutz see Farr Collection 1 (*Letters to William Farr*): 90, British Library of Economics and Political Science (London School of Economics).

24 W. Farr, 'Mortality and Diseases of Armies', *British Medical Almanack* 6 (1836): 109–11; 'Proportion of Sickness at Different Ages', *ibid.*, 111–13; 'On Benevolent Funds and Life Insurance in Health and Sickness', *Lancet* (1837–8, pt. i): 701–4, 817–23.

25 W. Farr, 'On a Method of Determining the Danger and the Duration of Diseases at every period of their progress', *British Annals of Medicine, Pharmacy, Vital Statistics and General Science* 1 (1837): 72–9.

26 W. Farr, 'On the Law of Recovery and Dying in Small Pox', *ibid.* 2 (1837): 134–43.

7 The granary of science

1 Charles Babbage, 'On the advantage of a Collection of Numbers, to be entitled the Constants of Nature and of Art [...] in a letter to Dr. Brewster,' *The Edinburgh Journal of Science*, new series **6** (1832): 334.

2 For a careful study, see H.J.M. Bos, 'Introduction', in *Christiaan Huygens' The Pendulum Clock or Geometrical Demonstrations Concerning the Motion of Pendula as Applied to Clocks*, ed. R.J. Blackwell (Ames, Iowa, 1986): xxi-xxv.

3 William Turnbull, *A Treatise on the Strength, Flexure, and Stiffness of Cast Iron Beams and Columns, shewing their fitness to resist Transverse Strains, Torsion, Compression, Tension, and Impulsion; with Tables of Constants* [etc.] (London, 1831). The *OED* cites the much enlarged 2nd edn of 1832.

4 *The Mathematical and Scientific Library of the Late Charles Babbage*, a catalogue compiled by R.T. (London, 1872).

5 *Annalen der Physik und Chimie* **21** (1824): 609.

6 Babbage's attack on the Royal Society is *Reflections on the Decline of Science in England and Reflection on Some of its Causes* (London, 1830). His German trip was reported in *Edinburgh Journal of Science* **10** (1829): 225–34.

7 *On the Economy of Machinery and Manufactures* (London, 1832).

8 'Sur l'emploi plus ou moins fréquent des mêmes lettres dans les différentes langues', *Correspondance mathématique et physique* **7** (1831): 135–7. Extracts from Quetelet's *éloge* in the *Annuaire de l'Observatoire Royal de Bruxelles* of 1873 are translated with a comment by Joseph Henry in *Annual Report of the Board of Regents of the Smithsonian Institution* (Washington D.C., 1873): 183–7.

9 Ole Immanuel Franksen, *Mr. Babbage's Secret: The Tale of a Cypher – APL* (n.p., n.d; IBM, Strandberg, Denmark, 1984?).

10 'A Letter to the Right. Hon. T.P. Courtenay, on the Proportionate Number of Births of the two Sexes under Different Circumstances', *Edinburgh Journal of Science*, new series **1** (1829): 85–104.

11 Babbage became a witness to the Select Committee on the strength of his study, *A Comparative View of the Various Institutions for the Assurance of Lives* (London, 1826).

12 Babbage, 'On Tables of the Constants of Nature and Art', *Annual Report of the Board of Regents of the Smithsonian Institution*, (Washington, D.C., 1856): 294. His 1826 proposal was summarized in *Edinburgh Journal of Science*, new series **1** (1829): 187.

13 See *Compte Rendu des Travaux du Congrès Général de Statistique* (Brussels, 1853); for Henry, see the Smithsonian *Annual Report* for 1873, p. 25.

14 T.S. Kuhn, 'The Function of Measurement in Modern Physical Science', *Isis* **52** (1961): 161–90; references are to the reprint in T.S. Kuhn, *The Essential Tension* (Chicago, 1977): 178–224.

15 Statements, origins and formulations of Kelvin's end-of-the-nineteenth-century saying are given in R.K. Merton *et al.*, 'The Kelvin Dictum and Social Science: an Excursion into the History of an Idea', *Journal of the History of the Behavioral Sciences* **20** (1984): 319–31.

16 See. K. Pearson, *The Life, Letters and Labours of Francis Galton* (4 vols., Cambridge, 1914–30): **2**, 347f.

17 Kuhn, *Essential Tension*, 220.

18 On institutions and 'big' revolutions, see Ian Hacking, 'Was There a Probabilistic Revolution 1800–1930?', in *The Probabilistic Revolution* 1, 45–58. For an account of the English statistical societies and their networks, see Michael Cullen, *The Statistical Movement in Early Victorian Britain: The Foundations of Empirical Social Research* (London, 1975).

19 Herbert Butterfield, *The Origins of Modern Science* (Cambridge, 1957): 1.

20 *Thoughts on the Principles of Taxation*, (London, 1848): 21.

21 This was part of a large investigation for studying diurnal and seasonal rhythms in plants and animals. A. Quetelet, *Bulletins de l'Académie Royale des Sciences et Belles-Lettres de Bruxelles* 9 (1842): 65–95.

22 Kuhn, *Essential Tension*, 219.

23 Babbage, 'Constants', 340.

8   Suicide is a kind of madness

1 George M. Burrows, 'Observations on the Comparative Mortality of Paris and London in the Year 1813', *The London Medical Repository* 4 (1814): 457.

2 Laurent Haeberli, 'Le Suicide à Genève au XVIIIe siècle' in *Pour une histoire qualitative: études offertes à Sven Stelling-Michaud* (Geneva, 1975): 115–29.

3 For a full study, see Jan Goldstein, *Console and Classify: The French Psychiatric Profession in the Nineteenth Century* (Cambridge, 1987).

4 J.-E.-D. Esquirol, 'Suicide', *Dictionnaire des sciences médicales* 53 (1821): 213. There are references to Burrows on p. 276.

5 Agatopisto Cromaziono, *Storia critica filosofica del suicidio ragionato* (Lucca, 1759).

6 In Esquirol's dictionary article, and in the summing up of his life work, *Des maladies mentales, considérées sous les rapports médical, hygiénique et médico-légal* (Paris, 1838).

7 G.M. Burrows, *An Inquiry into Certain Errors Relative to Insanity and their Consequences, Physical, Moral and Civil* (London, 1820): 87.

8 By George Cheyne (London, 1732). The work is largely a reply to those who queried diet as a cure for madness; for the diet itself, see p. 163 of the 2nd edn (London, 1734).

9 Anne-Charles Lorry, *De melancolia et morbis melancolicis* (Paris, 1765).

10 J.-P. Falret, *De l'hypochondrie et du suicide. Considérations sur les causes, sur le siège et le traitement de ces maladies, sur les moyens d'en arrêter le progrès et d'en prévenir le développement* (Paris, 1822). Falret eulogized Esquirol: *Discours sur la tombe de M. Esquirol le 14 décembre 1840* (Paris, 1841).

11 G.M. Burrows (unsigned), *The London Medical Repository* 18 (1822): 438–46.

12 G.M. Burrows, 'A Reply to Messieurs Esquirol's and Falret's Objections to Dr. Burrows' Comparative Proportions of Suicides in Paris and London', *ibid.*, 460–4.

13 It was widely understood that pellagra had suicide as one of its consequences. Burrows, in his *Inquiry*, said that 'intellectual derangement, with a propensity to suicide, is also consequent on the endemics [e.g.] the pellagra of Lombardy ...' (p. 84). Pellagra was horrible and mysterious, a seasonal and regional disease of degeneration, known to be endemic in the maize-eating localities of Italy. It was apparently a disease of recent origin. As late as 1910 it was thought

to be caused by bacteria that grew in stored corn. It is a niacin deficiency disease.

14 E.-J. Georget, *Dissertation sur les causes de la folie*, (Paris, 1820). The dissertation is dated 3 February; in an expanded form it is *De la folie: considérations de cette maladie ... suivies de récherches cadavériques* (Paris, 1820).

15 G.M. Burrows, *Commentaries on the Causes, Forms, Symptoms and Treatment, Moral and Medical, of Insanity* (London, 1828): 416.

16 F.-J.-V. Broussais, *De l'irritation et de la folie: ouvrage dans lequel les rapports du physique et du moral sont établis sur les bases de la médecine physiologique* (Paris, 1828).

17 J.-B. Cazauvieilh, *Du suicide, de l'aliénation mentale et des crimes contre les personnes* (Paris, 1840): 16. The author was formerly at Salpêtrière, but now practising in the country, where he found, contrary to Falret, that suicide was as endemic as in the city.

18 G.F. Etoc-Demazy, *Recherches statistiques sur le suicide, appliquées à l'hygiène publique et à la médecine légale* (Paris, 1844): 35. Etoc-Demazy had been more inclined to the organic view of some lunatics when he was a student. Referring to Esquirol and Georget, he defined *stupidité* as the 'accidental absence of the manifestation of thought' which is a 'functional disorder whose true cause is the alteration of an organ ...' *De la stupidité considérée chez les aliénées: recherches fait à Bicêtre et à la Salpêtrière*, 21 August 1833. One had to toe the organic line pretty closely to get one's degree. Thus Etoc-Demazy's thesis was presented the day after F.H. Chaillou's *Dissertation sur le délire nerveux*, 20 August 1833. On p. 1 of this work its title is explained: 'since it is desirable that the name of a disease should recall at the same time the organ affected and the nature of the affect'.

19 C.E. Bourdin, *Du suicide considéré comme maladie* (Batignolles, 1845). Bourdin was phrenological: *Essai sur la phrénologie considérée dans les principes généraux et son application pratique* (Paris, 1847).

20 François Leuret, *Traitement moral de la folie* (Paris, 1848): 4.

21 Leuret's approach to the insane had always been psychological rather than physiological; *cf.* his *Fragmens pyschologiques sur la folie* (Paris, 1834).

22 E. Lisle, *Du suicide: statistique, médecine, histoire et legislation* (Paris, 1856). This work was awarded the Prix Montyon in 1848. The insertions in proof presumably mark transitions between the prizewinning essay and the published book.

23 Burrows, *Inquiry*, 81–2.

9 The Experimental basis of the philosophy of legislation

1 Guerry's letter to A. Quetelet was published in the latter's 'Recherches sur le penchant au crime aux différents âges', *Nouveaux mémoires de l'Académie Royale des Sciences et Belles-Lettres de Bruxelles* 7 (1832), 84. Quetelet read his paper on 9 July 1831, and inserted this part of Guerry's letter for the published version. Guerry's insertion in the epigraph is from A.-M. Guerry, *Essai sur la statistique morale de la France*, Paris, 1833 (presented to the Academy of Sciences on 2 July 1832). The classic biography of Quetelet, rich in quotation

and analysis, is Joseph Lottin, *Quetelet, statisticien et sociologue* (Louvain, 1912). It contains extensive comparisons of Guerry and Quetelet, as of Quetelet and Comte.

2 *Recherches statistiques sur la ville de Paris et le département de la Seine* (4 vols., Paris, 1821–9).

3 See I. Grattan-Guinness, *Joseph Fourier 1768–1830: A Survey of His Life and Work* (Cambridge, Mass., 1970): 485f. Grattan-Guinness refers to numerous folios in the Bibliothèque Nationale on insurance, e.g. 22515, 22517. Fourier was by then the bureaucrat, and his unsigned introductions to the *Recherches statistiques* were his chief public commentaries on probability. The two sections from 1826 and 1829 that bear on the theory of errors were republished in *Œuvres de Fourier* (Paris, 1890) **2**, 523–45, 547–90. There was also his work on commissions, e.g. the report on tontines, signed by Lacroix, Laplace and Fourier, *Histoire de l'Académie Royale des Sciences* **5** (1826): 26–43 (for the session of 1821–2).

4 A. Quetelet, *Instructions populaires sur le calcul des probabilités* (Brussels, 1828). Lessons 13 and 14 follow closely pp. ix-xxxi of Fourier's introduction to the *Recherches statistiques* **3** (1826). A. Quetelet, 'Mémoire sur les lois des naissances et de la mortalité à Bruxelles', *Nouveaux mémoires de l'Académie Royale des Sciences et Belles-Lettres de Bruxelles* **3** (1825): 495–512. On Fourier's introducing Quetelet to Villermé, see Lottin, *Quetelet*, 112.

5 Henry Lytton Bulwer, *France: Social, Literary, Political* (London, 1834): 203. He had been reading Guerry: see the quotation in the present chapter for note 11.

6 A. Daquin, *La Philosophie de la folie, ou essai philosophique sur le traitement des personnes attaquées de la folie* (Paris, 1792; 2nd edn Chamberty, 1804).

7 E. Lisle, *Du suicide* (Paris, 1856), 3.

8 For Guerry's 1832 *Statistique morale*, published in 1833, see note 1. The second work was *Statistique morale de l'Angleterre comparée avec la statistique morale de la France* (Paris, 1864).

9 I know nothing of the *ordonnateur* except a fleeting reference in the article on Guerry for the *Dictionnaire de la XIXe siècle*.

10 H. Diard, *Statistique morale de l'Angleterre et de la France, par M. A.-M. Guerry: Etude sur cet ouvrage* (Tours, 1866): 4, 10.

11 Lytton Bulwer, *France*, 201.

12 See the *Proceedings* of the British Association for 1851 and 1865. For a popular account of the 1851 display, see *Athenaeum* (12 July 1851): 755.

13 A. Balbi and A.-M. Guerry, *Statistique comparée de l'état de l'instruction et du nombre des crimes dans les divers arrondissements des cours royales et des académies universitaires de France* (Paris, 1829).

14 One classic study is Louis Chevalier, *Classes laborieuses et classes dangereuses* (Paris, 1950).

15 Guerry, *Statistique morale de l'Angleterre comparée*, xliv.

16 Lisle, *Du suicide*, 3.

17 *Ibid.*, 101.

18 Diard, *Statistique morale*, 6.

19 In 1812 the book was published in Paris (once again in French) as a 'translation' of the work of the French priest. For some texts, see Charles B.-Maybon (ed.), *La Relation sur le Tonkin et la Cochinchine de Mr de La Bissachère*, Paris, 1920.

10 Facts without authenticity

1 Report by S.-D. Poisson, P.-L. Dulong, D.-J. Larrey and F.-J. Double, *Comptes rendus hebdomadaires des séances de l'Académie des Sciences* 1 (1835): 167–77.

2 E. H. Ackernecht, 'Broussais, or a Forgotten Medical Revolution', *Bulletin of the History of Medicine* 27 (1953): 321.

3 F.-J.-V.-Broussais, *De l'irritation et de la folie* (Paris, 1828): 263.

4 F.-J.-V. Broussais, *Examen de la doctrine médicale généralement adoptée, et des systèmes modernes de nosologie, dans lesquels on détermine, par les faits et par le raisonnement, leur influence sur le traitement et la terminaison des maladies, suivi d'un plan d'études fondé sur l'anatomie et la physiologie pour parvenir à la connaissance du siège et des symptômes des affections pathologiques et à la thérapeutique la plus rationelle* (Paris, 1816). Longer and longer editions with shorter and shorter titles appeared 1821–34.

5 F.-J.-V.Broussais, *Traité de physiologie appliquée à la pathologie* (2 vols., Paris, 1822–3). *Catéchisme de la médecine physiologique* (Paris, 1824).

6 F.-J.-V. Broussais, *Principles of Physiological Medicine in the Form of Propositions Embracing Physiology, Pathology and Therapeutics, with Commentaries on those Relating to Pathology*, trans. Isaac Hayes and R. Eglesfield Griffith (Philadelphia, 1832): 515. A translation of *Commentaires des propositions de pathologie consignée dans l'examen des doctrines médicales* (2 vols., Paris, 1829), Proposition CCLXX.

7 H. de Balzac, *La Messe de l'athée* (1830), in *La Comédie humaine* (13 vols., Paris 1976–80): 3, 391. References in the footnote are to *La Comédie du diable*, *ibid.*, **8**, 60. *Le Peau de chagrin*, *ibid.* **10**, 257–60. *Physiologie du mariage* (1829), *ibid.*, **11**, 1026; also in the 1826 version, *La Physiologie du mariage préoriginale*, ed. M. Bardèche (Paris, 1940): 124.

8 Deputy Puymaurin, quoted in J. Léonard, *Les Médecins de l'Ouest au XIXe siècle* (Paris, 1978): **2**, 693.

9 A. Miquel, *Lettres à un médecin de province: exposition critique de la doctrine médicale de M. Broussais* (Paris, 1825), a critique of the works cited in notes 4 and 5.

10 L.-C. Roche, *De la nouvelle doctrine médicale considerée dans les rapports des théories de la mortalité: Discussion entre MM. Miquel, Bousquet et Roche* (Paris, 1827). Roche defended Broussais against the other two.

11 P.C.A. Louis, *Recherches sur les effets de la saignée* (Paris, 1835).

12 F.-J.-V. Broussais, *Le Choléra-morbus vaincu, 1 mort sur 40 malades, nouveau traitement par le docteur Broussais* (Paris, n.d)

13 See Jean-François Braunstein, *Broussais et le matérialisme: médecine et philosophie au XIXe siècle* (Paris, 1986): 81f, to whom I also owe the preceding reference and the following one.

14 F. Magendie, *Leçons sur le choléra morbus* (Paris, 1832): 204f.

15 The official report of the Academy debate is given, in part, in J.-E. Belhomme's *éloge* of Broussais, 'Compte rendu des travaux de la Société phrénologique pendant le cours de l'année 1839', *Escalupe* 1 (1839): 78.

16 W. Coleman, 'Experimental Physiology and Statistical Inference: The Therapeutic Trial in Nineteenth-Century Germany', in Krüger *et al.*, *Probabilistic Revolution*, **2**, 201.

17 J. Civiale, *Parallèle des divers moyens de traiter les calculeux* (Paris, 1836). *Traité de l'affection calculeuse, suivi d'un essai statistique sur cette maladie* (Paris, 1838), of which the latter part is a slightly revised version of the earlier book.

18 In the essay judged by Poisson in 1835 for the Montyon prize, the data were not quite so extensive: *lithotomie* had killed 1,141 out of 5,715 patients, while *lithotétrie* had killed only six in 257.

19 H. Navier, 'Remarques a l'occasion du rapport fait a l'Académie dans la séance du 5 octobre 1835', *Comptes rendus hebdomadaires des séances de l' Académie des Sciences* **1** (1835): 247–51.

11 By what majority?

1 *Archives parlementaires*, 2e serie 1800 à 1860, **98** (1898): 353f. The debate starts on p. 271, and continues, with an admixture of other matter, to p. 432. For Arago's complaint about interruptions p. 347. The sentences quoted are not consecutive, but are taken, in order, from Arago's long and passionate speech. The comments are those of the official reporter. I have, however, altered the record. The *archives* have Arago saying in the second statement that the odds are one in eight that a simple majority voting seven to five is mistaken. I believe he said eight to four, for three reasons. (1) On four different occasions on three different days he said that the odds of error in a 7:5 vote are about $\frac{1}{4}$. (2) He said that he was referring to Laplace, who gave the odds for a mistaken 7:5 vote as better than $\frac{2}{7}$; Laplace's odds for an 8:4 vote were $\frac{1}{8}$. (3) His supporters on the left laughed jovially when he made his statement about the 7:5 vote but the entire centre was in an uproar when he made his statement about the 8:4 vote. I take (3) as evidence that the court reporter rather than Arago made a mistake; if Arago had mis-spoken, there would not have been the uproar.

2 Condorcet, *Essai sur l'application de l'analyse à la probabilité des décisions rendues à la pluralité des voix* (Paris, 1785): cxl and 267–304.

3 P.S. de Laplace, *Théorie analytique des probabilités* (Paris, 1815): 520–30. This is one of the supplements to the 1814 edition; see the *Œuvres complètes* (Paris, 1878–1912): 7, 520–9.

4 L. Daston, *Classical Probability in the Enlightenment* (Princeton, 1988).

5 Glenn Shafer has shown how this sort of combination of evidence was integral to Jacques Bernoulli's *Ars conjectandi*, Part IV: 'Non-additive Probabilities in the Work of Bernoulli and Lambert', *Archive for the History of Exact Sciences* **19** (1978): 309–70. See also 'Bayes' Two Arguments for the Rule of Conditioning', *Annals of Statistics* **10** (1982): 1075–89. For his own solutions, see *Probability and Evidence* (Princeton, 1976). *Cf.* Ian Hacking, 'Combining Evidence', in S. Stenlund, (ed.), *Logical and Semantic Analysis: Essays Dedicated to Stig Kanger on his Fiftieth Birthday* (Dordrecht, 1974): 113–24.

6 Condorcet, *Essai*, cxxvi and 241.

7 *Observations des cours d'appel sur le projet de Code Criminel* (Paris, l'an XIII): 7.

8 In l'an X the Institut set a prize essay, 'What are the means of perfecting the jury in France?' to which this is a response. Quoted in A. Esmein, *A History of Continental Criminal Procedure with Special Reference to France*, trans. J. Simpson (London, 1910): 471.

9 The simple majority stayed until the law of 6 March 1848 set the majority at nine out of twelve. On 18 October this was changed back to eight. On 10 June 1853 a mere majority sufficed once again. At the time of writing the current but controversial French model is nine jurors who vote with three magistrates and decide by simple majority in a secret ballot.

10 *Essai philosophique sur les probabilités* (2nd edn, Paris, 1814): 85. By the first edition I mean that which was published as the introduction to the 1814 edition of the *Essai*. *Essai* (3rd edn, Paris, 1816): 159. Laplace, 'Sur une disposition du code d'instruction criminelle' (Paris, 1816), issued as a separate pamphlet 15 November. See Bibliothèque Nationale Fp.1187 and the notice on pp.529–30 of the *Œuvres*, 7, 529f. Silvestre Lacroix, *Traité élémentaire du calcul des probabilités* (Paris, 1816): 241–5; the remarks on Article 351 are discussed in a footnote to the 2nd edn (Paris, 1822).

11 Details are given in Ian Hacking, 'Historical Models for Justice: What is Probably the Best Jury System?' *Epistemologia* 6 (1984): 191–212. The procedure is as follows. First obtain the conditional probability that a jury that splits $i{:}n{-}i$ is correct given that the unknown average reliability of a juror is r. Secondly, find the probability density for r conditional on a jury splitting $i{:}n{-}i$. Thirdly, multiply the quantities resulting from these two steps to obtain the probability density for a correct decision, conditional on $i{:}n{-}i$, and integrate assuming that r is uniformly distributed between $(\frac{1}{2}, 1)$. As is common in Laplace, what entered as a plausible but inconsequential assumption, that r is in $(\frac{1}{2}, 1)$ turns out to be what underpins the entire easy integration at this juncture. We obtain:

$$\text{Probability (Correct}/i{:}n - i) = \frac{1}{2^{n-1}} \sum_{j=0}^{j=n-1} \frac{(n-1)!}{(n-1)! \ (n+1-j)!}$$

12 Quantitatively, Laplace's method shows that when a jury splits 7:5 for conviction, there is a 0.28 chance of error. But when first a jury votes 7:5 for guilt, and then a group of five judges votes three for acquittal and two for conviction, the upshot (conviction by an overall vote of 9:8) is reliable only about 63 per cent of the time. By the above formula, the probability that a 3:2 tribunal decides correctly is 0.59, and the probability that a 7:5 jury decides correctly is 0.71. The two bodies are supposed to be independent. A conviction occurs if the accused is guilty (probability 0.71 by jury decision) and the minority of two in the tribunal is right (0.41 probability) or the accused is innocent and the majority of three is right (0.29, 0.59 probabilities). Hence the proportion of innocents among convictions is
$(0.29)(0.59)/\{(0.29)(0.59)+(0.71)(0.41)\} = 0.37$, even worse than 0.28.

13 G. Gergonne, 'Examen critique de quelques dispositions de notre code d'instruction criminelle', *Annales de mathématiques pures et appliquées* 9 (1816): 306–319.

14 For one survey of the school and its contributions to the mathematical theory of probability see L.E. Maistrov, *Probability Theory: A Historical Sketch*, trans. S. Kotz (New York, 1974).

15 Mikhail Vasilievich Ostrogradsky, 'Extrait d'un mémoire sur la probabilité des erreurs des tribunaux', *Mémoires de l'Académie de Saint-Petersbourg*, 6e série, 3 (1838): xix-xxv.

16 I mean that he *explicitly* represented probabilities in this way using just such a symbolism. As Shafer has shown, this representation is implicit in Jacques Bernoulli's treatment of testimony.

17 For details see Hacking, 'Models for Justice'. Ostrogradsky in brief: Laplace should assume neither that all jurors have the same reliability, nor that their reliability exceeds $\frac{1}{2}$. Make the minimum assumption. Assume that the reliability of juror j is in the interval (r_{j*}, r_j^*), contained in $(0,1)$. Assume only that the upper and lower bounds are the same for each juror, and that the reliabilities for each juror, r_j, are independently distributed for different j. Then essentially following Laplace's method one gets a very tidy integration. Let z be the difference between the upper and lower reliability; then the probability of a mistaken conviction is:

$$\frac{(2-z)^d}{(2-z)^d + z^d}$$

12 The law of large numbers

1 S.-D. Poisson, 'Recherches sur la probabilité des jugements principalement en matière criminelle', *Comptes rendus hebdomadaires des séances de l'Académie des Sciences* 1 (1835): 478. I.J. Bienaymé, 'Sur un principe que M. Poisson avait cru découvrir et qu'il avait appelé Loi des grands nombres', *Comptes rendus des séances et travaux de l'Académie des Sciences Morales et Politiques* 11 (1855): 386. He referred to a talk given on 16 April and reported in *Procès verbaux de la Société Philomathique*. His doubts were first expressed in I.J. Bienaymé, 'Théorème sur la probabilité des résultats moyens des observations. Sur la probabilité des résultats moyens lorsque les causes sont variables durant les observations', *Société Philomathique de Paris, Extraits* 5 (1839): 42–9.

2 S.-D. Poisson, *Recherches sur la probabilité des jugements en matière criminelle et en matière civile, précédées des règles générales du calcul des probabilités* (Paris, 1837).

3 S. Stigler, *The History of Statistics* (Cambridge, Mass., 1986): 188–91.

4 See O.B. Sheynin, 'S.-D. Poisson's work in Probability', *Archive for History of Exact Science* 18 (1978): 245–300. See also his 'On the Early History of the Law of Large Numbers', *Biometrika* 55 (1968): 459–67.

5 A.E. Gelfand and H. Solomon, 'A Study of Poisson's Models for Jury Verdicts in Criminal and Civil Trials', *Journal of the American Statistical Association* 68 (1973): 271–8. See also their 'Modeling Jury Verdicts in the American Jury System', *ibid.* 69 (1974): 32–7.

6 L. Daston, *Classical Probability in the Enlightenment* (Princeton, 1988) stems from a doctoral dissertation for Princeton University with the more informative title, 'The Reasonable Calculus: Classical Probability Theory 1650–1840'. It was in 1840 – maybe 1843, with the publication of Cournot's book, note 8 below – that the classical theory expired, long after the 'Enlightenment' had been replaced by 'Romanticism'. And the classical theory was not just a 'probability calculus'; it was a calculus of reason itself.

7 The mis-spelling of 'Blayes' for 'Bayes' is found in Poisson's papers throughout the 1830s, and is corrected in the *Recherches* only in proof, on page i. This

confirms the suggestion that Thomas Bayes's original work was not known at first hand in Poisson's circle.

8 A.A. Cournot, *Exposition de la théorie des chances et des probabilités* (Paris, 1843). Cournot held that he made the distinction between *chance* and *probabilité* independently of Poisson, at about the same time, and corresponded on the point in 1837. He quoted correspondence with Poisson to establish this, p. vii.

9 Poisson, *Recherches*, 30, 31. Poisson did define probability in the old-fashioned way, as a ratio of favourable cases to equally possible cases. But he noted that 'it seems to result from this definition that a probability is always a rational number'. He at once gave a geometrical example and said that probabilities don't have to be rational fractions; *ibid.*, 33.

10 Laplace, *Traité*, 3rd edn of 1820, pagination as in *Œuvres complètes de Laplace* 7 (Paris, 1886). What appears to be Laplace's equivocation between the two methods of reasoning is best illustrated by his derivation of interval estimates which are formally akin to confidence intervals. For a Bernoullian derivation, see p. 287. For a Bayesian derivation of 'essentially' the same formula, see p. 377.

11 I. Grattan-Guinness, *Joseph Fourier 1768–1830* (Cambridge, Mass., 1972): 486. I find Poisson's objectivism more ambivalent than does Grattan-Guinness.

12 Stigler, *History of Statistics*, 190. Poisson repeated Laplace's 'Bernoullian' derivation on p. 211 of the *Recherches*, where he derived a fiducial distribution for an estimate of objective probability (or chance). The word 'fiducial' is R.A. Fisher's. His 'fiducial argument' is one way to go with Bernoullian reasoning. My version of it is given in *Logic of Statistical Inference* (Cambridge, 1965), chapter 11. Another way is that of Peirce, Neyman and Pearson, discussed in chapter 23 below.

13 A.A. Cournot, *Recherches sur les principes mathématiques de la théorie des richesses* (Paris, 1838).

14 A follower of R.A. Fisher would say that Poisson was computing a fiducial probability of the reliability of the juror. A follower of J. Neyman and E.S. Pearson would say that Poisson was computing a confidence interval. Both anachronistic assertions are correct, because Poisson's intervals are among those that can be interpreted in either way. These twentieth century authors would insist that the probabilities in question were objective and indeed frequencies or based on frequencies. But for Poisson fiducial limits were *probabilités*, i.e. subjective, or, better, epistemic.

15 Poisson's study of the jury came only in the second half of his book, but it is clear from lectures given at the Academy between 1835 and 1837 that it was his chief research project in his later years. His teaching continued to be on traditional probability theory, augmented by his own theorems, and did not address jurisprudence. See Sheynin, 'Poisson', 269f, for Poisson's annual programme at the Polytechnique.

16 $c_{g,1} = \sum_{i}^{g+i} \left(k r^e (1-r)^{i + (1-k)ri} (1-r)^e \right)$

17 *Recherches*, 1.

18 *Ibid.*, 27.

19 S.D. Poisson 'Note sur la loi des grands nombres', *Comptes rendus hebdomadaires des séances de l'Académie des Sciences* 2 (1836): 377

20 i.e. the variance in the Poisson case is less than in the Bernoulli case. See C.C. Heyde and E. Seneta, *I.J. Bienaymé: Statistical Theory Anticipated* (New York, 1977): 41. This book is an excellent historical survey with explanation of the mathematics.

21 Poisson, *Recherches*, 144.

22 Poisson, 'Note' (11 April 1836), 382. Debate continued on 18 April, followed by 'Formules relatives aux probabilités qui dependent de très grands nombres'.

23 Heyde and Seneta, *Bienaymé*, 46–9.

24 See note 3.

25 Bienaymé, 'Sur un principe', 383.

26 *Ibid.*, 389.

27 Stigler discusses Cournot's criticism in *History of Statistics*. A.A. Cournot, 'Mémoire sur les applications du calcul des chances à la statistique judicaire', *Journal de Mathematiques Pures et Appliquées* 3 (1838): 257–334.

28 A. Guibert, 'Solution d'une question relative à la probabilité des jugements rendus à une majorité quelconque', *ibid.*, 25–30. 'Mémoires sur les probabilités des arrêts de deux sortes de cours d'appel', *Comptes rendus hebdomadaires des séances de l'Académie des Sciences* 7 (1838): 650–2.

29 James Jerwood, 'On the Application of the Calculus of Probabilities to Legal and Judicial Subjects', *Transactions of the Devonshire Association for the Advancement of Science, Literature and Art* 2 (1867–8): 578–98. This is a fairly thorough survey, citing Turgot, Condorcet, Laplace, Lacroix, Poisson, Cournot, De Morgan (from the *Encyclopaedia Metropolitanica*), Galloway (from the *Encyclopaedia Britannica*), Tozer (from the Cambridge Philosophical Society), etc.

30 P.L. Chebyshev, 'Démonstration élémentaire d'une proposition générale de la théorie des probabilités', *Journal für die reine und angewandte Mathematik*, 33 (1859): 259–67.

31 Sheynin, 'Poisson'.

13 Regimental chests

1 Adolphe Quetelet, 'Sur l'appréciation des documents statistiques, et en particulier sur l'application des moyens', *Bulletin de la Commission Centrale de la Statistique* (of Belgium) 2 (1845): 258, presented in February 1844, and also issued separately as *Recherches statistiques* (Brussels, 1844): 54.

2 'Recherches statistiques sur le royaume des Pays-Bas', *Nouveaux mémoires de l'Académie Royale des Sciences et Belles-Lettres de Bruxelles* 5 (1829): 28.

3 *Ibid.*, 35. Quetelet said this over and over again, for example in his own journal, the *Correspondances mathématiques et physiques* 5 (1829): 117–87, or *ibid.* 6 (1830): 273.

4 'Recherches sur le penchant au crime aux différents ages', *Nouveaux mémoires de l'Académie Royale des Sciences et Belles-Lettres de Bruxelles* 7 (1832): 20.

5 I should not leave the impression that Quetelet thought that conviction rates were absolutely constant. 63.5 per cent is his figure for French convictions in

1825; he thought that the rate was declining very slightly, showing some amelioration in society. Poisson did think that the rates were constant. For the difference between the two on this point, see S.M. Stigler, *The History of Statistics* (Cambridge, Mass., 1986): 190f.

6　Stigler, *History of Statistics*, 158.

7　As a valuable supplement to Stigler on the law of error, see O.B. Sheynin, 'On the Mathematical Treatment of Astronomical Observations', *Archive for the History of Exact Sciences* 11 (97–126); 'Laplace's Theory of Error', *ibid.*, 17 (1977): 1–61; 'C.F. Gauss and the Theory of Errors', *ibid.*, 20 (1979): 21–69.

8　The standard deviation of a set of observations is the square root of the arithmetic mean of the squares of the difference from the mean. The standard deviation of a theoretical error distribution is the continuous version of this. The probable error is 0.6745 times the standard deviation.

9　The dating is due to Mansfield Merriman, 'A List of Writings Related to the Method of Least Squares, with Historical and Critical Notes' *Transactions of the Connecticut Academy of Arts and Sciences* 4 (1877–82): 141–232. For further information, see H.M. Walker, *Studies in the History of Statistical Method* (Baltimore, 1931): 24f, 49–55. Walker describes a great many other measures of dispersion that have been used, together with their bizarre terminology. The name 'standard deviation' was introduced by Karl Pearson in 1894; see Walker, p. 54n.

10　A. Quetelet, *Sur l'homme et le développement de ses facultés ou essai de physique sociale* (2 vols., Paris, 1835), translated as *A Treatise on Man and the Development of his Faculties* (London, 1842). An expanded version reversed the title: *Physique sociale ou essai sur le développement des facultés de l'homme* (2 vols., Brussels, 1869).

11　*Athenaeum* 29 August 1835, p. 661. The review appeared in three parts during August: pp. 593–5, 611–13, 658–61.

12　S.S. Schweber, 'The Origin of the *Origin* revisited', *Journal of the History of Biology* 10 (1977): 232. Compare the effect on James Clerk Maxwell of John Herschel's review of *Lettres à S.A.R. le duc régnant de Saxe-Cobourg et Gotha, sur la théorie des probabilités, appliquée aux sciences morales et politiques* (Brussels, 1846): John Herschel (unsigned), 'Quetelet on Probabilities', *Edinburgh Review* 92 (1850): 1–57. For discussion of Maxwell, Herschel and Quetelet, and citation of earlier historical remarks, see T.M. Porter, *The Rise of Statistical Thinking* (Princeton, 1986): 118 and 'A Statistical Survey of Gases: Maxwell's Social Physics', *Historical Studies in the Physical Sciences* 12 (1981): 77–116.

13　Stigler thinks this stage of central importance to Quetelet, *History of Statistics*, chapter 5. He proposes that throughout this period Quetelet was deeply concerned with the problem of recognizing homogeneous groups, a problem forcefully put to him in 1827 by the Baron de Keverberg in 'Notes', *Nouveaux mémoires de l'Académie Royale des Sciences et Belles-Lettres de Bruxelles* 4 (1827): 175–92, appended to a paper of Quetelet's on Belgian population statistics.

14　Viz. just before the quotation used as my epigraph; the space between the second and third paragraphs of p. 54 of the monograph is *exactly* where the jump occurs.

15 *Appréciation*, 54. A rare source of heights available to Quetelet was F. Lelut, *Annales d'hygiène publique et de médecine légale* **31** (1844): 297–316.

16 *The Edinburgh Medical and Surgical Journal* **13** (1817): 260–4.

17 Stigler reproduces the 1846 version of this table (slightly less perspicuous than the 1844 version) and gives the correct figures as derived from the 1817 *Journal* (which, as I suggest in the footnote to p. 109, Quetelet may never have seen). Stigler, *History of Statistics*, 206–9.

18 *Lettres*, cf. note 12 above, trans. O.G. Downes, *Letters ... on the Theory of Probabilities* (London, 1859): 92.

19 A. Quetelet, 'De l'homme considéré dans le système social, ou comme unité, ou comme fragment de l'espèce humaine', *ibid.*, 2nd ser. **35** (1873): 201. The data had been presented at the International Statistical Congress in Berlin, 1863, but the moral had not then been drawn.

20 F. Galton, 'Typical Laws of Heredity', *Nature* **15** (1877): 512.

21 F. Galton, *Natural Inheritance* (London, 1889): 58.

22 Starting in 1875: W. Lexis, *Einleitung in die Theorie der Bevölkerungsstatistik* (Strasbourg, 1875).

23 T.M. Porter, 'The Mathematics of Society: Variation and Error in Quetelet's Statistics', *British Journal for the History of Science* **18** (1985): 51–69, and *The Rise of Statistical Thinking 1820–1900* (Princeton, 1986): 240–55.

24 On revolution and civilization, see A. Quetelet, 'Sur la possibilité de mesurer l'influence des causes qui modifient les éléments sociaux, Lettre à M. Villermé', *Correspondances mathématiques et physiques* **7** (1832): 326. The letter to Albert is quoted in H.H. Schoen, 'Prince Albert and the Application of Statistics to Problems of Government', *Osiris* **5** (1938): 286f.

25 Quetelet, 'Sur la possibilité', 346.

14   Society prepares the crimes

1 These sentences are excerpts, in the order in which they were read, from William Farr's address, *Fourth Session of the International Statistical Congress* (London, 1860): 4f. For Farr's biography, see J.M. Eyler, *Victorian Social Medicine: The Ideas and Methods of William Farr* (Baltimore, 1979).

2 A. D'Angeville, 'Influence de l'âge sur l'aliénation mentale et sur le penchant au crime,' *Bulletins de l'Académie Royale des Sciences et Belles-Lettres de Bruxelles* **3** (1836): 184f. The same worry is stated in his *Essai de la statistique de la population française, considérée sous quelques uns de ses rapports physiques et moraux* (Bourg, 1836). The latter expresses positivist sentiments: 'Statistics is the best torch of reason, when it is employed in good faith, without commitment to any particular system of opinion and with bases sufficiently large in number and in time.' It addresses many of the problems I have mentioned in various chapters, for example the correlation between education and crime. Guerry and Balbi had used information from the ministry of war about recruitment in the various departments, to judge the level of education by department. D'Angeville urged the ministries of justice, education and war to use the same measures of education level so that meaningful comparisons could be derived from their different experiences.

3 T. Young, 'Remarks on the probabilities of error in physical observations, and on the density of the earth, considered especially with regard to the reduction of experiments on the pendulums', *Philosophical Transactions of the Royal Society of London* **109** (1819): 71.

4 *Hard Times* (London, 1854): Book III, chapter 7.

5 'Observations on puerperal fever; containing a series of evidence respecting its Origin, Causes and Mode of Propagation', by Robert Storrs in Farr's *Letter, Annual Report of the Registrar-General of England and Wales* **4** (1842): 384–93, quoting from *The Provincial Journal* no. 166.

6 Farr's *Letter, Annual Report* **1** (1839): 89.

7 Farr's *Letter, Annual Report* **3** (1841): 84.

8 *Congrès international de statistique: programme de la sixième session* (Florence, 1867): 89.

9 *Ibid.*, 93. The movement in question was from country to town, or from district to district. The data to be collected about *les misérables* was of a sort that by 1867 had become standardized as relevant: sex, civil state, legitimate paternity? Education, place of origin, fixed address? Primary causes of *misère*? Imperfections (blind, deaf, dumb, maimed, insane, idiot)? Then one moved to the state of the family, the moral condition of the paternal family, etc.

10 Daniel Kevles, *In the Name of Eugenics: Genetics and the Uses of Human Heredity* (New York, 1985).

11 T.M. Porter, *Rise of Statistical Thinking*, 151–92; Lottin, *Quetelet*, chapter 5.

12 M. Moreau, 'Idée générale du système du docteur Gall' in *L'Art de connaître les hommes par la physiognomie de M. Lavater, augmentée des recherches ou des opinions de la Chambre, de Porta, de Campa, de Gall sur la physiognomie* (10 vols., Paris, 1806): **2**, 47.

13 See e.g. George Cruikshank, *Phrenological Illustrations, or the Artist's View of the Craniological System of Drs Gall and Spurzheim* (London, 1826).

14 Thomas Forster, *Sketch of the New Anatomy and Physiology of the Brain and Nervous System of Drs. Gall and Spurzheim Considered as Comprehending a Complete System of Zoonomy, with Observations on its Tendency to the Improvement of Education, of Punishment and of the Treatment of Insanity* (London, 1815). E.-J. Georget, *De la physiologie du système nerveux et spécialement du cerveau* (Paris, 1821): **1**, 104–11; for the recantation in 1828, see Jan Goldstein, *Console and Classify* (Cambridge, 1987): 256, n. 60.

15 R. Young, *Mind, Brain and Adaptation in the Nineteenth Century: Cerebral Localization and its Biological Context from Gall to Ferrier* (Oxford, 1970). Roger Cooter, *The Cultural Meaning of Popular Science: Phrenology and the Organization of Consent in Nineteenth Century Britain* (Cambridge, 1984).

16 P.M. Roget, *Essays on Phrenology, or an Inquiry into the Principles and Utility of the System of Drs Gall and Spurzheim, and into the Objections made Against it* (Edinburgh, 1819).

17 J.G. Spurzheim, *The Physiognomical System of Drs. Gall and Spurzheim* (London, 1815): 499.

18 *Ibid.*, 502.

19 *Ibid.*, 506.

20 A. Quetelet, 'Recherches sur le penchant au crime aux différents âges',

Nouveaux mémoires de l'Académie Royale des Sciences et Belles-Lettres de Bruxelles **7** (1832): 81.

21 A. Quetelet, *Sur l'homme et le développment de ses facultés ou essai de physique sociale* (2 vols., Paris, 1835): **1**, 16.

22 'Does the Progress of Physical Science tend to give any advantage to the opinion of Necessity (or Determinism) over that of the Contingency of Events and the Freedom of the Will?', in L. Campbell and W. Garnett, *The Life of James Clerk Maxwell* (London, 1882): 481.

23 H.T. Buckle, *History of Civilization in England* **1** (London, 1857): 20.

15 The astronomical conception of society

1 G.F. Knapp, 'Die neueren Ansichten über Moralstatistik', *Jahrbücher für Nationalökonomie und Statistik* **17** (1871): 239f; some sentences omitted from the end of the first paragraph. For his ambivalence about France, see G.F. Knapp, *Aus der Jugend eines deutschen Gelehrten* (Stuttgart, 1927).

2 C.R. Proffer (ed.), *The Unpublished Dostoyevsky 1860–1881: Diaries and Notebooks* (Ann Arbor, Mich., 1973): **1**, 32. The Russian translation of Buckle appeared three years later, in 1865, but a German edition was available in 1861.

3 Men such as Lord Acton and James Fitzjames Stephen began the onslaught. For a bibliography discussing several hundred retorts to Buckle, see John MacKinnon Robertson, *Buckle and his Critics: A Study in Sociology* (London, 1895).

4 *Physique Sociale* (Brussels, 1869). Herschel is referred to in **1**, pp.1, 32, 89, 108, 267, and **2**, pp. 38, 208; the full praise for Herschel is reserved until p. 445.

5 A. Quetelet, 'Notice sur Sir John Fréderic William Herschel', *Annuaire de l'Observatoire Royal de Bruxelles* **39** (1872): 153–97.

6 J. Venn, *The Logic of Chance* (London, 1866): 355.

7 *Ibid.*, 4.

8 A. De Morgan, *An Essay on Probabilities and on their application to Life Contingencies* (London, 1838): 7.

9 Venn, *Logic*, 61. He was chiefly referring to A. de Morgan, *Formal Logic* (London, 1847).

10 Robert Leslie Ellis, 'On the Foundation of the Theory of Probabilities', *Transactions of the Cambridge Philosophical Society* **8** (1842–5): 3. Reprinted in W. Walton (ed.), *The Mathematical and Other Writings of Robert Leslie Ellis* (Cambridge, 1863): 3.

11 J.F. Fries, *Versuch einer Kritik der Principien der Wahrscheinlichkeitsrechnung* (Brunswick, 1842). The most philosophically interesting German work on probability during the nineteenth century was Johannes von Kries, *Die Principien der Wahrscheinlichkeitsrechnung: eine logische Untersuchung* (Freiburg, 1886). It had a profound influence on J.M. Keynes and on Wittgenstein's remarks on probability in the *Tractatus*, and thus on Rudolf Carnap. The theory was subjective, but took seriously the estimation of 'real' objective probabilities by statistics. But once again it was the applied statistician grappling with actual observed frequencies who had the keenest insight, as in Wilhelm Lexis's review, 'Uber die Wahrscheinlichkeitsrechnung und deren Anwendung auf die Statistik', *Jahrbücher für Nationalökonomie und Statistik*, neue Folge **13** (1886):433–50.

12 Porter, *Rise of Statistical Thinking*, 168.

13 W. Wundt, *Beiträge zur Theorie der Sinneswahrnehmung* (Leipzig and Heidelberg, 1862): xxvi.

14 Ian Hacking, 'Prussian Numbers 1860–1882', in *Probabilistic Revolution* 1, 377–94.

15 E. Engel, in 'Mein Standpunkt der Frage gegenüber ob die Statistik eine selbständige Wissenschaft oder nur eine Methode sei' (1851), reprinted in *Zeitschrift des königlichen preussischen statistischen Büreaus* 11 (1871): 189. *Die Bewegung der Bevölkerung im Königreich Sachsen* (Dresden, 1852).

16 E. Engel, 'Die Volkzählung, ihre Stellung zur Wissenschaft und ihre Aufgabe in der Geschichte', *Zeitschrift des königlichen preussischen statistischen Büreaus* 2 (1862): 25–31.

17 Already in 1860 – after Buckle – Engel had made a note about Saxon suicides: 'Verunglückungen und Selbstmorde im königreich Sachsen', *Zeitschrift des statistischen Büreaus des königlich sächsischen Ministeriums des Innern* 6 (1860).

18 A. Wagner, *Vergleichende Selbstmordstatistik Europas, nebst einem Abriss der Statistik der Trauung*, published separately and in *Die Gesetzmässigkeit in den scheinbar willkürlichen Handlungen vom Standpunkt der Statistik* (Hamburg, 1864).

19 C.H., 'Selbstmord in Preussen', *Zeitschrift des königlichen preussischen statistischen Büreaus* 9 (1871): 1–76. The essay noted that there had not been any official and ongoing study of suicide in Prussia. It recorded Engel's work in Saxony, but stated that nowhere in Germany had there been regular studies of suicide.

20 E. Engel, 'L.A.J. Quetelet. Ein Gedächtnisrede', *ibid.* 16 (1876): 207–20; also as the 'Eloge de Quetelet', *Congrès international de statistique: Programme de la huitième session* (Budapest, 1876): 6.

21 F. Mehring, 'Die Hetze gegen den Kathedersozialismus', *Die neue Zeit* 15 (1897): 225–8.

22 A. Wagner, *Statistische-anthropologische Untersuchung der Gesetzmässigkeit in den scheinbar menschlichen Handlungen*, published in 1864 and as the introductory part of his *Gesetzmässigkeit*.

23 A. Wagner, in a review of E. Morselli, *Il suicido: saggio di statistiche morale comparata* (Milan, 1879), *Zeitschrift für die gesammte Staatswissenschaft* 36 (1880): 192.

24 'Die Idee einer ganz regel-und-gesetzlosen, absoluten *Willkühr* des Menschen', *Gesetzmässigkeit*, 47.

25 W. Dröbisch, 'Moralische Statistik', *Leipziger Repertorium der deutschen und ausländischen Literatur*, 2 (1849): 28–39; a review of two Flemish writers who argued from Quetelet's results to the old 'Newtonian' opinion that divine intervention was needed to explain statistical stability. P. De Decker and M. Van Meenen, 'De l'influence du libre arbitre de l'homme sur les faits sociaux', *Nouveaux mémoires de l'Académie Royale des Sciences, des Lettres et des Beaux-Arts de Belgique* 21 (1848): 69–112.

26 W. Dröbisch, *Die moralische Statistik und die menschliche Freiheit* (Leipzig, 1867).

27 G. Rumelin, 'Ueber den Begriff eines sozialen Gesetzes' (1867), in *Reden und Aufsätze* (Freiburg, 1875): 1–31.

28 G. Rumelin, 'Moralstatistik und Willensfreiheit', *ibid.*, 370–7.

29 G.F. Knapp, 'Die neueren Ansichten über Moralstatistik', *Jahrbücher für Nationalökonomie und Statistik* **16** (1871): 237–50; 'Bericht über die Schriften Quetelet's zur Sozialstatistik und Anthropologie', *ibid.* **17** (1871): 167–74, 342–58, 427–45; 'Quetelet als Theoretiker', *ibid.* **18** (1872): 89–124; and a review of one of Quetelet's last works, *Anthropométrie*, in *ibid.* **17** (1871): 160–7.

16 The mineralogical conception of society

1 Frédéric Le Play, *Les Ouvriers européens: Etudes sur les travaux, la vie domestique et la condition morale des populations ouvrières de l'Europe d'après les faits observés de 1829 à 1879* (6 vols., Paris, 1879): **1**, 157. His first collection of 36 studies is *Les Ouvriers européens* (Paris, 1855). He and collaborators published many more in *Ouvriers des deux mondes* (4 vols., Paris 1857–62).

2 H. de Balzac, *La Physiologie du mariage préoriginale* (1826), ed. M. Bardèche (Paris, 1940). *Physiologie du mariage, ou méditations de philosophie éclectique sur le bonheur et le malheur conjugal*, ed. A. Michel and R. Guise, in *La Comédie humaine* (Paris, 1980): **11**. The notes to the latter state grounds for dating the '1826' version, p.1733f; see also Moïse Le Yaouanc, 'Notes sur la première *Physiologie du marriage*', *Revue d'histoire littéraire de la France* (1953): 525–32.

3 M. Bardèche, Editor's introduction to *Physiologie*, 43.

4 The titles exemplify an unattractive genre of satire that flourished in the 1820s. It included mock versions of the penal code (*Code du littérateur et du journaliste, Code gourmand, Code galant*), 'How to' parodies (*The art of tying your tie, The art of dining in town and not dining at home*), and numerous jaded tracts on marrying well, on ensuring fidelity, on making your wife love you and so forth. Bardèche, 'Introduction' to *Physiologie préoriginale*, 13–17. Balzac himself provided a *Code pénal des honnêtes gens, contenant les lois, règles, applications et exemples de l'art de mettre sa fortune, sa bourse et sa réputation à l'abri de toutes les tentatives*.

5 Bardèche, *Introduction to Physiologie*, 45.

6 *Physiologie, Œuvres* **11**, 922. *Biman*, the species of two-handed mammals, is of course the more instructive equivalent of the 'featherless biped' provided by traditional logic. The reference is to A.-M. C. Duméril, *Zoologie analytique ou méthode naturelle de classification des animaux rendue plus facile à l'aide de tableaux synthétiques* (Paris, 1802): 8. The fifteen species of the human race were due to J.-B. Bory de Saint-Vincent, *Dictionnaire classique d'histoire naturelle* (Paris, 1804); *cf.* Yaouanc, 'Notes'.

7 The Moroccan and Syrian families come from the 1879 edition. The bulk of the northern (including English) and eastern (including east of the Urals) examples were in the first edition and put into the 1879 edition in vols. **3** and **2** respectively. Vol. **1** was introductory; **4**, **5**, and **6** were dedicated to western Europe (Rhineland, Austria, Switzerland, France, Spain, Italy). The families in

these three volumes were divided into three types: *stables, ébranlées* and *désorganisées*, another instance of the way in which Le Play deliberately mirrored the taxonomy of natural history.

8 Quoted in *Ouvriers* (1879): **1**, 436, n.1.

9 *Ibid.*, **1**, 38. For autobiography, see 17–49, 393–443.

10 See *ibid.*, 431 and Montesquieu, *Esprit des lois*, xv., 8.

11 *Ibid.*, 406. His straightforward statistical work ranged over other domains as well, e.g. *Recherches statistiques sur la production et l'élaboration de la soie en France* (Paris, 1839).

12 The most salient passages are reprinted in F. Le Play, 'Vue générale sur la statistique, *Journal de la Société de Statistique de Paris* **26** (1885): 6–11. Cf. C.B. Silver, *Frédéric Le Play* (Chicago, 1982): 45.

13 *Ouvriers* **1**, 444–79. Nor does the word 'statistics' occur in the subsequent *précis alphabétique*, nor, except in an adventitious way, in any other later writing that I have examined.

14 Le Play, *Ouvriers* (1879): **1**, 157.

15 Le Play, *La Réforme sociale en France, déduite de l'observation comparée des peuples européens* (2 vols., Paris, 1864); 4th edn (Paris, 1878): **2**, 17.

16 *La Constitution de l'Angleterre considérée dans ses rapports avec la loi de Dieu et les coutumes de la paix sociale* (2 vols., Paris 1875): **2** 247f.

17 *L'organisation du travail selon la coutume des ateliers et la loi du décalogue* (Tours, 1870): 474.

18 La Société d'Economie Sociale, 1856.

19 See notes 15–17 and *L'Organisation de la famille selon le vrai modèle signalé par l'histoire de toutes les races et de tous les temps* (Paris, 1870); *La Réforme en Europe et le salut en France* (Paris, 1876); *La Constitution essentielle de l'humanité: exposé des principes et des coutumes qui créent la prosperité ou la souffrance des nations* (Tours, 1881).

20 *L'Organisation du travail*, Sec. 70, n.17. The Dominion of Canada had been established by the British North America Act in 1867; in the first edition of 1870 Le Play got the terms of Confederation wrong, but he corrected this in the second edition that appeared later in the year. The quotation is from p. 469 of the first edition.

21 *Réforme sociale*, 64.

22 *Ouvriers* (1878): **1**, 48.

23 Anthony Oberschall, 'The Two Empirical Roots of Social Theory and the Probability Revolution', in *Probabilistic Revolution* **2**, 114.

24 *Ouvriers* (1878): **1**, 228.

25 *Ibid.*, 43.

26 Emile Cheysson, *Œuvres choisies* (Paris, 1911). See A. Desrosières, 'L'Ingénieur d'état et le père de famille', *Annales des mines: gérer et comprendre* (1986): 66–81.

27 As does Oberschall, 'The Two Empirical Roots', 113-15.

28 E. Engel, 'Der Arbeitsvertrage und die Arbeitsgesellschaft: Industrial Partnerships', *Die Arbeiterfreund* (1867): 371–94. See Hacking, 'Prussian Numbers', 385.

29 E. Engel, 'Das Gesetz der Dichtigkeit, *Zeitschrift des statistischen Bureaus des königlich sächsischen Ministeriums des Innern*, **2** (1857): 153–82, reprinted in

E. Engel, *Die Lebenskosten belgischer Arbeitfamilien früher und jetzt* (Dresden, 1895).

30 Carroll D. Wright, *Sixth Annual Report of the Massachussets Bureau of Statistics of Labour* 4 (1875): 438.

31 Chistopher Jencks, 'The Politics of Income Measurement', in W. Alonso and P. Starr (eds.), *The Politics of Numbers* (New York, 1987): 100f.

17 The most ancient nobility

1 E. Labiche and E. Martin, *Les Vivacités du Capitaine Tic: comédie en trois actes* (Paris, 1861): 19; the play opened on 16 May.

2 Edmond Gondinet, *Le Panache*, at the Palais Royal, 12 October 1875.

3 The source of the story is obscure. It may be Mark Twain.

4 Auguste Comte, *Système de politique positive* (Paris, 1851–3): **1**, 381 (my italics).

5 Alexis Bertrand, in Lyon, 'Cours municipal de sociologie: leçon d'ouverture (9 mars 1892)', *Archives d'anthropologie criminelle de médecine légale et de psychologie normale et pathologique* 7 (1892): 677.

6 Georges Canguilhem, *On the Normal and the Pathological*, (1943, 1966), trans. C.R. Fawcett (Dordrecht/Boston, 1978): 29–45 and index; William Coleman, 'Neither Empiricism nor Probability: The Experimental Approach', in M. Heidelberger *et al.* (eds.), *Probability since 1800: Interdisciplinary Studies of Scientific Development* (*Report Wissenschaftsforschung* 25, Bielefeld, 1983): 275–86; T.M. Porter, *The Rise of Statistical Thinking* (Princeton, 1986): 160–2.

7 F. Dostoyevsky, *Notes from Underground* (1864), trans. J. Coulson (Harmondsworth, 1972): 30.

8 *Ibid.*, 42.

9 *Ibid.*, 31. In *Notes* the chief point against Buckle is his ludicrous contention that the human race is becoming less and less cruel. 'Have you noticed that the most refined shedders of blood have been almost always the most highly civilized gentlemen, to whom all the various Attilas and Stenka Razins could not have held a candle?' (pp. 31f).

10 C.R. Proffer (ed.), *The Unpublished Dostoyevsky 1860–1881: Diaries and Notebooks* (Ann Arbor, Mich., 1973): 1, 106.

11 *Ibid.*, 35.

12 *Ibid.*, 30–2. There is much powerful material between the sentences that I have quoted.

13 Novalis, *Werke*, XXX **3** 441 no. 901. I owe this reference to Michael Murray.

14 F. Nietzsche, *Also Sprach Zarathustra*, *Werke in drei Bänden* (Munich 1976): **2**, 416. The German for 'by chance' or 'by accident', as in 'it happened by accident', is 'von Ohnegefähr', which punningly thus signified noble lineage.

15 F. Nietzsche, *Morgenröte: Gedanken über die moralische Vorurteile* (no. 123), trans. R.J. Hollingdale, *Daybreak Thoughts on the Origins of Morality* (Cambridge, 1982): 125.

16 Gilles Deleuze, *Nietzsche and Philosophy* (New York, 1983): sec. 11, 'The Dicethrow'. Talk of the abolition of chance, in Deleuze's exposition, obviously alludes also to Mallarmé, whose poem I mentioned at the end of chapter 1.

17 F. Nietzsche, *Morgenröte* (no. 130), *Daybreak*, 131.

18 Ian Hacking, 'The Inverse Gambler's Fallacy: The Argument from Design. The Anthropric Principle Applied to Wheeler Universes', *Mind* **96** (1987): 331–40.

19 *Daybreak*, 130. The phrase is *das Reich der Zufälle*, which in context is doubtless better rendered 'the realm of chance', as in Hollingdale's translation, or 'realm of chances'. My allusion is to G. Gigerenzer *et al.*, *The Empire of Chance: How Probability Changed Science and Everyday Life* (Cambridge, 1989).

20 *Zarathustra, Werke* **2**, 338.

21 *Nachlass, Werke* **3**, 912.

22 L. J. C. Tippett, *Random Sampling Numbers*, (Cambridge, 1927).

18   Cassirer's thesis

1 Emil Du Bois-Reymond, 'Ueber die Grenzen der Naturerkennens' in *Reden von Emil Du Bois-Reymond* (Leipzig, 1886): **1**, 107. The material omitted within my quotation includes a long quotation from Laplace's *Philosophical Essay*.

2 Ernst Cassirer, *Determinism and Modern Physics* (1936), trans. O.T. Benfey (New Haven, 1956): 3.

3 Alan Donagan, 'Determinism', *Dictionary of the History of Ideas* (New York, 1972): **2**, 18.

4 Christian Wilhelm Snell, *Ueber Determinismus und moralische Freiheit* (Offenbach, 1789). The first citation in the new *Grimm* is Georg Forster, *Geschichte der Englischen Literatur von Jahre 1789*, reprinted in *Georg Forsters Werke* (Berlin, 1967): **7**, 87. *Grimm* has a 1788 citation for *Determinist*.

5 I. Kant, *Die Religion innerhalb der Grenzen der Blossen Vernunft* (Königsberg, 1793); 2nd enlarged edn (Königsberg, 1794): 58.

6 *The Works of Thomas Reid*, ed. William Hamilton (London, 1846): 87n.

7 C.W. Sigwart, *Das Problem von der Freiheit und der Unfreiheit* (Tübingen, 1839): 21. W.T. Krug, *Allgemeines Handwörterbuch der philosophischen Wissenschaften* (Leipzig, 1832).

8 A.F.M. Willich, *Elements of the Critical Philosophy* (London, 1798): 154. On p. 159 'fatalism' is reserved for a Spinozan idea. I owe this example to Roland Hall, who extracted many other neologisms from this text: see *Notes and Queries* **212** (1967): 190–2. Even he had not noticed that 'determinism' is new, so deep is our conviction that it must be an 'old' word.

9 F.J. Gall and J.G. Spurzheim, *Des Dispositions innées de l'âme et de l'esprit du matérialisme, du fatalisme et de la liberté morale, avec des réflections sur l'éducation et sur la législation criminelle* (Paris, 1811): 55.

10 *Dictionnaire de l'Académie Française* (Supplément, 1836).

11 Claude Bernard, *Introduction à l'étude de la médecine expérimentale* (1865; Paris, 1903): 376.

12 *Ibid.*, 303.

13 *Ibid.*, 217. Bernard implied that the word *déterminisme* was his own creation, earning him a scathing commentary in A. Dechambre, *Dictionnaire encylcopédique des sciences médicales* **28** (1883): 455. It mentioned earlier German usage, with reference to Kant, and asserted that one finds the word *Determinismus* in a

Leipzig encyclopaedia of 1832. It also mentioned several French uses prior to Bernard, including one by Proudhon.

14 Charles Renouvier, *Essais de critique générale. Deuxième essai. L'Homme: la raison, la passion, la liberté, la certitude, la probabilité morale* (Paris, 1859): 190f, 335ff, 347ff, 397, 461, etc.

15 *Ibid.*, *Premier essai* (Paris, 1854): 247.

16 *Ibid.*, 589.

17 William James, 'The Dilemma of Determinism', *The Unitarian Review* **22** (1884): 193–224; reprinted with revisions in *The Will to Believe and Other Essays in Popular Philosophy* (New York, 1897): 145.

18 William James, 'The Experience of Activity', *The Psychological Review* **12** (1905): 1–17, reprinted with revisions in *Essays in Radical Empiricism* (New York, 1912): 155–88.

19 William James, *Some Problems of Philosophy* (New York, 1911): 164f.

20 William James, in *The Nation* **22** (1876): 367–9; reprinted in *Collected Essays and Reviews* (New York, 1920): 26–35.

21 L. Campbell and W. Garnett, *The Life and Letters of James Clerk Maxwell* (London, 1882): 483–9.

22 I owe this observation to Graeme Hunter. Thomas Baldwin reminded me of the Hume quotation.

23 G.W. Leibniz, *Textes inédits* ed. G. Grua (Paris, 1948): **1**, 412.

24 *Cf.* Giancotti Boscherini, *Lexicon Spinozarum* (Paris, 1970).

25 James Gregory, *Letters from Dr James Gregory in defence of his essay on the difference of the relation between motive and action and that of cause and effect in physics, with replies by Rev. Alexander Crombie* (London, 1819).

26 Julien Offray de Lamettrie, *Histoire naturelle de l'âme* (Paris, 1745); *L'Homme machine* (Leiden, 1747).

27 *Actes du premier congrès international d'anthropologie criminelle* (Rome, 1885).

28 Karl Pearson, *The History of Statistics in the 17th and 18th Centuries against the Changing Background of Intellectual, Scientific and Religious Beliefs* (London, 1978): 360.

29 Campbell and Garnett, *Maxwell*, 444.

30 Renouvier, *Premier essai*, 246; *Deuxième essai*, 344.

31 Renouvier, *Premier essai*, 489.

32 E. Boutroux, *De la contingence des lois de la nature* (Paris, 1875): 194.

33 E. Boutroux, *De l'idée de loi naturelle dans la science et la philosophie* (Paris, 1895): 82.

34 E. Durkheim, *Suicide*, trans. J.A. Spaulding and G. Simpson (Glencoe, Ill., 1951): 366.

35 *Ibid.*, 307.

36 *Ibid.*, 309.

37 Review of Simon Deplogie, *Le Conflit de la morale et de la sociologie*, in *L'Année sociologique*, **15** (1913): 327.

38 'Lettres au directeur', *Revue néo-scolastique* **14** (1907): 613.

39 E. Durkheim, review of L. Gumplowicz, *Grundriss der Sociologie*, in *Revue philosophique de la France de l'étranger* **20** (1885): 629.

40 Emile Durkheim, 'Cours de science sociale: leçon d'ouverture', *Revue internationale de l'enseignement* **15** (1888): 33.
41 Durkheim, *Suicide*, 325, note 20 (translation revised).

19 The normal state

1 A. Comte, *Système de politique positive* (Paris, 1851): **1**, 651, 652f. G. Canguilhem, *On the Normal and the Pathological* (1943, additions published 1966), trans. C.R. Fawcett, (Dordrecht, 1978): 22.
2 The essays about which the controversy was formed are collected in Jack Lively and John Rees (eds.), *Utilitarian Logic and Politics: James Mill's 'Essay on Government', Macaulay's Critique and the Ensuing Debate* (Oxford, 1978). Page references below are to this collection. As for the time frame, the sequence of essays was as follows. T.B. Macaulay, 'Mill's Essay on Government: Utilitarian Logic and Politics', *Edinburgh Review*, March 1829. James Mill, 'Greatest Happiness Principle', *Westminster Review*, July, 1829. Macaulay, 'Bentham's Defence of Mill', *Edinburgh Review*, June, 1829. Macaulay was here replying to an unsigned piece in the *Westminster*, which he mistakenly took to be by Bentham. Mill, 'Edinburgh Review and the "Greatest Happiness Principle"', *Westminster Review*, October 1829. Macaulay, 'Utilitarian Theory of Government and the "Greatest Happiness Principle"', *Edinburgh Review*, October 1829. Mill, 'Edinburgh Review and the "Greatest Happiness Principle"', *Westminster Review*, January 1830.
3 *Ibid.*, 51f.
4 *Ibid.*, 101.
5 *Ibid.*, 134.
6 E.O. Wilson, *On Human Nature* (Cambridge, Mass., 1978).
7 In *The New York Review of Books*, starting 1975, involving in addition to Wilson, R.C. Lewontin (the most active opponent), S.J. Gould, S. Hampshire, R. Hubbard, C.H. Waddington and others, collected in A. Caplan, *The Sociology Debate* (New York, 1978). For an overview, see Ullica Segerstrale, 'Colleagues in Conflict: An "in Vivo" Analysis of the Sociobiology Controversy', *Biology and Philosophy* **1** (1986): 53–87.
8 *Utilitarian Logic*, 118.
9 *Ibid.*, 234.
10 John Stark, *Elements of Natural History* (London, 1828): **2**, 216.
11 A. Giddens (ed.), *Durkheim on Politics and the State* (Stanford, 1986): 26.
12 *Nicomachean Ethics*, 1107a.
13 Canguilhem, *On the Normal*, 150.
14 Comte, *Politique positive*, **2**, 280.
15 F.-J.-V.-Broussais, *De l'irritation et de la folie* (Paris, 1828): 263.
16 *Ibid.*, 300.
17 *Ibid.*, 267.
18 See footnote on p. 82.
19 H. de Balzac, *Eugénie Grandet* (1833), in *La Comédie humaine* (13 vols., Paris, 1976–80) **3**, 1182.
20 H. de Balzac, *La Cousine Bette* (1847), *Ibid.* **6**, 201.
21 A. Comte, *Cours de philosophie positive*, 40th lecture, printed 1838, ed.

M. Serres *et al.* (Paris, 1975): 695. The editors note that Broussais's principle 'to which Comte grants a disproportionate importance ... goes back to Brown, Bichat and Pinel'.

22 Comte, *Politique positive*, **2**, 443.

23 For Blainville's own exposition of Broussais, see H.-M.D. de Blainville, *Histoire des sciences de l'organisation et de leur progrès comme bas de la philosophie* (Paris, 1845): **3**; for his physiology, *Cours de physiologie générale et comparée* (Paris, 1833).

24 His comment on the asylum is at the end of his review of Broussais, *Politique positive*, **4**, 472.

25 See e.g. Henri Gouhier, *La Philosophie de A. Comte* (Paris, 1987): 164.

26 In *Journal de France*, August 1828. *Cf.* Comte, *Politique positive*, **4**: 468–73.

27 *Ibid.*, 465. He also said that his review 'will ever possess an historical interest since it roused the great biologist [Broussais] to the noble effort which produced, at the close of his admirable career, his just appreciation of the masterly conception of Gall, till then disregarded by him'. In fact Broussais gave the elegy at the grave of Gall in August 1828, the month that Comte's review appeared, and the later admiration of phrenology was well expressed on that occasion. F.-J.-V. Broussais, 'Discours prononcé par M. Broussais sur la Tombe du docteur Gall', *Revue encyclopédique* **39** (1828): 526–31.

28 P.-C.-F. Daunou, *Cours d'études historiques* (Paris, 1849): **20**, 413.

29 Jean-François Braunstein, *Broussais et le matérialisme: médecine et philosophie au XIXe siècle* (Paris, 1986): 111–15. This book also develops the ramifications of the conflict long after Broussais's death in 1838.

30 Comte, *Politique positive*, **2**, 569.

31 A. Comte, *Discours sur l'esprit positif* (Paris, 1844): 55f.

20 As real as cosmic forces

1 Emile Durkheim, 'Suicide et natalité: Étude de statistique morale', *Revue Philosophique* **26** (1886): 447. For his lecture topics, see Steven Lukes, *Emile Durkheim, His Life and Work* (London, 1973): 617.

2 Emile Durkheim, *De la division du travail social: étude sur l'organisation des sociétés supérieures* (Paris, 1893): i.

3 At greater length: we find a practice or a phenomenon *P* in a society. Members of the society may have practical reasons for continuing *P*. However they are unaware that *P* actually is a necessary condition for the preservation of the society. Moreover there is a sort of feedback effect, that is, when the strength of *P* diminishes, the society tends to fall apart, but in such a way as to reinforce *P*, so that the society does persist as an organic unity, and *P* is kept in place. See Jon Elster, *Explaining Technological Change: A Case Study in the Philosophy of Science* (Cambridge, 1983). He argues that functional explanations work in biology but not in sociology. The most lively advocate of functional explanations in sociology defends Durkheim: Mary Douglas, *How Institutions Think* (Syracuse, N.Y., 1986).

4 *Division*, 450. The French is stronger: 'elle devient du même coup la base de l'ordre moral'.

5 *Division du travail*, 33.

6 'Suicide et natalité', 462.

7 *Ibid.*, 463.

8 Emile Durkheim, 'Les Règles de la méthode sociologique', *Revue philosophique* **37** (1894): 465–98, 577–607; **38** (1895): 14–59, 168–82. Reprinted with a preface under the same title (Paris, 1895). Page references are to the *Revue* series, in this case p. 579.

9 Lukes, *Durkheim*, 617.

10 *Division*, 395.

11 *Ibid.*, 396.

12 *Ibid.*, 590.

13 *Ibid.*

14 Emile Durkheim, 'Criminalité et santé sociale', *Revue philosophique* **39** (1895): 518, replying to Gabriel Tarde's criticism under the same title, *ibid.*, 148. For a full account of the Tarde/Durkheim polemics, see Lukes, *Durkheim*, 302–14. Tarde was a magistrate, then director of the statistics department of the ministry of justice, and professor at the Collège de France. His chief work at this time was *Les Lois de l'imitation* (Paris, 1890).

15 *Règles*, 589. This is Durkheim's second rule 'for distinguishing between the normal and the pathological'. It does not occur in the first formulation of the criteria in *Division*.

16 *Ibid.*, the first rule.

17 *Ibid.*, the third rule.

18 *Ibid.*, 72.

19 C. Lombroso, *Uomo delinquente* (Milan, 1876).

20 C. Lombroso, 'Introduction', in G. Lombroso-Ferrero, *Criminal Man According to the Classification of Cesare Lombroso* (New York, 1911): xxv.

21 E.g. M. Benedikt, 'Les Grands criminels de Vienne. II Raimond Hackler', *Archives d'anthropologie criminelle, de médecine légale et de psychologie normale et pathologique* **7** (1892): 237–63. One of a series of studies of 'brains in the Hoffmann collection' in Vienna.

22 'Troisième Congrès International d'Anthropologie Criminelle' *ibid.*, 472. On the congresses and related debates, see for example Robert A. Nye, *Crime, Madness and Politics in Modern France: The Medical Concept of National Decline* (Princeton, 1984): chapter 4.

23 Enrico Ferri, 'Le Crime comme phénomène sociale', *Annales de l'Institut International de Sociologie* **2** (1896): 411. He incorporated this chart into his *Sociologia criminale* (4th edn, Turin, 1900). The third edition of this book appeared in French in 1894. His doctoral thesis was a refutation of the possibility of free will, and a corresponding demand for radical revision of the system of criminal jurisprudence. *Teoria dell'imputabilità e la negazione del libro arbitrio* (Florence, 1878).

24 *A bibliography for a course of criminal anthropology, or criminal sociology, circa 1893–4.* For a complete bibliographical essay of 1893, consult Hans Kurella, *Naturgeschichte des Verbrechers* (Stuttgart, 1893). The following is based only upon Ferri's altogether typical list:

Journals: Lombroso's *Archivio di psichiatria, scienza penale ed'antropologia criminale* (Turin, 1880–), and Lacassagne's *Archives*, note 21 above (Lyon, 1886–)

Albrecht, Hans 'La Fossetta occipitale nei mammiferi', Lombroso's *Archivio*, **5** (1885): 105

Baer, Abraham Adolf *Der Verbrecher in anthropologischer Beziehung* (Leipzig, 1893)

Benedikt, M. note 21 above and *Kraniometrie und Kephalometrie (Vienna, 1888)*

Bleuler, Eugen *Der geboren Verbrecher: eine kritische Studie* (Munich, 1896). It will be seen that Bleuler was on Ferri's table, although this book would be too late for an 1894 bibliography. I include it here as a reminder that this celebrated psychiatrist began his career with criminal anthropology.

Bonfigli, Clodomiro *La Storia naturale del delitto* (Milan, 1893)

Colajanni, Napoleone *Socialismo e sociologia criminale* (Catania, 1884); *La delinquenza della Sicilia e le sue cause* (Palermo, 1885); *La Sociologia criminale* (Catania, 1889)

Dally, Eugène *Remarques sur les aliénés et les criminels au point de vue de la responsibilité morale et légale* (Paris, 1864)

Despine, Prosper *Du rôle de la science dans la question pénitentiaire* (Stockholm, 1878)

Ferri, Enrico *Socialismo e criminalità* (Turin, 1883, Rome 1884)

Garofalo, Raffaele *Criminalogia, studi sui delitto sulle sue cause e sui mezzi di repressione* (Turin, 1885); 2nd edn Turin, 1889. The translation used by Durkheim was *La Criminologie: étude sur la nature du crime et la théorie de la pénalité* (Paris 1890)

Gumplowicz, Ludwig *Der Rassenkampf: sociologische Untersuchungen* (Innsbruck, 1875). Durkheim reviewed his *Grundriss der Sociologie* in the *Revue philosophique* **20** (1885): 629

Jelgersma, Gerbrandus *De Befoening der Crimineele Anthropologie en Gerechtelijke Psychiatrie* (Utrecht, 1894)

Kirn, Ludwig 'Kriminalpsychologie', in F. von Holzendorff (ed.), *Handbuch des Gefangniswesens* (Hamburg, 1888)

Lacassagne, Alexandre *De la criminalité chez les animaux* (Lyon, 1882); *L'Homme criminel comparé a l'homme primitif* (Lyon, 1882)

Lewis, W. Bevan 'The Genesis of Crime', *Fortnightly Review* **54** (1893): 329–44

Liszt, Franz von *Der Zweckgedanke im Strafrecht* (Marburg, 1883); 'Kriminalpolitischeaufgaben', a series in his journal *Zeitschrift für die gesamte Strafrechtswissenschaft* (Berlin), between 1889 and 1891

Lombroso, Cesare see note 19 above

Loria, Achille *Problemi sociali contemporanei* (Milan, 1894)

Marro, Antonio *Cartteri dei delinquenti* (Turin, 1887)

Maudsley, Henry *Responsibility in Mental Disease* (London, 1874), translated as *La Crime et la folie* (Paris, 1874)

Prins, Adolphe   *Criminalité et répression; essai de science pénale* (Brussels, 1886), *Bulletin de l'Union Internationale de Droit Pénal* **30** (1891): 121

Raux, Paul   *Nos Jeunes coupables: étude sur l'enfance coupable avant, pendant et après son séjour au quartier correctionnel* (Lyon, 1886)

Roncaroni, P., and Ardu, P.   'Esame di 43 cranii di criminali', Lombroso's *Archivio* **12** (1891): 148

Tarde, Gabriel   see note 14 above

Turati, Filippo   *Il delito e la questione sociale* (Milan, 1883)

Topinard, P.   *L'Homme dans la nature* (Paris 1891)

Vargha, Julius   *Das Strafprocessrecht systematisch dargestellt* (Berlin, 1885). (This was to be followed by *Die Abschaffung der Strafrechtschaft: Studien zur Strafrechtsreform* (Graz, 1896))

Virgilio, Gaspare   *La Filosofia e la patologia de la mente* (Caserta, 1883); *Passanante e la natura morboso del delitto* (Rome, 1888)

25 C. Lombroso, 'Les Bienfaits du crime', *Nouvelle Revue* **95** (1895): 86–92.

26 *Règles*, 596.

27 Durkheim referred to Garofalo on pp. 77 and 87 of *Division*, but my discussion concerns the long note on p. 589 of *Règles*.

28 Emile Durkheim, *Le Suicide: étude de sociologie* (Paris, 1897); *Suicide*, trans. J.A. Spaulding and G. Simpson (Glencoe, Ill., 1951): 363.

29 *Ibid.*, 309.

30 Durkheim, *Division*, 324–6. See Alain Desrosières, 'Histoires des formes: statistiques et sciences sociales avant 1940', *Revue Française de sociologie* **26** (1985): 293.

31 Durkheim, *Suicide*, 300f.

32 I have in fact been doing that since my *Logic of Statistical Inference* (Cambridge, 1965).

21   The autonomy of statistical law

1 Francis Galton, *Typical Laws of Heredity* (London, 1877): 17. Also printed in *Proceedings of the Royal Institution of Great Britain* **8** (1877): 282–301 and in a sequence of three segments in *Nature* the same year. For illustrations of the quincunx see S. Stigler, *The History of Statistics* (Cambridge, Mass., 1986): 277–80. For Peirce's quincuncial projection, see C.S. Peirce, 'A Quincuncial Projection of the Sphere', *American Journal of Mathematics* **2** (1879): 394–6 plus map plate.

2 Mortimer Collins, *Marquis and Merchant* (London, 1871): 3, *141*. This is an isolated observation in a chapter that touches on fundamental issues. Two pages later the marquis says to the merchant, 'You English deem yourselves great by reason of your sordid utilitarian notions; whereas your greatness comes from the poetical side of the national character. Shakespeare has done more for the English than any other man, yet you believe in Adam Smith and John Stuart Mill.'

3 Stigler, *History of Statistics*, 265–99. T.M. Porter, *The Rise of Statistical Thinking* (Princeton, 1986): 128–48. Karl Pearson, *The Life, Letters and Labours of Francis Galton* (4 vols., Cambridge, 1914–30), esp. vol. **3A**, and also F. Galton, *Memories of My Life* (London, 1908). For a modern biography not

attending much to statistics, see D.W. Forrest, *Francis Galton: The Life and Work of a Victorian Genius* (New York, 1974).

4 See for example Jan von Plato, 'Probabilistic Physics the Classical Way', in *Probabilistic Revolution* **2**, 379–408.

5 The classic studies of explanation are by C.G. Hempel, in *Aspects of Scientific Explanation and Other Essays in the Philosophy of Science* (New York, 1965). For more recent discussion, see W.C. Salmon, *Scientific Explanation and the Causal Structure of the World* (Princeton, 1984). On explaining rare events, see R.C. Jeffrey, 'Statistical Explanation and Statistical Inference', in N. Rescher (ed.), *Essays in Honour of C.G. Hempel* (Dordrecht, 1969).

6 For a description plus modifications, see *Photographic News* **27** (1885): 244.

7 The photographs from *The Journal of the Anthropological Institute* **15** are reproduced in Pearson, *Life* **2**, Plates xxviii-xxxv. On the opinion of the neighbours, 'Note by Mr. F. Galton, appended to Joseph Jacobs, "On the Racial Characteristics of Modern Jews"', in J. Jacobs, *Jewish Statistics* (London, 1891): xl.

8 Donald MacKenzie, *Statistics in Britain, 1865–1930: The Social Construction of Scientific Knowledge* (Edinburgh, 1981). Daniel Kevles, *In the Name of Eugenics* (Chicago, 1984). Stephen Jay Gould, *The Mismeasure of Man* (New York, 1981).

9 One finds 'Normal curve' in e.g. *Natural Inheritance* (London, 1888): 56; also 'Normal Values' on p. 54. For signs of Galton's caution about the normal distribution, see Porter, *Statistical Thinking*, 299f.

10 The geologist was William Spottiswoode; see F. Galton, *Memories of My Life* (London, 1908): 304. John Herschel (unsigned), 'Quetelet on Probabilities,' *The Edinburgh Review* **92** (1850): 1–57.

11 F. Galton, *Hereditary Genius: An Inquiry into its Laws and Consequences* (London, 1869): *passim*.

12 Galton,'Typical laws', 512.

13 Victor Hilts, 'Statistics and Social Science', in R. Giere and R. Westfall (eds.), *Foundations of Scientific Method, The Nineteenth Century* (Bloomington, Ind., 1973): 206–33.

14 Of numerous accounts, the one most sympathetic to Darwin, and quoting many letters about the experiments, is to my mind the most interesting: Pearson, *Life*, 156–69, 174–7.

15 F. Galton, 'Presidential Address' *Journal of the Anthropological Institute* **15** (1886): 494.

16 *Natural Inheritance*, 86.

17 About the several generations of Bertillons who were statisticians, see B.-P. Lecuyer, 'Probability in Vital and Social Statistics: Quetelet, Farr and the Bertillons', in *Probabilistic Revolution*, 317–36.

18 Carlo Ginzburg, 'Morelli, Freud and Sherlock Holmes: Clues and the Scientific Method', *History Workshop* **9** (1980): 7–36; in U. Eco and T.A. Seboek (eds.), *The Sign of the Three: Dupin, Holmes, Peirce* (Bloomington, Ind., 1988): 81–118.

19 A. Bravais, 'Analyse mathématique sur les probabilités des erreurs de situation d'un point', *Mémoires présentés par divers savants à l'Académie Royale des Sciences de l'Institut de France* **9** (1845): 255–332.

20 C.M. Schols, whose work is described in H. L. Seal, 'The Historical Development of the Gauss Linear Model', E. S. Pearson and M. G. Kendall (eds.), *Studies in the History of Statistics and Probability* (London, 1970): 207–30.
21 MacKenzie, *Statistics in Britain*, 71.
22 Pearson, *Life and Letters* **3A**, 1f.

22 A chapter from Prussian statistics

1 Salomon Neumann, *Die Fabel von der jüdischen Masseneinwanderung: Ein Kapitel aus der preussischen Statistik* (Berlin, 1880): 2 (2nd edn, 22 November 1880).
2 Neumann, *Fabel* (3rd edn, Berlin, 20 May 1881); with supplements listed on the title page as *I. Antwort an Herrn Adolf Wagner. II. Herr Heinrich v. Treitschke und seine jüdische Masseneinwanderung. III. Die Antwort des königl. preussischen statistischen Büreaus.*
3 Engel was a National-Liberal deputy in the *Abgeordnetshaus*, 1867–70. His predecessor at the Prussian statistical bureau, Dieterici, had been a Centre-Liberal representative in the 1848 Parliament of Frankfurt-am-Main. Neumann was a Berlin city councillor from 1859 to 1905, devoting his political energies chiefly to health measures.
4 Biographical data are taken from the eulogy by Hermann Cohen, 'Salomon Neumann: Gedächtnisrede', *Lehranstalt für die Wissenschaft des Judenthums* **27** (1908): 39–54.
5 S. Neumann, 'Das Sterblichkeits-Verhältniss in der Berliner Arbeiter-Bevölkerung nach in den Genossenschaften des Gewerbskrankverein 1861–63 vorgekommenen Todesfallen', *Der Arbeiterfreund* **4** (1866): 46–67. E. Engel, 'Der Arbeitsvertrag und die Arbeitsgesellschaft: Industrial Partnerships,' *ibid.*, **5** (1867): 371–94.
6 R. Virchow, 'Atoms and Individuals'(1859), in L.J. Rather (ed.), *Disease, Life and Man. Selected Essays by Rudolf Virchow* (Stanford, 1958). I owe these references to Virchow to Gordon MacOuat.
7 'Zur medicinischen Statistik des preussischen Staates nach den Akten des statistischen Büreaus für das Jahre 1846', *Archiv für pathologischen Anatomie und Physiologie und für klinische Medicin* **3** (1851): 13–141. Cf. his *Die öffentliche Gesundheitspflege und das Eigenthum* (Berlin, 1847).
8 R. Virchow, 'Report on the Typhus Epidemic in Upper Silesia'(1848), translated in R. Virchow, *Collected Essays on Public Health and Epidemiology* (New Delhi, 1985): 307.
9 *Ibid.*, 85.
10 Cohen, 'Gedächtnisrede', 44. Little has been written about Neumann; one can glimpse his role as a solid committee man in lobbying the representatives of the great powers at the Berlin Congress of 1878. See 'The Intervention of German Jews at the Berlin Congress of 1878', *Publications of the Leo Baeck Institute* **5** (1960): 221–48.
11 These materials and some of the replies to them are collected in W. Boehlich (ed.), *Der Berliner Antisemitismusstreit* (Frankfurt-am-Main, 1965). These include an attack on Neumann's *Fabel*, to which the latter replied in the third edition.

12 L. Zunz, 'Grundlinien zu einer kunftigen Statistik der Juden', *Zeitschrift für die Wissenschaft des Judenthums* 1 (1823): 523–32; in Zunz, *Gesammelte Schriften* (Berlin, 1875): 134–41. Neumann's dedication to Zunz opens his *Zur Statistik der Juden in Preussen von 1816 bis 1880 aus den amtlichen Veröffentlichungen* (Berlin, 1884). The opening sentences of chapter 42 of *Daniel Deronda* are translated from L. Zunz, *Synagogale Poesie des Mittelalters* (Berlin, 1855).

13 *Zur Judenfrage. Statistische Erörterung. Anzahl und Vertheilung der Juden im preussischen Staat, nach einer Vergleichung der Zahlungen zu Ende der Jahre 1840 und 1842,* (Berlin, 1842). 'Statistische Uebersicht und Vergleichung der Zunahme der critischen jüdischen Bevölkerung in den Zeitperioden 1816 bis 1825, 1825 bis 1834, 1835 bis 1843 und 1843 bis 1846 in den einzelnen Regierungsbezirken des Preussischen Staats', *Mittheilungen des statistichen Büreaus in Berlin* 2 (1849): 356–83.

14 E. Glatter, *Uber die Lebenschancen der Israeliten gegenüber den christlichen Konfessionen: Biostatistischen Studien* (Wetzler, 1856).

15 *Uber Auswanderung und Einwanderung, letztere in besonder Beziehung auf dem preussischen Staat, vom statistichen Standpunkt* (Berlin, 1847).

16 *Uber die Zunahme der Bevölkerung im preussischen Staat in Bezug auf Vertheilung derselben nach Stadt und Land,* (Berlin, 1867).

17 The results are given in the *Zeitschrift des königlich preussischen statistischen Büreaus* 22 (1882): 239.

18 In a warm preface, Engel attributes the work to G. von Fircks. 'Rückblick auf die Bewegung der Bevölkerung im preussischen Staat 1816–1874,' *Jahrbuch des königlich preussischen statistischen Büreaus* 48A (1877): 22, 27.

19 S. Neumann (unsigned), 'Die Bilanz der preussische Bevölkerung von 1846–1867', *Vierteljahrschrift für Volkwirtschaft und Kulturgeschichte,* 29 (1870): 193–203.

20 'Die Fremdgeburten im preussischen Staat,' *Zeitschrift des königlich preussischen statistischen Büreaus* 20 (1880): 387–98.

21 He makes substantive errors because of this in his 'Die Sterblichkeit und die Lebenserwartung im preussischen Staat angewandten', *ibid.* 1 (1861): 321–53; 2 (1862): 50–69.

22 R. Boeckh, 'Die statistische Bedeutung der Volksprache als Kennzeichnis der Nationalität', *Zeitschrift für Völkerpsychologie und Sprachwissenschaft* 4 (1866): 259–402. *Die deutsche Volkzahl und Sprachgebiet in den europaischen Staaten* (Berlin, 1869).

23 Late in life Boeckh applied his interest in the German language to computing the number of real –in his cultural and linguistic sense – Germans in the United States. The US began to classify immigrants by country of origin only in 1898. In response to a publication showing 151,118 immigrants from the German empire between 1898 and 1904, Boeckh computed that in fact the US had admitted a further 289,438 Germans from other European countries. See B. Faust, *The German elements in the United States, with Special Reference to their Political, Moral, Social and Educational Influence* (New York, 1927): 2, chapter 1.

24 *Statistisches Jahrbuch der Stadt Berlin* 6 (1880) reporting data for 1878.

25 How should one be Olympian? In its overview of the the results of the census of 1 December 1880, Engel's bureau displayed data in this order: (1) The state;

(2) Berlin; (3) place of birth of citizens; (4) place of birth of the Christian and Jewish population in the four easternmost provinces and in the major cities of Berlin, Frankfurt-am-Main and Stolp in Pomerania; (5) breakdown of the population for each *Kreis* showing the confessional statistics – a breakdown into four groups, namely Evangelicals, Roman Catholics, Jews and Sects. *Die definitiven Ergebnisse der Volkzählung von 1 Dezember 1880 im preussischen Staate* (Berlin, 1883).

26 A. Nossig, *Materielien zur Statistik des Jüdischen Stammes* (Vienna, 1887).

27 See A. Nossig (ed.), *Jüdische Statistik* (Berlin, 1903) for the type of work conducted by the *Verein*, and an account of its activities and branches all over Europe.

28 Alex Benn, 'Arthur Ruppin', *Jewish Social Studies* 17 (1972): 117–41.

29 J. Jacobs, 'The Racial Characteristics of Modern Jews' (Read to the Anthropological Institute, 24 February 1885) in J. Jacobs, *Jewish Statistics* (London, 1891): iii.

30 J. Jacobs and Isidore Spielman, 'On the Comparative Anthropometry of English Jews', *ibid.*, 77.

31 J. Jacobs, 'The Comparative Distribution of Jewish Ability' (read to the Anthropological Institute, 10 November 1886), *ibid.*, xliii.

32 *Ibid.*, 1.

23   A universe of chance

1 'Reply to the Necessitarians', *The Monist* 3 (1893): 526–70; *Papers* 6, 425. References are to *Writings of Charles Sanders Peirce: A Chronological Edition* (Bloomington, Ind., 1982–) so far as the volumes have been printed; for material not yet published in that edition, to *Collected Papers of Charles Sanders Peirce* (8 vols., Cambridge, Mass., 1931–58). References to *Papers* is by volume and page, not by the decimal system indicating volume and paragraph. P. Carus, 'Mr. Charles S. Peirce on Necessity', *The Monist* 2 (1892): 442. 'Mr Charles S. Peirce's Onslaught on the Doctrine of Necessity', *ibid.*, 560–82. 'The Idea of Necessity, its Basis and its Scope', *ibid.* 3 (1893): 68–96. 'The Founder of Tychism, His Methods, Philosophy and Criticisms: In reply to Mr. Charles Sanders Peirce', *ibid.*, 571–622. J. Dewey, 'The Superstition of Necessity', *ibid.*, 362–79.

2 David Hume, *Inquiry* (1748), p. 95 of the Selby-Bigge edition.

3 Peirce, 'Reply', *The Monist* 3 (1893): 535; *Papers* 6, 409.

4 'Man's Glassy Essence,' *The Monist* 2 (1892): 1; *Papers* 6, 155.

5 C. Eisele, 'Charles Sanders Peirce', in the *Dictionary of Scientific Biography; Studies in the Scientific and Mathematical Philosophy of Charles Sanders Peirce* (The Hague, 1979); 'Peirce the Scientist', in C. Eisele (ed.), *Historical Perspectives on Peirce's Logic of Science* (2 vols., Berlin, 1985): 17–38. See also her editorial remarks in C. Eisele (ed.), *The New Elements of Mathematics by Charles Sanders Peirce* (Amsterdam, 1976). One philosopher who attends to Peirce's career in the Coast Survey, and to his work on measurement, is H.S. Thayer, *Meaning and Action: A Critical Exposition of American Pragmatism* (Indianapolis, 1973): 70, 349.

6 The story was on p. 1 of the *Washington Post*, and is copied in the Peirce fiche,

item 00322; see K. L. Ketner, *A Comprehensive Bibliography of the Published Works of Charles Sanders Peirce with a Bibliography of Secondary Sources* (2nd edn, Bowling Green, Ohio, 1986). Peirce replied in a letter to the *New York Post*, dated 10 August, reported in *Science* **6** (1895): 158.

7 To Lady Victoria Welby, 14 March 1909, in C.S. Hardwick, (ed.), *Semiotics and Significs: The Correspondence between Charles S. Peirce and Victoria, Lady Welby* (Bloomington, Ind., 1977): 113.

8 While employed at the Survey, Peirce worked concurrently at the Harvard Observatory, 1869–72, held various sorts of lectureship at Johns Hopkins University, 1880–4, gave occasional sequences of lectures in Cambridge and Boston, defined 7,069 mostly technical words for the *Century Dictionary*, wrote his most widely read and anthologized series of philosophical papers, the 'Illustrations of the Logic of Science' in *The Popular Science Monthly*, published, in the first English-language philosophy periodical, his three most innovative early philosophical essays, and commenced the sequence of essays in *The Monist* that includes his antideterminist 'Doctrine of Necessity Examined'.

9 *Papers* **6**, 28.

10 *Ibid.*, 36.

11 *Ibid.*, 43.

12 'The Doctrine of Chances' (1878), *Writings* **3**, 278.

13 'On the Theory of Errors of Observations', *Report of the Superintendent of the United States Coast Survey, 1870*, House Executive Document No. 112, 41st Congress, 3rd Session (Washington, 1873): 200–24 + plate + errata sheet. *Writings* **3**, 114–60.

14 J.F. Encke, 'Ueber die Methode der kleinsten Quadrate', *Berliner Astronomische Jahrbuch für 1834*, 249–312. This was a standard reference, and the source, for example, of the tables used for calculations in G.T. Fechner's *Elemente der Psychophysik* (Leipzig, 1860).

15 F.W. Bessel, 'Persönliche Gleichung bei Durchgangsbeobachtung', in R. Engelmann (ed.), *Abhandlungen von Friedrich Wilhelm Bessel* (vol. **3**, Berlin, 1876): 300–4. Encke and Bessel were collaborators, the former being a co-worker against whom the latter correlated the personal equation.

16 See Stigler, *History of Statistics*, 239–61.

17 G.T. Fechner, *Elemente der Psychophysik* (Leipzig, 1860): 78.

18 M. Heidelberger, 'Fechner's Indeterminism: From Freedom to Laws of Chance', in *Probabilistic Revolution* **1**, 117–56.

19 C.S. Peirce and J. Jastrow, 'On Small Differences of Sensation', *Memoirs of the National Academy of Sciences 1884* (Washington, 1885): 73–83.

20 S. Stigler, 'Mathematical Statistics in the Early States', *Annals of Statistics* **6** (1978): 239–65, esp. 248. Ian Hacking, 'Telepathy: Origins of Randomization in Experimental Design', *Isis* **79** (1988): 427–51.

21 Randomization was long ignored by psychologists. Likewise the subliminal error curve was scathingly dismissed by the leading American experimental psychologist. E.B. Titchener, *Instructor's Manual* (New York, 1905): 285–91, for *Experimental Psychology: A Manual of Laboratory Practice. 2 Quantitative Experiments, Pt. 2*. It was absurd, he said, to force subjects to make decisions when they did not 'feel' any difference between weights.

22 'Small Differences', 83.

23 Related in Hacking, 'Telepathy'.
24 'Probability of Induction' (1878), in *Writings* **3**, 304. In this passage, Peirce had a footnote connected to Gratry: 'The same is true, according to him, of every performance of a differentiation, but not of integration. He does not tell us whether it is the supernatural assistance which makes the former process so much the easier.' A.J.A. Gratry, *Logique* (4th edn, 2 vols., Paris, 1858). But although Gratry could make one smile, he was no figure of fun. For his attack on papal infallibility, see A.J.A. Gratry, *Mgr l'Evêque d'Orléans et Mgr. l'Archevêque de Malines. Lettres a Mgr Deschamps* (Paris, 1870; published in a series of editions, first as a first letter, then as two letters, and so on, concluding as a series of four letters, which went through seven editions all in 1870. A 'First American Translation' was published in Hartford, Conn. in 1870, and another translation in London, 1870). Deschamps was a cardinal. For the 'method of despotism', see Peirce, *Writings* **3**, 25f. For Peirce's admiration of Gratry, see *Writings* **1**, 163, and his review of M.E. Boole, *The Preparation of the Child for Science*, in *The Nation*, **80** (1905): 18.
25 Lecture VIII, written in the spring of 1865, *Writings* **1**, 267. Any index to any body of his works will turn up subsequent uses of this distinction.
26 'Deduction, Induction and Hypothesis' (1878), *ibid.* **3**, 326.
27 E.g. in 1905, *Papers* **2**, 478.
28 E.g. 1901, 'Hume on Miracles', *Papers* **6**, 358.
29 Anyone who prefers Peirce's unfortunate coinage 'abduction' should reflect on those whom Peirce listed as his authority for the phrase 'method of hypothesis': Descartes, Leibniz, 's Gravesande, Boscovitch, Hartley, Le Sage, Dugald Stewart, Chauvin, Newton, Sir W. Hamilton, J.S. Mill, Kant, Herbart, Beneke – 'There would be no difficulty in multiplying these citations.' 'Consequences of Four Incapacities' (1868), *Writings* **2**, 218f, note 1.
30 *Papers* **2**, 500.
31 George Boole, *An Investigation of the Laws of Thought on Which are Founded the Mathematical Theories of Logic and Probabilities* (London, 1854). Peirce's first elaboration of Boole's ideas was in his third lecture at Harvard in 1865, *Writings* **1**, 189–204.
32 For his vigintillions, see 'Treatise on Metaphysics' (1871) in *Writings* **1**, 70. The onslaught on parapsychology is in 'Criticism of *Phantasms of the Living*: An examination of the Arguments of Messrs. Gurney, Myers and Podmore', *Proceedings of the American Society for Psychical Research* **1** (1885–9): 150 (in 1887). E. Gurney, F.W.H. Myers and F. Podmore, *Phantasms of the Living* (London, 1886). The three authors of this remarkable book have, as Peirce put it, 'cipher[ed] out some very enormous odds in favor of the hypothesis of ghosts'. Gurney replied in the *Proceedings*, on pp. 157–79, and 'Mr Peirce's rejoinder' follows on pp. 180–215.
33 *North American Review* **105** (1867): 317; *Writings* **2**, 98.
34 *Papers* **6**, 590.
35 Arthur W. Burks, 'Peirce's Two Theories of Probability', in E.S. Moore and R.S. Robin (eds.), *Studies in the Philosophy of Charles Sanders Peirce* (2nd series, Amherst, Mass., 1964): 451–50.
36 For an account of 'facility' from the time of Leibniz, and with references to Lagrange and Laplace, see Hacking, *Emergence*, 154–71. Like his contempo-

raries and predecessors, Peirce sometimes used the Laplacian terminology, e.g. 'the equation which represents the facility of error', in 'Errors of Observations', *Writings* 3, 124.

37 'The Doctrine of Chances', *Popular Science Monthly* 12 (1878): 609; *Writings* 3, 281.

38 Lowell Lecture III, *Writings* 1, 400.

39 'Preliminary Sketch of Logic' (1869), *Writings*, 2, 294; Peirce's italics.

40 'Reasoning', *Baldwin's Dictionary*, 748.

41 J. Neyman and E. Pearson, 'On the Problem of the Most Efficient Tests of Statistical Hypotheses', *Philosophical Transactions of the Royal Society of London* A 231 (1933): 289–337. See E.S. Pearson, 'The Neyman-Pearson Story 1926–34', in F.N. David (ed.), *Research Papers in Statistics* (New York, 1966): 1–24.

42 For details of Wilson, see Ian Hacking, 'The Theory of Probable Inference: Neyman, Peirce and Braithwaite', in D.H. Mellor (ed.), *Science, Belief and Behaviour* (Cambridge, 1980): 143, note 1, and p. 160 for references. For Wilson on Peirce on error, see E.B. Wilson and M.M. Hilferty, 'A Note on C.S. Peirce's Experimental Discussion of the Law of Errors', *Proceedings of the National Academy of Sciences* 15 (1929): 120–5.

43 E.B. Wilson, 'Comparative Experiment and Observed Association', *ibid.* 51 (1964): 293.

44 Unfortunately Lehmann's paper has never been published, originally because he did not want to offend Neyman (personal letter, 5 July 1988). E.L. Lehmann, 'Some Early Instances of Confidence Statements', Statistical Laboratory, University of California, Berkeley; ONR 5 Technical Report to the Office of Naval Research, September 1958.

45 *Writings* 3, 116.

46 A proposed set of lectures for 1898, *Papers* 6, 3.

47 *Papers* 2, 480.

48 S. Stigler, 'Early States', 248.

49 I.J. Good, *Good Thinking: The Foundations of Probability and its Applications* (Minneapolis, 1983): 220–4 and see name index, Peirce. I.J. Good, 'A Correction Concerning my Interpretation of Peirce, and the Bayesian Interpretation of Neyman-Pearson "Hypothesis Determination"', *Journal of Statistical Computation and Simulation* 18 (1983): 71–4.

50 'Doctrine of Chances' (1878), *Writings* 3, 281.

51 *Ibid.*, 282. The point was more commonly made after the 1930s in a contretemps featuring Neyman and R.A. Fisher. Fisher said that Neyman's procedures were fine for quality control, when one was repeatedly testing batches of goods, but were not relevant to testing a unique scientific hypothesis.

52 *Ibid.*, 284f. Twenty-five years ago, in my first discussion of the Neyman-Pearson mode of inference, I admired Peirce's three sentiments; see *Logic of Statistical Inference* (Cambridge, 1965): 47. I thought them unsuitable for founding the Neyman-Pearson theory, and held this to be a decisive objection to it. Ten years ago, in 'Neyman, Peirce and Braithwaite', I realized that the theory really did provide one route (but only one of several viable routes) to induction in general, and again worried at faith, hope and charity (pp. 157–9).

53 'Consequences of Four Incapacities' (1868), *Writings* 2: 239. Peirce's capitalization.

54 *Ibid.*, 212. *Cf.* his italicized 'community' in his review, 'Fraser's *The Works of George Berkeley*', *Writings* 2, 487.

55 'A Neglected Argument for the Reality of God', *Hibbert Journal* 7 (1908): 90–112; *Papers* 6, 331. Peirce's italics.

56 In his 1893 reply to Carus on necessity, *Papers* 6, 420.

57 L. Laudan, 'Peirce and the Trivialization of the Self-correcting Thesis', in R. Giere and R. Westfall (eds.), *Foundations of Scientific Method: The Nineteenth Century* (Bloomington, Ind., 1973): 275–306.

58 'Preliminary Sketch of Logic', *Writings* 2, 294. The account of argument in full is that an *argument* is a statement intended to *appeal* to a person and is such that the person 'will regard the statement as if he would admit that every set of facts, taken as those stated have been taken, determines by certain relations another possible statement, and that this would be more apt to be true in the long run when the facts stated are true, than a random assertion would be'. Then follows the footnote. Peirce's italics for 'argument' and 'appeal'.

59 Benjamin Osgood Peirce, *A System of Analytic Mechanics* (Boston, 1855): 447.

60 'Evolutionary Love', *The Monist*, 3 (1893): 176–200. *Papers* 6, 190–215.

61 'The Architecture of Theories', *The Monist* 1 (1891): 175; *Papers* 6, 26. There is a whole litany of firsts, seconds and thirds in this passage, including Mind, Matter and Evolution.

62 Stéphane Mallarmé's *Un Coup de dés jamais n'abolira le hasard* (1897), trans. Brian Coffley, *Dice Thrown Never Will Annul Chance* (Dublin, 1965).

INDEX

Years of birth and death given for most people who figure in *The Taming of Chance*.

Ideas in Context

Forthcoming titles include works by Martin Dzelzainis, Mark Goldie, Noel Malcolm, Roger Mason, James Moore, Dorothy Ross, Nicolai Rubinstein, Quentin Skinner, Martin Warnke and Robert Wokler.